AF352455

THE CATHOLIC UNIVERSITY OF AMERICA
CANON LAW STUDIES
NUMBER 51

THE MATRIMONIAL IMPEDIMENTS
of
Mixed Religion
and
Disparity of Cult

A DISSERTATION

*Submitted to the Faculty of Canon Law of the
Catholic University of America in partial
fulfillment of the requirements for
the Degree of*

DOCTOR OF CANON LAW

by the

REVEREND FRANCIS J. SCHENK, A.B., S.T.B., J.C.L.,
of the Archdiocese of St. Paul.

THE CATHOLIC UNIVERSITY OF AMERICA
WASHINGTON, D. C.
MCMXXIX

To the

Most Reverend Austin Dowling, D. D.,
Archbishop of St. Paul

in

Reverence and Gratitude

TABLE OF CONTENTS

PART I
PRELIMINARY DISCUSSION

CHAPTER

PART II
HISTORICAL DEVELOPMENT

PRINCIPAL ABBREVIATIONS

AAS—Acta Apostolicae Sedis.

AER—The American Ecclesiastical Review.

AkKR—Archiv für katholisches Kirchenrecht.

ASS—Acta Sanctae Sedis.

CIC—Codex Iuris Canonici.

Coll.—Collectanea S. Congregationis de Propaganda Fide.

Denz.—Denzinger, H., - Bannwart, C., *Enchiridion Symbolo-
      rum Definitionum et Declarationum de Rebus Fidei et
      Morum.*

Fontes—Codicis Iuris Canonici Fontes.

HPR—The Homiletic and Pastoral Review.

IER—The Irish Ecclesiastical Record.

Jus Pont.—Jus Pontificium.

LQS—Theologisch-praktische Quartalschrift (commonly is
      known as *Linzer Quartalschrift*).

Mansi—Mansi, J. D., *Sacrorum Conciliorum Nova et Amplis-
      sima Collectio.*

MPL—Migne, J. P., *Patrologiae Cursus Completus - Series La-
      tina.*

NRT—Nouvelle Revue Théologique.

Thes.—*Thesaurus Resolutionum Sacrae Congregationis Con-
      cilii.*

ZkT—Zeitschrift für katholische Theologie.

INTRODUCTION

The background of any study of the impediments of
Mixed Religion and Disparity of Cult is the attitude of the
Church towards heresy and infidelity. That attitude is well
known and well established by the tradition of the Christian
ages. Both with regard to the pagan and hostile environment
of the Roman Empire and to the early assaults of heresy but
one policy under different names seems to have resulted. For
the one it was segregation, for the other it was excommunication. In both cases it was avoidance.

The games, the fashions, the daily life of peoples who
lived so much in the open and together betrayed in the stress
of patriotic crises the *gens lucifuga* which tried to maintain
its cultus and preach its doctrines in secret when its more
daring propaganda was opposed. The anathemas of early councils brought about new lines of separation. There was to be
no association of the orthodox with pagans, Jews, and heretics.

To what extent it was possible in the early centuries to
maintain this discipline of avoidance is a matter difficult to
determine. St. Augustine could complain that many of his
time did not consider it a sin to contract marriages with unbelievers. Nay more, the Church at Chalcedon found it necessary to reprimand the scandalous examples of such marriages
among clerics.

Whatever proportions such laxities assumed, it is significant that they met the incessant protests of the Fathers and of
the councils. Of particular constancy were the prohibitions of
the councils along the Mediterranean littoral against the marriages of Christians with Jews. Perhaps these enactments reflected the prevalence of abuses. More probably, they represented the growth of a popular aversion to any association with a
Jew. At any rate, they grew in number and severity with the
advance of the centuries until finally they appear to have
assumed the form of a diriment impediment.

But with the advent of the twelfth century new dangers threatened the Christian body. For years, the Moor, the Saracen, the Mohammedan, had been terrorizing the southern shores of Europe,—now he was thundering upon its eastern gates. The heretic again lurked at home. Perhaps he passed for a devout Catholic, as his training and environment implied that he was. But he was restless to spread his new evangel, and he gathered around him followers and presently raised his banner of religious revolt.

Christendom was aroused as never before to the sense of its perilous condition. Everything that had been raised to destroy it was to be exterminated. If St. Dominic and his companions could not subdue the stubborness of the heretic by exhortation and by prayer, Simon de Montfort would bring him to a sullen acquiesence by the might of his crusading sword. The Mohammedan would not only be held in check, —he would be driven from the very walls of his own strongholds.

There was, therefore, no question in the minds of the faithful of countenancing any such thing as a marriage of a Catholic with an unbeliever. That was high treason to their deepest interests and loyalties. The aversion that for many centuries had been confined largely to the marriages of Catholics with Jews now came to embody every marriage that the faithful might contract with those alien to the Faith. It is not surprising, therefore, to find in the writings of the authors of the twelfth century the repeated *dictum* that the marriages of Catholics with infidels, Jews, or heretics were in valid. There was not even an attempt on the part of these writers to defend this teaching. It was an accepted fact that seemed for the time to brook no challenge.

Under the studied scrutiny of the theologians and canonits of the thirteenth century the diriment force of the impediment would be restricted to the marriages of the baptized with the unbaptized, but even this modification would in no way affect the policy of the Church in its discipline of avoidance. The Inquisition would take care of heresy at home; the Crusades of infidelity abroad.

How then, and in what circumstances, was it ever possible for the Church who had so repeatedly and so strongly expressed her mind on the subject of infidels and heretics to bring herself to a position in which she would permit one of her own children to enter into the closest of human relations with either the heretic or the infidel?

Two leading events of the sixteenth century appear to have brought on this change. One was represented by the enthusiastic missionary activity in the Orient and in the newly discovered continents to the West, the other by the avalanche of heresy that swept over Europe. The Church felt constrained to provide by dispensations for the conditions that naturally arose in missionary regions. In Europe, however, it seemed utterly intolerable to the Church to permit a union of marriage founded upon a broken unity of the Faith in the very places where the Faith had flourished for centuries.

But when all doubt as to whether or not the Reformation had come to stay had finally passed, yet when there were still hopes that the conversion of a ruler might bring back his people to the Faith, it is then that one might expect to trace the beginnings of dispensation. The first sources that bring to light the procedure of the Roman *Curia* are furnished by the examples of the mixed marriages of Catholic rulers. Not only in the "Spanish Match" which ended in a fizzle, but also in the long drawn out discussions which accompanied the contract of Prince Charles with Henrietta Marie are found in embryo the development of this dispensation. It was an affair that concerned kingdoms rather than individuals. It involved the making of a treaty between nations. Everything had to be foreseen. There were to be the provisions for the religious freedom of the princess, for the Catholic education of the children, for the mitigation of the penal laws against the British Catholics. Such transactions were elaborate and prolonged for they were to serve as precedents for the years to come.

Of all these formalities only the *cautiones scriptae* remain. Even the causes, which in the beginning had been restricted to those of a manifest public concern, yielded to the recognition of those of a private nature when the mixed marriages of the common people were to be contracted with Papal dispensation.

The Code expresses the same ancient abhorrence of mixed marriages. *Severissime Ecclesia ubique prohibet!* Yet it is a discipline that has been modified by circumstances and experience. While the Church repeats in a language born centuries ago the prohibitions to such marriages, she also provides for exceptions through dispensation. She yields when greater evils would follow upon her absolute resistance. She reserves the right of dispensation to the Congregation of the Holy Office yet grants faculties to Bishops by way of exception. She insists that the pastors of her flock be ever vigilant in deterring her children from such marriages, yet admonishes them to temper their severity with prudence and patience.

The writer takes this occasion to express his sincere gratitude to the illustrious members of the Faculty of Canon Law for their timely and helpful assistance in the preparation of this study; to Archbishop Dowling for the opportunity of advanced studies, and for his kindly and unfailing interest; to the librarians of the University Library for their many courtesies; to all, and especially to the Reverend Rudolph E. Nolan, who have assisted in the revision of the text in preparing it for the press.

PART I

PRELIMINARY DISCUSSION

CHAPTER I

PROHIBITIONS OF THE DIVINE AND NATURAL LAW TO MARRIAGES OF CATHOLICS WITH NON-CATHOLICS

ART. I. FAITH AND THE SACRAMENT OF MARRIAGE

1. Marriage is the great social sacrament that has for its primary end the generation of human life. Baptism is the social sacrament of the regeneration of this life unto Christ. Men are born as the natural sons of men to be reborn as the adopted sons of God. Marriage is truly a sacrament of life; Baptism, a sacrament of the rebirth of life, and preëminently a sacrament of Faith, for through Baptism man receives the virtue of faith, which is the foundation of his reborn life.

2. Faith is a supernatural virtue that enables man to believe the revealed truths of God on the authority of God revealing. Though freely given, it is a gift that must be used as a means of salvation for it is the basis of the life of grace, the root of justification.[1] "The just man liveth by faith."[2]

3. The virtue of faith is intimately connected with the sacrament of marriage. The sacrament of marriage reflects a profound mystery, that of the union of Christ with His Church. Grace is the principle of Christ's union with the Church, wherein is kept the unity and integrity of the Faith. It is likewise the supernatural principle of the union of husband and wife, having its root in the virtue of faith received through Baptism, the sacrament of faith. The sacrament of marriage is possible because of the sacrament of faith. The grace of the sacramental union of marriage dwells in those united to the Church and in Christ through the unity of the profession of faith. The holiness of marriage has its full realization

---

[1] Conc. Trident., *sess.* VI, *de justificatione,* cap. 8,—Denz., n. 801.
[2] Rom., I, 17.

only in those who are united in the true Faith. Where there is a departure from this unity, though the husband and wife vow to each other in Christ to have their bodies united in one, yet they rend the body of Christ by belonging to different communions.[3]

ART II. PROHIBITIONS OF THE NATURAL LAW TO MARRIAGES OF CATHOLICS WITH NON-CATHOLICS

4. But far more than the violation of this sacred ideal is involved in the marriages of Catholics with non-Catholics. The very faith that binds the Catholic to the Church and to Christ is endangered by such a union. A daily familiarity with error or unbelief removes half the dread of it.

5. The common adjustments of marital difficulties are based largely on the sacrifice of individual selfishness. But when husband and wife adhere to different professions of faith, it is no far step from the normal, mutual concessions to the sinful compromises in matters of faith. The transition may at times be almost imperceptible, arising from a delusion of fairness or broadmindedness. It readily passes into the most dangerous indifference; it may even reach the length of a compromise in the religious education of the children. In the eyes of the world such concessions may bear the semblance of equity; in the eyes of God they are treason. To barter in matters of faith is to betray the means of salvation.

6. Where marriages represent a division in faith the danger to the faith of the children is even greater than that which exists for their Catholic parent. The convictions of children will not grow normally into those that are truly Catholic where the home is not thoroughly Catholic. To what rule of faith will they adhere when they see their parents divided on the question? What Catholic instruction will they receive in the home where the Catholic parent has succumbed to indifference? Even if a Catholic father or mother has not become indifferent, what convincing explanation will be given to the

---

[3] "Nonne ingemiscimus quod vir et uxor, ut fideliter coniungant corpora sua, iurant sibi plerumque per Christum, et ipsius corpus Christi diversa communione dilaniant?"—S. Augustinus, *Epist.*, XXIII, n. 5,—*MPL*, XXXIII, 97.

children for the indifference or open opposition of the non-Catholic parent to the truths that are taught them as the most sacred and fundamental in life?[4] *Verba movent, exempla trahunt!*

ART. III. PROHIBITIONS OF THE DIVINE LAW

The warnings found in both the Old and New Testament are authentic evidence that such marriages are full of perils, the hazards of the shipwreck of the faith.

§ I. THE OLD TESTAMENT

7. In the history of man before the coming of Christ the Jews were God's Chosen People. They were the special beneficiaries of God's favor, and of His Divine Revelation to man. They too were to be justified by faith.[5] But living amongst the pagans who still remained in large numbers in the Promised Land, the Jews often forsook their God. Through marriages with these pagans the hearts of many Jews were turned to the brazen creations of idolatry. God's laws were, therefore, directed especially towards preserving the faith of His people by deterring them from alliances with heathens.

8. Thus in the Book of Exodus (XXXIV, 16) God forbade the Jews to marry daughters of the pagans lest they too become idolators. More explicit was the prohibition to marital unions with the seven pagan nations in the land of Cana: "Thou shalt make no league with them, nor show mercy to them: Neither shalt thou make marriages with them. Thou shalt not give thy daughter to his son, nor take his daughter for thy son: *For she will turn away thy son from following me, that he may rather serve strange gods . . .*"[6]

9. Cardinal Bellarmine in referring to this prohibition says that though the precept was judicial and strictly bound

---

[4] For a further discussion of the dangers to the faith of the children see Clemens XIII, ep., *Quantopere,* 16 Nov. 1763, §§ 2-3,—*Fontes,* n. 460; Pius VII, rescript. (ad ep. et vicar. capit. Galliar.), 17 Feb. 1809,—Migne, *Theol. Curs. Complet.,* XXV, 710; Tanquery, *Theol. Mor.,* Tom. I, n. 907.

[5] Cf. Rom., IV.

[6] Deut., VII, 1-4; cf. Jos., XXIII, 12-13.

only the Jews, it was also moral in its nature, transcending, therefore, the abrogation of judicial enactments and passing with full vigor into the Christian Dispensation.[7]

10. The wisdom of the prohibitions saw ample confirmation in the evil results that so often followed when they were disregarded. The tragic defection of Solomon is memorable.[8] Such marriages were among the chief causes that deprived the Chosen People of God's protection and brought heathen worship into the very palaces of their kings and to the gates of the Temple.

§ II. THE NEW TESTAMENT

11. If in the Old Law the marriages of Jews with certain pagans were forbidden because of the attendant moral dangers, there is evident reason for similar precepts in the New and more perfect Dispensation. ". . . For what participation hath justice with injustice? Or what fellowship hath light with darkness? Or what part hath the faithful with the unbeliever"?[10]

12. At first sight St. Paul seems, therefore, to forbid the marriages of Christians with pagans when he writes: "Bear not the yoke with unbelievers."[11] Yet there is not an agreement as to the precise meaning of the text. In the opinion of some of the Fathers[12] and learned authors,[13] St. Paul's concern is centered especially on *marriages* with unbelievers. Others, again,

---

[7] Lib. I *De Sacram. Matr.*, cap. XXIII,—*Op. Omnia*, Tom. V, p. 119-120. Vide etiam Sanchez, *De Matr.*, Lib. VII, Disp. 71, n. 5.

[8] III Kings, XI, 1-11.

[9] Cf. Judges, III, 5-7; III Kings, XVI, 31-32; I Esdras, IX; Malach., II, 11-12.

[10] II Cor., VI, 14-15.

[11] II Cor., VI, 14.

[12] Cf. S. Cyprianus, *Ad Quirinium*, Lib. III, cap. 62,—*Corp. Scr. Eccles. Lat.*, Vol. 3, pars I, p. 240; S. Hieronymus, *Adv. Jovinianum*, Lib. I, n. 10,—*MPL*, XXIII, 225.

[13] Estius, *In Omnes B. Pauli Comment.*; Calmet, Tom. VIII; Tirinus, *Comment. in Univ. S. Script.* (Isti auctores ad vers. cit.); Binterim, *Denkwürdigkeiten*, VI, I, p. 427-428; Wernz, *Ius Decret.*, IV, n. 503, not. 9; Cappello, *De Sacram.*, III, n. 426; Blat, *Comment.*, Vol. III, P. I, n. 467.

derive a different meaning,[14] namely, that the Apostle is reminding the Corinthians that as Christians they have been
cleansed from their former pagan vices. Never again may they
return to them. Construed in this manner, the text has no
direct reference to marriage.[15]

13. A clearer instance of a warning or prohibition can
be found in St. Paul's First Epistle to the Corinthians (VII,
39) where, in permitting a widow to marry again, he adds
the warning, ". . . only in the Lord." Very frequently these
words are interpreted to mean "Christian" as St. Thomas,[16]
Estius, Cornelius a Lapide, Tirinus,[17] and Cornely[18] prefer.
Others, however, construe the words as referring to *the manner* of marrying, that is, with an upright and religious intention,—not from base motives.[19]

14. The opinion that the phrase refers to the *person*
rather than to the *manner* of the marriage is confirmed on an
examination of the twenty-second verse of this same chapter.[20]
Here the very same words are used, "in the Lord" ($\dot{\epsilon}\nu$ $\varkappa\nu\varrho\dot{\iota}\omega$),
and they seem to designate a *Christian person*. It would appear,
therefore, more in conformity with sound exegesis to interpret
a disputed passage of the *same chapter* by one that is clear,

---

[14] Thomas Aq., *In Omnes D. Pauli Epist. Comment.*, II Cor., cap. VI,
Lectio III; Cornely, *Comment. in S. Pauli Epist.*, III, ad II Cor., VI, 14;
Leitner, *Lehrb. des kath. Eherechts*, p. 183, not. 6. Other authors do not
subscribe definitely to a fixed opinion. Cf. Cornelius a Lap., *Comment. in
Sacram. Script.*, Tom. IX, ad II Cor., VI, 14; Van Steenkiste, *S. Pauli
Epist., vers. cit.*

[15] "Verum cavendum est, ne his verbis neophytis omne commercium cum
ethnicis, qui nomine infidelium designantur, interdici censeatur . . . Ad eius
[S. Pauli] mentem iugum cum infidelibus ducunt, quicumque iisdem, quibus
illi, perversis studiis dediti eosdem cum illis perversos fines sectantur eademque
perversa via incedunt; atque iugum cum infidelibus ducentes fiunt Christiani
illi qui a pristinis vitae suae ethnicae criminibus abluti et sanctificati ad eadem
revertuntur . . . Quapropter iis non assentimur, qui . . . his verbis speciatim
cautum esse arbitrantur ne fideles cum infidelibus matrimonia contraherent . . .
At de his consortiis Apostolus hos in loco diserte non agit, sed de vitiis
fugendis, quae eos ethnicis similes reddant."—Cornely *loc. cit.*

[16] *Op. cit.*, I Cor., cap. VII, Lectio VIII.

[17] Isti auctores in *op. cit.*

[18] *Comment. in S. Pauli Epist.*, II, ad *vers. cit.*

[19] Cf. Calmet, Tom. VIII, ad Cor. VII, 39. The Fathers themselves are
divided in their interpretation. Cf. Cornely, *loc. cit.*; Tournely, *Prael. Theol.
de Sacram. Matr.*, Quaest. II, concl. 4.

[20] Cf. Binterim, *Denkwürdigkeiten*, VI, 1, p. 427.

especially if the expression is identically the same, and the context freely permits it. St. Paul would here seem clearly to demand that Christians marry only Christians.

15. The same Apostle is quite explicit in condemning associations with idolators,[21] and those who taught contrary to his doctrine.[22] He writes to Titus (III, 10) "A man that is a heretic, after the first and second admonition, avoid." St. John is even more severe in his warning. He forbids the faithful to greet or to extend any hospitality whatsoever to false teachers.[23] While these latter references to passages from the New Testament do not, indeed, refer directly to marriage, the warnings to abstain from the ordinary associations of life would assuredly apply with even greater force to the most intimate and life-enduring society, the union of marriage.

ART. IV. VALIDITY OF SUCH MARRIAGES IN THE NATURAL AND DIVINE LAW

16. Great as the hazards may be, no valid inference can be adduced to show that such marriages are at the same time *invalid* by the natural or the divine law.[24] One instance in the Old Testament is at times cited as proof that the marriages of Jews with pagans were regarded as invalid. In the First Book of Esdras (X, 3) we read: "Let us make a covenant with the Lord our God, to put away all the wives, and such as are born of them, according to the will of the Lord, and of them that fear the commandments of the Lord our God: let it be done according to the law." In the eleventh verse of the same chapter Esdras commands: ". . . separate yourselves from the people of the land, and from your strange wives." Yet Pope Benedict XIV when commenting on this passage, says

---

[21] I Cor., V, 11.

[22] Rom., XVI, 17.

[23] II John, 10-11. Cf. Tirinus, *Comment. in Univ. S. Script.*, ad II Joan. 10-11.

[24] Cf. Benedictus XIV, ep. *Singulari,* 9 Feb. 1749,—*Fontes,* n. 394; Sanchez, *De Matr.*, Lib. VII, Disp., 71, n. 7; Bellarminus, Lib I *De Sacram. Matr.*, cap. XXIII, *Op. Omnia,* Tom. V, p. 118-119; Schmalzgrueber, *Jus Eccles. Univ.,* Tom. IV, P. II, Tit. VI, n. 127; Billuart, *Curs. Theol.,* Tom. XIII, Dissert. VII, art. 10; Pirhing, *Jus Can.,* Tom. IV, Tit. I, Sect. VI, n. 164.

that even here the text should be interpreted in the light of the prohibition in the Book of Deuteronomy (VII, 1-4). The marriages were, indeed, prohibited but not invalidated; the separation that was commanded is to be understood in the sense of a *separation from bed and board.*[25]

17. Even on the probable supposition that the marriages in question were regarded as invalid, the separation was, nevertheless, the verdict of a judicial decree. It extended only to those marriages contracted with the pagans in the land of Cana.[26] Since the judicial precepts of the Old Law ceased with the New Dispensation, the enactment of Esdras does not bind Christians.[27] Nowhere in the New Testament are such marriages prohibited under pain of invalidity. The natural law in like manner postulates no such sanction. The force of these prohibitions is to render such marriages illicit when the dangers to the faith are present.

ART. V. CESSATION OF THE PROHIBITIONS OF THE DIVINE AND NATURAL LAW

18. In individual cases it may happen, however, that the dangers contemplated in the divine and natural law are absent, or have at least been rendered remote. Since the hazards to the faith form the basis of the prohibitions of the natural and divine law, their absence removes the foundation of the prohibitions, and in such instances the prohibitions themselves cease.[28]

---

[25] Ep. *Singulari,* 9 Feb., 1749, § 6,—*Fontes,* n. 394.

[26] Benedictus XIV, *ep. cit.,* § 5; Bellarminus, Lib. I *De Sacram. Matr.,* cap. XXIII,—*Op. Omnia,* Tom . V, p. 119; Salmanticenses, Tract. IX, *de Matr.,* cap. XII, punct. VI, nn. 70-71. In other instances where such marriages were contracted, they are not referred to nor regarded as invalid. See Genesis, XLI, 45; Exodus, II, 21; Judges, XIV, 3-4; III Kings, XI, 1-11 & XVI, 31-32; Santi, *Prael. Juris Can.,* Lib. IV, Tit. I, n. 171.

[27] Santi, *op. cit.,* Lib. IV, Tit. I, n. 172.

[28] Cf. Tournely, *Prael. Theol. de Sacram. Matr.,* Quaest. VII, concl. 2; Bailly, *Theol. Dogm. et Mor.,* Tom. VI, Tract. *de Matr.,* pars II, cap. II, n. 6; Ballerini-Palmieri, *Op. Theol. Mor.,* Tract. X, Sect. VIII, n. 714.

CHAPTER II

DEFINITION OF MIXED RELIGION AND DISPARITY OF CULT—BASIS OF DISTINCTION

19. The Church in her divinely appointed mission of guarding faith and morals has repeated the prohibitions of the divine and natural law, and has added to them her own legal contributions. Juridically speaking, she has erected impediments to the marriages of Catholics with heretics and schismatics, and to the marriages of the baptized with the unbaptized. These canonical barriers are commonly known as the impediments of "Mixed Religion" and "Disparity of Cult".[1]

ART. I. DEFINITION

20. "Mixed Religion" may be defined as a *prohibitive* impediment to a marriage *between two baptized persons*, one of whom belongs to the Catholic Church, and the other to an heretical or schismatic sect. "Disparity of Cult", on the other hand, is a *diriment* impediment to a marriage between a person who is *baptized* and one who is *not baptized*.[2]

§ I. ETYMOLOGICAL DERIVATION

21. If the terms "Mixed Religion" and "Disparity of Cult" are examined in relation to each other, the connotation of a specific difference in the names themselves is not clear. The word "cult" is derived from the Latin "*colere*", meaning to cultivate, to take care of, to pay respect to, to worship. "Disparity" is derived from the Latin "*dispar*" (*dis+par*), meaning unlike, different, unequal. "Mixed" is from the Latin "*miscere*",—to mingle, to mix; and "Religion" is from the

---

[1] The term "Disparity of Worship" is also frequently used.

[2] The fundamental characteristic of the impediment rests on the difference existing between the baptized and the unbaptized. The restriction of the Code (canon 1070, § 1) to Baptism in the Catholic Church, is not considered for the present.

Latin *"relegere"*,—to read again, to treat carefully; or from *"religare"*,—to bind, to bind or to subject oneself to God.[3]

§ II. Significance of the Terms

22. "Cult" may be defined as a man's interior or exterior worship of God, or of a Supreme Being (or Beings). In an objective sense, "religion" is the sum total of beliefs and practices by which men are directed to God; in a subjective sense it is a voluntary subjection of oneself to God, or some invisible and superior Being (or Beings) on whom there is a consciousness of being dependent.

23. Though notable differences exist in the concepts of religion and cult, the attempt to explain the exact difference between Disparity of Cult and Mixed Religion, on the basis of the terms themselves, is beset with difficulties.[4] In the first place the term "disparity" is predicated of "cult" and the term "mixed" of "religion". There is, therefore, no common term of comparison. Wernz[5] attempts to bring out the distinction by the use of the Greek phrase ἡ διαφορὰ τῆς θρησκείας to designate Disparity of Cult, and the phrase ἡ διαφορὰ τοῦ δόγματος to designate Mixed Religion.[6] Some distinction between the two phrases appears to have been employed also in the Eastern Church though it was not sharply defined.[7] The use of the same word ἡ διαφορά as it is predicated of both ἡ θρησκεία and τό δόγμα does, indeed, establish a common term of comparison, yet the recourse to the Greek phrases does not seem to be conclusive in determining the decisive difference between the impediments.

---

[3] The discussion as to the correct derivation of the word *"religio"* has never been settled with finality. The question is of no vital consequence in the present discussion.

[4] "Quae terminologia nunc iam diu recepta sine dubio in praxi est retinenda, quamvis differentiam utriusque impedimenti clare obvioque sensu non exprimat. Nam tandem aliquando in utroque impedimento habetur diversitas *cultus* et disparitas *religionis*, quemadmodum quilibet infidelis est acatholicus, licet in causis matrimonialibus frequenter solummodo acatholici dicuntur christiani sive baptizati, qui sectis haereticis et schismaticis, non Ecclesiae catholicae sunt adscripti."—Wernz, *Ius Decret.*, IV, n. 503, not. 6.

[5] *Ius Decret.*, IV, nn. 502, 574.

[6] Cappello (*De Sacram.*, III, n. 306) uses the Greek phrase only in connection with the impediment of Mixed Religion.

[7] Cf. Zhishman, *Das Eherecht der orient. Kirche*, p. 506, not. 2.

§ III. Historical Usage

24. Historically, the first term is "Disparity of Cult", though it was not in use until the twelfth century. The Fathers[8] and the early councils do not employ a juridic term to designate their prohibitions,—they speak rather of "the marriages of the orthodox or faithful with infidels, gentiles, pagans, Jews, heretics, or schismatics". The title *"De Dispari Cultu"* seems to have been used first by Peter Lombard.[9] Thereafter, the term remained for centuries to designate both the marriages of the baptized with the unbaptized, and those of Catholics with heretics or schismatics.

25. The authors were wont to distinguish between the two by adding differentiating words.[10] Thus they added the term "antecedent" (referring to that disparity preceding a marriage), and "subsequent" (referring to that disparity taking place after the marriage). These terms were again distinguished. Antecedent Disparity of Cult in the *strict sense* designated that disparity existing between the baptized and the unbaptized; in a *broad sense* it connoted a difference of a profession of faith of two baptized persons, one of whom belonged to the Catholic Church, and the other to an heretical or schismatic sect.[11] Subsequent Disparity of Cult in the *strict sense* arose when one of two unbaptized parties (to the same marriage) received Baptism. In a *broad sense* it arose between two married baptized Catholics, upon one of the parties apostatizing from the Cath-

---

[8] St. Ambrose uses the phrases *"dispares devotione"* and *"dispares fide"* in a rather free sense, not in the juridic sense as serving to designate an impediment. Cf. *De Abraham,* Lib. I, cap. 9, n. 84,—*MPL,* XIV, 451 (the passage is quoted in No. 37, note 28); Epist. 19 *Ad Vigilium,* - *MPL,* XVI, 984-985 (the passage is quoted in No. 36, note 24). The same may be said of the phrase *"qui veri Dei cultus esset prorsus ignarus"* used by Eadbaldus in his answer to King Edwin. See No. 53, note 20.

[9] *Sent.,* IV, D. XXXIX.

[10] The distinctions were not employed in the twelfth and early thirteenth centuries. In this brief period the one *diriment* impediment of Disparity of Cult included the marriages of Catholics with infidels, Jews, heretics, or schismatics.

[11] The authors also spoke of the "improper" and "proper" use of these terms. Cf. De Angelis, *Prael. Juris Can.,* Lib. IV, Tit. I, n. 21. Vlaming (*Prael. Iuris Matr.,* n. 207) says that the terms "imperfect" and "perfect" were employed also in documents of the Holy See.

olic Faith, joining an heretical or schismatic sect, or becoming an adherent of Judaism or Mohammedanism.[12]

26. The term "Mixed Religion" (*Mixta Religio*) was, perhaps, not employed until the nineteenth century.[13] Even in Papal letters, or in the instructions and decrees of the Congregations, the prohibition was under the heading of the title, "Mixed Marriages" (*matrimonia mixta* or *nuptiae mixtae*),[14] or it was designated by longer expressions such as "the marriages of Catholics with those ascribed to heretical or schismatic sects." The term "*Mixta Religio*" in all probability has its more immediate origin in the term "*matrimonia mixta*". In the Code, the connotation of the terms "*Mixta Religio*" and "*Disparitas Cultus*" is fixed and definite.[15]

ART. II. BASIS OF DISTINCTION

27. The specific difference between the two impediments is centered, however, rather on the fundamental issues underlying both impediments than on the names by which they are known. The presence or absence of Baptism in the parties to the marriage is a basic consideration. Baptism marks the inequality or difference between a Christian and an infidel.[16] Because of the nature of Baptism, which is a birth to the supernatural life, the difference between the baptized and the unbaptized is *radical*. On the other hand, Baptism marks the basic

---

[12] In the *strict sense*, subsequent Disparity of Cult established a condition that, together with given circumstances, might serve as a foundation for invoking the *Pauline Privilege*. Cf. c. 7, X, *de divortiis*, IV, 19. This was not true, of course, of subsequent Disparity of Cult in the *broad sense*. Cf. Conc. Trident., sess. XXIV, *de Sacram. Matr.*, can. 5,—Denz., n. 975; Benedictus XIV, ep. *Singulari*, 9 Feb. 1749, § 11,—*Fontes*, n. 394.

[13] One will look in vain among the older authors for the specific term "*Mixta Religio*".

[14] "Quare cum mixta religione non est confundenda [Disparitas Cultus], etsi in nonnullis documentis *matrimonia mixta* dicantur ea quae cum disparitate cultus et quae cum mixta religione inita sunt."—Vermeersch-Creusen, *Epitome*, II, n. 344.

[15] Cf. canons 1061, § 1; 1063, § 1; 1071; 1120, § 2. The phrase "*mixtae nuptiae*" continues to designate the marriages of Catholics with members of heretical or schismatic sects. Cf. canon 1064, nn. 1, 3. The phrase "*matrimonium mixtum*" in canon 2375 may, perhaps, refer to marriages contracted with either impediment.

[16] The terms "Christian" and "infidel" are here used in a strict sense with reference to reception or the non-reception of Baptism.

likeness or parity that exists between a Catholic and a heretic or a schismatic,—the difference that exists between them is *modal*[17] rather than radical. The *radical* difference arises on the basis of the *sacrament of faith*; the *modal* on the basis of the *profession of faith*.

N. B. In the chapters that follow, whenever the term "mixed marriages" is employed, it will refer to the marriages of Catholics with heretics or schismatics. The term "disparate marriages" will refer to the marriages of the baptized with the unbaptized, or, in the restricted sense of the impediment in the Code, i. e., the marriages of those baptized in the Catholic Church or converted to the Catholic Church, with the unbaptized.

---

[17] The term "modal" does not mean, however, that a truly grave difference does not exist.

PART II

HISTORICAL DEVELOPMENT

Foreword

The available evidence for the Church's early legislation on the marriages of the faithful with unbelievers is derived largely from the Fathers, ecclesiastical writers, and particular councils.

Particular or provincial legislation and practice has, of itself, authority only over the limited region for which it was established.* The strictly chronological arrangement is inadequate to show its development into universal legislation and practice. A sameness of discipline exhibited in a chronological series of Spanish councils would have no force in France or Italy. On the other hand the degree of universality that a certain discipline possessed is more easily ascertained if attention is centered on discovering its presence in *all* the provinces of the heart and center of Christendom. In the present study, therefore, the chronological is subservient to the regional or geographical arrangement of the Church's early legislation.

---

* "Et propterea quamvis sola confirmatio Pontificia non efficiat, ut leges in illis latae ultra territorium suum extendantur, usu tamen, et traditione Ecclesiae approbatio, et confirmatio Papae operatur, ut etiam ultra territorium proprium extendantur, et deserviant pro norma Ecclesiae Universalis . . ." Albitius, *De Inconstantia in Fide*, Cap. XXXVI, n. 184. Cf. Feije, *De Matr. Mixtis*, p. 60-61.

CHAPTER III

THE ECCLESIASTICAL PROHIBITIONS OF THE FIRST FIVE CENTURIES

28. The Church set forth to win souls for Christ in a world that was grossly pagan, in a world that sought to dismiss her by the sophistries of its philosophers, in a world that saw foolishness in the Cross of Christ. Heresies, moreover, arose on every side to imperil the faith of the early Christians. From the very beginning, therefore, the Church saw the necessity of providing safeguards that the faith of her members might remain one and unblemished. Although some associations of the Christians with the world as it existed were inevitable, the Church knew the dangers and sought to deter the faithful from them as much as possible. While many fled to the deserts to keep a virgin tryst with Christ, the larger number remained in the world to marry. Here arose a vital need for the Church's vigilance that the marriages of the faithful would not lead them to a shipwreck of their faith. The Church repeated the warnings of Sacred Scripture, and in her councils legislated practical prohibitions to such marriages as were perilous to the Faith.

Art. I. The Church in the East

29. Thus the Council of Laodicaea (between 343 and 381) decreed that the members of the Church ought by no means to unite their children "indifferently" with heretics in matrimony.[1] Fuchs draws attention to the proper interpretation of the word "indifferently" (*indiscriminatim*), urging that the council did not refer to a discrimination in the selection of heretics, but rather rebuked those to whom it was of little concern whether they gave their children in marriage to here-

---

[1] Can. 10: "Non oportere eos qui sunt ecclesiae, *indiscriminatim* suos filios haereticis matrimonio coniungere."—Mansi, II, 565.

tics or to Catholics.[2] This opinion apparently receives confirmation in a later canon of this council, which ruled that it was not lawful to enter marriage with all sorts of heretics or to give their children to them; they were rather to receive them if they professed themselves as future Catholics.[3]

ART. II. THE CHURCH IN NORTHERN AFRICA

30. With his characteristic vehemence of expression Tertullian severely condemns the marriages of Christians with pagans,—at times almost insinuating their invalidity.[4] Such marriages, he says, are against the divine law,[5] and the Christians are not to enter them lest they be led into idolatry and unbelief.[6] When he refers to St. Paul's words, "only in the Lord", he argues that they were written not as a matter of advice but in the sense of a command.[7] Much of Tertullian's argument must, however, be received with caution since his reference to the words of St. Paul often serves as an occasion for a withering denunciation of second marriage.

---

[2] The observation is cited and approved by Hefele, *Conciliengeschichte*, I, 756. Feije (*De Matr. Mixtis*, p. 30) gives the same interpretation to canon 67 of the Council of Agde (506) which repeated substantially the provisions of this council. See No. 42, note 1.

[3] Can. 31: "Quod non oportet *cum omni haeretico* matrimonium contrahere, vel dare filios aut filias: sed magis accipere, si se Christianos futuros profiteantur."—Mansi, II, 569. The readings of this canon as given by Dionysius Exiguus (Mansi, II, 580) and Isidor Mercator (Mansi II, 588) have the word "*Christianos*" though the context of the canon in its dealing with heretics seems to demand the translation of "*Christianos*" by the word "Catholics". The phrase "*cum omni haeretico*" seems to offer a close parallel to the word "*indiscriminatim*" of canon 10. For a critical discussion of the Greek text of both canons 10 and 31 see Feije, *De Matr. Mixtis*, p. 48-53.

[4] "Igitur cum quaedam istis diebus nuptias suas de Ecclesia *tolleret*, id est, gentili coniungeretur, idque ab aliis retro factum recordarer, miratus ut ipsarum petulantiam aut consiliariorum praevaricationem, quod nulla scriptura eius facti licentiam profert."—*Ad uxorem*, Lib. II, cap. 2, — *MPL*, I, 1290. In referring to this passage, Binterim (*Denkwürdigkeiten*, VI, I, p. 432) thinks that by the word "*tolleret*" Tertullian meant to say that such marriages were invalid. While the expression is, perhaps, one of the most forceful of any found in the early centuries, yet it must be remembered that Tertullian often exaggerates and that too great a stress must not be laid on a word in a passage from his writings.

[5] *De Monogamia*, cap. 7,—*MPL*, II, 938; *Adversus Marcion*, Lib. V. cap. 7,—*MPL*, II, 487.

[6] *Liber de Corona*, cap. 13,—*MPL*, II, 96; *De Monogamia*, cap. 11,—*MPL*, II, 945-946; *Ad uxorem*, Lib. II, cap. 3,—*MPL*, I, 1292-1293.

[7] *Ad uxorem*, Lib. II, cap. 1,—*MPL*, I, 1290.

St. Cyprian, Bishop of Carthage in the third century, likewise denounces the marriages of Christians with pagans as a prostitution of the members of Christ.[8] He emphasized in particular the dangers arising from such unions, citing as proof the evil that befell Solomon.[9]

31. In the light of the writings of Tertullian and St. Cyprian, the statement of St. Augustine that in his time such marriages were not thought to be sinful, may, at first sight, afford an element of surprise.[10] But if the entire context of the passage be examined carefully it will be apparent that St. Augustine did not express this as his own attitude nor as that of the Church, but rather as that of certain lax Christians who were of that opinion.[11] He inveighs, moreover, against the marriages of the faithful with heretics.[12]

32. The councils held in Northern Africa may be grouped together since their legislation concerned itself in each instance with the marriages of clerics and their children with those outside of the Church. Thus the Council of Hippo (393) forbade the children of clerics to marry pagans, heretics and schismatics.[13]

---

[8] " . . . iungere cum infidelibus vinculum matrimonii, prostituere gentibus membra Christi."—*De Lapsis*, cap. 6,—*Corp. Scr. Eccl. Lat.*, Vol. 3, pars I, p. 240.

[9] *Ad Quirinium*, Lib. III, cap. 62,—*Corp. Scr. Eccl. Lat.*, Vol. 3, pars I, p. 166.

[10] See the following note and *De coniugiis adulterinis*, Lib. I, cap. 25,— *MPL*, XL, 468-469.

[11] " . . . Sed quoniam malorum christianorum mores, qui fuerunt antea etiam pessimi, habuisse non videntur hoc malum, ut alienas uxores ducerent viri, aut alienis viris feminae nuberent; inde fortasse apud quasdam Ecclesias negligentia ista subrepsit, ut in catechismis competentium nec quaererentur nec percuterentur haec vitia; atque inde factum est, ut inciperent et defendi . . . Hinc autem existimandum est non ea primum apparuisse in moribus quamvis malorum christianorum, quoniam beatus Cyprianus in epistola de Lapsis, cum deplorando et arguendo multa commemoraret, quibus merito dicit indignationem Dei fuisse commotam, ut intolerabili persecutione Ecclasiam suam sineret flagellari, haec ibi omnino non nominat: cum etiam illud non taceat, et ad eosdem mores pertinere confirmet, iungere cum infidelibus vinculum matrimonii nihil aliud esse asserens, quam prostituere Gentibus membra Christi: quae nostris temporibus iam non putantur esse peccata; quoniam revera in Novo Testamento nihil inde praeceptum est, et ideo, aut licere creditum est, aut velut dubium derelictum."—*De fide et operibus*, Lib. I, cap. 19,—*MPL*, XL, 220-221. Cf. *De coniugiis adulterinis*, Lib. I, cap. 21,— *MPL*, XL, 465-466; Binterim, *Denkwürdigkeiten*, VI, I, p. 436.

[12] Sermo XLVI, *De Pastoribus in Eziechiel*, cap. VII,—*MPL*, XXXVIII, 278-279; Epist., XXIII, n. 5,—*MPL*, XXXIII, 97 (See No. 3, note 3).

[13] Can. 12,—Mansi, III, 921.

The same canon is repeated, practically verbatim, in the Third Council of Carthage (397).[14] A somewhat similar prohibition for clerics, though not explicitly concerned with marriage, is repeated in the seventieth canon of the Fourth Council of Carthage (436).[15] The Bishops assembled in these councils appear to have been concerned principally with the scandal that would naturally be given by clerics entering such unions. Since the opinion that such marriages were not unlawful was prevalent at this time the correction of the abuse would certainly have to begin with the clergy.[16]

ART. III. THE CHURCH IN SPAIN

33. In point of time, the Council of Elvira (306) was apparently the first council to legislate on the marriages of the faithful with unbelievers. At an early date the problem in Spain became particularly acute because of the large and influential Jewish population.[17] In its reference to marriage, however, the council seems to be equally severe against heretics. "If heretics will not enter the Catholic Church, the daughters of Catholics must not be given to them in marriage.[18] They are not to be given to Jews or to heretics because there can be no society between believers and unbelievers. If parents violate this law they must be withheld from communion for five years."[19]

34. Though marriages with pagans were also forbidden,[20] the danger to the Faith from that source was not as great as it was from heretics and Jews. The pagans were not as bitter, nor did they possess the obstinate convictions characteristic of the Jews. It is worthy of note that the Council of Elvira marks the beginning of a severity in condemning the marriages of Christians with Jews that in the course of time seems to have taken the form of a diriment impediment.

---

[14] Can. 12,—Mansi, III, 882.

[15] Mansi, III, 957.

[16] Cf. Feije, *De Matr. Mixtis*, p. 29-30.

[17] Cf. Dale, *The Synod of Elvira*, p. 254-262.

[18] The prescription of this clause is much the same as that incorporated into the Council of Laodicaea a half century later.

[19] Can. 16,—Mansi, II, 8. See also canons 17, 50, and 78.

[20] Can. 15: "Propter copiam puellarum, Gentibus minime in matrimonium dandae sunt virgines Christianae, ne aetas in flore tumens in adulterio animae resolvatur."—Mansi, II, 8.

ART. IV. THE CHURCH IN FRANCE

35. Hefele, in speaking of the Council of Arles (314),
says that it may be considered a General Council of the Roman
Patriarchate.[21] In its eleventh canon the council decreed that
Christian maidens, who had married pagans, were to be denied
communion for a time.[22] In its reference to young women the
canon may be closely allied with the fifteenth canon of the
Council of Elvira, though its addition of punishment is new.[23]

ART. V. THE CHURCH IN ITALY

36. Much significance is contained in the prohibitions of
St. Ambrose. In a letter to St. Vigilius he writes that there
could scarcely be anything more grave than marriages with
aliens to the Faith, for such unions were seared with the flames
of lust and dissension, and branded with the crimes of sacrilege.[24] By impugning such marriages on the involved crimes
of sacrilege he emphasizes a prohibition that centuries later was
repeated almost verbatim by the Popes.[25] It is not entirely apparent, however, that in using the term *"sacrilegii flagitia"* St.
Ambrose employed it in precisely the same sense as did the
Roman Pontiffs. Their use of the term refers, perhaps, more
immediately to the "profanation of the sacrament" and to the
"communicatio in sacris".[26] While these elements may have
been foremost in the mind of St. Ambrose, he would seem to

---

[21] *Conciliengeschichte,* I, 202.

[22] Mansi, II, 472.

[23] Hefele, *op. cit.,* I, 211.

[24] ". . . Nihil gravius, quam copulari alienigenae, ubi et libidinis et dis-
cordiae incentiva, et *sacrilegii flagitia* conflantur. Nam cum ipsum coniugium
velamine sacerdotali, et benedictione sanctificari oporteat; quomodo potest
coniugium dici, ubi non est fidei concordia? Cum oratio communis esse debeat, quomodo inter dispares devotione potest esse coniugii communis cha-
ritas? Saepe plerique capti amore feminarum fidem suam prodiderunt . . ."
Epist. 19, *Ad Vigilium,*—*MPL,* XVI, 984-985.

[25] Benedictus XIV, Const. *Matrimonia,* 4 Nov. 1741,—*Coll.,* n. 333;
ep. encycl. *Magnae Nobis,* 29 Iun. 1748, § 2,—*Fontes,* n. 387; Pius VI,
rescript. ad Card. Archiep. Mechlinien., 13 Iul. 1782, n. 1,—*Fontes,* n. 471;
Pius VII, rescript. (ad ep. Galliar.), 17 Feb. 1809,—Migne, *Theol. Curs.
Complet.,* XXV, 710; Gregorius XVI, allocut. *Officii memores,* 5 Iul.
1839,—*Fontes,* n. 492; litt. ap. *Quas vestro,* 30 Apr. 1841, n. 1,—*Fontes,*
n. 497.

[26] Cf. Eichmann, *Kath. Mischehenrecht nach dem C. I. C.,* p. 13-14.

include also other evils that were *consequent* upon such unions, rather than those immediately present in the very act of form ing them.

37. His prohibition includes the marriages of the faithful with pagans, Jews and heretics, and he adduces the divine law in support of his reasons.[27] With regard to the marriages with pagans, however, he introduces a reason for their prohibition which is both striking and significant since it turns on the sacrament of Baptism and on the grace of the sacrament of marriage.[28] The passage is, perhaps, the only one to be found in the writings of the Fathers wherein the factor of Baptism is used in connection with this prohibition. Centuries later, the element of Baptism was to be of primary importance in determining the impediment of Disparity of Cult.

St. Zeno,[29] Bishop of Verona, and St. Jerome[30] stress the dangers that usually accompany such marriages. St. Jerome seems to be of the opinion that St. Paul strictly prohibited them.[31]

ART. VI. THE ECUMENICAL COUNCIL OF CHALCEDON

38. The Council of Chalcedon is the only Ecumenical Council that has legislated directly on the marriages of the

---

[27] *De Abraham*, Lib. I, cap. 9, n. 84,—*MPL*, XIV, 451; *Expositio in Ps. CXVIII*, Sermo 20, n. 48,—*MPL*, XV, 1499; *Expositio Evang. sec. Lucam*, Lib. VIII, n. 2,—*MPL*, XV, 1765.

[28] "Cave, inquam, gentilem aut Iudaeam atque alienigenam, hoc est, haereticam, et omnem alienam a fide tua uxorem arcessas tibi . . . *Si Christiana sit, non est satis, nisi ambo initiati sitis sacramento baptismatis . . . Non possunt hoc dispares fide credere, ut ab eo quem non colit, putet sibi connubii impartitam gratiam* . . . Primum ergo in coniugio religio quaeritur."—*DeAbraham*, Lib. I, cap. 9, n. 84,—*MPL*, XIV, 451. The passage does not indicate in any way that St. Ambrose regarded such marriages as invalid. Cf. Astesani de Asta, *Summa*, Lib. VIII, Tit. XV, art. 1.

[29] *Tractatus*, Lib. I, Tract. V, nn. 7-9,—*MPL*, XI, 307-311.

[30] St. Jerome is a witness of both the Eastern and Western discipline. His intimate association with Pope Damasus should justify the insertion of his testimony under the present grouping.

[31] *Adversus Jovinianum*, Lib. I, n. 10,—*MPL*, XXIII, 225.

faithful with those outside of the Church.[32] In its fourteenth canon this Council forbade chanters and lectors (to whom marriage was permitted in certain regions) to marry heretical women. Those who already had children of such marriages and had had them baptized by heretics, were to bring these children into the communion of the Church. The unbaptized children were not to be baptized in an heretical sect, nor were they to be married to heretics, Jews, or pagans, unless such unbelievers would be converted to the Catholic Faith.[33]

39. The force of the prohibition may at first sight appear to be somewhat limited since it speaks only of the lower order of clerics and their children. Yet the canon must be regarded in much the same light as the legislation of the councils of Northern Africa. The councils of prominent centers of Christendom[34] and the Fathers had been unanimous in prohibiting such marriages, though it appears that practice did not always con-

---

[32] The sixty-seventh and sixty-ninth canons of the Arabic Collection of the Council of Nicaea (Mansi, II, 975) have been cited at times to show the great antiquity of the diriment force of the impediment of Disparity of Cult. While the text of these canons seems to suppose the dirimency of the impediment, yet the argument drawn from them has little or no value. It is generally agreed that this Arabic Collection of Nicaea is spurious, and that the only authentic canons are the *twenty* usually attributed to this Council. Cf. Hefele, *Conciliengeschichte*, I, 367; Ballerini-Palmieri, *Op. Theol. Mor.*, Tract. X, Sect. VIII, n. 702. On the other hand see Scherer, *Handbuch des Kirchenrechtes*, II, p. 373, not. 7. Whoever compiled the collection evidently considered the marriages of Christians with infidels as invalid. But who was the compiler, and when and where was the collection made? The collection was not discovered to the Western world until the sixteenth century. No decisive evidence exists to show at what time it was known in the East. Trombellius (*Tract. de Matr.*, Tom. III, Dissert. IX, cap. II, art. 1, n. 14) says that these canons are very old and represent the early discipline of the Church. At best, the statement is vague. Binterim (*Denkwürdigkeiten*, VI, I, p. 444) states that they were known in the seventh century but he offers no conclusive proofs. Even if the canons were known at an early date the evidence is wanting to show that they had any function in the development of the law of the Church. They do, indeed, represent the mind of the man or men who made the spurious collection. but unless these canons can be shown to have had their influence on the mind and practice of the Church, they are of negligible value.

[33] Mansi, VII, 388. For the various versions of canon 14 of the Council of Chalcedon see Feije, *De Matr. Mixtis*, p. 4-6. In effect all the readings are substantially the same.

[34] The condition enacted by the Council of Chalcedon for licit entrance into marriages with those outside the Church was the same as that demanded at Elvira and Laodicaea, namely, the conversion of the unbeliever. The faith of the children is an added concern of the Council of Chalcedon.

form to law.[35] In its concern over this laxity the Church at Chalcedon, as well as at Hippo and Carthage, directed its attention to a source of evil, the scandalous conduct of certain clerics.[36] This concentration represents rather a determined effort of the Church to remove the evil entirely than a toleration of such marriages among the laity.

ART. VII. SUMMARY

40. The marriages of the faithful with aliens to the Faith were, therefore, universally forbidden at the close of the fourth century.[37] The Council of Chalcedon in the fifth century merely enacted a practical measure to safeguard what had already been established *as law* in all the Christian communities. At this period there is no indication that a distinction existed universally between the marriages of Catholics with heretics or schismatics, and the marriages of Catholics with Jews and infidels. All marriages with those outside the Church were forbidden under one prohibition. Nor is there any apparent provision for dispensation. The instances of such marriages that are commonly cited[38] afford no information of a dispensation having been given; they exemplify rather the ultimate conversion of the unbeliever. The promise of conversion was the condition of licit entrance into such marriages.[39] The opinion of Westermarck,[40] however, that such marriages were *encouraged*, seems to lack an historical foundation. It was almost inevitable that some such

---

[35] See No. 31, note 11.

[36] Cf. Feije, *De Matr. Mixtis*, p. 4, 7.

[37] Cf. Hergenröther, P., *Lehrb. des kath. Kirchenrechts*, p. 728; Scherer, *Handb. des Kirchenrechtes*, II, p. 407; Binterim, *Denkwürdigkeiten*, VII, II, p. 23-24. St. Leo the Great also gave a general warning as to the dangers of association with pagan women. (Cf. Sermo XVI, *De Ieiunio decimi mensis V.*, cap. 5,—*MPL*, LIV, 179.) The prohibition was not, however, in the form of a diriment impediment. Cf. Sanchez, *De Matr.*, Lib. VII, Disp. 71, n. 8 (and all modern authors).

[38] Cf. Binterim, *op. cit.*, VI, I, p. 451-456.

[39] In that age Baptism was often received late in life, a fact which may account for some marriages of the Christians with the catechumens.

[40] *History of Human Marriage*, Vol. II, p. 58. Westermarck refers to Winroth, *Offentlig Ratt. Familjeratt; Äktenskapshindren*, p. 212.

marriages would take place[41] for the early Christian communities were often small and in the midst of a pagan population. St. Augustine complains of the laxity of his age. The protests of the Fathers and the councils afford clear evidence that it was entirely foreign to the mind of the Church to encourage such marriages.

---

[41] Binterim (*Denkwürdigkeiten*, VI, I, p. 452) calls attention to the fact that all the well known cases of such marriages are those of Christian *women* with pagan men. The Council of Elvira, too, refers to the "*copia puellarum*". The marked concern of the Church that Christian *women* should not enter into such marriages may receive some explanation in the fact that in Roman Law women were to follow the religion of their husbands. Cf. Vlaming, *Prael. Iuris Matr.*, I, p. 183, not. 2. Feije (*De Matr. Mixtis*. p. 29) in referring to the concern expressed by the Council of Elvira that Catholic women be not given in marriage to Jews and heretics, says: "Ratio est, quod filiae solebant nuptui tradi a parentibus, filii vero non ita."

CHAPTER IV

THE SIXTH TO THE TWELFTH CENTURY

41. The one prohibition that existed in the early ages of the Church to the marriages of Catholics with heretics, schismatics, pagans, and Jews, had been established primarily because of the attendant dangers to the Faith. Accordingly, as the presumption of this peril attached itself in a more definite and marked way to any one of the enumerated classes of unbelievers, the councils legislated with a proportionate severity. Yet it appears that the gradual evolution of the one prohibition into two distinct impediments left the original prohibition to the marriages of Catholics with heretics and schismatics substantially the same.

Art. I. Marriages of the Faithful with Heretics

42. When the councils of the sixth and seventh centuries directed their attention to the marriages of Catholics with heretics and schismatics, their enactments represented repetitions of the canons of former councils rather than a development or formation of new elements to the prohibition already existing.[1]

43. The most singular decree is found in the Council in Trullo (692) held after the Sixth Council of Constantinople. In its seventieth canon it erected a diriment impediment to the

---

[1] The collection made in Northern Africa by Fulgentius Ferrandus contains the Law of Laodicaea. Cf. *Breviatio Canonum*, nn. 180, 182,—*MPL*, LXVII,958-959. The Council of Agde (506) in its sixty-seventh canon (Mansi, VIII, 336) repeated substantially the provisions of Laodicaea. For a discussion as to the authenticity of this canon see Feije, *De Matr. Mixtis*, p. 31, not. 1. In all probability it has a spurious origin. With regard to the dependent relation of this canon of the Council of Agde see Berardi, *Gratiani Can.*, Vol. I, p. 254; Feije, *op. cit.*, p. 30; Binterim, *Denkwürdigkeiten*, VII, II, p. 26. The thirteenth canon of the Council of Lerida (524) [Mansi, VIII, 614] contains a fragment of the legislation of Chalcedon. Cf. Binterim, *loc. cit.* Canon twenty of the Seventeenth Council of Toledo (694) [Mansi, XII, 106] depends for its wording and context on the canons of the councils of Agde, Laodicaea, and Elvira.

marriages of the orthodox with heretics.[2] In the present study, however, the enactment is of little significance for the decree of the Council in Trullo, while exerting an influence in the Eastern Church for centuries,[3] was disregarded in the Western Church, and even repudiated by Pope Sergius.[4]

44. It appears that marriages with heretics were not an infrequent occurence among the Franks[5] though Binterim argues that the early canons, by being incorporated into civil laws, were faithfully observed.[6]

ART. II. MARRIAGES OF THE FAITHFUL WITH PAGANS AND JEWS

45. The councils of this period exhibit no definite line of demarcation from the orginal prohibition regarding the marriages of the faithful with *pagans* and *infidels*. The real concern

---

[2] "Non licere virum orthodoxum muliere haeretica coniungi, neque vero orthodoxam cum viro haeretico copulari. Sed et si quid eiusmodi ab ullo ex omnibus factum apparuerit, *irritas nuptias* existimare, et *nefarium coniugium dissolvi* . . ."—Mansi, XI, 975. Wernz, (*Ius Decret.*, IV, n. 504 cum not. 19) in estimating the date when Disparity of Cult became a diriment impediment, draws attention to this canon of the Council in Trullo as a possible starting point. Yet, from the wording and context of the entire canon it is not clearly evident that the marriages of the orthodox with *infidels* were included under the diriment impediment to the marriages of the orthodox with heretics. Though the marriages of Catholics with heretics were regarded as invalid by some authors of the twelfth century (cf. No. 66, note 6) there is no evidence that the opinion was in any way influenced by the enactment of the Council in Trullo. The Western Church, moreover, did not accept this discipline. Cf. Benedictus XIV, *Opera Inedita*, p. 432.

[3] Cf. Vering, *Lehrb. des kath. orient. und prot. Kirchenr.*, p. 915.

[4] Sanchez, *De Matr.*, Lib. VII, Disp. 28, n. 7; Pichler, *Jus Can.*, Tom. I, Lib. IV, Tit. I, n. 130; Reiffenstuel, *Jus Can. Univ.*, Lib. IV, Tit. I, n. 358; Feije, *De Matr. Mixtis*, p. 85; Wernz, *Ius Decret.*, IV, n. 576; De Becker, *De Spons. et Matr.*, p. 275.

[5] Loening, *Das Kirchenr. im Reich der Merowinger*, II, p. 566, and not. 2. "Desiderius, rex Longobardorum, persuadere voluerat Carolo et Carlomanno regibus Francorum, ut eorum alteruter uxorem duceret Desideratam, filiam Desiderii, Arianam. In Epistola quam hac de re anno 770 ad eos dedit Stephanus IV haec leguntur: 'Nullus . . . qui mentem sanam habet, hoc vel suspicari potest, ut tales nominatissimi reges, tanto detestabili atque abominabili contagio implicentur: quae enim societas luci ad tenebras? aut quae pars fideli cum infideli'"?—Feije, *op. cit.*, p. 8.

[6] *Denkwürdigkeiten*, VII, II, p. 27. As a reason for no tangible development in legislation he adduces an argument from the fact that no heresies of importance arose at this period,—that the early legislation, therefore, sufficed for the needs of the time.

of the councils was centered rather on the marriages of the faithful with *Jews*. The dangers arising from such marriages were deemed so great that in the course of time they appear to have given rise to a diriment impediment.

§ I. THE CHURCH IN SPAIN

46. The marked discipline against marriages with Jews had already received an impetus in the Council of Elvira. It was to grow in severity, especially in the succeeding councils of Spain. Thus the fourteenth canon of the Third Council of Toledo (589)[7] forbidding marriages with those outside the Church, directed its attention solely to such unions with Jews.

47. In the following century the discipline assumed an additional element at the Fourth Council of Toledo (633) where is was decreed that converted wives of Jewish husbands were to be separated from them unless they too became Christians. In any event, the children were to follow the faith of their Christian mother.[8] Though the enactment considers rather the separation from a union already contracted in Judaism than the antecedent invalidity of a marriage between a Christian and a Jew, it does offer striking evidence of the absolute abhorrence of the Church in Spain to the marital union of a Christian with a Jew. The renewed and vigorous condemnations in the subsequent councils of Toledo[9] of marital or any other association with Jews, served as a foundation for the rise of a diriment impediment to the marriages of Christians with Jews.

48. In the eighth century Pope Hadrian I wrote to the Spanish Bishops deploring the fact that some Christians in Spain did not think it sinful to associate with Jews and un-

---

[7] Mansi, IX, 996.

[8] Canon 63: "Iudaei qui christianas mulieres in coniugio habent, admoneantur ab episcopo civitatis ipsius, ut si cum eis permanere cupiunt, Christiani efficiantur. Quod si admoniti noluerint, separentur . . . Filii autem ex talibus nati existunt, fidem atque conditionem matris sequantur . . ." Barbosa (*Coll. Doct.—Decret. Gratiani*, Tom. V, Causa XXVIII, cap. X, n. 1) and Sanchez (*De Matr.*, Lib. VII, Disp. 73, n. 11) give as a reason for the restricted reference of the canon to *wives*, the fact of the greater danger of perversion due to the subjection of wives to their husbands.

[9] Toletanum X (656), cap. 7,—Mansi, XI, 37; Toletanum XII, (681), cap. 9,—Mansi, XI, 1035-1036; Toletanum XVI (693), cap. 1,—Mansi, XII, 68-69; Toletanum XVII (694), cap. 8,—Mansi, XII, 101-102.

baptized pagans, and adds: ". . . *et illud* QUOD INHIBITUM EST, *ut nulli liceat iugum ducere cum infidelibus, ipsi enim filias suas cum alio benedicent, et sic populo gentili traden- tur . . .*"[10] By the use of the more general term *"infidelibus"* the Pope appears to refer to the universal prohibition of the Church covering all marriages of the faithful with those outside of the Church. The force of the phrase, *"quod inhibitum est"*, has, therefore, no reference to the Spanish legislation against marriages with Jews, (a discipline which by this time may have taken on the form of a diriment impediment), but rather to the discipline of the universal Church.

§ II. THE CHURCH IN FRANCE

49. As in Spain, the Church in France was confronted with the same problem of the marriages of Christians with Jews. The legislation of the councils of this region appears to be even more severe. The nineteenth canon of the Second Coun- cil of Orleans (533) represents, perhaps, the clearest evidence of the probable development of the prohibition into a diriment impediment. *"Placuit ut nullus Christianus Iudaeam, neque Iudaeus Christianam in matrimonio ducat uxorem, quia inter huiusmodi personas* ILLICITAS NUPTIAS *esse censemus. Qui si commoniti* A CONSORTIO HOC SE SEPARARE *distulerint, a com- munionis gratia sunt sine dubio submovendi."*[11] Binterim is of the opinion that the word *"illicitas"* has the force of *"irri- tas"* since the Christians who enter such marriages are excom- municated if they will not separate from their Jewish consorts.[12] While the separation may, perhaps, be understood in the sense of a separation *from bed and board*, yet the context of the canon seems to favor Binterim's interpretation,—the very denial of the *ius coniugale*. The Second Council of Orleans appears, there- fore, to offer the first instance of a *diriment* impediment to the marriages of Christians with Jews.

50. The Council of Auvergne (535) decreed that Christ- ians were not to marry Jews under penalty of excommunica-

---

[10] Ep. *Institutio universalis*, a. 785.—*Fontes*, n. 24.
[11] ˙Mansi, VIII, 838.
[12] *Denkwürdigkeiten*, VI, I, p. 441-442.

tion.[13] The canon itself seems to offer no indication that such marriages were regarded as invalid.[14] The severity of the penalty and the council's proximity in time and place to the Second Council of Orleans may indicate, however, that the *invalidity* of marriages between Christians and Jews was taken for granted. Though the inference is somewhat hazardous the argument from silence must not be pressed too far. The Third Council of Orleans (538), held but five years after the second council, does not repeat the decree of its predecessor to the extent of invalidating such marriages,[15] but by its silence it does not thereby revoke the discipline already established. It seems rather to emphasize the added punishment of excommunication.

51. A further indication of an accepted diriment impediment is derived from the thirty-first canon of the Fourth Council of Orleans (541) whereby a Jew marrying his Christian female slave, thereby lost his slave.[16] The decree of separation does not appear to derive its greatest force from the fact that the woman was a slave, but from the fact that she was a Christian.

52. The Council of Meaux (845) recalled the ancient disciplinary measures that had been decreed against the Jews. It quoted the sixth canon of the Council of Auvergne, many of the enactments of the Fourth Council of Toledo, and several decrees of Roman civil law.[17]

Rhabanus Maurus, referring to the discipline concerning the marriages of Christians with Jews, quotes the eleventh canon of the Council of Arles, the seventy-eighth canon of the Council of Elvira, and the fourteenth canon of the Third Council of

---

[13] Can. 6,—Mansi, VIII, 861.

[14] Barbosa (*Coll. Doct.*—*Decret. Gratiani*, Tom. V, Causa XXVIII, cap. XVII) writes of this canon: "Vulgo notatur hic text. ad hoc quod Iudaeus contrahens matrimonium cum Christiana *separari statim* debet, ut per Masquard, *de Iudae. part 2, cap. 3, a num. 1.*" He adds three other authorities to substantiate the statement.

[15] Can. 13,—Mansi, IX, 15. Dom Chardon (*Histoire du Sacrement de Mariage*, chap. XIII,—Migne, *Theol. Curs. Complet.*, XX, 1117), however, seems to attribute an invalidating force to this canon of the Third Council of Orleans, while regarding canon 19 of the Second Council of Orleans as merely referring to their unlawfulness.

[16] Mansi, IX, 118.

[17] Can. 73,—Mansi, XIV, 836-839.

Toledo. He does not comment upon these canons to indicate his attitude with reference to the validity of such marriages.[18]

§ III. THE CHURCH IN ENGLAND

The problem in England was not the same as that in the Mediterranean countries. England at this time was confronted with paganism; the Mediterranean countries were menaced by the Jews.[19]

53. When the pagan King Edwin wished to marry the Christian Ethelburga he was opposed by her brother, Eadbaldus.[20] Even Pope Boniface V (625) wrote to King Edwin urging him to renounce his paganism entirely[21] and communicated his desire to Ethelburga that she bring her pagan husband to the Christian faith.[22] Though his words do not in any way insinuate the invalidity of the marriage, (the condition for its licit entrance had already been fulfilled), it is significant that the Pope in an individual instance deemed it necessary to write both the king and queen concerning their marriage.

§ IV. THE CHURCH IN ITALY

54. The First Council of Rome (743) held under Pope Zacharias anathematized a Christian who would give his daughter in marriage to a Jew. The same censure was decreed for a widow who would marry a Jew, unless the Jew would be converted and baptized.[23]

§ V. THE CHURCH IN GERMANY

55. The evidence derived from a council held under the saintly Henry II of Germany is of no particular value. Very

---

[18] *Poenitentiale*, cap. 26-27,—*MPL*, CX, 490.

[19] "The Jew came to England in the wake of the Norman Conqueror. That no Israelites had ever dwelt in this country before the year 1066 we dare not say; but if so, they have left no traces of their presence that are of importance to us."—Pollock-Maitland, *History of English Law*, I, 468.

[20] ". . . non esse licitum Christianam virginem pagano in coniugem dari, *ne fides et sacramenta* coelestis Regis consortio *profanaretur* regis, qui veri Dei cultus esset prorsus ignarus."—Beda Ven., *Hist. Eccl. Gentis Angl.*, Lib. II, cap. 9. The clause "*ne fides et sacramenta . . . profanaretur*" places an unusual emphasis on the dignity of the sacrament.

[21] Beda Ven., *op. cit.*, Lib. II, cap. 10.

[22] "Quomodo ergo unitas vobis coniunctionis inesse dici poterit, si a vestrae fidei splendore, interpositis detestabilis erroris tenebris, ille remanserit alienus?"—Beda Ven., *op. cit.*, Lib. II, cap. 11.

[23] Can. 10,—Mansi, XII, 384.

little of the deliberations of this council has been preserved.
Mansi gives a mere outline of it.[24] Hefele is also brief but mentions that this council forbade the marriages of Christians with
pagans.[25] The very brevity and vagueness of the evidence does
not permit a conclusion further than that such marriages were
forbidden and, perhaps, punished with excommunication.

§ VI. THE CIVIL LAW

56. The provisions of Roman Law referring to the marriages of Christians with non-Christians restricted their concern
to the marriages of Christians with Jews. The decree of the
Emperor Constantius (339) threatened capital punishment to
those Jews who would marry Christian women.[26] The Theo-
dosian law branded such marriages as adulterous.[27] Opinions
are somewhat divided as to the real force of these decrees. Some
would seem to deny that the marriages in question were regarded as invalid.[28] Others, however, admit that these laws did
establish a diriment impediment.[29] Though the imposed penalties or the words of the decrees do not, of themselves, clearly

---

[24] Concilium Tremoniense (1005),—Mansi, XIX, 279-281.

[25] In referring to the testimony of Thietmar on this council Hefele says:
"Den Ort gibt er nicht an, und widmet ihr überhaupt nur ein einziges Sätz-
chen des Inhalts: durch Synodalentscheidung habe der König die Ehen zwischen Christen und Heiden verboten, und die Zuwiederhandelnden mit dem
geistlichen Schwert zu strafen befohlen. Es waren damit wohl die Ehen der
Christen mit den benachbarten Slaven gemeint."—*Conciliengeschichte,* IV, 663.

[26] ". . . ne Christianas mulieres suis iungant flagitiis vel, si hoc fecerint,
capitali periculo subiugentur."—*C. Th.,* XVI, 8, 6. An interesting quotation reflecting the mind of the Emperor Constantine toward the marriages
of Christians with infidels is cited by Binterim, *Denkwürdigkeiten,* VI, 1,
p 446-448. Cf. Zhishman, *Das Eherecht der orient. Kirche,* p. 510.

[27] "Ne quis Christianam mulierem in matrimonio Iudaeus accipiat, neque
Iudaeae Christianus coniugium sortiatur. Nam si quis aliquid huiusmodi ad-
miserit adulterii vicem commissi huius crimen obtinebit, libertate in accusan-
dum publicis quoque vocibus relaxata."—*C. Th.,* III, 7, 2. This law was
taken up in the Justinian Code.—C., I, 9, 6.

[28] "Leges autem Imperatorias dicendum est, dicta matrimonia ut adulteria
punire propter gravitatem peccati, *non propter nullitatem* matrimonii . . ."—
Estius, *In IV Lib. Sent. Comment.,* Dist. 39, § 3. This passage from
Estius is cited and apparently approved by Pope Benedict XIV, ep. *Singulari,*
9 Feb. 1749, § 7,—*Fontes,* n. 394.

[29] Cf. Pappiani, *De Sacram.,* Tract. VII. § 53; Schulte, *Handb. des kath.
Eherechts,* p. 223; Scherer, *Handb. des Kirchenrechtes,* II, p. 372, and not. 6.

postulate a diriment impediment, it is well to bear in mind that Roman Law did not distinguish between prohibitive and diriment impediments. A marriage contracted against the prescriptions of the law *was not recognized as valid by Roman Law*; every impediment was, therefore, a diriment impediment.

57. What is of importance is to determine the relation of such legislation to the practice and law of the Church. Pope Benedict XIV calls attention to the fact that these laws did not bind the Church.[30] On the other hand, they did appear to lend an impetus to the growth of the custom which came to regard such marriages as invalid.[31] Particular councils were wont to incorporate enactments of Roman Law against the Jews.[32] Again, civil laws incorporated the decrees of particular councils. Thus the sixty-third canon of the Fourth Council of Toledo was incorporated into the laws of the Visigoths.[33] It appears, therefore, that the civil law not only contributed to the formation of a diriment impediment to the marriages of Christians with Jews, but also reflected in some measure the growth of the custom in the particular regions where it became a diriment impediment.

ART. III. SUMMARY OF DEVELOPMENT

58. On the ground that the punishments of Roman Law were not invoked, Loening, in speaking of the relation of the prescriptions of the councils in France to Roman Law, seems to be of the opinion that the severity of the discipline against

---

[30] Ep. *Singulari*, 9 Feb. 1749, § 7,—*Fontes*, n. 394. Tournely (*Prael. Theol. de Sacram. Matr.*, Quaest. VIII, concl. 2) and Pappiani (*loc. cit.*) are of the opinion that the Church consented to this legislation. This may be true at a later date but the evidence of ecclesiastical approval is wanting for the period when the laws were formed.

[31] "Videtur tamen ab illa aetate increbrescentibus prohibitionibus Episcoporum, *et concurrentibus legibus Imperatorum* fundamentum iactum, unde cultus disparitas per consuetudinem ad effectum dirimendi Matrimonium erecta est . . ."—Rupprecht, *Notae Hist. in Univ. Jus Can.*, Lib. IV, Tit. I, n. 149.

[32] Concilium Meldense (Meaux), can. 73,—Mansi, XIV, 836-839. Cf. Regino Prumiensis Abbas, *De Ecclesiasticis Disciplinis*, Lib. II, CXLIII,—*MPL*, CXXXII, 311; Augustine, *Commentary*, V, p. 180.

[33] Cf. Berardi, *Gratiani Can.*, Vol. I, p. 192.

marriages of Christians with Jews gradually fell into desuetude.[34] The assumption, however, that the severity of conciliar legislation in France was mitigated because it substituted excommunication for the punishments of Roman Law, would seem to be somewhat gratuitous. *Every council cited for Spain, France, and Italy* enacted rigorous laws to deter the faithful from such marriages. The severity of the discipline is the dominant note of the period.[35] In Spain such marriages were on the verge of being regarded as invalid (if, actually, they were not) in the seventh century. In France there is sufficient evidence to postulate a diriment impediment in the sixth century. The close relation between the legislation of Spain and France would eventually tend to a uniformity of discipline in both regions.[36]

---

[34] "Diese canones drohen Excommunication an, wenn die Ehe auf Ermahnung des Bischofs hin nicht gelöst werde, 'si commoniti a consortio hoc separare distulerint'. *Sie setzen also Gültigkeit und Straflosigkeit solcher Ehen nach weltlichem Recht voraus.* Da die Juden nach römischem Rechte lebten, so hatten auch auf Ehen zwischen ihnen und Franken die römischen Strafbestimmungen Anwendung finden können. Uebrigens scheinen auch in Rom, obgleich der Cod. Just. die alten Strafgesetze wiederholte, solche Ehen im 8. Jahrhundert straflos gewesen zu sein. Römisches Concil von 743, c. 10."—*Das Kirchenr. im Reich der Merowinger*, II, p. 567, not. 3. But see also *Jus Pont.*, VII (1927), 122, not. 1; infra No. 58, note 36. The fact that the First Council of Rome employed an "*anathema*" instead of an "*excommunicatio*" does not seem to support the contention that such marriages were free from punishment. It is very probable that the "*anathema*" represented at that time even a greater severity than the "*excommunicatio*". Cf. Hyland, *Excommunication*, p. 24. It is of more than passing significance that this council, the first in Italy to legislate on the marriages of the faithful with Jews, used a term more severe than councils of other regions. It was not necessary, moreover, for the Church to incorporate Justinian legislation.

[35] Though the Council in Trullo in the Eastern Church does not deal with the problem, the prescriptions of the Justinian Code, if they bound anywhere, would have their greatest force in the region about Constantinople. Cf. Zhishman, *Das Eherecht der orient. Kirche*, p. 509-510. No conciliar evidence is available from Northern Africa for that Church had been destroyed by the Vandals in the fifth century. In England or Germany the problem does not appear to have existed before the eleventh or twelfth centuries.

[36] "Die fränkische und spanische Kirche anerkannte den rechtlichen Bestand einer zwischen Juden und Christen geschlossenen Ehe seit dem 6. Jahrhundert nicht mehr. Wurde auch deren Nichtigkeit mit klaren Worten nicht ausgesprochen, so wurde bei Excommunication Trennung aller zwischen Juden und Christen bestehenden Verbindungen aufgetragen und diesbezüglich zwischen Ehe und Concubinat nicht unterschieden."—Scherer, *Handb. des Kirchenrechtes*, II, p. 372. Vide etiam Linneborn, *Grundriss des Eherechts*, p. 199, not. 5. Other authors, while admitting the presence of a diriment impediment in Spain and France, deny that it ever bound the entire Church.

In Italy the prohibition was given the sanction of an "anathema".

59. It appears quite reasonable, therefore, to infer that the diriment impediment of Disparity of Cult had its beginning in a diriment impediment to the marriages of Christians with Jews.[37] Though the discipline of Spain and France in the sixth and seventh centuries did not bind all Christendom,[38] yet if the ample time of three to four centuries be allowed for the custom to take firm root also in Italy, it does not seem improbable that the impediment was recognized as diriment in the tenth or eleventh centuries for every community where the problem existed.[39] Spain, France, and Italy formed the heart of Christendom. No evidence is available, however, that a diriment impediment existed also for the marriages of the faithful with other infidels. The prohibition of the early centuries remained also in this period as a mere prohibition.

Cf. Alexander, Nat., cap. IV *De Sacram. Matr.*, art. 8,—*Theol. Dogm. et Mor.*, Tom. II; Wernz, *Ius Decret.*, IV, n. 504; Chelodi, *Ius Matr.*, n. 79.

[37] Cf. Glossa ad c. 10, C. XXVIII, 2, 1; Thomas Aq., *Summa Theol.*, IIIa suppl., q. 59, art. 3, ad 2; Sanchez, *De Matr.*, Lib. VII, Disp. 73, nn. 11-12; Scavini, *Theol. Mor.*, Lib. III, n. 795.

[38] See No. 58, note 35.

[39] A curious passage regarding the marriages of Christians with Jews is found in the writings of Abelard: "Christianus etiam Iudaeam posset ducere, si recompensatio inde sequeretur."—*Epitome Theologiae Christianae*, cap. 31,—*MPL*, CLXXVIII, 1747. Though the meaning of the clause "si recompensatio inde sequeretur" is not altogether clear, it is interesting to note that later when Albertus Magnus speaks of dispensation, he defines it as "relaxatio iuris in opere, aliqua de causa utilitatis vel necessitatis, PER QUAM IUS IN OPERE RELAXATUM RECOMPENSABITUR."—Brys, *De Dispens.*, p. 260, not. 3. It does not appear improbable, therefore, that Abelard's "recompensatio" may perhaps be understood in the sense of a dispensation. Abelard seems, however, to have regarded the marriages of Christians with pagans (perhaps also with Jews) as valid. Cf. Linneborn, *Grundriss des Eherechts*, p. 199, not. 6; De Smet, *De Spons. et Matr.*, p. 520, not. 4.

CHAPTER V

THE TWELFTH TO THE SIXTEENTH CENTURY

60. For several centuries Islam had gradually advanced farther and farther upon the boundaries of Western civilization. The Moors had penetrated into Spain until they finally possessed the larger part of the peninsula. Sicily had been taken by the Saracens; inroads had been made even on the southern shores of Italy. From the East the Mohammedans were advancing closer by repeated victories over the Christians.

61. It was not until the eleventh century that Christendom seemed to realize the full menace, and then with a suddenness of awakening it arose in a mighty force to free itself of the peril. In Spain the Moors were pressed back to the confines of the small kingdom of Granada. With the meteoric appearance of the Normans the Saracens were driven from the kingdom of Sicily. Before the close of the century two great Crusading armies had been sent to redeem the Sanctuaries of the Holy Land.

62. On the northern boundaries of the Empire the pagans had stubbornly resisted all invitations of conversion and had even harassed the neighboring Christian communities. It was not until the twelfth and early thirteenth centuries that their resistance was gradually subdued.

63. With the accumulated laxities in Church discipline of the preceding age, other dangers had arisen within the very centers of Christendom. The Waldensian sect, that had begun as a protest to the existing evils, came to be imbued with the most flagrant heresy. The Cathari, or Albigenses, went even to further extremes in doctrine and practice that were subversive not only of Christian faith and morality but even of the foundations of civil society. For a time they existed in scattered communities, but in the twelfth century they commanded a considerable following in southern France and northern Italy,—spreading into England, Germany, Bohemia, and

Poland. Civil rulers themselves became alarmed at their excesses and with the failure of the persuasive methods of the Church a crusade was sent against them. Under the leadership of Simon de Montfort the crusade crushed the power of the Albigenses. The vigilance of the established Inquisition held further eruptions in check.

64. Western Christendom was revived in a spirit of faith. Its heart pulsed with the beginnings of noble ventures; its mind was bent on a great ideal, a great unity,—the unity of the Faith. The very dangers that beset it on every side but whetted the desire for its realization. Everything that endangered or was destructive of this unity was to be exterminated. The possibility of a marriage with those alien to the Faith was, therefore, a thought inconceivable. The abhorrence of such marital unions converted itself into a diriment impediment. The center of Christendom had already regarded the marriages of the faithful with Jews as invalid,—it now came to regard their marriages with *anyone outside of the Church as invalid.*

ART. I. THE TWELFTH CENTURY

65. When Gratian brought forth his monumental Concordance he incorporated the prescriptions of the early centuries of the Church on the marriages of the faithful with heretics, pagans and Jews.[1] A passage from St. Ambrose[2] he prefaced with the *dictum:* ". . . *Illa itaque auctoritate* IUBENTUR SEPARARI AB INVICEM *qui contra Dei ecclesiae decretum copulati sunt, utpote* INFIDELES CUM FIDELIBUS, *consanguinei cum consanguineis, vel affines cum affinibus.* HII OMNES, *si sibi invicem copulati fuerint,* SEPARANDI SUNT." The wording and context of the *dictum* seems to justify the opinion that Gratian deemed the marriages of the faithful with infidels as invalid,[3] though some athors do not agree with this interpretation, or at

---

[1] C. 10, 15, 16, 17, C. XXVIII, q. 1; C. XXXI, q. 2; c. 15, D. XXXII.

[2] C. 15, C. XXVIII, q. 1—(*De Abraham,* Lib. I, cap. 9, n. 84).

[3] Mercerus, *Comment. in Tertiam part. S. Thomae, suppl.,* Quaest. 59, prop. 1, n. 3; Scherer, *Handb. des Kirchenrechtes,* II, p. 373, not. 7; Sägmüller, *Lehrb. des kath. Kirchenr.,* Buch IV, § 139, n. 1; Linneborn, *Grundriss des Eherechts,* p. 199, not. 6; Prümmer, *Theol. Mor.,* III, n. 823.

least regard it as doubtful.[4] The fact that the incorporated passage from St. Ambrose does not demonstrate the implication of the *dictum* offers no serious difficulty. There was no authentic canon of any council, no passage from ony of the Fathers, that Gratian might have used to show the invalidity of marriages with *infidels*. The very absence of such evidence may of itself offer an explanation of the wording and the context of the *dictum*.

66. It is quite probable, moreover, that by the term *"infideles"* Gratian included *all*, without exception, who were not Catholics. Yet this fact scarcely affords a cogent reason for tempering the more obvious contextual significance of the expression *"separandi sunt"*.[5] The authors of the twelfth century who followed him included also the marriages with heretics in the diriment impediment.[6] The inclusion of all aliens to the

---

[4] Cf. Wernz, *Ius Decret.*, IV, n. 503, not. 20; Leitner, *Lehrb. des kath. Eherechts*, p. 184; Chelodi, *Ius Matr.*, n. 79.

[5] In view of the popularity that the *Decretum Gratiani* enjoyed among canonists, the observation of Pope Benedict XIV is well taken when he calls attention to the fact that it did not bind the Church.—ep. *Singulari*, 9 Feb. 1749, § 9.—*Fontes*, n. 394.

[6] Peter Lombard does not, perhaps, teach this so clearly, yet he makes no distinction of discipline for pagans, Jews or heretics. He seems to include all these classes under the one diriment impediment: *"Post haec de dispari cultu videndum est. Haec est enim una de causis, quibus personae* ILLEGITIMAE FIUNT AD CONTRAHENDUM MATRIMONIUM . . . *Item Ambros. Cave Christiane Gentili vel Iudaeo filiam tuam tradere: cave ne Gentilem vel Iudaeam vel alienigenam, id est,* HAERETICAM, ET OMNEM ALIENAM A FIDE TUA, *uxorem accersas tibi . . . Ex his aliisque pluribus testimoniis apparet non posse contrahi coniugium ab his qui sunt* DIVERSAE RELIGIONIS ET FIDEI."—*Sent.*, IV, D. XXXIX, A. Bernard of Pavia is quite explicit: *"Dispar cultus impedit matrimonium contrahendum et* DIRIMIT CONTRACTUM, *si ab initio intercesserit, v. g. fidelis aliquis paganam, iudaeam vel* HAERETICAM *accipere in coniugium non potest; quod si acceperit separatur . . . Hic haeretici nomine solus ille accipitur, qui falsam de fide opinionem gignit vel sequitur; in hoc enim solo potest disparis cultus impedimentum notari."*—*Summa Decret.*, p. 291-292. Tancred is of a like opinion: *"Sequitur de dispari cultu, scilicet, quando unus eorum est Catholicus et alter* HAERETICUS, *vel unus Christianus et alter iudaeus, vel paganus, qui contrahere volunt, quando sunt* DISPARIS PROFESSIONIS, *non potest contrahi matrimonium inter eos, et si contrahunt* NULLUM EST MATRIMONIUM."—The passage is cited by Featherston, *Disparity of Cult*, p. 28. Chelodi's opinion: *"At iam Petrus Lombardus, Rolandus, Tancredus, aliique saec. XII dirimens esse docent,* RESERVATO IMPEDIENTI PRO HAERETICIS," (*Ius Matr.*, n. 79), seems to be at variance with the preceding quotations, and with the fact that some of the Glossators deemed that the marriages of Catholics with heretics were invalid. Cf. Leurenius, *Jus. Can. Univ.*, Lib. IV, quaest, 116; Sägmüller, *Lehrb. des kath. Kirchenr.*, p. 560, not. 5.

Faith in the diriment impediment marks a sudden and singular change,—as unique as the century that was responsible for it. Yet it represented rather an intense reaction toward the dangers to the Faith than a true expression of the mind of the Church. The wholesale inclusiveness of the impediment lacked an *ultimate* theological and canonical foundation.

67. Perhaps the prevailing teaching of the twelfth century appeared at least in some minor capacity in the question of the Bishop of Farrara when he asked whether a lapse into heresy constituted a canonical ground for the Catholic's entering another marriage. The answer of Pope Innocent III called attention for the first time to the *fundamental difference* existing between the marriages of the *baptized* and the *unbaptized*.[7] It clearly asserted the doctrine that, while a marriage of the unbaptized was a *matrimonium verum,* a marriage of the baptized was in addition a sacrament, a *matrimonium ratum,* effected through the sacrament of Baptism. Because of its sacramental character through Baptism, a marriage of the baptized could not, therefore, be dissolved on the ground of a lapse into heresy even though the contumely of the Creator be greater.[8]

ART. II. THE THIRTEENTH TO THE SIXTEENTH CENTURY

68. Though the answer of Pope Innocent III was not concerned with an antecedent impediment it served, nevertheless, as a guide whereon the great scholastics of the thirteenth century were to base their teaching regarding the marriages of the faithful with aliens to the Faith. Hitherto, the development in particular legislation, and even widespread custom, had struck its root in the presumption of danger to the Faith.[9] The theologians of the thirteenth century went further to turn their attention to the very requirements of the sacrament of marriage. Since a parity arising from the reception of Baptism was required for the very existence of a "*matrimonium ratum*" it followed that the *sacrament* of faith was a more fundamental issue than the *profession* of faith. A marriage *between the bap-*

---

[7] Cf. Smisniewicz, *Die Lehre von den Ehehind. bei P. Lomb.,* p. 129.

[8] C. 7, X, *de divortiis,* IV, 19.

[9] Cf. Santi, *Prael. Juris Can.,* Lib. IV, Tit. I, n. 175; Sägmüller, *Lehrb. des kath. Kirchenr.,* Buch IV, § 139, n. 1

tized and the unbaptized represented a disparity that frustrated the realization of a *"matrimonium ratum"*. In the teaching of Albertus Magnus,[10] St. Thomas,[11] St. Raymond of Pennafort,[12] St. Bonaventure,[13] William Durandus,[14] and Duns Scotus,[15] this disparity served as the *ultimate* basis of a diriment impediment. On the other hand, the requirements of a *"matrimonium ratum"* were fulfilled in a marriage of *two baptized persons* even though a disparity of a *profession* of faith existed. This disparity was regarded as a *prohibitive* impediment.[16]

69. In their restatement of the limits and foundation of a diriment impediment, the authors of the thirteenth century departed, therefore, from the opinion of the writers of the twelfth. In view of the fact that their teaching prevailed in the centuries that followed, the complete omission in the *Corpus Iuris Canonici* of any reference to a diriment impediment of Disparity of Cult is somewhat surprising. The lack of legisla-

---

[10] ". . . tamen peccatum non ex magnitudine sua habet impedire matrimonium, sed potius *ex contrarietate quam habet ad fundamentum* vel actum."—*Comment. in IV Sent.*, Dist. XXXIX, art. II, ad 4,—*Op. Omnia*, Vol. XXX, 429.

[11] ". . . matrimonium est sacramentum; et ideo *quantum pertinet ad necessitatem sacramenti, requirit paritatem*, quantum ad sacramentum fidei, scilicet *baptismum*, magis quantum ad interiorem fidem."—*Summa Theol.*, IIIa suppl., q. 59, art. 1, ad 5.

[12] *Summa*, Lib. IV, Tit. X.

[13] ". . . Si autem sit infidelis, *quia caret fidei Sacramento, utpote baptismo*; quia Sacramentorum ecclesiasticorum et fidelium ianua et fundamentum est baptismus, fidelis, qui contrahere habet secundum Sacramenta Ecclesiae, si cum tali contrahat, nihil facit, etiam si sit fidelis, dum tamen non habeat baptismum, unde dirimit contractum."—*Comment. in IV Lib. Sent.*, Dist. XXXIX, art. 1, q. 1,—*Op. Omnia*, Tom. IV, 833.

[14] *Spec. Iuris*, Lib. IV, Partic. 4, Tit. *de divortiis*, n. 2.

[15] ". . . nec honestum est fidelem contrahere, *cui contractui non sit annexum Sacramentum fidei Christianae, et etiam ubi non sit bonum Sacramenti, id est, indissolubilitas*, quia coniugium Christianorum natum est habere haec bona."—*Quaest. in IV Lib., Sent.*, Dist. XXXIX, Quaest. un., art. 2,—*Op. Omnia*, Vol. XIX, 510.

[16] ". . . *non tamen ordinatur ex contrarietate* contra fundamentum matrimonii omne segregans a consortio fidelium, et ideo non dissolvit contractum matrimonium; sed verum *est quod contrahi non debet*."—Albertus Magnus, *op. cit.*, Dist. XXXIX, art. IV. ". . . si aliquis fidelis cum haeretica baptizata matrimonium contrahat, *verum est matrimonium, quamvis peccet contrahendo*, si sciat eam haereticam; sicut peccaret, si cum excommunicata contraheret; non tamen propter hoc matrimonium dirimeretur . . ."—Thomas Aq., *loc. cit.* St. Raymond of Pennafort, St. Bonaventure, William Durandus, and Duns Scotus (isti auctores ad *loc. cit.*) uphold the same teaching.

tive evidence[17] may, perhaps, be partially explained upon the fact that the numbers of the unbaptized in the Christian countries of Western Europe were, in all probability, limited largely to Jews, against whom the popular feeling ran so high that its excesses called forth the condemnation of the Holy See. The very spirit, moreover, that prompted the Crusades against the Mohammedans precluded the possibility of frequent marriages with them.[18]

ART. III. SUMMARY OF DEVELOPMENT

70. All authors are agreed that the diriment impediment of Disparity of Cult arose rather from a universal *custom* than from any positive, written law of the Church,[19] but in assigning a date when the custom became universal, they are arrayed in a wide divergence of opinion, covering a span of eight centuries. Some authors select a date as early as the sixth century.[20]

---

[17] The seventeenth canon of the Synod of Mainz (1233) supposes an impediment of Disparity of Cult when it mentions it as one of the impediments to be disclosed *in facie ecclesiae*. The German text in Hefele (*Conciliengeschichte*, V, 1028) designates it as *"verschiedene Religion"* to which *"dispar cultus"* is added in parenthesis. Though its definite nature is not indicated, its enumeration with the impediments that were regarded as diriment may indicate that it too was regarded as diriment.

[18] Zhishman (*Das Eherecht der orient. Kirche*, p. 511-512), however, cites rather frequent examples of members of the royalty in the East entering such marriages.

[19] Cf. Benedictus XIV, ep. *Singulari*, 9 Feb. 1749, § 10,—*Fontes*, n. 394; Sanchez, *De Matr.*, Lib. VII, Disp. 71, n. 8; Bellarminus, Lib. II *de Sacram. Matr.*, cap. XXIII,—*Op. Omnia*, Tom. V, 119; Pirhing, *Jus Can.*, Tom. IV, Lib. I, Sect. VI, n. 164; Schulte, *Handb. des kath. Eherechts*, p. 224; Gasparri, *De Matr.*, n. 695.

[20] Mercerus (*Comment. in Tertiam part. S. Thomae,—suppl.*, Quaest. 59, prop. 1, n. 3) says that it arose after the year 500. Pope Benedict XIV (*Opera Inedita*, p. 430-431) places the beginning of the custom in the Patristic age (cf. Prümmer, *Theol. Mor.*, III, n. 823), though his own reference to the marriages of saints Monica, Anastasia, und Cecelia, does not offer conclusive foundation for the opinion. Elsewhere (ep. *Singulari*, 9 Feb. 1749, § 10,—*Fontes*, n. 394) he says that it had existed for many centuries with the force of law. Binterim (*Denkwürdigkeiten*, VI, 1, p. 444) seems to favor the seventh century though in another instance (*ibid.*, p. 445) he refers to the ninth and tenth. Others select the period from the seventh to the twelfth century. Cf. Wernz, *Ius Decret.*, IV, n. 504; Cappello, *De Sacram.*, III, n. 426. Philipp Hergenröther (*Lehrb. des kath. Kirchenrechts*, p. 761) prefers the eighth; Petrovits (*New Church Law on Matrimony*, n. 219) the ninth to the twelfth. Scherer (*Handb. des Kirchenrechtes* II, p. 372-373) says that it arose before the twelfth century. Cf. etiam Alexander, Nat., cap. IV *De Sacram. Matr.*, art. 8,—*Theol. Dogm. et Mor.*, Tom. II.

Most authors accept the twelfth century,[21] though a few place
it as late as the thirteenth.[22]

71. It appears that a century earlier than the eleventh
would afford little more than fragmentary evidence of the
probable existence of a diriment impediment for the marriages
of Christians with Jews. Those who accept the twelfth century offer by way of confirmation the testimony of the writers
of that century. What then is the import of such evidence?
Are the twelfth century authors witnesses to an existing custom?
They appear to be for they do not speak with the accents of in-
novators,—they exhibit no hesitation in their opinions.[23] The
unanimous testimony of the theologians and canonists in the
centuries that followed to the existence of a diriment impediment of Disparity of Cult seems to leave no reasonable doubt
of its universal existence in the twelfth century. Yet the diriment impediment of the twelfth is not altogether the same
as that of the succeeding centuries. Perhaps the custom of the
twelfth remained; perhaps the thirteenth century also accepted
it but gave it a new foundation and pared it of its excessive
inclusiveness.

72. Was the custom of the twelfth century accepted by
the *Church*? The practically unanimous opinion of the authors
in denying that the marriages of Catholics with heretics were
ever regarded as invalid by the Church in the West, suggests
a negative answer. Yet St. Bonaventure[24] and Duns Scotus[25]

---

[21] Cf. Estius, *In IV Lib. Sent. Comment.*, Dist. 39, § 3; Billuart, *Curs. Theol.*, Tom. XIII, Dist. VII, art. 10; Pappiani, *De Sacram.*, Tract. VII. cap. IV, § 53; Gasparri, *De Matr.*, n. 695; Esmein, *Le mariage en droit canonique*, I, p. 216; De Smet, *De Spons. et Matr.*, n. 592 cum not. 4, p. 520; Vlaming, *Prael. Iuris Matr.*, n. 286; Farrugia, *De Matr.*, n. 168. Cardinal Bellarmine (Lib. I *De Sacram. Matr.*, cap. XXIII,—*Op. Omnia*, Tom. V, 119) says that it arose at least four hundred years before his time.

[22] Leitner, *Lehrb. des kath. Eherechts*, p. 184; Noldin, *Theol. Mor.*, III, p. 665, not. 1; Augustine, *Commentary*, V, p. 180.

[23] The custom may have had its beginnings in the century preceding. No evidence, however, exists for its universality.

[24] ". . . Sic et in nova [lege] impedit non simpliciter sive de se, sed ob vitationem periculi et diversitatem Sacramenti baptismi *et inhibitionem eccle-siastici statui, quae ortum habet a duobus praedictis.*"—*Comment. in IV Lib. Sent.*, Dist. XXXIX, art. 1, q. 1,—*Op. Omnia*, Tom. IV, 833.

[25] ". . . Sed *de Iure positivo Ecclesiae* simpliciter non potest [contrahi], quia *Ecclesia illegitimavit* fidelem, non simpliciter, sed respectu infidelis . . ." —*Quaest. in IV Lib. Sent.*, Dist. XXXIX, Quaest. un., art. 2,—*Op. Omnia*, Vol. XIX, 510.

of the thirteenth century, and Durandus of St. Porcian[26] of
the fourteenth, refer to the *law of the Church*. They do not
speak of it as something novel; they seem rather to take it for
granted as though it were not even a matter for discussion.
They seem almost to suppose a formal positive law of the
Church yet they never refer to it, nor quote it,—nor is there
any record of such a law within this period. They may be
justifying their teaching by an indirect reference to the legislation of the earlier centuries,[27] attributing to it the logical deduc-
tions of their teaching as completing what had not been explicitly enacted. Perhaps they refer to that custom which had
gained the force of law in the twelfth century? More probably, their testimony indicates at least a *tacit acceptance* by the
Church of the custom as it existed with the force of universal
law *in the thirteenth century.*

73. That the Church in the thirteenth century accepted
only a *prohibitive* impediment to the marriages of Catholics
with heretics or schismatics, as distinct from the diriment impediment affecting the marriages of the baptized with the unbaptized, seems to be clearly implied in a decree of Pope Innocent
IV wherein the dowry of a woman, knowingly marrying a
heretic is confiscated,—yet the existence of a valid marriage is
supposed.[28]

In the fourteenth century the prohibition (without an
invalidating clause) of such marriages enacted in the particular
council of Pressburg (1309)[29] was confirmed and approved in
1346 by Pope Clement VI.[30]

---

[26] Durandus says that as far as the law of the Church is concerned, a
disparity of cult existing *between two infidels* would not invalidate their
marriage, "*. . . et idem esset de fidelibus quod possent contrahere cum infidelibus,* NISI OBVIARET STATUTUM IURIS *et dictum Apostolici.*"—*In Sent.
Comment. lib. IV,* Lib. IV, Dist. XXXIX, Quaest. 1, n. 10.

[27] The authors of the later centuries frequently refer to early legislation
to demonstrate the constant abhorrence of the Church. Even the Holy See
has at times referred to the enactments of early councils. The following instruction of the Holy Office refers to the councils of Laodicaea, Agde, and
Chalcedon: S. C. S. Off., instr. (ad omnes Ep. Ritus Orient.), 12 Dec.
1888, n. 3,—*Fontes,* n. 1112.

[28] C. 14, *de haereticis,* V, 2, in VI°.

[29] Can. 8,—Mansi, XXV, 222.

[30] Cf. Binterim, *Denkwürdigkeiten,* VII, II, p. 28; Feije, *De Matr.
Mixtis,* p. 9; Wernz, *Ius Decret.,* IV, n. 576.

74. The acknowledgment by the Church of a distinct prohibitive impediment to the marriages of Catholics with heretics, confirms the opinion that the Church accepted only that diriment impediment which was limited to the marriages of the baptized with the unbaptized. Since this arose only as late as the thirteenth century, it may, therefore, be stated without serious hesitation that the two impediments as distinct from each other, one,—the diriment impediment of Disparity of Cult, the other,—the prohibitive impediment of Mixed Religion, were accepted by the Church in the *thirteenth century.*

75. With the severe discipline of the late Middle Ages against heresy and heretics; in the light of the stringent laws against all association with the unbaptized as they were represented for the most part by Jews and Saracens, the possibility of entering such marriages was not even discussed. The question of dispensation did not arise. It was altogether foreign to the mind of an age bent on the *extermination* of heresy and infidelity.[81]

---

[81] Cf. Scherer, *Handb. des Kirchenrechtes*, II, p. 407; De Becker, *De Spons. et Matr.*, p. 275; Wernz, *Ius Decret.*, IV, n. 576; AkKR, XIV (1865), 322.

CHAPTER VI

THE SIXTEENTH CENTURY TO THE CODE

With the religious revolt of the sixteenth century and the missionary awakening of the Church following the discovery of America, the question of dispensation became suddenly an issue of instant importance.

76. The missionary activities in the Orient and in the newly discovered continents of the Western Hemisphere saw conditions develop similar in many respects to those which had existed in the early centuries of Christianity. Again the same problem arose concerning the relation of the new converts to those who still remained in paganism, and marriages between Christians and pagans would again engage the attention of the Church.

77. Severe as had been the discipline regarding such marriages in the Middle Ages, the Church took cognizance of missionary conditions and granted faculties to the Apostolic Vicars of these regions to dispense from the impediment of Disparity of Cult. The faculty was to be used only in regions where pagans outnumbered the Christians, and upon the existence of grave causes. There was also to be due precaution that such marriages be contracted without contumely of the Creator, and that the children be educated as Catholics.[1] While the provision

---

[1] "Etenim novimus a Clemente IX, 23 Ianuar. 1669, concessam fuisse episcopo Heliopolitano tam pro se, quam pro aliis vicariis apostolicis in regnis Sinarum, Tunchini, Cocincinae, aliisque finitimis facultatem, ad annos quindecim proxime futuros 'dispensandi super impedimento disparitatis cultus, gravibus tamen ex causis, in quibus, dispensandum erit, et in locis tantum ubi sunt plures infideles quam Christiani, ita ut in eo matrimonio postmodum, quatenus absque Creatoris contumelia fieri possit, contrahentes remanere libere et licite valeant, prolesque exinde suscipiendas legitimas decernendi, super quibus eorumdem vicariorum apostolicorum conscientia oneratur, et praedictae dispensationes gratis concedantur'."—Perrone, *De Matr.*, Tom. II, cap. VII, art. 2. Vide etiam Benedictus XIV, 15 Feb. 1756,—*ibid.*; S. C. S. Off. (Albaniae), 19 Sept. 1671,—*Fontes*, n. 749; (Tunkin. Orient.), 5 Sept. 1736,—*Fontes*, n. 790; 29 Ian. 1767,—*NRT*, XV

for the safety of the faith of the Catholic party and the children was strictly enjoined, it appears to be stated more in the form of a general principle of observance than in the form of a definite and specific engagement. There is no mention of an exclusive method of observance to bring about the realization of this condition. In all probability it may have been left to the prudence and good judgment of those enjoying the faculty of dispensing. By custom and tradition the religious authority of a family in these countries was vested completely in the husband.[2] In the absence of a provision for formal *cautiones*, as they are known today, the Catholic faith of the husband may frequently have been accepted as a sufficient safeguard.[3]

78. Europe, on the other hand, presented a scene of confusion and disorder. Heresy was making fearful inroads in England, Germany, and Poland. Even certain sections of France had been infected. The Church was confronted as never before with the issue of holding the loyalty of those who still kept the Faith, and of bringing back those who had deserted.

79. The prohibitions of ancient councils to mixed marriages were to be renewed and enforced for such marriages would occasion only further apostasies. How could the Church depart from its traditional policy towards heretics and heresy?[4]

(1883), 423-424; 12 Ian. 1769,—*Fontes*, n. 822; S. C. de Prop. F., 28 Iulii 1760,—*Coll.*, n. 432 (a more complete text is given by Perrone, *loc. cit.*); instr. (ad Vic. Ap. Fokien.), 13 Sept. 1760,—*Coll.*, n. 435. See infra No. 244 note 66. While Pope Clement XI in 1702 granted faculties of the most surprising extent to De Tournon, sent as Apostolic Legate to the missionary regions of the Orient, it appears somewhat strange that in his matrimonial faculties there is no mention of the faculty to dispense from the impediment of Disparity of Cult. (Cf. P. Norbert, *Memoires Historiques Presentes au Souverain Pontife Benoit XIV sur les Missions des Indes Orientales*, Luques, 1745, Tom. I, par. I, p. 115-129). Did he possess the faculty by virtue of the fact that he was given every faculty extended to the Vicars Apostolic? In all probability he did.

[2] See No. 285, note 28.

[3] In view of the peculiar conditions in China an extraordinary dispensation for that country as to the manner of exacting the *cautiones* was given by the Holy Office on April 5, 1918. Cf. Winslow, *Vicars and Prefects Apostolic*, p. 106-107. Vide etiam S. C. S. Off. (Pekin.), 29 Apr. 1891,—*Fontes*, n. 1134.

[4] To understand the legislation of the Church on mixed marriages it is necessary to understand the attitude of the Church toward heresy. In her mind, heresy, apart from the hatred of God, is the most heinous of sins. (Cf. Thomas Aq., *Summa Theol.*, IIa-IIae, q. 10, art. 3; Malderus, *De*

Were she in any way to permit a Catholic to marry a heretic it would seem equivalent to an acknowledgment of the
right of heresy to exist. No, she would dispense from no
impediment existing between a Catholic and a heretic unless
the abjuration of heresy preceded.[5] Where the abjuration did
not take place, or where only the impediment of Mixed Religion existed, the Church would not dispense except for reasons
of a manifest public concern, i. e., for the marriages of Catholic rulers with someone of their rank but of an heretical form
of religion.[6] For a Catholic to associate himself with a heretic

---

Virtutibus Theol., q. 10, art. 3). Other sins, indeed, deprive the soul of
the life of grace (Conc. Trident., sess. VI, *de justificatione*, can.. 27,—
Denz., n. 837), yet faith, which is the root of this life, still remains (*ibid.*,
can. 28,—Denz., n. 838). But to tear out the root of the supernatural
life is a violence that leaves the soul only with the indelible mark of the
sacrament of faith as a terrible reproach to the vandal of the faith. This
is the awful malice of heresy or apostasy,—it is high treason to Christ.

[5] "Et licet de stylo, huius Supremae, et Universalis Inquisitionis commit-
terentur Nunciis, vel Ordinariis tales dispensationes cum clausula, *Abiurata
prius haeresi*, Innocentius Decimus sanctae memoriae mandavit, ut in futurum prius haberetur testimonium abiurationis, antequam concederetur dispensatio."—Albitius, *De Inconstantia in Fide*, Cap. XVIII, n. 44. Cf. Clemens XI, 16 Iun. 1710,—Migne, *Theol. Curs. Complet.*, XXV, 628; Benedictus XIV, ep. encycl. *Magnae Nobis*, 29 Iun. 1748, §§ 4-5,—*Fontes*,
n. 387; ep. *Ad tuas*, 8 Aug. 1748, § 6,—*Fontes*, n. 389; Pius VI, rescript. ad Card. Archiep. Mechlinien., 13 Iulii 1782, n. 1,—*Fontes*, n. 471;
S. C. S. Off., 16 Iun. 1710,—Migne, *op. cit.*., XXV, 628; Petra, *Comment. ad Const. Apost.*, Tom. IV, Const. XII, Ioannis XXII, nn. 13-39;
Scherer, *Handb. des Kirchenrechtes*, II, p. 408; De Angelis, *Prael. Iuris Can.*,
Lib. IV, Tit. I, n. 22; Chelodi, *Ius Matr.*, n. 58. As a precaution against
the possibilities of deception the Holy See demanded that petitions for dispensation mention either the fact that both parties were Catholics, or that
the abjuration had been given. Cf. Albitius, *op. cit.*, Cap. XVIII, n. 45.
The heretic's abjuration as a condition for dispensation from impediments
of relationship was at times designated in the early seventeenth century as
the *causa pro Germania*, upon which Corradus remarks: "Haec causa . . .
pariter in unum tendunt: nam movetur Papa ad dispensandum, ut matrimonium in pares Religione contrahatur [cum in illis partibus non satis
tutum sit, cum quibusvis personis matrimonium contrahere] . . . Hanc
causam audio non admitti hodie in Dataria pro Germania, sed tamen pro
nobilibus Orthodoxis . . ."—*Praxis Dispens.*, Lib. VII, cap. II, nn. 96-99.
The same author (*loc. cit.*) gives examples of three petitions for dispensation which were granted in the early seventeenth century: one for affinity,
and two for consanguinity. In each of these petitions the marriage had been
contracted invalidly and with heretics. The mention of the "*abiuratio haere-
sis*" occurs in each. The abjuration was demanded also of schismatics. Cf.
Schulte, *Handb. des kath. Eherechts*, p. 251.

[6] Cf. Benedictus XIV, ep. encycl. *Magnae Nobis*, 29 Iun. 1748, § 5,—
Fontes, n. 387; De Justis, *De Dispens. Matr.*, Lib. II, cap. XV, n. 16;
Albitius, *De Inconstantia in Fide*, Cap. XVIII, n. 45.

in a union as intimate as that of marriage would, in a certain sense, be abetting the cause of heresy, even though it be material and indirect.⁷ All who lent such favor could be proceeded against as *"suspecti de haeresi vel eiusdem fautores"*.⁸

80. Though the Council of Trent had enacted no legislation referring directly to mixed marriages, indirectly, such marriages were prohibited by the decree *"Tametsi"*, which demanded under pain of invalidity that marriages be celebrated before the proper pastor (or his, or the Ordinary's delegate),

---

⁷ Throughout the Middle Ages the discipline regarding any association whatever with heretics had been most severe. While this discipline was somewhat modified by Pope Martin V (Const. *Ad evitanda* [in Conc. Constantien.], a. 1418,—*Fontes*, n. 45), the constant aversion of the Church to such associations may readily explain De Lugo's opinion (*Tract. de Vir!. Fidei Div.*, Disp. XXII, Sect. II, n. 30) which maintained that one of the principal elements of the prohibitive impediment to the marriages of Catholics with heretics was *the punishment of heretics*. See infra No. 115.

⁸ Cf. Albitius, *De Inconstantia in Fide*, Cap. XXXVI, nn. 163, 185, 187-191, Cap. XXII, n. 129; Suarez, Trac. I, *De Fide Theol.*, Disp. XXIV, Sect. I, n. 9; Dandino, *De Suspectis de Haeresi*, Cap. III, Sect. I, Subsect. I, § IV, nn. 1-2; Petra, *op. cit.*, Tom. IV, Const. XII, Ioannis XXII, nn. 2-5. When Pope Paul III in 1542 established the Inquisition as a Congregation and as a Tribunal the question of mixed marriages became its immediate concern. "Huic porro congregationi expresse attribuebatur iudicium de *haereticis quomodo libet suspectis de haeresi, deque eiusdem fautoribus.* Iamvero communiter censebatur contrahentem matrimonium cum persona heretica esse suspectum de fide ·et contra illum inquisitores posse procedere."—Arendt, "De Exclusiva S. Officii Competentia circa Matrimonium Mixtum", *Jus Pont.*, VII (1927), 122. Early instructions and responses of the seventeenth century coming from the Holy Office indicated likewise the competency of this Congregation upon questions concerning disparate marriages. Yet it is doubtful whether the Holy Office from the very beginning reserved to itself the *exclusive* right of judging of the validity of disparate marriages. It appears that in at least one instance the Congregation of the Council gave a declaration of nullity. "Aliter suadere posset canonicum illud impedimentum, quod vocatur cultus disparitas; nam absolute prohibetur coniugium baptizati cum non baptizato . . . irritumque declaratur . . . probavitque Sacra haec Congregatio [Concilii] die Septembris 1623 per decretum illud: *Sacra Congregatio* [Concilii] *censuit, matrimonium, ut proponitur, cum infideli contractum nullum prorsus, atque irritum esse.*"—S. C. Conc., (Brixien. Dubia Baptismi, et Matrimonii), 27 Aug. 1796,—*Thes.*, LXV, 218. Admittedly, too much stress may not be placed on this evidence since the full context of the decision is not given. The Congregation of the Council may have acted merely in the capacity of transmitting the decree which may have been given by the Holy Office [?], though the text scarcely warrants such an assumption. for on the next page of the *Thesaurus* (*Thes.*, LXV, 219) the consultor refers to the Holy Office to confirm the evidence he has already given from the Congregation of the Council. The Congregation of the Council, moreover, gave decisions pertaining to the impediment of Mixed Religion. See No. 80, note 11.

and at least two witnesses.[9] Only Catholic pastors could be *parochi proprii*[10] and since they were forbidden to assist at marriages between Catholics and heretics unless an abjuration preceded or a Papal dispensation had been given,[11] all avenues to mixed marriages seemed to be closed.

81. Yet in spite of the obstacles which stood in the way of mixed marriages in the universal law of the Church and in a host of particular synods of the sixteenth and seventeenth centuries[12] many diversities in discipline existed from the very beginning of the religious revolt in the hinterland of Catholic influence,—in Germany, England, Poland, and the Netherlands. Here mixed marriages were contracted with such frequency and at the same time without an abjuration or Papal dispensation that among many canonists and theologians of

---

[9] Conc. Trident., sess. XXIV, *de reform. matr.*, cap. 1,—Mansi, XXXIII, 152-153. Schulte (*Handb. des kath. Eherechts*, p. 243) draws attention to the fact, that such marriages were contrary, moreover, to the urgent admonition of the same decree that both parties receive the sacraments of Penance and the Eucharist. It seems to be laboring the point too far, however, to say that the Tridentine legislation was enacted primarily against heretics. Cf. Dandino, *op. cit.*, Cap. III, Sect. I, Subsect. VI, n. 21. There can, however, be no doubt that the decree comprehended all marriages between those subject to the Latin Church, whether it be a question of a marriage between two Catholics, a Catholic and a heretic, or two heretics. Cf. Petra, *Comment. ad Const. Apost.*, Tom. IV, Const. II, Ioannis XXI, n. 20. Feije, *De Matr. Mixtis*, p. 94-121.

[10] "... Unde est, ut etiam priventur [parochi qui postea in haeresim incidunt] beneficio Parochiali, et consequenter matrimonia coram ipsis inita, nulla sunt, perinde ac si coram non Parocho facta fuissent, ut resolvit Sacr. Congr. Conc. quae sub die 19 Maii 1572 censuit: *Nullum esse matrimonium contractum coram Parocho haeretico, si Decretum Concilii cap. I de reformat. Matrimon. publicatum fuerit in Parochia, et lapsi erant triginta dies a die primae publicationis* . . ."—Petra, *op. cit.*, Const. XII, Ioannis XXII, n. 27.

[11] "Unde Parochis permissum non est iis assistere, ut pluries respondit Sac. Congr. Concilii, praesertim sub die 22 Iunii 1624 . . . dum censuit, quod sive alter tantum ex coniugibus sit haereticus, sive ambo, nullatenus debeat Parochus huiusmodi matrimoniis assistere. Cum enim a Iure Canonico prohibita est, et illicita, permissum non erit Parochis eis assistere, et sua praesentia auctorizare, nisi pro tali contractu ineundo Summi Pontificis dispensatio concurrat, . . . ut etiam respondit eadem Sacr. Congregat. in *Dubio Iurisdictionis Capellanorum Exercitus* die 6 Mart. 1694 ubi cum dubitaretur, An milites Acatholici, contrahentes cum Mulieribus Catholicis teneantur servare formam a Concilio praescriptam; Sacr. Congreg. respondit: *Affirmative, sed ulterius indigere dispensatione, ut praedicta matrimonia licite contrahantur.*"—Petra, *op. cit.*, Const. XII, Ioannis XXII, n. 8. Cf. Albitius, *De Inconstantia in Fide*, Cap. XVIII, n. 47.

[12] Cf Binterim, *Denkwürdigkeiten*, VII, II, p. 30-33; Feije, *De Matr. Mixtis*, p. 33-48; Scherer, *Handb. des Kirchenrechtes*, II, p. 408.

name[13] this laxity came to be accepted as a custom established contrary to the law of the Church.[14]

82. Amid such uncertainties and informalities there was no provision for formal *cautiones*, as they are known today, nor was there question of the necessity of a formal canonical cause. True, even the authors who accepted the custom insisted that no mixed marriages could be permitted without a grave reason and especially those which would represent a violation of the divine or natural law, but the norms deduced for the lawfulness of such marriages were based rather upon the application of reflex principles than upon an adherence to formal observances. It was a discipline wholly devoid of such formalities as dispensations, formal canonical causes, or *cautiones*,— a situation perhaps somewhat surprising to us of a modern day, yet one that would readily develop in the perilous conditions of countries where the Old Church and the new Religion were meeting and uncertain which would prevail.[15] It was a period in which the Holy See seemed to be beset with misgivings and uncertainties as to the mold and form which her discipline would assume.

------

[13] Though the postulation or admission of the contrary custom does not appear to have originated with Sanchez (*De Matr.*, Lib. VII, Disp. 72, n. 5) yet he seems to have lent it considerable weight. Thereafter it was accepted by many illustrious authors. Cf. Pontius, *De Matr.*, Append., cap. VIII, n. 4; De Lugo, *Tract. de Sacram. in genere*, Disp. VII, n. 225; *Tract. de Virt. Fidei Div.*, Disp. XXII, Sect. II, n. 16; Schmalzgrueber, *Jus Eccl. Univ.*, Tom. IV, Pars II, Tit. VII, n. 148; Castropalao, *Op. Mor.*, Tract. XXVIII, *De Spons.*, Disp. 4, Punct. 11, nn. 10-11; Salmanticenses, *Curs. Theol. Mor.*, Tract. *de Matr.*, Cap. XII, Punct. VI, n. 69; Laymann, *Theol. Mor.*, Lib. V, Tract. X, Pars IV, cap. XIV, n. 2; Alphonsus, *Theol. Mor.*, Lib. VI, n. 56; Dandino, *De Suspectis de Haeresi*, Cap. III, Sect. I, Subsect. I, § IV, n. 12; Pirhing, *Jus Can.*, Tom. IV, Tit. I, Sect. VI, n. 166; Cornelius a Lapide, *Comment. in Sacram Script.*, Tom. IX, ad I Cor., VII, 39. A few, however, dissented. Cf. Reiffenstuel, *Jus Can. Univ.*, Lib. IV, Tit. I, nn. 366-370; Pichler, *Jus Can.*, Tom. I, Lib. IV, n. 130; Petra, *Comment. ad Const. Apost.*, Tom. IV, Const. XII, Ioannis XXII, nn. 9-10, 13-15; Mazzei, *De Matr. personarum div. Relig.*, cap. II, § IX. De Coninck (*De Sacram.*, Tom. II, Disp. 31, Dub. 3, n. 45) is very hesitant in accepting it.

[14] Lessius had taught that the custom of a diriment impediment of Disparity of Cult had never passed to the Orient, and that, therefore, the marriages between the baptized and the unbaptized of those regions were valid without dispensation. Pope Benedict XIV called attention to the error and reasserted the universality of the law. Cf. ep. *Singulari*, 9 Feb. 1749, § 19.—*Fontes*, n. 394; *Opera Inedita*, p. 431.

[15] See No. 104, notes 53-54.

83. Even Cardinal Albitius, grown gray in the service of the Inquisition, the very touchstone of orthodoxy, seemed to recognize the existence of a kind of double discipline. In his opinion mixed marriages among the common people might be contracted without Papal dispensation in those regions where heresy existed with impunity,[16] and the decisions forbidding the assistance of pastors were to be understood as not applying to such conditions.[17] Nay more, he would permit pastors to impart the nuptial blessing.[18] But on no condition would he subscribe to the opinion sponsored by Cardinal De Lugo[19] who had so completely accepted the custom in these regions regarding mixed marriages among the common people that he was at a loss to explain why Catholic rulers living in those countries seemed to regard themselves bound to seek a dispensation when marrying heretics.[20]

84. An entirely different discipline, says Cardinal Albitius, existed for the marriages of Catholic rulers with heretics. Here the welfare of the Church and of the Catholic faith of kingdoms and of states was in far greater jeopardy than in the mixed marriages of the common people.[21] It was still the day of the formula which wrought such havoc for the peace of the world,—"*cuius regio, eius et religio*". The Church, therefore, insisted upon the necessity of abjuration or dispensation.

85. The negotiations in such proposed unions were practically equivalent to the processes involved in diplomatic treaties. To read the stories of such transactions is to enter into the

---

[16] *De Inconstantia in Fide*, Cap. XVIII, nn. 43-44, 47-48; Cap. XXXVI, n. 203.

[17] Sed haec declaratio debet intelligi, ut habeat locum in iis locis, in quibus non vivunt haeretici permixtum impune cum Catholicis, quia ubi impune vivunt, Parochus Catholicus potest assistere etiam matrimonio haereticorum, cum post Concilium Constantien. Haeretici nec in Sacris, nec in Politicis negotiis vitandi sint, nisi sint denunciati."—*De Inconstantia in Fide*, Cap. XVIII, n. 48.

[18] *Loc. cit.* Pope Clement VIII had, however, forbidden the imparting of a blessing for such marriages. Cf. Benedictus XIV, *De Synodo Dioec.*, Lib. VI, cap. V, n. 5; *Rituale Romanum*, Suppl. pro Prov. Am. Septentr. Foed., p. 10. See infra No. 388, note 66.

[19] There were evidently others too in Rome who shared De Lugo's opinion. Cf. Albitius, *op. cit.*, Cap. XXXVI, n. 163.

[20] De Lugo, *Tract. de Virt. Fidei Div.*, Disp. XXII, Sect. II, n. 16; *Tract. de Sacram. in genere*, Disp. VIII, n. 225.

[21] *De Inconstantia in Fide*, Cap. XXXVI, n. 205. Cf. Petra, *Comment. ad Const. Apost.*, Tom. IV, Const. XII, Ioannis XXII, n. 17.

councils of kings, and to be entangled in the politics of Europe, where it seems that the controversy over a dispensation from the impediment of Mixed Religion became the turning point of the discussions. The stipulations, exactions, guarantees, and signatures were all of the deepest concern to the Holy See. These it would demand, these it would examine to see if sufficient safeguards had been provided for the faith of the Catholic party, of the children, and even of the subjects under their present or future rule.

86. The first record of such a proceeding concerns Henry of Bavaria who without dispensation had married his Calvinist cousin Catherine of Navarre, the sister of Henry IV of France. The impediment of Mixed Religion, writes Spondanus,[22] was of far greater concern to the Holy See than that of Consanguinity. Pope Clement VIII was altogether unwilling to dispense until Catherine would at least promise to become a Catholic. Even though she began to take instructions, and Henry had gone to Rome to seek the dispensation personally, it was granted only with the greatest reluctance and after years of discussion.[23] Catherine died before the dispensation could be executed, upon which Spondanus offers the reflection: *"Singulari et inscrutabili providentia divina."*[24]

---

[22] *"Potissima difficultas erat de diversitate religionis.* Quamvis enim cognatio in gradibus prohibitis secundum leges Ecclesiasticas irritaret per se matrimonium; facilis tamen est dispensatio, cum causa. At diversitas religionis, etiamsi ea sola inter christianos baptizatos non irritet matrimonium contractum; impedit tamen ne contrahi possit absque gravissimo peccato partis catholicae, ob periculum seductionis, ac perversionis, et pravae institutionis liberorum, rixarumque, et odiorum quae facile inter coniugatos inde oriuntur: quae causae sunt, propter quas eiusmodi matrimonia prohibita sunt; et quarum ratione fixus in eo manebat Clemens, ut non dispensaret cum Barrensi, nisi prius Catharina haereism eiuraret."* (Quoted by Feije, *De Matr. Mixtis*, p. 9-10.)

[23] Pope Clement VIII in granting the dispensation wrote to Catherine: ". . . Atque una spe freti, ut nostra erga te benignitate inducaris ad cognoscendam veritatem, ad quam Nos te in primis antea hortati sumus, et frater tuus Rex Christianissimus, et Dux Bariensis et universa Ecclesia Catholica te invitant; Dispensationem, quam litteris tuis a Nobis humiliter petiisti, matura nonnullorum Venerabilium fratrum nostrorum Sanctae Romanae Ecclesiae Cardinalium, et Theologorum, et Iuris Canonici peritissimorum virorum consultatione adhibita, et certa forma praescripta, prout in re tanti momenti fieri debuit, quanquam ut verum ingenue fateamur, propter ipsius difficultatem, et novitatem quodammodo renuentes, et inviti concessimus . . ."—Albitius, *De Inconstantia in Fide*, Cap. XXXVI, n. 208.

[24] Cited by Juenin, *Comment. de Sacram.*, Dissert. X, Q. VII, cap. VI, art. 3. Cf. Albitius, *op. cit.*, Cap. XXXVI, n. 206.

87. The efforts of King James I of England to effect a union with Spain through the marriage of his son, Charles, to the Infanta, Donna Maria, exemplify well the endless negotiations, hesitations, stipulations, and guarantees which were required to overcome the one outstanding difficulty that rested in the difference of religion.[25]

88. Philip III of Spain was reluctant to see his daughter a mere child of twelve, enter a royal court where she might easily be seduced from the Catholic Faith. He placed the matter before Pope Paul V, who commended his stand and directed that only upon Charles' conversion could the union be countenanced.[26]

89. Negotiations were renewed with the accession of Philip IV who looked with favor upon the marriage, and petitioned the Holy See for a dispensation. In his eagerness, James I had also sent Catholic envoys to the same purpose, to whom the Pontiff replied that the dispensation could not be given unless it were for the benefit of the Church. James had promised much to Philip III but as yet he had done nothing. There might be a sufficient cause if he were to relieve the Catholics of England from the pressure of the penal laws.

90. James I lost no time in following this suggestion and instructed the judges to issue pardons. Twenty-three articles safeguarding the Catholic faith of the Infanta and the children were subscribed and sworn to by James and Charles.[27] The negotiations might have ended here had not Charles in a rash spirit of adventure gone to Madrid to sue in person for the hand of the Infanta. The Spanish minister, Olivarez, who had been eager for more favorable terms, saw his advantage in this unexpected turn of events. The dispensation was granted but at the request of Olivarez it had been accompanied by two sets

---

[25] The story of both the Spanish and the French match, which is given here in synoptic form, is told in intimate detail by Lingard, *History of England*, VII, 237-276.

[26] Cf. Pastor, *Geschichte der Päpste*, XII, 453-454; Gardiner, *History of England*, II, 255-256.

[27] The twenty-three articles may be found in Rushworth, *Historical Collections*, I, 86-88. The twentieth article granted the Infanta the custody of the children to the age of ten. Pope Gregory XV corrected this to the age of twelve for the girls and fourteen for the boys.

of instructions to the nuncio, Massimi,—one to be made public, and the other to be given only to the Spanish minister. By the first the nuncio was forbidden to part with the dispensation except upon Charles' promise of conversion and the repeal of the penal laws. By the other the nuncio was ordered to procure for the British Catholics every possible indulgence but to deliver the dispensation to the King of Spain whenever it should be required. Olivarez was thus given the opportunity to reopen discussions. The result was a public and private treaty. By the first it was stipulated that the marriage was to be celebrated in Spain and that the children should remain in the care of the mother to the age of ten. The private treaty stipulated that none of the penal laws should be executed, and that the king should strive to have them repealed. Catholic worship was to be tolerated in private houses and there must be no attempt to seduce the Infanta from her religion. King James and the Lords of the Council swore to the observance of the public treaty; the king privately, but before four witnesses, to the secret treaty.

91. A new cause of delay came with the death of Pope Gregory XV. Since his dispensation had not been executed, it was deemed necessary to procure another from his successor, Urban VIII. A new treaty was concluded and a second dispensation granted, but further threatened delays exhausted the patience of Charles who returned to England, and there the Spanish treaty was declared at an end.

92. But James would have an alliance and he now turned to France to begin negotiations for the marriage of Charles with Henrietta Maria, the sister of Louis XIII. Both the Pope and Philip of Spain made several attempts to dissuade Louis from consenting to the union, but Louis finally yielded to the suggestions of his mother who saw in the marriage a political advantage for France. An agreement was again drawn up which stipulated that the marriage take place in France; that on the arrival of the princess in England the contract should be publicly ratified without any religious ceremony; that she and her servants should be allowed the free exercise of their religion as fully as had been stipulated for the Infanta, and that the children should remain under her care to the age of thirteen.

93. Cardinal Richelieu observed, however, that it would be an affront to his sovereign if less were conceded in favor of a French than had been granted to a Spanish princess. He asked that every indulgence promised to English Catholics in the treaty at Madrid would likewise be secured in the treaty with the French king. To James and Charles this difficulty seemed insurmountable for after the Spanish negotiations both had given a sworn promise to Parliament that they would never permit in any treaty whatsoever the insertion of any clause granting indulgence or toleration to the English Catholics. A compromise was effected upon the stipulation of a secret engagement whereby the English king promised to grant his Catholic subjects a greater freedom than they would have enjoyed by virtue of the Spanish treaty.[28]

94. On December 30, 1624, Pope Urban VIII granted the dispensation,[29] but forbade the nuncio, Spada, to deliver it unless some better security would be offered in favor of the English Catholics. The dispensation was finally executed upon an oath taken by Louis XIII by which he bound himself and his successors to employ the power of France in compelling the fulfillment of the treaty should this be necessary.

95. It is well to note that for at least a century and a half the mixed marriage dispensations of the Holy See were given only for the marriages of the Catholic nobility.[30] Since

---

[28] The conditions of the final treaty may be found in Albitius, *De Inconstantia in Fide*, Cap. XXXVI, n. 218.

[29] ". . . Idque ob maximas, et gravissimas causas universae Christianae Reipublicae bonum, et Catholicae fidei propagationem concernentes notas exponere Nobis propterea, etc. Idcirco Nos, etc. licet probe teneamus, Catholicorum cum Haereticis Matrimonia omnio fugienda esse, et quantum in Nobis est a Catholica Ecclesia procul arcere intendamus. Tamen cum grande verae fidei, et animarum plurimarum bonum speretur: negotium prius accuratissime examinatum cum pluribus gravibus viris, ac Doctrina, et prudentia praestantibus Venerabilibus Fratribus Nostris Sanctae Romanae Ecclesiae Cardinalibus mandavimus, qui post longam rei consultationem, videri sibi huiusmodi Matrimonium permittendum Nobis retulerunt . . ."—Albitius, *op. cit.*, Cap. XXXVI, n. 217.

[30] See No. 79, note 6. Other examples of such dispensations or their refusal, may be found in Albitius, *De Inconstantia in Fide*, Cap. XXXVI, nn. 209-213; Mazzei, *De Matr. personarum div. Relig.*, cap. II, § XIV; Feije, *De Matr. Mixtis*, p. 11-14; Giovine, *De Dispens. Matr.*, Tom. I, § CLXXII, n. 1; Binterim, *Denkwürdigkeiten*, VII, II, p. 49; Schulte, *Handb. des kath. Eherechts*, p. 251-252. Feije (*op. cit.*, p. 12) cites an instance of where Pope Clement XI on June 25, 1706 refused a Catholic noble (Comes de Hohenlohe) a dispensation from the impediment of Disparity of Cult.

both a *causa publica* and formal *cautiones* always existed for such dispensations, both came to be demanded as a necessary condition for every mixed marriage dispensation.[31] There were no dispensations, therefore, for mixed marriages among the common people of Catholic countries, for in such cases the *causa publica* was wanting.[32] In countries where heresy existed with impunity, the very necessity of Papal dispensation, and therefore of formal causes and *cautiones* for the mixed marriages of the common people, was entirely disregarded. It may accordingly be said without serious hesitation that the *Stylus Curiae* of the Holy See in reference to dispensations for mixed marriages had its derivation in the formalities of religious-political treaties. Perhaps the *cautiones* as they are known today may be regarded as a survival of these first formal guarantees.

96. In the meantime, however, mixed marriages among the common people in the countries where heresy was rampant continued to grow in number. For lack of observance of the decree *"Tametsi"* many of these unions were invalid. It was a trying situation, and accordingly Pope Benedict XIV declared that marriages between Protestants, and mixed marriages contracted in the United Provinces of Belgium were no longer to be subject for validity to the Tridentine form required by the decree *"Tametsi"*.[33] Similar declarations were extended to other regions by later Pontiffs.[34]

----

[31] Cf. Benedictus XIV (ep. encycl. *Magnae Nobis*, 29 Iun. 1748, § 5,—*Fontes*, n. 387; Pius VII, rescript. ad ep. et vicar. capit. Galliar., 17 Feb. 1809,—Migne, *Theol. Curs. Complet.*, XXV, 710; S. C. de Prop. F., instr. (ad Vic. Ap. Sveciae), 6 Sept. 1785,—*Coll.*, n. 579.

[32] "Quae autem causa sit sufficiens, ut Pontifex dispenset ad huiusmodi matrimonia contrahenda: Ego nunquam vidi concessas fuisse similes dispensationes, nisi suadente causa boni publici."—Albitius, *op. cit.*, Cap. XVIII, n. 46.

[33] Const. *Matrimonia*, 4 Nov. 1741,—*Coll.*, n. 333. A *dubium* had already been proposed on August 23, 1681 to the following effect: "*An in Provinciis Belgii confoederatis valeant matrimonia Catholicorum cum Heterodoxis contracta coram magistratu haeretico, non obstante decreto Concilii de solemnitatibus matrimonii in illis Provinciis publicato, et recepto.* Sacr. Congreg. Concilii respondit: *Secretario cum Sanctissimo ad mentem, quae erat, quod si respondendum esset ad dubium, dicendum esset matrimonia non valere; attamen animadversum fuit id non expedire, quia potius deberent permitti in eorum bona fide permanere quam tot periculis exponere Catholicos.*"—Petra, *Comment. ad Const. Apost.*, Tom. IV, Const. XII, Ioannis XXII, n. 24. Vide etiam S. C. Conc., 13 Feb. 1683,—*ibid*.

[34] Pius VI, 19 Iun. 1793,—Migne, *Theol. Curs. Complet.*, XXV, 681; Pius VIII, litt ap. *Litteris altero*, 25 Mart. 1830, *Fontes*, n. 480. Cf.

97. But slowly, and with patience, the Holy See began to gather the loose ends of straying customs to fashion one discipline that would apply everywhere and for all mixed marriages. Pope Benedict XIV condemned the practice of those who sought dispensations from the Holy See without mentioning that one of the parties was a heretic.[35] He would not, however, inaugurate too drastic a reform of a sudden lest dire consequences follow in its wake. The Holy See had indeed reserved to itself the exclusive right to dispense from the impediment of Mixed Religion,[36] yet where this right had been disregarded the abuse was to be corrected gradually. A certain dissimulation could even be tolerated as long as there was no danger of violating the divine and natural law.[37]

Schulte, *Handb. des kath. Eherechts*, p. 271. With regard to the extension of the law in the United States see Conc. Plen. Balt. III (1884), p. CV-CIX. The marriages of Catholics with schismatics were also valid, even though they were contracted before a non-Catholic minister. Cf. S. C. de Prop. F., 21 Mart. 1759,—*Coll.*, n. 415; 18 Feb. 1783,—*Coll.*, n. 562; S. C. S. Off., 5 Aug. 1846,—*Coll.*, n. 1009; 10 Feb. 1892.—*Fontes*, n. 1150. The reason whereby a Catholic who was bound to the observance of the Tridentine form could clandestinely marry a heretic or schismatic, rested on the principle that those who were exempt (heretics and schismatics) communicated the exemption to those who were not,-"*propter individuitatem contractus.*" Cf. Litterae Clementis XIII ad Archiep. Mechlinien., 15 Maii 1767, —Migne, *op. cit.* XXV, 684; Benedictus XIV, *De Synodo Dioec.*, Lib. VI, cap. VI, n. 12. As far as the requirements of the form were concerned, the same principle applied to the marriages of the baptized with the unbaptized since they were not bound to observe the form. Cf. S. C. S. Off., instr. (ad Archiep. Quebecen.), 16 Sept. 1824, ad 2,—*Fontes*, n. 866; Gasparri, *De Matr.*, n. 710; Chelodi, *Ius Matr.*, n. 81.

[35] Ep. encycl. *Magnae Nobis*, 29 Iun. 1748,—*Fontes*, n. 387; *De Synodo Dioec.*, Lib. VI, cap. V, n. 2; Lib. IX, cap. III, nn. 1-3.

[36] S. C. Conc., 22 Iun. 1624,—Petra, *Comment. ad Const. Apost.*, Tom. IV, Const. XII, Ioannis XXII, n. 8; 6 Mart. 1694,—*ibid.* Both decrees are quoted in No. 80, note 11.

[37] Pope Pius VI seems to have tolerated the same practice for he quotes the passage from Pope Benedict XIV with approval: "Quamvis tamen nequaquam velimus Tibi et Coepiscopis tuis vel in minimo adaugere angustias, neque criticas istas sequelas, quas credunt merito a se timeri, super illos attrahere; et ideo quantum ad id, quod punctum spectat simplicis permissionis seu veniae dandae, dicemus idem quod in responsoriis suis de 12 Sept. 1750 Episcopo Wratislaviensi dixit praenominatus Benedictus XIV scilicet: 'non posse se positivo actu approbare, ut dispensationes concedantur inter haereticos, vel ipsos inter et catholicos, sed tamen se posse hoc dissimulare'; additque: 'scientia haec nostra et tolerantia sufficere debet ad tuam assecurandam conscientiam, quandoquidem in materia, de qua agitur, non occurat oppositio cum iure divino aut naturali, sed tantummodo cum iure ecclesiastico'."—rescript. ad Card. Archiep. Mechlinien., 13 Iul. 1782, n. 2,—*Fontes*, n. 471.

98. In Belgium the civil law had enacted the forced assistance of pastors at mixed marriages. The Cardinal Archbishop of Mechlin wished, therefore, to know whether the assistance of the pastors could be permitted.[38] The answer given by Pope Pius VI represents a step in reform through an insistence upon the observance of formal *cautiones*.

99. If the Catholic party could not be dissuaded from his purpose, and the proposed mixed marriage was certain to take place, the pastor might be present as a material or informal witness ("*poterit tunc parochus catholicus* MATERIALEM SUAM EXHIBERE PRAESENTIAM") but only on the following conditions. There was to be no publication of the banns; the marriage was not to be celebrated *in loco sacro*; no liturgical prayers, rites, or vestments could be used, and on no pretext could the nuptial blessing be given. Furthermore, the heretic must give a formal declaration in writing, sealed with an oath and signed conjointly with two witnesses that the Catholic be left the free exercise of the Catholic religion, and that all the children, regardless of sex, be educated in the Catholic faith. The Catholic was likewise to give a sworn, written, and witnessed declaration foreswearing all apostasy, promising to educate all the children in the Catholic faith, and to employ effective means to procure the conversion of the non-Catholic spouse.[30]

---

[38] It is interesting to note that the question did not turn upon the necessity of dispensation, but rather upon the liceity of the pastor's assistance.

[30] ". . . poterit tunc parochus catholicus *materialem suam exhibere praesentiam*, sic tamen, ut sequentes observare teneatur cautelas. *Primo*, ut non assistat tali matrimonio in loco sacro, nec aliqua veste ritum sacrum praeferente indutus, neque recitabit super contrahentes preces aliquas ecclesiasticas, et nullo modo ipsis benedicet. *Secundo*, ut exigat et recipiat a contrahente haeretico *declarationem in scriptis*, qua cum *iuramento*, praesentibus duobus testibus, qui debebunt et ipsi subscribere, *obliget se ad permittendum comparti usum liberum religionis catholicae et ad educandum in eadem omnes liberos nascituros sine ulla sexus distinctione* . . . *Tertio*, ut et ipse contrahens catholicus declarationem edat a se et duobus testibus subscriptam, in qua cum iuramento promittat, non tantum se nunquam apostaturum a religione sua catholica, sed educaturum in ipsa omne prolem nascituram, et procuraturum se efficaciter conversionem alterius contrahentis acatholici. *Quarto*, quod attinet *proclamationes*, decreto Caesareo imperatas, quas Episcopi apprehendunt actus esse civiles potius quam sacros, respondemus; quum praeordinatae illae sint ad futuram celebrationem matrimonii, et ex consequenti positivam eidem co-operationem contineant, quod utique excedit simplicis tolerantiae limites, *non posse nos, ut hae fiant, annuere* . . ."—rescript. ad Card. Archiep. Mechlinien., 13 Iul. 1782, n. 4,—*Fontes*, n. 471.

100. The answer of Pope Pius VI involves a striking combination of formality and informality. There is an insistence upon written, sworn, and witnessed declarations and stipulations,—a prescription as formal as possible without an actual abjuration, in conjunction with the utter informality of a pastor's material presence, and the absence of even a suggestion as to the necessity of dispensation.

101. At first sight such a union of two opposites may appear somewhat strange, yet it is easily understood if the origin of the Roman *Stylus Curiae* be kept in mind. In fact it is what one might expect in the process of a gradual reform which would impose upon the laxities of practice some of the formalities of a discipline born of state treaties. The observance of the entire *stylus* implying the strict necessity of Papal dispensation might not at first be insisted upon,—the reform would begin rather with a definite provision for the safeguarding of the divine law; it would begin with an insistence upon a partial observance of a *stylus* which of its nature was formal. It is not surprising, therefore, to find much of this formality in the *cautiones* demanded for mixed marriages among the common people for which, up to that time, no *Stylus Curiae* as yet existed. Thereafter such *cautiones* were strictly insisted upon for all mixed and disparate marriages.[40] While they were indeed

-----

[40] Cf. Pius VII, litt. (ad Vic. Treviren.), 23 Apr. 1817,—Gasparri, *De Matr.*, n. 490; Pius VIII, litt. ap. *Litteris altero*, 25 Mart. 1830,—*Fontes*, n. 482; instr., 27 Mart. 1830,—Ballerini-Palmieri, *Op. Theol. Mor.*, Tract. X, Sect. VIII, n. 724; Gregorius XVI, ep. encycl. *Summo iugiter*, 27 Maii 1832, § 1,—*Fontes*, n. 484; allocut. *Officii memores*, 5 Iul. 1839,—*Fontes*, n. 492; ep. *Dolorem*, 30 Nov. 1839, n. 2,—*Fontes*, n. 493; litt. ap. *Quas vestro*, 30 Apr. 1841, nn. 2-3,—*Fontes*, n. 497; instr. (ad Archiep. et Ep. Austriacae ditionis), 22 Maii 1841,—Ballerini-Palmieri, *op. cit.*, Tract. X, Sect. VIII, n. 724; ep. 25 Iun. 1845,—*ibid.*, n. 720; ep. *Non sine gravi*, 23 Maii 1846, n. 1,—*Fontes*, n. 503; Instr. Secret. Stat. iussu Pii PP. IX, 15 Nov. 1858,—*Coll.*, n. 1169; litt. Secret. Stat. (ad Archiep. Strigonien.), 7 Iul. 1890,—*NRT*, XXIII (1891), 387-388; Card. Rampolla, litt. (ad Card. Simor), 26 Sept. 1890,—*NRT*, XXIII (1891), 388-391; S. C. S. Off. (Quebec.), 10 Sept. 1820,—*Fontes*, n. 859; instr. (ad Archiep. Quebecen.), 16 Sept. 1824, ad 5,—*Fontes*, n. 866; 20 Dec. 1837, —*ASS*, XXVI (1893-1894), 512; 30 Iun. 1842,—*Fontes*, n. 890; 15 Mart. 1854,—*LQS*, XLVI (1893), 21-22; (Helvetiae), 21 Ian. 1863,— *Fontes*, n. 973; (ad Ep. Osnabrugen.), 17 Feb. 1864,—*Fontes*, n. 976; (ad Archiep. Corcyren.), 3 Ian. 1871, nn. 3, 6-7,—*Fontes*, n. 1013; litt. (S. Germani), 17 Feb. 1875,—*Fontes*, n. 1039; (ad Ep. Aurelianen.), 6 Iun. 1879,—*Fontes*, n. 1064; litt. (ad Card. Simor), 21 Iul. 1880,— *NRT*, XIX (1887), 4-9; 12 Mart. 1881,—*NRT*, XV (1883), 121-122;

relieved of some of their formality[41] they would have to be given in a form of a promise *"quae in pactum deducta praebeat morale fundamentum de veritate executionis, ita ut prudenter eiusmodi executio expectari possit."*[42] Nor would the Church dispense from them[43] for they were founded on the divine law,[44] and were necessary to safeguard it.

102. In France, where the Revolution had broken down the last barriers that had existed between Catholic and heretical communities, mixed marriages became a matter of frequent occurrence. The French Bishops presented an urgent request to Pope Pius VII asking for the faculty to dispense for mixed marriages. Apparently, the faculty had never before been ex-

---

instr. (ad omnes Ep. Ritus Orient.), 12 Dec. 1888,—*Fontes*, n. 1112; 10 Dec. 1902,—*Fontes*, n. 1262; 21 Iun. 1912,—*AAS*, IV (1912), 442-443.

[41] "The Bishops of the First Plenary Council of Baltimore (*Acta et Decreta*, p. 53) determined to petition the Holy See to substitute a solemn promise of the Catholic party for the oath. On three occasions the Holy See demanded it. Cf. S. C. S. Off., instr. (ad Archiep. Quebecen.), 16 Sept. 1824, ad 5,—*Fontes* n. 866; litt. (S. Germani), 17 Feb. 1875,—*Fontes*, n. 1039; (ad Ep. Aurelianen.), 6 Iun. 1879,—*Fontes*, n. 1064. Those who were occult Catholics were also to give the *cautiones* under oath. Cf. S. C. S. Off., instr. (ad Archiep. Scopien.), 15 Nov. 1882,—*Fontes*, n. 1074. It was generally admitted by the authors before the Code, however, than an oath of the Catholic party was not required. Cf. Bangen, *De Spons. et Matr.*, Tit. IV, p. 16; Wernz, *Ius Decret.*, IV, n. 587, not. 32; Gasparri, *De Matr.*, n. 499. In a letter of the Holy Office of Feb. 17, 1875 (*Fontes*, n. 1039) it was declared that the oath of the non-Catholic party was not always necessary. See also rescript. Poenitentiariae, 17 Ian. 1836, —Roskovány, *De Matr. Mixtis*, III, p. 156, not.* Its prescription was, however repeated in a later decree. Cf. S. C. S. Off. (ad Ep. Aurelianen.), 6 Iun. 1879,—*Fontes*, n. 1064. "Et quidem hoc ultimum [iuramentum] tunc erit necessarium, ubi religionis gubernium eiusmodi reversales non attendit, vel ubi nupturientes in locum acatholicum se transferunt, in quo promissionis impletio difficillima futura est."—Aichner, *Compend. Juris Eccles.*, § 183.

[42] S. C. S. Off., 30 Iun. 1842, ad 5,—*Fontes*, n. 890.

[43] Instr. Secret. Stat. iussu Pii PP. IX, 15 Nov. 1858,—*Coll.*, n. 1169; Card. Rampolla, litt. (ad Card. Simor), 26 Sept. 1890,—*NRT*, XXIII (1891), 388-391.

[44] Pius VIII, litt. ap. *Litteris altero*, 25 Mart. 1830,—*Fontes*, n. 482; Gregorius XVI, litt. 25 Iun. 1845,—Ballerini-Palmieri, *Op. Theol. Mor.*, Tract. X, Sect. VIII, n. 720; S. C. S. Off., instr. (ad Archiep. Corcyren.), 3 Ian. 1871, nn. 6-7,—*Fontes*, n. 1013; litt. (ad Card. Simor), 21 Iul. 1880,—*NRT*, XIX (1887), 4-9; instr. (ad omnes Ep. Ritus Orient.), 12 Dec. 1888, n. 6.—*Fontes*, n. 1112; litt. Secret. Stat. (ad Archiep. Strigonien.), 7 Iul. 1890,—*NRT*, XXIII (1891), 387-388; S. C. de Prop. F., 25 Mart. 1858,—*NRT*, XV (1883), 582; litt encycl., 11 Mart. 1868,—*Coll.*, n. 1324.

tended to Bishops,—at least not in Europe,[45] and the Pope was altogether unwilling to grant it.[46] He would not, however, disregard the gravity of the conditions that had arisen, so he had the question submitted to a group of theologians and Cardinals. Their decision would be transmitted to the French Bishops soon and all would receive the same formulary of faculties.[47]

103. It appears, therefore, that Bishops were given the faculty to dispense from the impediment of Mixed Religion only towards the close of the eighteenth or the beginning of the nineteenth century.[48] The Church seemed to be hesitant in

---

[45] "Episcopis vero, licet instantissime postulantibus eamdem licentiam dare, in Europa praesertim, nunquem concessit . . ."—Pius VII, rescript ad ep. et vicar. capit. Galliar., 17 Feb. 1809,—Migne, *Theol. Curs. Complet.*, XXV, 710. Mergentheim is of the opinion, however, that the Bishops of Germany enjoyed the faculty at a very early date. "Der Erzbischof Ferdinand von Köln [1612-1650] frug bei dem römischen Stuhle an, wie er sich angesichts der jetzt so häufig vorkommenden Mischehen verhalten solle, und ferner, wie 'auch in allen anderen Ehehindernissen, und in welchen Graden der Anverwandtschaft er ohne Gewissensverletzung und Missbrauch der oberhirtlichen Gewalt am sichersten zu dispensieren hätte'. Er erwartete auf diese Anfrage eine päpstliche Belehrung. Statt der gewünschten Instruktion bekam er aber unter dem erwähnten Datum vom Papste ein 'ungebetenes und ganz unerwartetes' Indult worin ihm von der Kurie die Vollmacht erteilt wurde, auf sieben Jahre auctoritate Apostolica tanquam Sedis Apostolicae delegatus bis zum zweiten Grade zu dispensieren."—*Die Quinquennalfakultäten pro Foro Externo*, I, 51. The indult given by Pope Paul V on December 23, 1619 (the complete text may be found in Mergentheim, *op. cit.*, II, 256-257) contains, however, no explicit reference to marriages between Catholics and heretics, and it does not, therefore, appear entirely obvious that the faculty to dispense from the impediment of Mixed Religion or from impediments of relationship existing between Catholics and heretics was granted or implied. Yet Mergentheim (*op. cit.*, II, 118-119) writes: "In einer der Streitschriften lesen wir dass eine Korrespondenz über die impedimenta mixtae religionis und consanguinitatis et affinitatis die Veranlassung der ersten Quinquennalendelegation gewesen sei [here he refers to the paragraph already quoted above]. Dass es sich hier nur um eine 'Belehrung' gehandelt habe, ist undenkbar. Hätte der Erzbischof wirklich die Ehedispensbefugnisse iure proprio in Anspruch genommen, so wäre, war die Anfrage, 'wie er in allen anderen Ehehindernissen (ausser dem impedimentum mixtae religionis), und in welchen Graden der Anverwandtschaft er ohne Gewissensverletzung und ohne Missbrauch seiner oberhirtlichen Gewalt am sichersten zu dispensieren hätte', ein Ding der Unmöglichkeit."

[46] "Quare si a nobis petitioni huic respondendum nunc esset, responsum certe nostrum a constanti huius Sanctae Sedis regula et praedecessorum nostrorum exemplo agendique ratione dissidere non posset."—*rescript. cit.*

[47] *Ibid.*

[48] See No. 102 note 45; Feije, *De Matr. Mixtis*, p. 220; *De Imped. et Dispens.*, n. 613. Yet Pope Benedict XIV seems to suggest that Bishops in his time did occasionally possess the faculty: "Tales enim re ipsa concurrere possunt circumstantiae, quae cum ab eo, qui *facultatem dipensandi habet*, expensae fuerint, aditum aperiant concessioni legitimae dispensationis, cuius vi

granting the faculty,—perhaps with a fear of a return to old abuses.[49] Whenever it was delegated thereafter its exercise was confined to a limited time or to a specified number of cases.[50]

104. But all this time the disregard of the necessity of Papal dispensation for mixed marriages among the common

---

matrimonium inter partes, haereticam unam, alteramque Catholicam, licitum reddatur, ut alibi demonstrabimus."—*De Synodo Dioec.*, Lib. VI, cap. V, n. 4.   Vide etiam *ibid.*, Lib. IX, cap. III, n. 2.   Cf. Scherer, *Handb. des Kirchenrechtes*, II, p. 422, not. 74; Bangen, *De Spons. et Matr.*, Tit. II, p. 160-161; Wernz, *Ius Decret.*, IV, nn. 576, 584; *AkKR*, XIV (1865), 324 for a confirmation of the opinion accepted as the more probable in the present study.   The Bishops of the United States enjoyed the faculty at least in the second half of the nineteenth century.   "In haereticorum cum catholicis nuptiis etiam nostrates [Episcopi] ex eadem speciali venia dispensant, conditionibus tamen appositis . . ."—Kenrick, *Theol. Mor.*, II, Tract. XXI, n. 217.   Cf. Conc. Plen. Balt. II (1866), n. 339; Vermeersch, *De Form. Facult. S. C. de Prop. F.*, n. 26; *Facult. Extr.*, Form. D, art. 3, 4,—Konings-Putzer, *Comment. in Facult.*, p. 388-389.

[49] In 1888 Pope Leo XIII, through the Holy Office, conferred on the *Ordinarii locorum* the power to dispense from public diriment impediments ("*excepto sacro Presbyteratus ordine, et affinitate lineae rectae ex copula licita proveniente*") those joined in civil marriage or living in concubinage, who, being in danger of death, wished to contract a valid marriage to obtain peace of conscience. Cf. S. C. S. Off., litt. encycl. 20 Feb. 1888,—*Fontes, n.* 1109; O'Keeffe, *Matrimonial Dispensations*, p. 47-49.   While the faculty thus included the impediment of Disparity of Cult, it did not include that of the impediment of Mixed Religion. Cf. S. C. S. Off. (Leopolien.), 18 Mart. 1891,—*Fontes*, n. 1132;; 12 Apr. 1899,—*Fontes*, n. 1219.

[50] Cf. Rescript. Poenitentiariae, 19 Ian. 1836,—Roskonávy, *De Matr. Mixtis*, III, p. 156, not.*; Wernz, *Ius Decret.*, IV, n. 584, not. 28. Further stipulations existed to keep the exercise of this faculty within well defined limits.   Already in the sixteenth century, Pope Clement VIII (*Cum sicut*, 26 Iul. 1596,—*Bullarium Diplomatum et Privilegiorum Sanctorum Romanorum Pontificum Taurinensis Editio*, [Augustae Taurinorum, 1865], X, 279-280) had forbidden the Italians to go to regions where Catholic worship was not held, and especially prohibited them from marrying heretics. The Inquisition could proceed against them, if they disregarded this prohibition, as *contra suspectos de haeresi*,—Albitius, *De Inconstantia in Fide*, Cap. XXXVI, n. 238, quoad 2um dub. When, therefore, the faculty of dispensing from the impediment of Mixed Religion was granted to Bishops it carried the exception: "*exceptis Italis, de quibus non constat Italicum domicilium deseruisse.*" Cf. S. C. de Prop. F., 30 Aug. 1865,—*ASS*, II (1866), 672.   Later the exception was removed. Cf. S. C. S. Off., 4 Maii 1887,—*NRT*, XX (1888), 37; 17 Iun. 1891,—*LQS*, XLIV (1891), 976. The limitation of the faculty regarding its exercise within the boundaries of the diocese, was abrogated in 1896.   Cf. S. C. S. Off., 6 Iul. 1896,—*Coll.*, n. 1945.   Other limitations existed to the effect that dispensations could be given only to the subjects of the one employing the faculty (S. C. S. Off., 14 Dec. 1882,—*Coll.*, n. 1583) and that the faculty to dispense from the impediment of Disparity of Cult did not comprehend the marriages of Catholics with Jews. Cf. *Facult. Extr.*, Form. D, art. 3,—Konings-Putzer, *op. cit.*, p. 379.

people continued in countries where heresy was rampant.[51] It was time that such laxity be corrected and the fact was emphasized that a dispensation was always to be sought from the Holy See,[52]—that the Church, though she had been silent with regard to the conditions existing in those countries in order to avoid greater evils,[53] had never by her silence approved of the abuses that under the plea of a contrary custom had derogated from her law.[54]

105. The final reform in discipline came, therefore, only with the insistence upon the observance of the entire *Stylus Curiae,* which, as we have seen, had its origin in the formalities of religious-political treaties. The *stylus* was subject also to a modification in this final step in reform. Formerly only the *causa publica* had been admitted since dispensations had been given only to members of the Catholic nobility. Now, with

---

[51] The laxity in Germany continued well into the nineteenth century. Cf. Scherer, *Handb. des Kirchenrechtes,* II, p. 409-410; Hergenröther, P., *Lehrb. des kath. Kirchenrechts,* p. 729, not. 2; Wernz, *Ius Decret.,* IV, n. 576; Leitner, *Lehrb. des kath. Eherechts,* p. 235; Hilling, *Das Eherecht des C. I. C.,* p. 54.

[52] Pius VIII, litt. ap. *Litteris altero,* 25 Mart. 1830,—*Fontes,* n. 482; Gregorius XVI, ep. encycl. *Summo iugiter,* 27 Maii 1832, §§ 2, 6,—*Fontes,* n. 484; ep. *Dolorem,* 30 Nov. 1839, n. 2,—*Fontes,* n. 493; litt. ap. *Quas vestro,* 30 Apr. 1841, n. 3,—*Fontes,* n. 497; Instr. Secret. Stat. iussu Pii PP. IX, 15 Nov. 1858,—*Coll.,* n. 1169; S. C. S. Off., instr. (ad Archiep. Corcyren.), 3 Ian. 1871, nn. 3-4,—*Fontes,* n. 1013. Cf. Giovine, *De Dispens. Matr.,* Tom. I, § CLXXI, nn. 2-4; Scherer, *op. cit.,* II, p. 413, not. 30.

[53] ". . . Tolerat quidem in aliquibus locis Apostolica Sedes matrimonia inter Catholicum, et Haereticam, vel Haereticum, et Catholicam, cum nequeat impedire; et ecclesiastica quadam prudentia, ne maiora mala enascantur, dissimulat, ac tacet."—Benedictus XIV, ep. *Ad tuas,* 8 Aug. 1748, § 6,—*Fontes,* n. 389. Cf. Pius VI, rescript. (ad Ep. Rosnavien.), 20 Aug. 1780, —Feije, *De Matr. Mixtis,* p. 178-179.

[54] "Et licet in quibusdam regionibus propter locorum et temporum difficultatem eadem connubia [catholicorum cum haereticis] tolerari contingat, id quidem ad eam referendum est aequanimitatem, quae nulla ratione approbationis et consensus cuiuspiam loco habenda sit, sed merae patientiae, quam ad maiora vitanda mala offert necessitas, non voluntas . . ."—Pius VII, breve ad Archiep. Moguntin., 8 Oct. 1803, n. 5.—*Fontes,* n. 477. "Quamobrem etsi iamdiu, uti affirmas, opinio isthic inoleverit, licite posse mixtas iniri nuptias absque Sancate Sedis dispensatione, haec tamen opinio, qualibet non obstante consuetudine, tolerari nequit."—S. C. S. Off., instr. (ad Archiep. Corcyren.), 3 Ian. 1871,—*Fontes,* n. 1013. Cf. Pius VII, rescript. (ad Vic. Treviren.), 25 Apr. 1817,—Feije, *De Matr. Mixtis,* p. 179; Gregorius XVI, ep. encycl. *Summo iugiter,* 27 Maii 1832. § 1,—*Fontes,* n. 484; litt. ap. *Quas vestro,* 30 Apr. 1841, n. 1,—*Fontes,* n. 497; Petra, *Comment. ad Const. Apost.,* Tom. IV, Const. XII, Ioannis XXII, nn. 13-15.

the insistence on the requirement of dispensation for mixed marriages among the common people, the *causa publica* was replaced by the *causa gravis.*[55]

106. The formal *cautiones* which had been the first wedge of reform now came to be so intimately connected with the necessity of dispensation and the existence of a grave cause that the three elements were to be regarded as inseparable in the reformed discipline.[56] The absence of a grave cause would render the dispensation invalid. No dispensation would be granted unless the *cautiones* were given. Rather than dispense in the absence of the *cautiones*, the Church continued to tolerate the practice that existed in certain sections of Germany and Austria[57] of permitting the passive assistance of a pastor at mixed marriages,[58] i. e., the pastor was to act merely as a qualified or authorized witness ("*testis qualificatus seu auctorizabilis*") without asking the consent of the parties.[59]

---

[55] See No. 104, note 52; S. C. de Prop. F., litt. encycl., 11 Mart. 1868, —Coll., n. 1324.

[56] See No. 244, note 65.

[57] Cf. Schönsteiner, *Grundriss des kirchl. Eherechts*, p. 35. This forced toleration could be invoked only for those regions where it was permitted by the Holy See. Cf. Feije, *De Imped. et Dispens.*, n. 570; Wernz, *Ius Decret.*, IV, n. 589, not. 53; S. C. S. Off., 21 Iun. 1912,—*AAS*, IV (1912), 443-444.

[58] Pius VI. instr. 19 Iun. 1793.—Migne, *Theol. Curs. Complet.*, XXV. 681-682; Pius VII, litt. (ad Vic. Treviren.), 23 Apr. 1817,—Gasparri. *De Matr.*, n. 490; Pius VIII litt. ap. *Litteris altero*, 25 Mart. 1830,— *Fontes*, n. 482; instr. ad Archiep. Colonien. et ad Ep. Treviren. Paderbornen. et Monasterien., 27 Mart. 1830,—Schulte, *Handb. des kath. Eherechts*, p. 259-262; Gregorius XVI, instr. ad Archiep. et Ep. Bavariae, 12 Sept. 1834. —*NRT*, XV (1883), 512-513; litt. ap. *Quas vestro*, 30 Apr. 1841, n. 6, —*Fontes*, n. 497. This tolerance often became necessary because of civil prescriptions forcing a pastor to assist at such marriages under threat of civil penalties. Cf. Gasparri, *De Matr.*, n. 490; Feije, *De Imped. et Dispens.*, p. 446, not. 3. Again soldiers, especially officers, were at times prohibited under threat of severe penalties to give the *cautiones*. Cf. S. C. S. Off., 10 Dec. 1902,—*Fontes*, n. 1262. In two decrees which apparently had reference only to particular regions, the Holy Office demanded that priests assist only passively at the marriages of Catholics with those who had left the Church, or who had joined condemned societies. Cf. S. C. S. Off. (Leodien.), 30 Ian. 1867,—*Fontes*, n. 998; instr. (ad Ordinarios Imperii Brasil.), 2 Iul. 1878,—*Fontes*, n. 1056. The toleration of passive assistance was never extended to the United States. Cf. Wernz, *Ius Decret.*, IV, n. 589, not. 55. For an enumeration of the places where it was tolerated for mixed marriages see Schönsteiner, *op. cit.*, p. 80-81; Prümmer, *Manuale Iuris Can.*, Q. 334, Schol., not. 1.

[59] The term "passive assistance" is here employed in its strict sense, name-ly, "*audito consensu.*" Among the authors and even in instructions of the

107. In her further concern that by dispensing she would in no way appear to approve such marriages, the Church prohibited all liturgical rites at their celebration, and only to avoid greater evils would she permit their limited use.[60] That the faithful might not be scandalized she began to forbid the publication of the banns, permitting it only for reasons of necessity and on the condition that the religion of the non-Catholic be not mentioned.[61] On this point, however, it does not appear that there was always a uniformity of disipline.[62]

Holy See the term is often used in a much broader sense, i. e., in the sense of forbidding any active cooperation by use of liturgical rites or the publication of the banns. Cf. Hergenröther, P., *Lehrb. des kath. Kirchenrechts*, p. 733; Feije, *De Imped. et Dispens.*, n. 571; Wernz, *Ius Decret.*, IV, n. 588, not. 43. The distinction should, however, be born in mind since the broad sense of the term referred also to those marriages that were contracted with a dispensation. See the following note.

[60] Pius VI rescript. ad Card. Archiep. Mechlinien., 13 Iul. 1782, n. 4,—*Fontes*, n. 471; instr. 19 Iun. 1793,—Migne, *Theol. Curs. Complet.*, XXV, 681; Pius VIII, litt. ap *Litteris altero*, 25 Mart. 1830,—*Fontes*, n. 482; Gregorius XVI, instr. ad Ep. et Archiep. Bavariae, 12 Sept. 1834,—*NRT*, XV (1883), 512-513; allocut. *Officii memores*, 5 Iul. 1839,—*Fontes*, n. 492; litt. ap. *Quas vestro*, 30 Apr. 1841, nn. 5-6,—*Fontes*, n. 497; ep. *Non sine gravi*, 23 Maii 1846, n. 2,—*Fontes*, n. 503; Instr. Secret. Stat. iussu Pii PP. IX, 15 Nov. 1858,—*Coll.*, n. 1169; S. C. S. Off., 1 Aug. 1821,—*Fontes*, n. 863; instr. (ad Archiep. Quebecen.), 16 Sept. 1824, ad 5,—*Fontes*, n. 866; 26 Nov. 1835,—*Fontes*, n. 873; instr. (ad Ep. S. Alberti), 9 Dec. 1847,—*Coll.*, n. 1427; (Vic. Ap. Sandwic.), 11 Dec. 1850, ad 22,—*Fontes*, n. 913; litt. (ad Vic. Ap. Myssurien.), 26 Nov. 1862,—*Fontes*, n. 971; instr. (ad Archiep. Corcyren.), 3 Ian. 1871,—*Fontes*, n. 1013; 17 Ian. 1872,—*Fontes*, n. 1020; 17 Ian. 1877,—*NRT*, XX (1888), 462-464; (Rosen), 16 Iul. 1885,—*Fontes*, n. 1094; 29 Nov. 1899,—*Fontes*, n. 1230; S. C. de Prop. F., instr. (ad Vic. Ap. Sveciae), 6 Sept. 1785,—*Coll.*, n. 579; ep. 4 Dec. 1862,—De Smet, *De Spons. et Matr.*, p. 446, not. 1; litt. encycl., 11 Mart. 1868,—*Coll.*, n. 1324.

[61] Pius VI, rescript. ad Card. Archiep. Mechlinien., 13 Iul. 1782, n. 4,—*Fontes*, n. 471; instr. 19 Iun. 1793,—Migne, *Theol. Curs. Complet.*, XXV, 681; Gregorius XVI, ep. encycl. *Summo iugiter*, 27 Maii 1832, §§ 2, 7,—*Fontes*, n. 484; S. C. S. Off., litt. (ad Vic. Ap. Myssurien.), 26 Nov. 1862,—*Fontes*, n. 971.

[62] Their publication was apparently taken for granted in the Apostolic letter of Pope Pius VIII (*Litteris altero*, 25 Mart. 1830,—*Fontes*, n. 482): "Quae quidem salubria monita erunt etiam, prout prudentia suggesserit, iteranda, eo praesertim tempore, quo nuptiarum dies instare videatur, *dumque consuetis proclamationibus disquiritur*, utrum alia sint, quae illis obstent, impedimenta canonica." In the previous centuries there appears to have been no universal prohibition to their publication. In a seventeenth century petition to the Holy See seeking a dispensation from the impediment of consanguinity existing between a Catholic and a heretic, it is explicitly stated that the impediment was discovered through the proclamation of the banns. Cf. Corradus, *Praxis Dispens.*, Lib. VII, cap. II, n. 99.

108. In the United States of America the discipline regarding the publication of the banns was, as a matter of fact, marked by many uncertainties. The Sixth Provincial Council of Baltimore held in 1846 decreed that the banns should be published in accordance with the provisions of the Councils of the Lateran and Trent.[63] On July 3, 1847 Cardinal Fransonius, the Prefect of the Congregation of the Propaganda, wrote to Archbishop Eccleston commending especially the decree on the banns, and added: *"Quapropter, cum haberi debeat, nulla ratio satis firma videtur obesse, quominus proclamationes, etiam quando agitur de matrimoniis mixtis fiant, quae tamen matrimonia nullo adhibito religioso ritu celebrari oportet."*[64] In view of this letter the first synod of the diocese of Milwaukee held in 1847,[65] and a diocesan synod held at St. Louis in 1850[66] decreed that the banns should be published also for mixed marriages. A diocesan synod of Baltimore in 1853[67] and the First Synod of the Diocese of Richmond in 1856[68] seemed to suppose the *necessity* of their publication when they extended faculties to the priests of their jurisdiction to dispense from all three publications in the case of mixed marriages.[69] Yet a diocesan synod of Baltimore held in 1857 issued the following decree:[70] *"Mixtis matrimoniis banna non sunt praemittenda iuxta constantem Ecclesiae Romanae disciplinam; quod enim in quadam S. Congregationis responsione ad concilii provincialis Baltimorensis VI decreta insinuatum est errore scribae contingit, prout certiores nos fecit dum Romae versamur anno 1854 Illmus Secretarius S. Congregationis, qui nunc Praefecti munere fungitur."*

---

[63] Decretum n. IV.

[64] Conc. Balt. Prov. VI (1846), p. 26-27.

[65] N. 15. The constitutions of this synod were not published until 1853.

[66] Decretum n. XVII. A synod of the diocese of St. Louis held in 1839 had decreed that the banns should not be published for mixed marriages. Cf. Feije, *De Matr. Mixtis*, p. 236.

[67] Decretum n. XIV.

[68] Decretum n. LXI.

[69] The statutes of the diocese of Pittsburgh compiled from synods held in 1844, 1846 and 1854 (cf. cap. VI, n. 11) demanded that the banns be published for *all* marriages.

[70] Decretum n. V.

109. On the other hand, the Baltimore Ritual of 1866 (note on page 189 of this ritual) read: *"ut fiant proclamationes etiam quando agitur de matrimoniis mixtis."*[71] The Archbishop of Oregon having received a reply from Cardinal Antonelli (28 Feb. 1874) that ten years before (May 11, 1864) had been given to the Bishop of Natchez,[72] wished to know further how the note in the Baltimore Ritual was to be reconciled with the letter of Cardinal Fransonius to Archbishop Essleston. Cardinal Franchi replied on September 28, 1874 that the note in the Ritual had been affixed without the knowledge of the Congregation; that it was to be rejected on a double score, namely, inasmuch as it implied an absolute precept to publish the banns, and (apparently) because the urgent conditions that would render the publication necessary and, therefore, reasonable, did not exist everywhere and in every case. The banns for mixed marriages were to be published only when it was deemed necessary and opportune by the Ordinary.[73] In the meantime a Roman Ritual published in 1873 by John Murphy of Baltimore directed: *"In ineundis istius modi, Ecclesia ea generatim omittenda indixit, per quae Catholicorcum matrimonia decorantur, inclusis etiam promlamationibus"* (p. 544, not.*).

110. On the 4th of July 1874 the Bishop of Nesqually (Seattle) received a reply from the Holy Office[74] to the same effect as that sent to the Bishop of Natchez, with the added explanation that if the publications were not made, which in certain circumstances and on the prudent judgment of the Bishop might be advisable to avoid the danger of scandal, the free state of the parties should be determined in accordance with the norms laid down by Pope Clement X in the instruction of August 21, 1670.[75]

---

[71] The reference and the quotation is found in a letter of Cardinal Franchi to the Archbishop of Oregon. Cf. Konings, *Theol. Mor.*, Vol. II, p. 395.

[72] ". . . posse fieri proclamationes in mixtis nuptiis, quae Ap[osto]lica dispensatione contrahuntur, suppressa tamen mentione religionis contrahentium."—Konings, *loc. cit.*

[73] Konings, *Theol. Mor.*, Vol. II, p. 395.

[74] *Fontes*, n. 1031. A Latin translation is found in Gasparri, *De Matr.*, I, p. 497, not. 1-2.

[75] *Fontes*, n. 742.

111. At the beginning of the following year (January 30, 1875) the Archbishop of Baltimore received a letter from Cardinal Franchi: ". . . *certum est S. Sedem hisce postremis temporibus declarasse fieri proclamationes in mixtis nuptiis, quae Apostolica dispensatione contrahuntur.*"[76] Eleven years later (1886) the Fifth diocesan Synod of Natchez, citing the reply of May 11, 1864,[77] decreed that the banns should be published also for mixed marriages.[78] Ten synods of other dioceses ruled, however, that they were not to be published.[79]

112. With the decree "*Ne Temere*"[80] a uniformity of discipline with regard to the form of marriage was again established.[81] Though it did not bind baptized or unbaptized non-Catholics when contracting among themselves,[82] it did bind all Catholics when marrying baptized or unbaptized non-Catholics, even after obtaining a dispensation from the impediment of Mixed Religion or Disparity of Cult,—except in those regions for which the Holy See had provided otherwise.[83] Practically, it implied the necessity of dispensation even for the validity of mixed marriages since a priest was forbidden to witness such marriages unless a dispensation had been granted,

---

[76] Konings, *loc. cit.*

[77] See No. 109, note 72.

[78] Decretum n. XLI.

[79] Synodus Dioecesana Bostoniensis (1868), n. 121; (1886), n. 139, footnote; Ludovicopolitana IV (1874), cap. VIII, n. VI; Novarcensis III (1878), n. 82, c; Omahanensis I (1887), n. 98; Sancate Fidei I (1888), § 8, n. 4; Dubuquensis II (1902), n. 103; Davenportensis II (1904), n. 101; Sioupolitana II (1909), n. 117, f; Kansanopolitana II (1912), n. 133.

[80] The text of the decree may be found in many canonical textbooks,—among them the following treatise: Wouters, *Comment. in Decret. "Ne Temere"*, p. 5-9.

[81] The decree was promulgated August 2, 1907 and took effect Easter Sunday, April 19, 1908.

[82] Art. XI, § 3. Article III of the apostolic letter "*Provida*" (*Fontes*, n. 670) had gone further and granted a *sanatio in radice* to all marriages of heretics or schismatics contracted among themselves, and to mixed marriages between a Catholic and a heretic or schismatic, which had been contracted in violation of the form prescribed by the decree "*Tametsi.*"

[83] Art. XI, § 2 of the decree "*Ne Temere.*" "*Sequitur igitur, non valere principium antea satis communiter admissum: Pars immunis communicat cum altera parte suam immunitatem; atque pro eo substitutum esse contrarium; Pars ligata communicat cum altera parte suum ligamen.*"—Wouters, *Comment. in Decret. "Ne Temere"*, p. 79.

—except in those regions where passive assistance was apparently still tolerated.[84] To a great extent these regions were governed by the prescriptions of the apostlic letter *"Provida"* which existed as an exception to the decree *"Ne Temere"*.

113. The apostolic letter *"Provida"*[85] which had taken effect on Easter Sunday, April 5, 1906, and which had established a uniform discipline for Germany[86] regarding the form of marriage was (together with the continued tolerance of passive assistance in certain regions) the only exception in the Latin Church that retained its force after the decree "Ne Temere".[87] Both the decree *"Ne Temere"* and the apostolic letter *"Provida"* remained in force up to the time of the Code.

---

[84] Cf. S. C. S. Off., 21 Iun. 1912,—*AAS*, IV (1912), 443-444; 5 Aug. 1916,—*AAS*, VIII (1916), 316.

[85] Pius X, litt. ap., 18 Ian. 1906,—*Fontes*, n. 670.

[86] While, indeed, the *"Declaratio Benedictina"* had been extended to parts of Germany, and though passive assistance was tolerated in certain localities, these two regulations of the form of marriage were, of course, in no way identical in nature. A certain confusion, moreover, existed regarding the places actually governed by the Tridentine rule of the *"Tametsi."* The purpose of the apostolic letter *"Provida"* was, therefore, to establish a uniformity of discipline for Germany. It did not, however, extend to Germany's foreign possessions.

[87] Cf. S. C. Conc., 25 Ian. 1907, ad IV,—*ASS*, XLI (1908), 108 sq. While the apostolic letter *"Provida"* emphasized the prohibition to the marriages of Catholics with heretics and schismatics, such marriages were not to be subject thereafter to the Tridentine law *for validity*. Only those who were born in Germany came under the exception. Cf. S. C. Conc., 28 Mart. 1908, ad III,—*ASS*, XLI (1908), 288. On February 23, 1909 the same discipline was extended also to Hungary, where it was likewise restricted to those born in Hungary. Moreover, those born in Germany could not use this privilege in Hungary, nor, *viceversa*, those born in Hungary marrying in Germany; nor could one born in Germany marry clandestinely another born in Hungary,—in either Germany or Hungary. Cf. S. C. de Sacram., 18 Iun. 1909, ad I, II, III,—*AAS*, I (1909), 516-517.

PART III

Present Legislation in the Code

CHAPTER VII

FUNDAMENTAL ELEMENTS IN THE LAW OF THE CHURCH

Art. I. Relation of the Ecclesiastical to the Divine and Natural Law

114. From an historical study of the discipline regarding
mixed and disparate marriages, a gradual development in the
Church's legislation becomes apparent.   While the Scriptural
warnings of the Apostles apparently implied a general presumption of danger to the Faith attendant upon the association of the faithful with unbelievers, the Church gave this
presumption a more specific determination by directing its attention especially to the *marriages* of the faithful with unbelievers.[1] If her members were to marry pagans, Jews, or heretics,
they might do so only on the condition of the conversion of
such unbelievers.   For centuries, this condition represented the
Church's practical safeguard; the baptism and conversion of
the pagan or Jew, and the abjuration of heresy by the heretic.
When finally the Church began to issue dispensations it was
again only on the condition that she have the assurance of the
absence of a proximate danger to the Faith through the *prima
facie* evidence of formal promises demanded especially of the
non-Catholic providing for the freedom of the Catholic party's
profession of the Catholic Faith, and for the Catholic education of the children.   This safeguard of reserving to herself

---

[1] Augustine expresses the relation of the impediments of Mixed Religion
and Disparity of Cult to the divine law in the following manner: "Impediments of the divine-natural law are . . . also disparity of worship and
mixed religion in cases where the faith of the Catholic party is in danger.
However, since this is rather an ethico-dogmatical consequence of the impediment, we should say that both these impediments of disparity and mixed
religion belong directly (*in directo*) to the impediments of ecclesiastical law,
but indirectly (*in obliquo*) to the impediments of divine law."—*The Pastor*, p. 130.

the judgment of the absence of danger to the Faith is a fundamental element in the law of the Church with regard to mixed and disparate marriages. She does not permit an interested individual to judge for himself, but reserves this decision to herself.[2]

ART. II. THE *"Communicato in Sacris"*

115. But in addition to this measure of safety, which has its more immediate foundation in the implied presumptions of the divine and natural law, the Church has reasons of her own for prohibiting mixed and disparate marriages. From the very beginning she has had a vital consciousness of the mysteries of grace that were left in her custody to dispense. Thus she permitted the presence of the catechumens only at the preparatory part of the Mass lest by their presence or participation in the Sacrifice itself they profane its sacredness. In like manner catechumens, heretics, and the excommunicated, were excluded from the reception of the sacraments. Their participation represented a communion in sacred things that the Church could not tolerate. While this element of a *"communicatio in sacris"* does not appear to have been urged as a formal part of the prohibition to the marriages of the faithful with unbelievers, yet it was hinted at.[3] The more complete development in the Middle Ages of the theology of the sacraments but re-emphasized the traditional discipline of the Church regarding a *"communicatio in sacris"* with those outside of the Church. When, therefore, the Holy See in later centuries repeated the constant prohibition of the Church to mixed marriages it emphasized the disgraceful communion in sacred things (*"flagitiosa in rebus sacris communio"*).[4] Since a valid marriage between baptized

---

[2] "Leges latae ad praecavendum periculum generale, urgent etiamsi in casu particulari periculum non adsit."—*CIC*, canon 21.

[3] See No. 3, note 3; No. 36, note 24; No. 53, note 20.

[4] Gregorius XVI, ep. encycl. *Commissum divinitus*, 17 Maii 1835, § 4.—*Fontes*, n. 490; litt. ap. *Quas vestro*, 30 Apr. 1841, n. 1,—*Fontes*, n. 497; Leo XIII, ep. encycl. *Arcanum*, 10 Feb. 1880, n. 26,—*Fontes*, n. 580; S. C. S. Off., instr. (ad omnes Ep. Ritus Orient.), 12 Dec. 1888, n. 2,—*Fontes*, n. 1112; instr. Secret. Stat. iussu Pii PP. IX, 15 Nov. 1858, n. 2, —*Coll.*, n. 1169; instr. S. C. de Prop. F., a. 1858 (ad Ep. Graeco Rumenos),—*Coll.*, n. 1154; litt. encycl. 11 Mart. 1868,—*Coll.*, n. 1324. Vide etiam Conc. Plen. Balt. III (1884), n. 130; Feije, *De Matr. Mixtis*, p. 175-176.

persons is at the same time a sacramental bond.[5] and since the parties themselves are the ministers of the sacrament, the "*communicatio in sacris*" becomes apparent.[6]

116. The general term "*communicatio in sacris*"[7] includes those communions which are forbidden to Catholics both by the divine and natural law, and by the law of the Church. A "*communicatio in sacris*" may be *active* or *passive*. It is *active* where there is formal participation in religious service; it is *passive* where there is mere material assistance or physical presence. The communion, whether active or passive, may be regarded from two viewpoints, namely; the assistance of a Catholic at non-Catholic rites, or the assistance of a non-Catholic at Catholic rites.[8]

117. A Catholic is never permitted to assist actively at non-Catholic services for such a communion would involve a denial of the Catholic Faith by at least an implicit profession for a false religion.[9] The prohibition is one of the divine and

---

[5] See No. 403.

[6] The "*communicatio in sacris*" is much more apparent in mixed than in disparate marriages since in a disparate marriage at least the unbaptized party cannot receive the sacrament. If the opinion be accepted that the baptized party to a disparate marriage receives the sacrament, the "*communicatio in sacris*" involved would rest on the fact that the sacrament is received from the unbaptized party. The opinion that neither party to a disparate marriage receives the sacrament is sponsored, however, by far the greater majority of modern canonists and theologians. See infra No. 400, note 2. Since the Church has not formally decided the question, the element of a "*communicatio in sacris*" cannot be attributed (*per se*) as a primary factor in her legislation on disparate marriages. There are reasons sufficient for establishing a prohibition and even a diriment impediment to such marriages without invoking doubtful matter.

[7] The phrase "*in sacris*" when applied to religious rites outside of the Catholic Church is used in a broad sense. These rites often involve flagrant errors against Faith, or, as is the case among pagans, gross superstitions. The phrase "*in sacris*" in such instances refers rather to the rite itself than to any intrinsic character of sacredness.

[8] Noldin (*Theol. Mor.*, II, n. 34) gives to *active* communion the meaning: "*quando nos aliorum sacris participamus,*" and to *passive*: "*qando infideles vel haereticos in nostris sacris permittimus.*" He then distinguishes both active and passive communion into *formal* and *material*. While the distinction thus becomes well defined, it is less confusing to retain the one distinction of *active* and *passive* as it is understood in canon 1258 of the Code. While this canon refers explicitly only to the communion of Catholics in non-Catholic rites, the same distinction of *active* and *passive* may readily be applied to the assistance of non-Catholics at Catholic services.

[9] Noldin, *Theol. Mor.*, II, n. 38. Cf. canon 1258, § 1.

natural law.[10] Moreover, the participation of non-Catholics at Catholic services which woud involve an acknowledgment of religious unity is likewise forbidden by the natural and divine law.   A passive communion of this kind, however, which would imply no acknowledgment of religious unity does not appear to be under divine prohibition.   A mixed marriage represents this latter type of *"communicatio in sacris"*. If the non-Catholic party complies with the requisite conditions demanded by the Church in dispensing from the impediment, he really renounces the rights he would claim as a non-Catholic and implicitly acknowledges the right of the Catholic Church.[11] Yet the Church abhors this communion between a Catholic and a non-Catholic in the ministration and reception of the sacrament of matrimony.   It is an element of the Church's prohibition to mixed marriages which is her own,—apart from the prohibition of the natural and divine law.[12]

ART. III. PROFANATION OF THE SACRAMENT

118. Parallel to, and intimately connected with, the prohibition of a *"communicatio in sacris"* is the element of the unworthy reception of the sacrament by the baptized non-Catholic.   Since the sacraments are intrinsically sacred and holy, a certain worthiness is required on the part of those who receive them,—especially with regard to the sacraments of the living. In the mind of the Church there is a profanation of the sacrament of matrimony when it is administered by a Catholic to one who is not united to the external communion of the

---

[10] Cf. Pontius, *De Sacram. Matr.*, Append., cap. II, n. 8; Jeunin, *Comment. de Sacram.*, Dissert. X, Q. VII, cap. VII, art. 3; Ferre, *De Virtutibus Theol.*, Tom. I, Tract. II, Q. IX, pr. For grave reasons a material assistance may at times be permitted, though this question has but an indirect bearing on the present discussion.   Decisions that deal with the various phases of the *"communicatio in sacris"* may be found in Blat, *Comment.*, Vol. III, P. III, n. 125.

[11] Cf. Noldin, *op. cit.*, II, n. 37; Vlaming, *Prael. Iuris Matr.*, n. 214.

[12] Cf. Giovine, *De Dispens. Matr.*, Tom. I, § CLXX, n. 7; Carriere, *Prael. Theol.*, Tom. II, n. 756; Feije, *De Imped. et Dispens.*, n. 567; Blieck, *Theol. Univ.*, Vol. IV, p. 329; Blat, *Comment.*, Vol. III, P. I, n. 458; Vermeersch-Creusen, *Epitome*, II, n. 330; Leitner, *Lehrb. des kath. Eherechts*, p. 238, De Smet, *De Spons. et Matr.*, p. 440, not. 3; Gasparri, *De Matr.*, n. 487.

Church.[13] The Popes have repeatedly spoken of such marriages as sacrilegious.[14]

ART. IV. THE ULTIMATE FOUNDATIONS OF THE IMPEDIMENTS OF MIXED RELIGION AND DISPARITY OF CULT

119. The elements discussed so far do not, however, give an ultimate explanation of the law of the Church on the impediments in question. Danger to the Faith does not, of itself, account for the fact that Disparity of Cult is a diriment impediment, while Mixed Religion is but prohibitive. If danger to the Faith were a sufficient explanation of the discipline as it has existed for centuries, on what score in the law before the Code were the marriages of baptized non-Catholics with the unbaptized invalid? Why should the marriage of a bap-

---

[13] Only a grave cause and the dispensation of the Church will save the Catholic from committing a sin by this profanation. That it may be suffered at times and without sin to the party ministering the sacrament to the unworthy is deduced from the practice of the Church and the common teaching of the authors. The principal arguments may be summed up as follows: a) It would be temerarious to say that because of the profanation involved the Church can never dispense and thereby at least implicitly permit the marriage to take place, for *de facto* the Church has given thousands of such dispensations. b) No theologian now seriously contends that a person in the state of grace (and who without a special revelation, can say absolutely that he is?) may never contract a marriage with one who is in the state of sin. Yet in this case there is a profanation just as there is in the ministration of the sacrament of matrimony by a Catholic to a heretic or schismatic. c) It is an admitted principle that one may seek the cooperation of another and with him posit an act good in itself or indifferent. For a grave reason, and in the present case with the dispensation of the Church, this may be done even though an evil effect follows accidentally which is contrary to the intention of the agent. d) With few exceptions a minister of a sacrament sins mortally if he is ordained and deputed for the purpose of administering the sacraments, and in this capacity solemnly confers a sacrament while in the state of mortal sin. The ministers of the sacrament of matrimony, however, are the contracting parties themselves acting not as public ministers of the Church, whose duty it is by virtue of their office to safeguard and administer the sacraments, but as private ministers entering a sacramental contract, and attending primarily to their own interests and advantge. Cf. De Lugo, *Tract. de Sacram. in genere*, Disp. VIII, nn. 225-229; Benedictus XIV, *De Synodo Dioec.*, Lib. IX, cap. III, n. 5; Carriere, *Prael. Theol.*, Tom. II, n. 756; Moser, *De Impedimentis Matrimonii*, cap. XIII, n. 10,—apud Migne, *Theol. Curs. Complet.*, XXV, 630; Scavini, *Theol. Mor.*, Lib. III, n. 727, not. 3; Cappello, *De Sacram.*, III, n. 37; Vlaming, *Prael. Iuris Matr.*, n. 215; Noldin, *Theol. Mor.*, III, nn. 32-33; Hyland, *Excommunication*, p. 99-100. *A fortiori*, after the Church has granted a dispensation the assistance of a priest and two witnesses becomes entirely lawful.

[14] See No. 36, note 25.

tized Catholic with another professed Catholic, though actually unbaptized, be invalid?   Why (*per se*) should the marriage of a baptized Catholic with a baptized, sworn enemy of the Church be valid?

§ I. MIXED RELIGION

120. If the elements of a "*communicatio in sacris*", and the profanation of the sacrament be taken conjointly with that of danger to the Faith, an adequate explanation still seems to be wanting why the Church on the basis of these three elements should not erect a formal prohibitive impediment to the marriages of Catholics with apostates and other baptized aliens to the Faith even if they are not enrolled in an heretical or schismatic sect.[15] In the law of the Church, Mixed Religion is a prohibitive impediment to a marriage between two baptized persons, one of whom belongs to the Catholic Church and the other to an heretical or schismatic sect.[16] Perhaps the restriction to formal membership in an heretical or schismatic sect may be explained on the ground that the limitation offers a more certain norm of determining the limits of the impediment.[17] But why should not notorious apostates and those who are already recognized as heretics through a declaratory or condemnatory sentence be included even though they have not joined an heretical or schismatic sect?   Other reasons must, therefore, be found that will give a more fundamental explanation of the actual limits of the impediment.

------

[15] The "*communicatio in sacris*" is not so evident in cases where the non-Catholic party is not a member of a sect. The note of a profanation of the sacrament, however, remains. Cf. Leitner, *Lehrb. des kath. Eherechts*, p. 251.

[16] Canon 1060.

[17] This explanation seems to derive some confirmation from the fact that apparently no such limitation was clearly defined until the nineteenth century. But see Benedictus XIV, ep. encycl. *Magnae Nobis*, 29 Iun. 1748, § 1, —*Fontes*, n. 387. One of the very arguments used by some authors in demonstrating why heresy should not be a diriment impediment was the element of uncertainty in determining who was a heretic, since a person might secretly profess heresy or be confused in his beliefs. Cf. Estius, *In IV Lib. Sent. Comment.*, Dist. 39, § 4; Mazzei (who quotes the opinion of Semelier), *De Matr. personarum div. Relig.*, cap. II, § VII; Feije, *De Imped. et Dispens.*, n. 666; Wernz, *Ius Decret.*, IV, n. 503, not. 6. The need of a certain norm, however, does not seem to explain why the Church placed the limitation of the impediment as it exists today when on the basis of other well defined lines she might have included others.

121. In the first place, membership of one party in an heretical or schismatic sect seems to imply a greater presumption of danger to the faith of the Catholic. It is less common for an individual who has fallen away from the Faith, or who has been brought up outside of the Church in a non-sectarian belief, to seek to draw others to his particular form of worship or belief.[18] But a sect of its nature, if it is to continue to exist, must make every effort to propagate itself. It is a demand of the very instinct of self-preservation. A member of a sect may be presumed to be identified, at least in some measure, with this aim. He has, moreover, the support of an organized society to secure this end. The greater constancy derived from a unity of purpose produces in an individual member of a sect a bias or prejudice against the truths of the Catholic faith that renders him less apt to respond to the efforts of a Catholic consort to convert him. The danger to the faith of the Catholic may, therefore, be justly presumed to be augmented by a union in marriage with a *sectarian* non-Catholic. Yet even this consideration does not seem to offer an adequate reason for the limits of the impediment.

122. The marriage of a Catholic (presumably in the state of grace) with a public sinner who refuses to be reconciled with the Church, or with a notorious apostate, or with a member of a condemned society, bears the mark of a deformity arising from an inequality or difference existing between the two parties. This deformity[19] is accentuated when it is based on the inequality existing between a Catholic and one who, in addition to a denial of the Faith, is also a member of an heretical or schismatic sect.[20]

---

[18] Cf. Wernz-Vidal, *Ius Canonicum*, V, 201.

[19] The Church has frequently referred to the deformity of mixed marriages as a reason for her abhorrence. Cf. Clemens XI, litt (ad Gustavum Leopoldum), 23 Iulii 1707,—Ballerini-Palmieri, *Op. Theol. Mor.*, Tract. X, Sect. VIII, n. 718; Pius VII, rescript. (ad ep. et vicar. capit. Galliar.), 17 Feb. 1809,—Migne, *Theol. Curs. Complet.*, XXV, 710; Pius VIII, litt. ap. *Litteris altero*, 25 Mart. 1830,—*Fontes*, n. 482; Gregorius XVI, ep. encycl. *Summo iugiter*, 27 Maii 1832, § 1,—*Fontes*, n. 484; S. C. S. Off., instr. (ad omnes Ep. Ritus Orient.), 12 Dec. 1888, n. 2,—*Fontes*, n. 1112.

[20] Theoretically, a schismatic sect may exist without heretical belief,— practically, the taint of heresy always accompanies it. Cf. Pignatelli, *Const. Can.*, Tom. IV, consult. CXXXIX, n. 1; Augustine, *Commentary*, V, p. 145, note 25; S. C. de Prop. F., 18 Feb. 1783,—*Coll.*, n. 562. (This decree speaks of Photians and other heretics).

123. It is a truly grave sin for an individual to deny the Faith or to leave the Church in schism. But the breach of separation is further widened when it assumes a social or corporate resistance to the Church, when it represents an adherence to a sect whose sole reason for existence is based on an objectively false profession of faith or an avowed and organized hostility to the Church which Christ founded.[21] Through the reception of Baptism, the sacrament of faith, a certain equality, however, exists between a Catholic and a sectarian non-Catholic, an equality which renders possible the contracting of a sacramental marriage, a *matrimonium ratum*. The inequality arises through the difference of a profession of faith, accentuated by a formal adherence to an heretical or schismatic sect. With reference, therefore, to the possibility of contracting a *matrimonium ratum*, the difference between a Catholic and a sectarian non-Catholic is *modal*. Because of the grave difference that does exist, the Church has established an impediment to such a union; inasmuch as the difference is *modal* the impediment is prohibitive instead of diriment. The ultimate foundation seems to be the *modal difference of a profession of faith* as it exists in its most pronounced form between a Catholic and a *sectarian* non-Catholic.

§ II. Disparity of Cult

124. On the other hand, the diriment impediment of Disparity of Cult is founded on the inequality existing between the baptized and the unbaptized. In the teaching of the great scholastics the very possibility of a sacramental marriage is frustrated since a *matrimonium ratum* demands an equality through Baptism, the sacrament of Faith. Since the union of marriage between the baptized and the unbaptized cannot subsist "*ratione sacramenti*" the deformity consists in this very frustration of the sacramental bond that Christ established and intended the baptized to enter.[22] The difference between

---

[21] Cf. Wernz, *Ius Decret.*, IV, n. 580.

[22] This teaching of the scholastics was accepted by the later authors. Cf. Bellariminus, Lib. 1 *De Sacram. Matr.*, cap. XXIII,—*Op. Omnia*, Tom. V, 120; Perez, *De S. Matr. Sacram.*, Disp. XXXVI, Sect. II, n. 2; Reiffenstuel, *Jus Can. Univ.*, Lib. IV, Tit. I, n. 358; Astesani de Asta, *Summa*, Lib. VII,

the baptized and the unbaptized is more than modal, it is *radical*, based on the inequality arising from the reception and non-reception of Baptism, the sacrament of Faith. On the ground of this existing difference the Church has accepted an impediment (even though the custom that established it seems to have contemplated rather the element of danger to the Faith) and inasmuch as this difference is *radical* she has made of it a *diriment* impediment. The ultimate foundation, therefore, of the diriment impediment of Disparity of Cult appears to be the *radical difference* existing between the baptized and the unbaptized.

125. All these elements,—the danger to the Faith, the *"communicatio in sacris"*, the profanation of the sacrament, the modal and radical differences, are represented in the discipline of the Church as it is expressed in its crystalized form in the Code.[23]

Tit. XV, art. I; Pirhing, *Jus Can.*, Tom. IV, Tit. I, Sect. VI, n. 164; Dandino, *De Suspectis de Haeresi*, cap. III. Sect. I, Subsect. I, § IV, n. 4; De Justis, *De Dispens. Matr.*, Lib. II, cap. XV, nn. 2-3; De Coninck, *De Sacram.*, Tom. II, Disp. 31, n. 43; Mazzei, *De Matr. personarum div. Relig.*, cap. I, § I; Leurenius, *Jus Can. Univ.*, Lib. IV, quaest. 116. A few appear to have overemphasized the element of danger to the Faith in accounting for the dirimency of the impediment. Cf. Soto, *Comment. in IV Sent.*, Tom. II, Dist. 39, Q I, art. 2; Pappaini, *De Sacram.*, Tract. VII, cap. IV, § 53.

[23] The element of scandal has not received a formal discussion for, though it enters into the disciplinary enactments of the Church, it is rather consequent upon the existence of the divine and ecclesiastical law that refers more immediately to the impediments themselves.

CHAPTER VIII

THE PROHIBITIVE IMPEDIMENT OF MIXED RELIGION

Canon 1060

Severissime Ecclesia ubique prohibet ne matrimonium ineatur inter duas personas baptizatas, quarum altera sit catholica, altera vero sectae haereticae seu schismaticae adscripta; quod si adsit perversionis periculum coniugis catholici et prolis, coniugium ipsa etiam lege divina vetatur.

126. The clause *"severissime Ecclesia ubique prohibet"* represents a concise summary of the constant discipline of the Church regarding mixed marriages. Even a casual study of the history of the impediment will leave no doubt as to the Church's attitude to marriages of her children with those who are members of non-Catholic sects. By the term *"ubique"* the canon enacts a precaution lest there be a revival of any teaching that might be similar to the once widespread opinion that a contrary custom in certain countries had abrogated the necessity of dispensation for mixed marriages among the common people.[1]

127. The basis of the impediment and its prohibitive nature (*"Ecclesia* PROHIBET") totally distinguish it from the diriment impediment of Disparity of Cult. In order that the impediment of Mixed Religion exist in contradistinction to that of Disparity of Cult, both persons must be validly bap-

---

[1] Cf. Cappello, *De Sacram.*, III, n. 306. Chelodi (*Ius Matr.*, n. 58) remarks: *sane ad superambundantiam in C. aposita est particula 'ubique'."* The precaution does not at all appear to be superfluous. A *prohibitive* impediment always faces the danger of being minimized or reduced to its least possible stringency when the pressing urgencies of periods and localities render its strict enforcement difficult. With the rising ascendancy of religious indifference in many regions it would require no far stretch of imagination to visualize a laxity contrary to both the spirit and the letter of the law.

tized. An essential condition to the existence of the impediment of Disparity of Cult is the non-baptism of one of the parties. Herein lies the radical difference that marks the basis of the impediment. In the impediment of Mixed Religion, however, valid Baptism marks the parity or likeness that exists between the parties (*"inter duas personas baptizatas"*). The *modal* difference rests fundamentally upon the difference of the profession of faith.

ART. I. THE TERM "CATHOLIC" IN CANON 1060

128. One of the parties must be a Catholic (*"quarum altera sit catholica"*). The term "Catholic" may be taken in a *strict* and in a *broad* sense. In the *strict* sense it connotes one who is by external profession an actual member of the Catholic Church. In a *broad* sense it designates not only those who are professed Catholics, but also those who at any time were members of the Catholic Church by Baptism or by conversion.[2]

129. In canon 1060 the term "Catholic" must be understood in the strict sense, i. e., as designating one who, at the time of the marriage, is an actual professed member of the Catholic Church.[3] The following, therefore, are included in the *strict* sense of the term "Catholic"; a) those who have been baptized in, or converted to, the Catholic Church and who at the time of marriage are actual, professed Catholics; b) those Catholics who are occult heretics;[4] c) those Catholics who are sus-

---

[2] Cf. De Smet, *De Spons. et Matr.*, p. 114, not. 1.

[3] Cf. De Smet, *op. cit.*, n. 500; Farrugia, *De Matr.*, n. 131; Blat. *Comment.*, Vol. III, P. I, n. 455; Cappello, *De Sacram.*, III, n. 306, c; Woywod, *A Practical Commentary*, I, n. 1039. In the term "Catholic" are included not only those who are members of the Latin Church, but also those who are members of the Uniate Eastern Churches. Cf. S. C. de Prop. F., 18 Feb. 1783,—*Coll.*, n. 562; instr. (ad Ep. Graeco-Rumenos), a. 1858,—*Coll.*, n. 1154; S. C. S. Off., instr. (ad omnes Ep. Ritus Orient.), 12 Dec. 1888,—*Fontes*, n. 1112; Duskie, *The Canonical Status of the Orientals in the United States*, p. 172; Cappello, *op. cit.*, III, nn. 898-900; Binders, *Handb. des kath. Eherechts*, p. 269. The phrase in canon 1060, *"ubique prohibet"*, likewise seems to preclude the possibility of any exception for those of the Uniate Eastern Churches. It is more accurate, however, to say that the impediment of Mixed Religion binds them by reason of their own discipline which in this respect is fundamentally the same as in the Latin Church.

[4] Since the impediment is *natura sua publicum*, the fact of the occult heresy cannot be urged in determining the allegiance to the Catholic Church in the external forum.

pected of heresy;[5] d) those who have been excommunicated for moral delinquencies other than heresy or apostasy,[6] and public sinners who refuse to be reconciled with the Church; e) those Catholics who are members of condemned societies.[7] The term "Catholic" excludes: a) those who notoriously have left the Church as heretics or apostates;[8] b) those who

---

[5] Cf. canons 2316; 2319, § 2; 2320; 2340, § 1. In these canons suspects of heresy seem to be regarded as Catholics though they are under suspicion of heresy. By virtue of canon 2315, if, after six months, and after due warnings, the suspect of heresy does not remove the cause of suspicion or amend his ways, he is then regarded as a heretic and may be punished as such. "*Ideo nulla opus est sententia iudicis: ipso facto* QUASI HAERETICUS, *etsi forte haereticus non sit, incurrit excommunicationem.*"—Cipollini, *De Censuris.* Lib. II, n. 15. Whether he be a "quasi heretic" or a heretic in the full sense of the term, canon 2315 says: "*habeatur tanquam haereticus,*" and it seems that a person so designated is not to be comprised in the term "Catholic" as it is used in canon 1060. If the provisions of canon 2315 are realized, the person becomes juridically a heretic. This seems to exclude him from the juridic term "Catholic" as it is used in canon 1060. Cf. Sole, *De Delictis et Poenis*, n. 320.

[6] Canon 2340, § 1 must, however, be considered: "*Si quis, obdurato animo, per annum insorduerit in censura excommunicationis, est de haeresi suspectus.*" Blat (*Comment.*, V, n. 181) in explaining why such an individual becomes a suspect of heresy, says: "*. . . est suspectus de haeresi, qua erret circa necessitatem communionis ecclesiasticae ad salutem consequendam.*" See the preceding note and Augustine, *Commentary*, VIII, p. 362; Hyland, *Excommunication*, p. 167.

[7] See No. 129, notes 5 & 6; No. 131, note 15; Nos. 139-140, 142-147.

[8] Eichmann (*Kath. Mischehenrecht nach dem C. I. C.*, p. 11) includes in the term "Catholic" those who have been baptized in the Catholic Church and have left the Church without joining a non-Catholic sect. In a sense, everyone who has ever been a member of the Catholic Church is a Catholic and remains bound by the laws of the Church. But by virtue of canon 1325, § 2, one who leaves the Church seems to be designated more accurately as a heretic, apostate, or schismatic,—at least he does not appear to be comprised in the term "Catholic" of canon 1060. If a heretic who was once a Catholic is to be regarded as a Catholic then Eichmann's opinion would stand. Yet the terms "heretic" and "Catholic" are apparently mutually exclusive of each other in canon 1060. An important difference exists between the concept of a Catholic who remains bound by the laws of the Church as long as he lives, and a Catholic who is an actual, professed member of the Church in the sense of canon 1060. The objection that by this interpretation the Catholic who became a heretic or an apostate would be granted a favor since the impediment would not bind him, might be urged with equal force in the case of a Catholic joining a non-Catholic sect. This is placing no premium on heresy or apostasy. Such a heretic or apostate remains bound to the prescriptions of canon 1099, § 1, n. 1 and, practically speaking, he could not enter a valid marriage with another ascribed to a sect unless he renounced his heresy or apostasy. A priest would not be permitted to assist at his marriage. Yet the term "Catholic" in canon 1060 is not to be confused with the broader sense of the term in canon 1099, § 1, n. 1. Cf. De Smet, *De Spons. et Matr.*, nn. 140, 500; Leitner, *Lehrb. des kath. Eherechts*, p. 217. One of the reasons for the impediment of Mixed Religion is the presumption of danger to the faith of the Catholic

by a declaratory or condemnatory sentence are recognized as heretics or apostates; c) those Catholics who have joined an heretical or schismatic sect or a false religion.

ART. II. *"Altero vero sectae haereticae seu schismaticae adscripta"*

130. On the other hand the non-Catholic party to the marriage must be a member of an heretical or schismatic sect or of a false religion. "A sect may be described as a group of Christians who, banded together, refuse to accept the supreme authority of the Catholic Church. They constitute merely a religious party under human unauthorized leadership, or a sect. Hence, the term 'sect'[9] connotes a group of individual heretics or schismatics morally united by a common bond of belief or purpose."[10]

131. The Code does not explicitly include the term "false religion" which former decisions were wont to use.[11] Is the term left out with design or is it implied in the term "heretical or schismatic sect"? If the interpretation be accepted that only strictly heretical or schismatic sects are implied, it would force the rather grotesque conclusion that a Catholic wishing to marry a baptized person who had become an adherent of the religion of the Jews or Mohammedans,[12] would not need a dispensation from the impediment of Mixed Religion. In the light of canon 6, nn. 2, 4,[13] it is quite legitimate

---

party. The presumption loses most of its force when it regards one who has renounced the Faith, or is guilty of heresy, apostasy, or schism. Cf. De Smet, *loc. cit.;* Mazella, Camillus, *De Religione et Ecclesia,* ed. 4., Romae, 1892, n. 600; Billot, L., *Tractatus de Ecclesia Christi,* ed. 3., Prati, 1909, p. 291; Tanquery, *Theol. Dogm.,* I, n. 903.

[9] The quotation marks about the word "sect" do not appear in the quotation cited,—they have been inserted for clarity.

[10] Kearney, *Sponsors at Baptism,* p. 83-84.

[11] Cf. S. C. S. Off. (Leodien.), 30 Ian. 1867,—*Fontes,* n. 998; (in statutis synodalibus pro dioecesi Ostiensi), a. 1886,—Gasparri, *De Matr.,* n. 485. The juxtaposition of the term "false religion" to the term "sect" apparently indicates an *organized* religious body.

[12] Binders (*Handb. des kath. Eherechts,* p. 269) regards such baptized adherents as apostates. The term "apostate", however, is not used in canon 1060.

[13] Canon 6, n. 2—"Canones qui ius vetus ex integro referunt. ex veteris iuris auctoritate, atque ideo ex receptis apud probatos auctores interpretationibus, sunt aestimandi; n. 4—In dubio num aliquod canonum praescriptum cum veteri iure discrepet, a veteri iure non est recedendum."

to extend the meaning of "*sectae haereticae*" to include the "false religion" of older decrees.   Admittedly, the strict sense of the term "heretical sect" would prohibit this usage.[14] An heretical or schismatic sect does not, however, include a condemned society.[15]

To avoid confusion and cumbersome expressions, the terms "sectarian non-Catholics" and "non-Catholic sects" are to be understood in the present study as including a false religion. The term "sect" has been applied by the Church also to Judaism and Mohammedanism,[16] though it usually connotes a Christian denomination.[17]

132. What is the precise meaning of "*altera vero sectae haereticae seu schismaticae adscripta*"?   Does membership in a non-Catholic sect refer only to those who have once been Catholics?   The Code in canon 1064, n. 1 demands of Ordinaries and pastors: "*Fideles a mixtis nuptiis, quantum possunt, absterreant.*"   When canon 1065 prescribes that the faithful are also to be deterred from marriages with those who have rejected the Catholic faith, "*etsi ad sectam acatholicam non transierint*", it seems to supply by a prohibition what canon 1060 has not included in the impediment of Mixed Religion. But canon 1065 refers *explicitly* only to those who have once

---

[14] Though the distinction between Judaism, Paganism, and Heresy is not rigidly fixed, it does appear, nevertheless, to exist. Cf. De Lugo, *Tract. de Virt. Fidei Div.*, Disp. XVIII, Sect. 3; Suarez, Tract. I, *De Fide Theol.*, Disp. XVI, Sect. IV; Bouquillon, *Inst. Theol. Mor. Spec.*, n. 218; Kenrick, *Theol. Mor.*, II, Tract. XIII, n. 41; Noldin, *Theol. Mor.*, III, nn. 26-27. "*Secta acatholica proprie non est nec iudaismus, nec paganismus . . .*"—Vermeersch-Creusen, *Epitome*, I, n. 625. See No. 174, note 61.

[15] Cf. S. C. S. Off. (Portus Aloisii), 1 Aug. 1855,—*Fontes*, n. 932; (Marysville), 21 Aug. 1861,—*Fontes*, n. 967; (Leodien.) 30 Ian. 1867,—*Fontes*, n. 998; (S. Bonifacii), 23 Apr. 1873,—*Fontes*, n. 1026; instr. (ad Ordinarios Imperii Brasil.), 2 Iul. 1878,—*Fontes*, n. 1056; (Bombay), 21 Feb. 1883,—*Fontes*, n. 1079; 26 Nov. 1896,—*AkKR*, LXXVIII (1898), 523-524; 25 Maii 1897,—*AkKR*, LXXIX (1899), 741-742 (also in *Fontes*, n. 1186); Vermeersch-Creusen, *Epitome*, I, n. 625.

[16] Cf. S. C. S. Off., instr. (ad omnes Ep. Ritus Orient.), 12 Dec. 1888, n. 1,—*Fontes*, n. 1112.

[17] Cf. Kearney, *Sponsors at Baptism*, p. 83; *Catholic Encyclopedia*, art. "Sect and Sects", XIII, 674. Augustine's restriction (*Commentary*, V, p. 143) of the term "*sectae haereticae seu schismaticae*" to Christian denominations alone, appears to be too limited. In a broad sense the sects of the Socinians, Unitarians, and Mormons, might be called Christian, yet the designation may readily be challenged.

been Catholics.[18] Again the Pontifical Commission for the Authentic Interpretation of the Code decided that the clause *"qui sectae acatholicae adhaeserunt"* of canon 542, n. 1 referred only to those who had left the Faith to join a non-Catholic sect.[19] Does membership in a non-Catholic sect contemplated in canon 1060 likewise refer only to those *Catholics* who have joined such sects? The decree most frequently referred to by the authors[20] as forming the background of the clauses in question in canons 1060 and 1065, is one issued by the Holy Office on January 30, 1867. Again there is *explicit* reference only to those who have once been Catholics.[21]

133. The restriction of the clause *"altera vero sectae haereticae seu schismaticae adscripta"* of canon 1060 to those who had formerly been Catholics does a manifest violence to the sense of the canon. It would thereby either exclude those who had been members of such sects from infancy, or it would include all non-Catholics (who had never been members of the Catholic Church), whether they were members of sects or not. Both hypotheses must be rejected. If those who are members of sects *by baptism* from infancy are to be excluded, a distinction is introduced that is not warranted by the wording of the canon. If all non-Catholics are to be included irrespective of membership in a sect, then the clause *"sectae haereticae seu schismaticae adscripta"* becomes meaningless. Membership in a sect has no limited reference to those who have once been Catholics,

---

[18] Implicitly canon 1065 has reference also to all non-sectarian non-Catholics.

[19] "Utrum verba *qui sectae acatholicae adhaeserunt* canonis 542 sint intelligenda de iis, qui Dei gratia moti ex haeresi vel schismate, in quibus nati sunt, ad Ecclesiam pervenerint; an potius de iis qui a fide defecerunt et sectae acatholicae adhaeserunt." *Resp.* "Negative ad primam partem, affirmative ad secundam."—Pont. Comm., 6 Oct. 1919, n. 7,—*AAS*, XI (1919), 477.

[20] Cerato, *Matr.*, n. 54; Chelodi, *Ius Matr.*, p. 58 cum not. 2; Farrugia, *De Matr.*, n. 131; Wernz, *Ius Decret.*, IV, n. 574 cum not. 1; Wernz-Vidal, *Ius Canonicum*, V, n. 168 cum not. 1.

[21] "Quoties agatur de matrimonio inter unam partem catholicam et alteram *quae a fide ita defecit,* ut alicui falsae religioni vel sectae sese adscripserit, requirendum esse consuetam et necessariam dispensationem cum solitis ac notis praescriptionibus et clausulis. Quod si agatur de matrimonio inter unam partem catholicam et alteram *quae fidem abiecit,* at nulli falsae religioni, vel haereticae sectae sese adscripsit, quando parochus nullo modo potest huiusmodi matrimonium impedire . . . rem deferendam esse ad R. P. D. Episcopum . . ." —*Fontes*, n. 998. Gasparri (*De Matr.*, n. 485) quotes a similar decree of the year 1886.

—it includes all who at the time of the marriage are such members.

134. Nor is it necessary to postulate novelty of the clause in canon 1060.[22] The decree of January 30, 1867 concerns itself only with those who have once been Catholics because the question which it answered concerned itself only with those who had been Catholics. Implicitly the decree may readily suppose the necessity of sectarian membership of those who have always been non-Catholics.[23] The decision of the Pontifical Commission regards only canon 542, n. 1, wherein the clause *"qui sectae acatholicae adhaeserunt"* has not the same meaning or purpose as the clause *"altero vero sectae haereticae seu schismaticae [sit] adscripta"* of canon 1060. In like manner, Catholics wishing to marry non-sectarian non-Catholics are to be ruled by the prescriptions of canon 1065. All authors who have written since the Code agree that for the existence of the impediment of Mixed Religion it is necessary that one of the parties be truly a member (*"adscripta"*) of a non-Catholic sect at the time of the marriage.[24]

135. To an inquiry as to who were to be considered as heretics with reference to mixed marriages, the Holy Office replied that those described in the inquiry were to be designated as heretics. The classification given in the inquiry was as follows:[25]

---

[22] The necessity of membership in a sect was clearly stated by authors who wrote before the Code. Cf. D'Annibale, *Theol. Mor.*, III, p. 344. not. 3; Wernz, *Ius Decret.*, IV, n. 503, not. 6; n. 574. Pope Benedict XIV (ep. encycl. *Magnae Nobis*, 29 Iun. 1748, § 1,—*Fontes*, n. 387) likewise seems to suggest the necessity of membership in a sect.

[23] See No. 135, note 28.

[24] Cf. Cappello, *De Sacram.*, III, n. 306; Cerato, *Matr.*, n. 54; Chelodi, *Ius Matr.*, n. 58; Petrovits, *New Church Law on Matrimony*, n. 187; Wernz-Vidal, *Ius Canonicum*, V, n. 168 cum not. 1; De Smet, *De Spons. et Matr.*, n. 500; Eichmann, *Kath. Mischehenrecht nach dem C. I. C.*, p. 12; Leitner, *Lehrb. des kath. Eherechts*, p. 235; Blat, *Comment.*, Vol. III, P. I, n. 455; Vermeersch-Creusen, *Epitome*, II, n. 330; Ayrinhac, *Marriage Legislation*, p. 113-114; Augustine, *Commentary*, V, p. 143.

[25] S. C. S. Off., litt. (ad Ep. Harlemen.), 6 Apr. 1859,—*Fontes*, n. 950. Ayrinhac (*Marriage Legislation*, p. 114) considers all the classes enumerated as members of heretical sects, while Augustine (*Commentary*, V, p. 144) classes them simply as heretics and remarks: "However it must not be overlooked that our text says: 'sectae haereticae adscripta', i. e., the non-Catholic party must be a member of an heretical sect, or at least must have adhered to a sect sometime previously to the marriage." With reference to

1). "*Illi qui catholice baptizati, a pueritia nondum septennali, inhaeresi educantur, ac haeresim profitentur.*" Those who have received Baptism in the Catholic Church but who from the age of infancy ("*a pueritia nondum septennali*") have been brought up in heresy and profess it, are regarded as having lost their character of being a Catholic. They are deemed to be members of the heretical sect ("*haeresi*") in which they have been educated and whose doctrines they still profess.

2). "*Qui non tam in haeresi, quam ab haereticis educantur, nulla scilicet, vel vix nulla haereticae doctrinae instructione accepta, et cultu non frequentato, licet aliquoties participato.*" Since there is no evident transition to a different or a larger class, it seems that those here under consideration are they who, though baptized as Catholics, have been brought up from infancy by heretics. Those in the preceding class had been educated *in heresy.* The question here turns rather on the fact of an education *by heretics* than in heresy. The mention of infrequent attendance at worship would again seem to imply the adherence of the children's tutors to an heretical sect for "*cultus*", as it is used here, connotes worship in an organized religion. Even if such children have little to do with the teaching or worship of the sect, they are regarded as belonging to the sect of their guardians.[26]

3). "*Qui adhuc pueri in manus haereticorum incidentes, haereticae sectae adiunguntur.*" The case here considered is that

---

sectarian membership, it has already been shown (No. 133) that canon 1060 is concerned with membership in a sect *at the time of the marriage,*—not with a past adherence. Ayrinhac's opinion may well be sustained and the classification given in the decree serves as the most complete statement of the law before the Code. It is somewhat surprising that among the authors consulted, Ayrinhac and Augustine seem to be the only ones who refer to the decree in connection with canon 1060. While the answer was concerned primarily with the exception from the *form* of marriage, which exception has been partially abrogated by the Code, the implied affirmation as to the inclusiveness of the term "heretics" in *mixed marriages* does not appear to have undergone any change. Cf. Chelodi, *Ius Matr.*, n. 139. It is for this reason that an interpretation of the meaning of each clause is deemed helpful in connection with the present question.

[26] In the light of the two classifications already given the following statement of Petrovits (*New Church Law on Matrimony*, n. 187) may be questioned: "A Catholic child, even if he should be brought up by heretics from his very infancy, is not considered as a heretic, unless they enrolled his name on the official register of such a sect, or unless he worshipped in it even without such enrollment."

of children baptized as Catholics who, after the age of reason ("*pueri*"), have fallen into the hands of heretics.   These are not regarded as following *ipso facto* the sect of their guardians; they must be positively affiliated with a sect before they are classed as members of an heretical sect.

4). "*Apostatae ab Ecclesia catholica ad haereticam sectam transeuntes.*"   Those who after the age of reason leave the Catholic Faith must formally join a sect before they will be regarded as heretics in the question of mixed marriages.   A mere favorable inclination toward a sect is not sufficient.[27]

5). "*Qui nati et baptizati ab haereticis, adoleverunt quin ullam sollemnem haereseos professionem emiserint, ac veluti nullius religionis.*"   Those born of heretics (members of an heretical sect) and baptized by them (in a sect) remain members of the sect of their parents even though they quite neglect their religious duties.   They continue to remain as members of the sect until *by a positive act* they separate themselves from it.[28]

ART. III. THE DIVINE AND ECCLESIASTICAL LAW

136. The last clause of canon 1060 draws attention to the fact that when there is danger of perversion of the Catholic party and the offspring the marriage is forbidden also by the divine law,—"*quod si adsit perversionis periculum coniugis catholici et prolis, coniugium ipsa etiam lege divina vetatur.*" The conjunction "*et*" in the phrase "*coniugis catholici et prolis*" should not, however, be interpreted to mean that the danger of perversion must exist for *both* the Catholic party *and* the offspring before the divine law would urge its prohibition. If either the Catholic party *or* the children, or both, were thus endangered, the divine law would forbid the union.[29] The

---

[27] Cf. Leitner, *Lehrb. des kath. Eherechts*, p. 235.

[28] Cf. Blat, *Comment.*, Vol. III, P. I, n. 455. The same rules will apply also for schismatics.   While the older decisions do not explicitly use the term "sect" with reference to schismatics, the membership in a sect was in all probability required. Cf. S. C. de Prop. F., 21 Mart. 1759,—*Coll.*, n. 415; 18 Feb. 1783,—*Coll.*, n. 562 (See No. 122, note 20); 11 Apr. 1894,—*ASS*, XXVII (1894-1895), 383; S. C. Conc., 28 Mart. 1908,—*ASS*, XLI (1908), 288. Marriages of Latin Catholics with members of the Uniate Eastern Churches are, of course, permitted.

[29] In a particular instance it might readily be possible that through steadfastness of faith the danger of perversion would be remote for the Catholic party while a valid presumption would exist concerning the proximate danger of perversion for the children.

last clause of canon 1060 indicates the province of the divine law; the first clause refers to the prohibition of the Church in the form of an impediment. The Church dispenses from the impediment but not from the divine law. When the Church does grant a dispensation from the impediment she implicitly declares the cessation of the divine prohibition.

Art. IV. Canons 1065 and 1066

137. With regard to the marriages of Catholics with those who have notoriously left the Faith or joined condemned societies, or with public sinners or those notoriously under censure, the Code has established the following discipline.

Canon 1065, § 1

Absterreantur quoque fideles a matrimonio contrahendo cum iis qui notorie aut catholicam fidem abiecerunt, etsi ad sectam acatholicam non transierint, aut societatibus ab Ecclesia damnatis adscripti sunt.

Canon 1066

Si publicus peccator aut censura notorie innodatus prius ad sacramentalem confessionem accedere aut cum Ecclesia reconciliari recusaverit, parochus eius matrimonio ne assistat, nisi gravis urgeat causa, de qua, si fieri possit, consulat Ordinarium.

It is well to note that canons 1065 and 1066 are not to be included under the impediment of Mixed Religion. They deal with a prohibition distinct from the impediment of Mixed Religion.

§ I. *"Qui notorie catholicam fidem abiecerunt"*

138. Most authors regard those who have notoriously left the Faith as apostates,[30] though the note of heresy seems likewise to be included.[31] The following may be regarded as having

---

[30] Cf. Augustine, *Commentary,* V, p. 155; Ayrinhac, *Marriage Legislation,* p. 131; Blat, *Comment.,* Vol. III, P. I, n. 460; Cerato, *Matr.,* n. 59; Chelodi, *Ius Matr.,* n. 66; De Smet, *De Spons. et Matr.,* p. 163, not. 3; Farrugia, *De Matr.,* n. 139; Wernz-Vidal, *Ius Canonicum,* V, n. 201; Vlaming, *Prael. Iuris Matr.,* n. 244.

[31] Cf. Cappello, *De Sacram.,* III, n. 330; De Smet, *loc. cit.*

rejected the Faith in the sense of canon 1065: atheists, deists, pantheists, rationalists, modernists in religion, and materialists;[32] those, moreover, who have rejected the Catholic Faith by frequent and public denials of the teachings of the Church; those who have exposed the teachings of the Church to ridicule; those who have openly professed an avowed disobedience to the Church;[33] those who publicly deny they are Catholics;[34] and those who are notoriously[35] under censure for heresy or apostasy. Those baptized non-Catholics who *by a positive act* have left the sect in which they were baptized, or to which they were ascribed, and who at the time of the marriage remain unattached to a non-Catholic sect, must come under the provisions of this canon. Excluded from those who have notoriously rejected the Faith in the sense of canon 1065 are the following: a) those who, though neglecting their religious duties, have not renounced the Faith publicly by word or act; b) those who are members of non-Catholic sects; c) those laboring under excommunications incurred *latae sententiae* for heresy or apostasy, but who have not been juridically declared as excommunicated; d) and those who are suspected of heresy.

§ II. *"Qui notorie societatibus ab Ecclesia damnatis adscripti sunt"*

139. Under the heading of condemned societies the following classes may be enumerated: Anti-Social, Secret, Bible, and Cremation Societies.[36] Anti-Social Societies are those that

---

[32] Cerato, *loc. cit.*; Farrugia, *loc. cit.*

[33] Vermeersch-Creusen, *Epitome*, II, n. 335.

[34] Wernz-Vidal, *loc. cit.*; Vlaming, *loc. cit.*; De Smet, *loc. cit.*

[35] A declaratory or condemnatory sentence of excommunication would establish this notoriety.

[36] Catholics are forbidden to join Theosophical Societies. Cf. S. C. S. Off., 18 Iul. 1919,—*AAS*, XI (1919), 317. "There is an esoteric section to which only members of a year's standing are admitted, and which is admittedly a secret society."—Quigley, *Condemned Societies*, p. 9. Cerato (*Matr.*, n. 59) includes Theosophical Societies among those contemplated in canon 1065. In their capacity of religious sects, however, such groups come under the provisions of canon 1060. It appears that the Jansenists come under the heading of an heretical sect. Cf. Vlaming, *Prael. Iuris Matr.*, Vol. I, p. 194, not. 1.

conspire or plot against either the Church or State or both.[37] Secret societies are organizations, the members of which are bound to secrecy concerning their constitutions, purposes, means, and the like. Bible Societies are Protestant associations founded for the purpose of translating the Sacred Scriptures, publishing them without note or comment, rejecting usually the Deutero-Canonical Books as apocryphal, and distributing the Bibles at cost, less than cost, or gratis.[38] Cremation Societies are associations whose purpose is the furtherance of the practice of cremation.[39]

140. Societies may be condemned *explicitly* ("*nominatim*"), i. e., by name, or *implicitly*, i. e., inasmuch as they bear those characteristics which designate them as societies that are under general condemnation. Membership in condemned societies may be forbidden *under censure*, i. e., under pain of excommunication, or *sub gravi*, i. e., under pain of mortal sin.[40] By way of example, the following societies are condemned: Masons, Sons of Temperance, Knights of Pythias, Odd Fellows, and the Independent Order of Good Templars.[41] In order

---

[37] Quigley, *op. cit.*, p. 7; Cerato, *Matr.*, n. 59. Under Anti-Social Societies may be grouped anarchistic, nihilistic, and communistic societies. Cappello (*De Sacram.*, III, n. 330) includes *truly* socialistic societies. De Smet (*De Spons. et Matr.*, p. 164, not. 1) quotes De Brabandere-Van Coillie to the effect that socialism is to be classed with the Masonic Order, yet he limits it to those members who are truly imbued with socialistic principles. He would, therefore, relieve from the censure of canon 2335 the ordinary rank and file members. Cf. Genicot-Salsmans, *Theol. Mor.*, II, n. 594. Farrugia (*De Matr.*, n. 139) includes those socialistic societies that would not hesitate to overthrow the government to attain their end. Vlaming (*op. cit.*, n. 245) seems to object to the inclusion of socialists on the ground that membership in their ranks is not condemned under censure.

[38] The British and Foreign Bible Society, The American Bible Society, and the Gideons, are the best known examples.

[39] The preceding definitions have been taken practically verbatim from Quigley, *Condemned Societies*, p. 8-9.

[40] Quigley, *op. cit.*, p. 9-10. Using the argument that the question at hand treats on matter "*de odiosis*", Petrovits (*New Church Law on Matrimony*, n. 200) restricts the phrase "*societatibus ab Ecclesia damnatis*" to those which are condemned "*nominatim*". See also Augustine, *Commentary*, V, p. 156; Vlaming, *Prael. Iuris Matr.*, n. 245. The argument does not seem to be conclusive and Quigley's opinion (*op. cit.*, p. 102-103) which includes all societies that are condemned explicitly, implicitly, under pain of censure, or mortal sin, appears to have a more solid foundation. Canon 1065, § 1 makes no distinction with regard to the manner of the condemnation of a society.

[41] Though several authors (Farrugia, *De Matr.*, n. 139; Cappello, *De Sacram.*, III, n. 330; Leitner, *Lehrb. des kath. Eherechts*, p. 251) list the

that the conditions postulated in canon 1065, § 1 be realized, it is necessary that those concerned be true members ("*adscripti*") of condemned societies. The notoriety required may be one of fact or of law.[42]

§ III. *"Publicus peccator aut censura notorie innodatus"*

141. A public sinner is one whose grave delinquency is known to many in the community in which the marriage is to take place. The publicity may be one of fact or of law.[43] The notoriety of law may also be established through a sentence of a civil court, in matters that lie within its competence.[44] The Roman Ritual[45] in speaking of those who are to be denied communion directs: *"Arcendi autem sunt publici indigni, quales sunt excommunicati, interdicti, manifestoque infames . . ."* Those notoriously under censure are those who are recognized as excommunicated by a condemnatory or declaratory sentence. Those also are included who have committed a crime which, "publicly known to be punished by excommunication, is committed under such circumstances that it cannot be concealed by any artifice or excused by any subterfuge of law."[46]

§ IV. Prohibition or Impediment?

142. Catholics are, indeed, to be deterred from entering marriages with those who notoriously have renounced the Faith

---

Carbonari, the Fenians, and the Clerico-Liberalists, their inclusion is of little practical value for they no longer exist. Cf. Quigley, *op. cit.*, p. 102. Cappello (*loc. cit.*), Farrugia (*loc cit.*), and Cerato (*Matr.*, n. 59) may be justified in listing "Old Catholics" among condemned societies (cf. S. C. S. Off., 17 Sept. 1871,—*AkKR*, XXVII [1872], CLXXI), though they are probably more accurately designated as a schismatic sect. Quigley (*loc. cit.*) characterizes them as a sect. The latter author is also of the opinion that the Y. M. C. A. is not a condemned society though Cappello and Farrugia deem it to be such. Cf. S. C. S. Off., 5 Nov. 1920,—*AAS*, XII (1920), 595-597. The London Society for the Propagation of Christian Unity seems to come under the heading of a condemned society. Cf. S. C. S. Off., 4 Iul 1919,—*AAS*, XI (1919), 309.

[42] Cf. Cappello, *De Sacram.*, III, n. 330; Quigley, *Condemned Societies*, p. 101.

[43] Cf. Cappello, *De Sacram.*, I, n. 74; III, n. 332; Cerato, *Matr.*, n. 60; Chelodi, *Ius Matr.*, n. 67; Petrovits, *New Church Law on Matrimony*, n. 201; De Smet, *De Spons. et Matr.*, p. 162, not. 5.

[44] Chelodi, *Ius Poenale*, p. 6, not. 1.

[45] Tit. IV, cap. I, n. 8.

[46] Hyland, *Excommunication*, p. 101. See canon 2197, n. 3.

or who are members of condemned societies, with public sinners, or with those notoriously under censure, yet the prohibition, in the opinion of the vast majority of authors who have written after the Code, is not to be regarded as an impediment.[47]

143. The reasons alleged by the few authors who have discussed the question as to why unworthiness is not an impediment do not, however, seem to be entirely adequate. Cerato,[48] when speaking of canon 1065, is of the opinion that the canon does not establish an impediment reserved to the Holy See, on the probable ground that such unions do not bear so great a presumption of perversion as do mixed marriages; that they are more frequent [?]; that prudence, therefore, would designate the local Ordinary as the best judge of the safeguards to be employed. Wernz-Vidal[49] maintains that the Church in establishing the impediments regards marriage *in se* and not under the aspect of a sacrament,—that the Church cannot remove the unworthiness of reception of the sacrament by dispensation.

144. Quigley[50] gives by far the most complete discussion of the question, developing the idea suggested by Wernz-Vidal.[51] The argument, as he presents it, may be summarized as follows. A matrimonial impediment directly affects marriage as a contract, and only indirectly as a sacrament. The sacrament of matrimony is unlawfully or invalidly received because the matrimonial contract is illicit or invalid. Unworthiness is found-

---

[47] Cf. Cerato, *Matr.*, n. 61; Chelodi, *Ius Matr.*, n. 65; Vlaming, *Prael. Iuris Matr.*, n. 243; Wernz-Vidal, *Ius Canonicum*, V, nn. 173, 200-201; Hilling, *Das Eherecht des C. I. C.*, p. 55; Farrugia, *De Matr.*, n. 139; Ayrinhac, *Marriage Legislation*, p. 132; Blat, *Comment.*, Vol. III, P. I, n. 460; Vermeersch-Creusen, *Epitome*, II, n. 335; Augustine, *Commentary*, V, p. 135; Genicot-Salsmans, *Theol. Mor.*, II, n. 509; Noldin, *Theol. Mor.*, III, nn. 562, 567; Quigley, *Condemned Societies*, p. 97-100; O'Keeffe, *Matrimonial Dispensations*, p. 187-188. Petrovits (*New Church Law on Matrimony*, n. 199) seems, however, to regard it as an impediment. With reference to the opinions of canonists who wrote before the Code, the following representative authors may be consulted: Sanchez, *De Matr.*, Lib. VII, Disp. 9; Pontius, *De Sacram. Matr.*, Lib. VI, cap. 10; Alphonsus, *Theol. Mor.*, Lib. VI, n. 54; Benedictus XIV, *De Synodo Dioec.*, Lib. VIII, cap. XIV, n. 5; De Becker, *De Spons. et Matr.*, p. 265-274; Gasparri, *De Matr.*, nn. 476, 526-537.

[48] *Matr.*, n. 59.

[49] *Ius Canonicum*, V, n. 200.

[50] *Condemned Societies*, p. 97-99.

[51] See also O'Keeffe, *Matrimonial Dispensations*, p. 187-188.

ed on mortal sin which does not impede the reception of the sacrament but rather places an *obex* to the reception of the grace of the sacrament. Since matrimonial impediments directly affect the contract of marriage and unworthiness merely suspends the effects of the sacrament, it remains that unworthiness is not a canonical impediment. Moreover, impediments are removed by dispensation, but no dispensation could remove unworthiness.

145. The statement that an impediment directly affects the contract and only indirectly the sacrament is not to be challenged. Nay more, the very prohibition of canon 1065 demands that the faithful be deterred from contracting marriage with the unworthy,—"*Absterreantur quoque fideles* A MATRIMONIO CONTRAHENDO." Some inaccuracy in the discussion seems to result in confusing the juridic fact of the prohibition itself with unworthiness, which is its basis. While unworthiness directly impedes the effect of the sacrament (and not the contract), it is not correct to say that *the prohibition* directly impedes the effect of the sacrament. If unworthiness is not an impediment because dispensation cannot remove it, it would be equally logical to say that Mixed Religion is not an impediment because adherence to a non-Catholic sect is not removed by dispensation. In like manner, Disparity of Cult would not be an impediment because a dispensation cannot remove the non-baptism of the unbaptized. The argument seems to be based on the assumption that an impediment or a prohibition which directly affects the contract of marriage may not derive the reason for its existence from a consideration of the *sacrament* of marriage.

146. The very foundation of the diriment force of the impediment of Disparity of Cult is derived from the nature of the sacrament of Matrimony. Mixed Religion has a partial foundation in the same reason. A dispensation from these impediments removes *only the impediments*, which, however, have a foundation in the very sacrament of Matrimony. Permissions given by the Ordinary to pastors to assist at the marriage of a Catholic to an unworthy person cancel the *prohibition* which is derived from a consideration of the holiness of a sacrament. *The basis of the prohibition* in canon 1065 should not be compared with the impediments but with the *basis* of the impe-

diments. The reason assigned by Wernz-Vidal and Quigley does not seem to clarify the issue why an impediment should stand in the way of marriages with the unbaptized and sectarian non-Catholics, and why only a prohibition should stand in the way of a pastoral witnessing of the marriages of Catholics with notorious apostates, heretics, members of condemned societies, public sinners, and the notoriously censured. Perhaps a few of the difficulties may be removed by comparing the *basis* of the prohibition with the *basis* of the impediments of Mixed Religion and Disparity of Cult.

147. Disparity of Cult is a diriment impediment because it is founded on the radical inequality existing between the baptized and the unbaptized. Mixed Religion is a prohibitive impediment because it represents *an accentuated modal inequality* between Catholics and sectarian baptized non-Catholics. The marriages contemplated in canons 1065 and 1066 are prohibited likewise on the basis of a modal difference existing between practical Catholics and the unworthy. The reason why unworthiness is not the basis of an impediment, but rather of a prohibition appears to rest on the fact that unworthiness does not represent the *accentuated* modal difference implied in the impediment of Mixed Religion.[52]

---

[52] See Nos. 119-124.

CHAPTER IX

THE DIRIMENT IMPEDIMENT OF DISPARITY OF CULT

Canon 1070, § 1

Nullum est matrimonium contractum a persona non baptizata cum persona baptizata in Ecclesia catholica vel ad eandem ex haeresi aut schismate conversa.

Art. I. *"Nullum est matrimonium contractum a persona non baptizata"*

148. The nature of the impediment of Disparity of Cult is wholly distinguished from that of Mixed Religion by the fact that it is a diriment impediment ("NULLUM *est matrimonium*"). The reason, moreover, which forms the very basis of the dirimency of the impediment is founded on the radical disparity existing between the baptized and the unbaptized. One essential condition, therefore, for the existence of the impediment of Disparity of Cult is that one of the parties to a marriage must be unbaptized ("*persona non baptizata*"),—that one party should lack the baptismal character which is required for a sacramental marriage. The other party must be baptized in order that the radical disparity exist.

149. In the law before the Code the conditions of the impediment were realized when one party was validly baptized and the other was not baptized. It mattered not that the Baptism was conferred in an heretical or schismatic sect, provided that the Baptism was valid.[1] The diriment force of the impe-

---

[1] Cf. Benedictus XIV, ep. *Singulari*, 9 Feb. 1749,—*Fontes*, n. 394; S. C. S. Off., instr. (ad Archiep. Quebecen.), 16 Sept. 1824, ad 5,—*Fontes*, n. 866; 3 Apr. 1878,—Aichner, *Compend. Juris Eccles.*, § 173, not. 4; (ad Vic. Ap. Iaponiae Merid.), 4 Feb. 1891,—*Fontes*, n. 1130; Feije, *De Imped. et Dispens.*, n. 459; Wernz, *Ius Decret.*, IV, n. 506; Schulte, *Handb. des kath. Eherechts*, p. 224; Gasparri, *De Matr.*, n. 685.

diment did not rest upon the difference of a profession of faith at the time of the marriage[2] but upon the disparity arising between those who had been baptized and those who had not been baptized.

ART. II. *"Cum persona baptizata in Ecclesia catholica vel ad eandem ex haeresi aut schismate conversa"*

150. The change that was introduced by the Code did, indeed, restrict the extension of the impediment, but it did not thereby alter in any way the fundamental reason for the dirimency of the impediment which in the Code, as in the law that preceded it, still has its ultimate foundation in the radical disparity existing between the baptized and the unbaptized. The restriction to Baptism in the Catholic Church, or conversion to the Church from heresy or schism, did, however, introduce a momentous change. Heretics and schismatics who have not received Baptism in the Catholic Church or who have never at any time been converted to it were for the future thereby liberated from the ambit of the impediment when contracting marriage with the unbaptized.

§ I. REASON FOR THE CHANGE

151. But why the restriction? The authors who have attempted to explain the change allege several reasons which may be briefly summarized under three headings: 1) the doubtful validity of Baptism as it it administered in many sects;[3] 2) the non-reception of Baptism by many non-Catholics;[4] 3) the reduction of the number of invalid marriages amongst heretics and schismatics.[5] The reasons summarized under the last two headings appear to be sufficiently adequate without introducing the question of the doubtful validity of Baptisms conferred in

---

[2] The profession of faith has, likewise, nothing to do with the law of the Code as it is expressed in canon 1070, § 1.

[3] Cappello, *De Sacram.*, III, n. 414; Chelodi, *Ius Matr.*, n. 79; Wernz-Vidal, *Ius Canonicum*, V, n. 265; De Smet, *De Spons. et Matr.*, p. 513, not. 6; Noldin, *Theol. Mor.*, III, n. 578, 3c.

[4] Ayrinhac, *Marriage Legislation*, p. 149.

[5] The authors enumerated in the preceding two notes offer also this reason. Vermeersch (*Theol. Mor.*, III, n. 779) and Farrugia (*De Matr.*, n. 169) give it as the principal reason.

some sects. The doubt of the validity of a Baptism may on investigation be either solved or remain unsolved. If the doubt admits of a solution and both parties are found to be baptized there is no question of the impediment. If one party is found to be unbaptized, the existence of the impediment will be demonstrated. When the doubt cannot be solved by direct proofs it may be solved by a resort to various presumptions that have been established by the Holy See as norms.[6]

152. The fact, as Ayrinhac[7] well observes, that many non-Catholics of today have never received Baptism gives rise to a condition truly grave, for, since their marriages with those validly baptized in the sects are quite frequent, the number of invalid marriages among non-Catholics would thereby be greatly increased. While in many instances such marriages would in all probability be putative,[8] thus conferring legitimacy to the children, the fact of their objective invalidity was a public evil that the Church seemed bent on relieving. Much of the reason that prompted the release of non-Catholics by the decree *"Ne Temere"* from the form of marriage, to which baptized non-Catholics had been bound by the decree *"Tametsi"*, may well have exerted its cogency in determining the Church's restriction of the impediment of Disparity of Cult. In both instances it was a merciful release on the part of the Church.[9]

A. CANONS 1070, § 1 and 1099, § 2

153. The reason which is drawn from an analogy to the exemption of the decree *"Ne Temere"* has its limitations, however, for though the Church under the law of the decree *"Ne Temere"* appeared reluctant to commit herself on the question of releasing from the form of marriage those born of non-Catholic parents, baptized in the Catholic Church, but raised

---

[6] The question of doubtful Baptism is discussed in the next Chapter.

[7] *Loc. cit.*

[8] See No. 264, note 107.

[9] "Haec sapienti provisione Ecclesia sinit esse valida quam plurima matrimonia quae, sine eius dispensatione, *haeretici* cum non baptizatis contrahunt."—Vermeersch, *Theol. Mor.*, III, n. 779. Vide etiam Vermeersch, "De canone 1070, § 1 eiusque opportunitate", *Periodica* (II novae seriei, Fasc. II), Romae, 1928, XVII, 55.

from infancy in heresy, schism, or irreligion,[10] she did release
them definitely in the Code.[11] Canon 1070, § 1, does not, however, grant this latter exception and here the parity fails.

154. Some authors, indeed, have sought to draw the exception of canon 1099, § 2 to canon 1070, § 1,[12] or at least
to raise the question of its doubtful application,[13] though they
are outnumbered by those who deny the exception.[14] The probability that the more liberal opinion may have enjoyed for a
time appears to have lost its force with a decision of the Holy
Office transmitted by the Congregation of the Propaganda on
April 1, 1922. A certain man born in 1898 of infidel parents
was, at the danger of death in infancy, baptized (*"insciis parentibus"*) by a Catholic doctor. He was raised from infancy in
infidelity. Towards the end of the year 1918 he married an
unbaptized woman. The case was sent to the Holy See, and
the answer received ordered the declaration of nullity to be
given on the ground of the impediment of Disparity of Cult.[15]

155. On the other hand the provision of canon 1099, §
1, n. 1 holds also for canon 1070, § 1 so that those who have

---

[10] Cf. S. C. S. Off., 31 Mart. 1911,—*AAS*, III (1911), 163-164.

[11] Canon 1099, § 2.

[12] Cf. Durieux, *The Busy Pastor's Book on Matrimony*, p. 93, note 120.

[13] Genicot-Salsmans (*Theol. Mor.*, II, n. 491) would refer the matter to
the Holy See. Vlaming (*Prael. Iuris Matr.*, n. 289) takes refuge in the decree of March 31, 1911 (*AAS*, III [1911], 163-164) and arrives at the
same conclusion. Cf. Knecht, *Grundriss des Eherechts*, p. 72. Cappello (*De
Sacram.*, III, n. 412, not. 3) denies the force of an argument based on the decree of March 31, 1911, but with Wernz-Vidal (*Ius Canonicum*, V, n. 263,
not. 24) admits the doubt.

[14] Cf. De Smet, *De Spons. et Matr.*, n. 586; p. 513, not. 7; p. 514, not.
1; Petrovits, *New Church Law on Matrimony*, n. 230; Hilling, *Das Eherecht
des C. I. C.*, p. 29; AkKR, CVII (1927), 178-179; Ayrinhac, *Marriage
Legislation*, p. 149; Vermeersch, *Theol. Mor.*, III, n. 779; Vermeersch-
Creusen, *Epitome*, II, n. 344; Creusen, "L'empêchement de disparité de culte",
NRT, LII (1925), 495-497; Augustine, *Commentary*, V, p. 182-183;
Woywod, *A Practical Commentary*, I, n. 1053; Blat, *Comment.*, Vol. III,
P. I, n. 501.

[15] "1. An matrimonium a viro Thac in fine anni 1918 contractum fuerit
validum? 2. Si fuit validum, an possit rescindi vi privilegii paulini, ita ut
Thac possit uxore interpellata negative respondente, aliud connubium cum
muliere catholica inire?" R. "Amplitudini Tuae communico Sacram Con-
gregationem S. Officii examinasse casum matrimonialem Thac-Nam istius
Vicariatus, et respondisse matrimonium hoc Thac-Nam a te declarandum esse
nullum, ob impedimentum *disparitatis cultus*."—S. C. de Prop. F., 1 Apr.
1922,—*NRT*, LII (1925), 497-498; AkKR, CVII (1927), 179-180.

been baptized in the Catholic Church or converted to it, are
not liberated from the impediment of Disparity of Cult by a
rejection of the Catholic Faith.[16] The reason why the exception
of canon 1099, § 2, does not hold for canon 1070, § 1, may
rest in the fact that since a disparate marriage does violence
(*per se*) to the sacramental character of marriage, it is of graver
moment than the matter of clandestinity. The exemption from
the law regarding the form of marriage seems to have a further
reason in the fact that the law pertaining to clandestinity covers
a much wider field than the impediment of Disparity of Cult,—
it affects every marriage where one of the parties is bound to
the form, whereas the impediment of Disparity of Cult affects
only those marriages in which one of the parties is unbaptized.
It may well be that for such reasons the Church, in granting
an exception from the law regarding the form in canon 1099,
§ 2, was unwilling to extend it to her discipline on disparate
marriages.

B. ORIENTALS

156. The restriction of the Code to Baptism in the Catholic Church, or conversion thereto from heresy or schism, does
not, however, affect the Oriental Churches, whether they be
united to Rome or separated through schism or heresy.[17] Not,
indeed, that Baptism in the Uniate Churches or conversion to
them would not be Baptism in the Catholic Church or conversion to the Catholic Faith, but rather by reason of the fact
that the Latin discipline with regard to the limited extension
of the impediment of Disparity of Cult does not affect the
Oriental Churches.[18] The Orientals are bound, however, to the
universal prescriptions regarding the conditions, causes, and
promises that arise in conection with the impediments of Mixed

---

[16] Cerato, *Matr.*, n. 69; Chelodi, *Ius Matr.*, n. 79; Vlaming, *op. cit.*, n.
288; Wernz-Vidal, *op. cit.*, V, n. 262; De Smet, *op. cit.*, n. 586; Hilling,
op. cit., p. 29; Genicot-Salsmans, *op. cit.*, II, n. 491; *Casus Consc.*, n.
1007; Linneborn, *Grundriss des Eherechts*, p. 200; Blat, *Comment.*, Vol.
III, P. I., n. 467; Noldin, *Theol. Mor.*, III, n. 578.

[17] Cf. Petrovits, *New Church Law on Matrimony*, nn. 223, 228; Cappello, *De Sacram.*, III, n. 906; De Smet, *De Spons. et Matr.*, n. 140; Linneborn, *op. cit.*, p. 199.

[18] "Licet in Codice iuris canonici Ecclesiae quoque Orientalis disciplina saepe
referatur, ipse tamen unam respicit Latinam Ecclesiam, neque Orientalem ob-
ligat, nisi de iis agatur, quae ex ipsa rei natura etiam Orientalem afficiunt."—
Canon 1.

Religion and Disparity of Cult.[19] The discipline in the Oriental Churches united to Rome is substantially the same as it existed in the Latin Church before May 19, 1918.

157. Those born of parents belonging to an Oriental rite may not be baptized into the Latin rite,[20] nor transferred thereto after Baptism without the permission of the Holy See. Perhaps even an Oriental schismatic or heretic may not be received into the Latin Church without this permission.[21] If one of the parents belongs to the Latin rite and the other to an Oriental, the children are to be baptized in the rite of the father unless a special provision rules otherwise for a particular group of the Orientals. If one of the parents be a Catholic, the child is to be baptized in the rite of the Catholic.[22] The descendants, therefore, of those who had been received illicitly into the Latin rite do not appear to come under the Latin discipline. If in this line of descendants some would have fallen into heresies or schisms which represent a separation from the Latin Church, their progeny, if baptized in such heresy or schism, would still seem to be bound to the Oriental discipline. When, therefore, the Code in canon 1070, § 1 speaks of conversion from heresy or schism, it seems to regard primarily a conversion from heretical or schismatic sects which represent separations from the Latin Church. If there is to be a conversion from Oriental schism or hersy to the Latin Church, it is to be in accordance with the norms established by the Holy See.[23]

§ II. *"Cum persona baptizata in Ecclesia catholica"*

A. WHAT IS BAPTISM IN THE CATHOLIC CHURCH?

158. Everyone that is validly baptized is, strictly speaking, by that very fact baptized into the Catolic Church and rendered

---

[19] Cf. S. C. S. Off.. instr. (ad omnes Ep. Ritus Orient.), 12 Dec. 1888, nn. 4-6,—*Fontes*, n. 1112; Cappello, *loc. cit.*

[20] Cf. canon 756, § 1; Duskie, *The Canonical Status of the Orientals in the United States*, p. 72-84.

[21] Cf. canon 98, § 3. The Holy See has declared that an Oriental schismatic or heretic could choose any one of the recognized Oriental rites when returning to the Church. Cf. S. C. de Prop. F., 20 Nov. 1838,—*Coll.*, n. 878; 7 Apr. 1859,—*Coll.*, I, p. 500, not. 1, May not this imply that the choice is restricted to *Oriental* rites?

[22] Canon 756. §§ 2-3.

[23] See No. 157, note 21.

subject to it.[24] Yet canon 1070, § 1, in using the clause *"bap-tizata in Ecclesia catholica"* speaks of Baptism in a more restrict-ed sense,[25] having regard rather for the *finis operantis* than the *finis operis* of the sacrament of Baptism.[26] ". . . All who are baptized are, and must be, baptized *into* the Catholic Church, by whomsoever they may be baptized. But this is not the same as being baptized *in* the Catholic Church. Heretics and schismatics administer the sacrament of Baptism, as well as the Catholic Church, and so the phrase 'baptized in the Catholic Church' is used in the Decree [*"Ne Temere"*][27] to distinguish those who are baptized as *Catholics*, as *acknowledged* members of the Cath-olic Church, from those who are baptized as schismatics or here-tics."[28]

B. Who Are Baptized in the Catholic Church?

159. In determining who are baptized in the Catholic Church it will be necessary to keep constantly in mind: the intention of the parents or guardians with regard to infants; the intention of the person himself who is an adult; and the intention of the one administering the sacrament. Infants are those who at the time of Baptism have not yet arrived at the use of reason. Those who have been insane from infancy are likewise to be regarded as infants, regardless of age.[29] Adults are

---

[24] Cf. Conc. Trident., sess. VII, *de baptismo*, can 7-8; *CIC*, canon 87; Vermeersch, *Theol. Mor.*, III, n. 779.

[25] "Allatae sunt Supremae huic Congregationi Sancti Officii preces Ampli-tudinis Tuae quibus petis num impedimentum disparitatis cultus, de quo in can 1079 [manifestly a misprint and should read can. 1070] CJC restringa-tur ad matrimonium catholicorum cum non baptizatis, an etiam applicandum sit ad matrimonia baptizatorum acatholicorum cum non baptizatis. Significo Tibi, nomine eiusdem Congregationis, impedimentum hoc ad normam ipsius can. 1070 tenere catholicos, non autem acatholicos, nisi hi fuerint baptizati in Ecclesia catholica aut ad eam conversi. Res adeo clara est, ut nullum de ea dubium habere liceat."—Card. Merry del Val,— S. C. S. Off. (ad Archiep. Friburgen.), 21 Dec. 1924,—*AkKR*, CV (1925), 202.

[26] Cf. Cappello, *De Sacram.*, III, n. 411; Vlaming, *Prael. Iuris Matr.*, n. 289; Wernz-Vidal, *Ius Canonicum*, V, n. 263. Vide etiam Wouters, *Com-ment. in Decretum "Ne Temere"*, p. 77.

[27] The clause "baptized in the Catholic Church" of canon 1070, § is used in the same sense as in the decree *"Ne Temere"*, art. XI, § 1, leaving out the possibility of exemption for the *form* of marriage that may be sug-gested by the decree of the Holy Office of March 31, 1911, (*AAS*, III [1911], 163-164). Cf. Petrovits, *New Church Law on Matrimony*, n. 222.

[28] Cronin, *The New Matrimonial Legislation*, p. 273.

[29] Canon 745, § 2, n. 1.

those who at the moment of Baptism enjoy the use of reason, or, in the case of the insane, those who have at any time enjoyed the use of reason.[30] Parents are the natural interpreters of the child's intention who in the age of infancy cannot determine it.[31]

1. OUTSIDE OF URGENT NECESSITY

160. In normal cases, therefore, the Baptism that an infant receives (i. e., with reference to Baptism in the Catholic Church or in a non-Catholic denomination) will be manifest by the intention of the parents when presenting the child for Baptism to the minister of that church in which they wish to have the infant enrolled.[32] The same will be true of infants presented by guardians who have become the legitimate interpreters of the child's intention through the transfer of parental authority.[33]

161. In mixed and disparate marriages which have been contracted with a dispensation conditioned on the giving of the *cautiones*, the intention of the parents will normally be presumed to be that of seeking Baptism in the Catholic Church for their children, unless their intention is manifest to the contrary. The Baptism of children born of mixed or disparate marriages contracted without the *cautiones* may present some difficulties, especially if the parents themselves disagree on the matter and if the child is presented by the non-Catholic before a non-Catholic minister against the will of the Catholic.[34] If

---

[30] Cf. canons 745, § 2, n. 2; 754, § 1.

[31] "Si vero nondum habent usum liberi arbitrii, secundum ius naturale sunt sub cura parentum, quamdiu ipsi sibi providere non possunt; unde etiam de pueris antiquorum dicitur, quod salvabantur in fide parentum . . ."— Thomas Aq., *Summa Theol.*, IIIa, q. 68, art. 10, resp.. Vide etiam IIa - IIae, q. 10, art. 12.

[32] Cf. Petrovits, *New Church Law on Matrimony*, n. 224, 4. Normally, parents will present the child to the minister of the church to which they themselves are ascribed. If, however, they willingly present the child to a minister of a denomination other than their own, the child is to be regarded as baptized in the church of that minister.

[33] Cf. Benedictus XIV, ep. *Postremo mense*, 28 Feb. 1747, n. 14,—*Fontes*, n. 377. Guardianship may be invested, for example, through the death of the parents, through a testament, or through their unconditional release of their rights over the child in favor of another.

[34] Perhaps in this latter case the child is not to be regarded as having received Baptism in the Catholic Church. But see infra Nos. 170, 182.

the child is presented to a Catholic minister by either one of
the parents, even against the will of the other, the Baptism is
to be regarded as Catholic, especially if it is administered in
conformity with the norms established by the Church.[35]

a. Baptism Conferred in Violation of Canons 750 and 751

162. If there is due provision for their Catholic education,
a Catholic may licitly baptize the infant children of infidels,
heretics, schismatics, and fallen-away Catholics provided: that
at least one of the parents or guardians consent; or that at the
time of the Baptism the child has no parents, grandparents, or
guardians,—or that they have lost their right over the child,
or cannot in any way exercise it.[36] If Baptism is conferred in accordance with these rules demanded by canons 750 and 751, the
Baptism is to be regarded as Catholic Baptism and those infants receiving it will be bound by the impediment of Disparity
of Cult when marrying the unbaptized.[37]

163. On the other hand, if Baptism is administered illicitly, i. e., contrary to the provisions of canon 750, § 2, nn.
1-2, it will be in violation of the natural right of the parents,
with the consequent moral certainty of the children's perver-

---

[35] These norms will be found in the following instructions and decisions:
Benedictus XIV, ep. encycl. *Inter omnigenas*, 2 Feb. 1744, § 8,—*Fontes*,
n. 339; ep. *Postremo mense*, 28 Feb. 1747, nn. 15-16.—*Fontes*, n. 377; S.
C. S. Off., 12 Oct. 1600,—*Fontes*, n. 714; 8 Feb. 1624,—*Fontes*, n.
718; 17 Sept. 1671,—*Fontes*, n. 747; (Hiberniae), 29 Nov. 1672,—
Fontes, n. 751; 14 Oct. 1676,—*Fontes*, n. 753; 18 Nov. 1745,—*Fontes*,
n. 796; (Sutchuen.), 12 Ian. 1769,—*Coll.*, n. 471; (Promont. Bonae
Spei), 22 Iul. 1840,—*Fontes*, n. 882; 6 Iul. 1898, ad 4-5,—*Fontes*, n.
1200. (The last decision regards the case of a dying Catholic parent, married
civilly to a non-Catholic.)

[36] Cf. canons 750, § 2, nn. 1-2; 751; Benedictus XIV, ep. *Postremo
mense*, 28 Feb. 1747, n. 14,—*Fontes*, n. 377; instr. S. C. de Prop. F., 17
Apr. 1777, nn. VII-VIII,—*Coll.*, n. 522.

[37] Vlaming, Genicot-Salsmans, Cappello, and Wernz-Vidal (see infra No.
154, note 13) doubt the validity of this conclusion, and the first two
authors would have recourse to the Holy See. Vermeersch-Creusen (*Epitome*,
II, n. 344), though disagreeing with the first three authors, admits the probability of their opinion. Hilling (*Das Eherecht des C. I. C.*, p. 30) admits
that they are bound. The decision of the Congregation of the Propaganda
of April 1, 1922 (see infra No. 154, note 15) seems to remove the probability of the opinion sponsored by the first four authors mentioned.

sion.[38] Cappello,[39] Wernz-Vidal,[40] Hilling,[41] and Woywod[42] are of the opinion that an infant (whose parents are non-Catholics) baptized by a Catholic in violation of canons 750 and 751, and raised from infancy in heresy or schism, will not be bound by the impediment of Disparity of Cult when marrying an unbaptized person. It cannot be urged, however, that the Baptism thus illicitly administered, is not Baptism in the Catholic Church,[43] for the basic reason in forbidding it seems to rest on the danger of perversion.[44] Yet the supposition of a danger of perversion implies *Baptism in the Catholic Church.*[45]

164. The liberation sponsored by the authors may, or may not, be in conformity with the mind of the Church. In as much as the Church forbids under pain of sin the illicit ad-

---

[38] ". . . et ideo contra iustitiam naturalem esset, si tales pueri invitis parentibus baptizarentur; sicut etiam si aliquis habens usum rationis baptizaretur invitus. Esset etiam periculosum taliter filios infidelium baptizare; quia facili ad infidelitatem redirent, propter naturalem affectum ad parentes."—Thomas Aq., *Summa Theol.*, IIIa, q. 68, art. 10, resp.; IIa - IIae, q. 10, art. 12. Cf. Suarez, Quaest. LXVIII, *De Suscipientibus Baptismum*, art. 10, sect. 3-5; Benedictus XIV, ep. *Postremo mense*, 28 Feb. 1747, nn. 6-7, 22-23, 27,—*Fontes*, n. 377.

[39] *De Sacram.*, III, n. 412.

[40] *Ius Canonicum*, V, n. 263.

[41] *Das Eherecht des C. I. C.*, p. 29-30. Cf. AkKR, CVII (1927), 180-181.

[42] *A Practical Commentary*, I, n. 1053. Wouters (*Comment. in Decretum "Ne Temere"*, p. 78) also seems to insinuate an agreement when he says: "si quis baptizatur in ordine ad Ecclesiam catholicam ex sola intentione *legitime* seu *licite* baptizantis, etiamsi ii qui infantibus praesunt, non consentiant." Cf. Vermeersch, *De Forma Spons. ac Matr. post Decretum "Ne Temere"*, n. 87.

[43] Vlaming (*Prael. Iuris Matr.*, n. 598), however, in speaking of canon 1099, seems to deny that those baptized contrary to canons 750 and 751 receive Catholic Baptism. Hilling (*AkKR*, CVII [1927], 180-181) is of the same opinion. ". . . es liegt gar kein Grund vor, Kinder protestantischer Eltern, die unrechtmässiger Weise in der katholischen Kirche getauft, aber von Jugend auf in der protestantischen Religion erzogen sind, anders zu behandeln, als solche Kinder, die nach dem Willen der protestantischen Eltern in der protestantischen Kirche getauft und erzogen sind."

[44] A study of the sources quoted in Cardinal Gasparri's notes to canons 750 and 751 will serve as confirmation. Cf. Labauche, *Three Sacraments of Initiation*, p. 104, note 1.

[45] There is no violation of parental rights with regard to the group enumerated in canon 751. Cf. King, *The Administration of the Sacraments to Dying Non-Catholics*, p. 36-37; Suarez, Quaest. LXVIII, *De Suscipientibus Baptismum*, art. 10, sect. 3, n. 2; Noldin, *Theol. Mor.*, III, n. 67; Labauche, *Three Sacraments of Initiation*, p. 103, note 2.

ministration of Baptism in the Catholic Church, it may be reasonable to suppose that she would be unwilling, in the light of her present legislation, to bind those baptized contrary to her law. In much the same manner as she would refuse to bind an Oriental to the Latin discipline through his illicit Baptism into the Latin rite, she may likewise refuse to bind by an impediment (which she restricts to those baptized in the Catholic Church or converted thereto) those unlawfully baptized in the Catholic Church, who from infancy have been brought up as non-Catholics. On the other hand, canon 1070, § 1 rules that those who have been baptized in the Catholic Church (regardless of their future profession of faith are bound by the impediment,—it offers no suggestion of an exception. The canon seems to be concerned with the *fact* of Catholic Baptism rather than with its licit or illicit administration. The matter lies wholly with the positive disposition of the Church. The question calls for practical solution only after a marriage has been contracted. In the absence of a definite pronouncement, it seems that a case of this kind should be sent to the Holy Office for decision.

b. Adults and the Insane

165. The words "Catholic Baptism" are applicable to those adults who in the reception of Baptism were actuated by the motive of becoming Catholics.[46] An adult who (while in a conscious state expressed his absolute unwillingness to receive Baptism) is baptized in an unconscious state; or an adult who, though conscious, is forced unwillingly to receive Baptism, would not be baptized validly for the intention of an adult is required for the validity of the sacrament.[47] An adult so baptized by a Catholic would not be bound by the impediment of Disparity of Cult. The Baptism of the insane (with reference to the impediment of Disparity of Cult) is to be judged according to the norms established in canon 754. The cases of urgent necessity will be discussed in due order.

---

[46] Petrovits, *New Church Law on Matrimony*, n. 224.

[47] Cf. canon 752, § 1; Cappello, *De Sacram.*, I, n. 154; Thomas Aq., *Summa Theol.*, IIIa, q. 68, art. 7-8. Suarez (Quaest. LXVIII, *De Suscipientibus Baptismum*, art. 7-8) after quoting the passage from St. Thomas, considers the question sufficiently clear to preclude the necessity of commenting on it.

2. URGENT NECESSITY

166. The Baptisms administered to infants in danger of death will present some difficulties and it will be well, therefore, to examine some of the possibilities in order to determine the nature of the Baptism conferred. Often the expressed or interpretative will of the parents or guardians may not be in accord with that of the baptizing minister. Cases may also arise where those who present the children for Baptism act contrary to the will of the parents.

a. Baptism *in utero*

167. The Baptism of an infant baptized *in utero* in accordance with canon 746, § 2 is to be judged according to the intention of the mother. *Antecedently* to a marriage with an unbaptized person of a person baptized *in utero* in violation of canons 750 or 751 the question of a pastor's assistance will normally arise only if the party under consideration is an actual professed Catholic. If this party has ever been a convert to the Catholic Church there is, indeed, need of a dispensation from the impediment of Disparity of Cult that he may contract a valid marriage, but the dispensation can be given only on the condition that at the time of the dispensation he is actually a professed Catholic. If, as a non-Catholic, he should seek to be married to an unbaptized person before a Catholic pastor, the pastor cannot assist until one or both parties to the marriage are received into the Church through conversion or (in the case of the unbaptized party) through Baptism. If one of the parties remains a sectarian non-Catholic or unbaptized there is need of the proper dispensation, either from the impediment of Mixed Religion or Disparity of Cult.

Post factum, if a person baptized *in utero* in violation of canons 750 or 751 (who from infancy has been brought up as a non-Catholic) has married an unbaptized person, the case should be referred to the Holy Office for decision. Baptism administered conditionally in accordance with canon 746, §§ 3-4 is doubtful Baptism and a marriage contracted by a person so baptized with an unbaptized person cannot be declared invalid.[48] This would be true, of course, only on the condition

---

[48] Cf. canon 1070, § 2.

that the doubtful Baptism has not been rendered certainly valid by the reception of conditional Baptism in the Catholic Church,[49] or by conversion to the Catholic Church if such a doubtful Baptism had been repeated conditionally (and rendered certainly valid) in heresy or schism.[50]

b. Two Catholic Parents, or Parents in a Mixed or Disparate Marriage Contracted with the *Cautiones*

168. If a child (infant) of two Catholic parents be baptized in urgent necessity by a Catholic, the Catholic Baptism of the child cannot be questioned.[51] Even if the child were baptized by an infidel, a baptized sectarian non-Catholic or non-sectarian non-Catholic, or by a fallen-away Catholic, the child should be regarded as having been baptized in the Catholic Church. The intention of the non-Catholic minister to incorporate the child into his sect would be impotent against the expressed or interpretative intention of the Catholic parents. The same may be said with regard to the expressed or interpretative intention of Catholic guardians who have become the legitimate interpreters of the child in infancy.[52]

---

[49] Cf. canon 746, § 5.

[50] By virtue of the doubtful Baptism under consideration, the person would presumptively, indeed, be bound to the laws of the Church, (see infra No. 201, note 46; Nos. 220-221) but not to the prejudice of the validity of a marriage. The question would become practical only after a person thus doubtfully baptized (in the Catholic Church) had contracted a marriage with an unbaptized person. If the doubtful (Catholic) Baptism were known antecedently to the contracting of such a marriage, the person would first be baptized conditionally before proceeding to procure the necessary dispensation. If the person were not again conditionally baptized (canon 746, § 5) at the time of the contracting of the marriage with an unbaptized person, the rule *"standum est pro valore matrimonii"* would have to be applied. See canons 1014; 1070, § 2. In the light of canon 1070, § 2, a marriage between a person baptized in accordance with the prescriptions of canon 746, §§ 3-4 and an unbaptized person could not be declared invalid. A truly doubtful Baptism *in utero* (cf. canon 746, §§ 3-4) can never be proved (a condition demanded by canon 1070, § 2 for a declaration of nullity) to be valid.

[51] Cf. Vermeersch, *De Forma Spons. ac Matr. post Decretum "Ne Temere"*, n. 87.

[52] Petrovits (*New Church Law on Matrimony*, n. 277) postulates a case of two Catholic parents in urgent necessity, presenting in good faith their infant child for Baptism by a non-Catholic minister. It appears that unless an expressed wish of the parents signified their intention of incorporating the child into a non-Catholic sect, their interpretative intention of wishing it to be baptized into the Catholic Church is to be presumed. Cf. Wouters, *Comment. in Decretum "Ne Temere"*, p. 77.

169. Children born of mixed or disparate marriages, which have been contracted on the giving of the *cautiones*, should be regarded in the same light as those born of Catholic parents, when the question of Catholic Baptism arises. It is to be presumed that the parents by the *cautiones* have interpreted the intention of having the child baptized in the Catholic Church until the contrary is proved.[53]

c. Parents in Mixed or Disparate Marriages Contracted without the *Cautiones*

170. Children born of mixed or disparate marriages contracted without the *cautiones* and baptized by a Catholic in danger of death, must be regarded as baptized in the Catholic Church, and bound by canon 1070, § 1.[54] If such children were baptized by a non-Catholic, a serious doubt would arise as to whether they are to be regarded as baptized in the Catholic Church. Though the Church has a right to have them baptized as Catholics, the expressed or interpretative intention of the parents is not clearly determined as being in accord with this right, or as opposed to the intention of the non-Catholic minister. The marriage of those so baptized (who from infancy have been brought up as non-Catholics) contracted with the unbaptized should be submitted to the Holy Office for a decision as to their validity.[55]

d. Two Non-Catholic Parents

171. If, in the case of danger of death, a Catholic baptizes the children of non-Catholic parents, even against the will of the parents or without their knowledge, the child is to be regarded as baptized in the Catholic Church and bound by can-

---

[53] Cf. Petrovits, *op. cit.*, n. 225.

[54] Cf. S. C. S. Off., 3 Mart. 1633,—apud Benedictus XIV, ep. *Postremo mense*, 28 Feb. 1747, n. 27,—*Fontes*, n. 377; 6. Iul. 1898, ad 4,—*Fontes*, n. 1200; Wernz, *Ius Decret.*, IV, Pars I, p. 305-306; King, *The Administration of the Sacraments to Dying Non-Catholics*, p. 31-32; Augustine, *Commentary*, V, p. 297.

[55] Cf. Petrovits, *New Church Law on Matrimony*, n. 227. Antecedently to such marriages the norms given in No. 167 will apply also to the cases under consideration.

on 1070, § 1.[56] If such children were baptized by a fallen-away Catholic who was not a member of a non-Catholic sect, the presumption would favor Catholic Baptism until his intention to the contrary could be proved. If a non-Catholic minister (one who had never been a Catholic) intended to administer Catholic Baptism, the intention would be effective. The presumption, however, is against such an intention and it would have to be proved.

e. Adults and the Insane

172. If dying adults are baptized by a Catholic by virtue of canon 752, § 2, they are to be regarded as baptized in the Catholic Church and bound by canon 1070, § 1. If they are baptized conditionally by virtue of canon 752, § 3, and upon their recovery the doubt concerning the validity of their Baptism still remains, they are to be baptized conditionally.[57] If they have not received this second conditional Baptism (in the Catholic Church) and contract a marriage with the unbaptized, their marriage cannot be declared invalid.[58]

173. Those insane from infancy are to be baptized as infants,[59] and the determination of the kind of Baptism they have received should follow the rules established for infants. If the insane, who have evinced their desire for Baptism in a lucid interval, are baptized by a Catholic, they will be baptized in the Catholic Church.[60] The Baptisms of the feeble-minded, who can distinguish right from wrong, follow the rules prescribed for adults. The Baptisms of those in a state of coma or delirium, when in danger of death, are to be judged as those of canon 754, §§ 3 (4).

§ III. *"Vel ad eandem ex haeresi aut schismate conversa"*

174. The same reasons that suggest a wider interpretation of the clause *"sectae haereticae seu schismaticae adscripta"* of

---

[56] S. C. de Prop. F., 1 Apr. 1922,—*NRT*, LII (1925), 497-498. In cases of this kind even the rights of infidel parents are not violated,—the natural cedes to the supernatural right. Cf. Benedictus XIV, ep. *Postremo mense*, 28 Feb. 1747, n. 16.—*Fontes*, n. 377; King, *op. cit.*, p. 36.
[57] Canon 752, § 3.
[58] Cf. canon 1070, § 2; No. 167, note 50.
[59] Canon 754, § 1.
[60] Cf. canon 754, § 3.

canon 1060 than strict heresy or schism[61] will apply with equal cogency to the clause *"ex haeresi aut schismate conversa"* of canon 1070, § 1. Conversion to the Catholic Faith may be from schism, heresy, or any false religion, yet the baptism of the convert is supposed by the term *"conversion"*. Conversion is a change from non-Catholic belief or infidelity to the Catholic Faith. In the case of those who enjoy the use of reason, it is a personal and volitional act, i. e., a free act performed by the person himself, and not passively through the will of another.

A. Adults

175. Normally, a conversion takes place after due instructions in the mysteries of Faith, whereupon the following order of procedure is observed: 1) If the Baptism is conferred absolutely, no abjuration of heresy or absolution from censures is required since the Sacrament of Regeneration wipes out all. 2) If Baptism is to be repeated conditionally the following order is to be observed:[62]

a) The abjuration or profession of faith.

b) Conditional Baptism.

c) Sacramental confession with conditional absolution.[63] If adults are received into the Church in the manner thus prescribed they are undoubtedly to be regarded as converts to the Catholic Church.[64]

---

[61] Creusen ("L'empêchement de disparité de culte",—*NRT*, LII [1925], 496) accepts this wider meaning by including conversions from schism, heresy, and infidelity, i. e., Judaism, paganism, or the religion of the Mohammedans. See No. 131, note 14.

[62] In both the first and second hypothesis the person so converted will be bound by the impediment of Disparity of Cult through the reception of Baptism in the Catholic Church. By virtue of an Indult granted to the Archbishop of Philadelphia January 4, 1914, and later to Cardinal Gibbons, a short formula for the conditional Baptism of adult converts was permitted in the Provinces of Philadelphia and Baltimore. Cf. *The Priest's New Ritual*, (compiled by Rev. Paul Griffith), 4 ed., Baltimore, 1914, p. 58-58b.

[63] This order of procedure is contained in *The Priest's New Ritual*, p. 46-56, and also in the Appendix for the United States inserted in the *Rituale Romanum*, p. 1-2. It was prescribed by an instruction of the Holy Office sent to the Bishop of Philadelphia on July 20, 1859,—*Fontes*, n. 953. Vide etiam S. C. S. Off.,20 Nov. 1878,—*Fontes*, n. 1058; 8 Mart. 1882,—*Fontes*, n. 1073.

[64] Cf. Petrovits, *New Church Law on Matrimony*, n. 224.

B. *Impuberes*

176. According to the rule of Cardinal Albitius, those validly baptized converts who enjoyed the use of reason but who had not yet completed their fourteenth year were required to make only the profession of faith.[65] The New Ritual prescribes the manner of procedure required in the law before the Code only in the supplement that is added for the United States. In the Ritual itself there is no reference to a manner of procedure.[66] The omission does not necessarily abrogate the former discipline but some doubt might readily be entertained with regard to the binding force of the particular mode in which this reconciliation is to take place.[67] It would be rash to say that the Church would recognize no conversion of a minor or an adult unless a formal abjuration or profession were made. If, in addition, the absolution from censure (apparently necessary only for those above the age of 14) were given in the internal, sacramental forum, what criterion is left in the external forum whereby the fact of conversion may be judged? It appears that the reception of the sacraments would serve as a sufficient evidence in the absence of the formal abjuration of heresy, the profession of faith, and the absolution from censure in the external forum.

----

[65] Cf. *De Inconstantia in Fide*, Cap. XIV, n. 58; *Fontes*, IV, p. 389, not. 2; S. C. S. Off., litt., 8 Mart. 1882,—*Fontes*, n. 1073; Vermeersch, *De Forma Spons. ac Matr. post Decretum "Ne Temere"*, n. 87; Cronin, *The New Matrimonial Legislation*, p. 279. The Code likewise excuses "*impuberes*" from punishments incurred *latae sententiae*. Cf. canons 2230; 2204. For the definition of "*impuberes*" and "*minores*" see canon 88, §§ 2-3. It seems to be a probable opinion, based at least on external authority, that the age of 14 is to be the norm for both sexes. Cf. Cappello, *De Censuris*, n. 17, 4; Sole, *De Delictis et Poenis*, n. 120, cum not. 1, 3; Vermeersch-Creusen, *Epitome*, III, n. 424; Cocchi, *Comment.*, Vol. 8, n. 44. Chelodi (*Ius Poenale*, p. 12, not. 1), Eichmann (*Das Strafrecht des C. I. C.*, p. 65-66, and Blat (*Comment.*, Vol. V, n. 50) employ the distinction in canon 88, § 2 and aver that girls at the completion of the age of twelve are subject to penalties incurred *latae sententiae*.

[66] The *Rituale Romanum* (Tit. II, cap. III, n. 12) prescribes only the following norm: "Haeretici vero ad Catholicam Ecclesiam venientes, in quorum Baptismo debita forma, aut materia servata non est, rite baptizandi sunt; sed prius errorum suorum pravitatem agnoscant et detestentur, et in fide Catholica diligenter instruantur; ubi vero debita forma et materia servata est, omissa tantum suppleantur, nisi rationabili de causa aliter loci Ordinario videatur." Here there is no mention of the procedure demanded in the instruction of the Holy Office of July 20, 1859 (*Fontes*, n. 953).

[67] Cf. *AER*, LI (1914), 86-88.

C. Infants

177. A division of opinion exists among the authors regarding the status of infants, validly baptized in a non-Catholic sect, whose parents become converts to the Catholic Church. Some are inclined to believe that children in the age of infancy become converts to the Catholic Church by the very conversion of their parents.[68] This opinion is opposed by some, either on the ground that the act is not personal,[69] or that it is not external.[70] Others turn to Catholic education as a solution of the question and regard those children converts, who, having been validly baptized in heresy, are subsequently (on the acquisition of the use of reason) educated in the Catholic faith.[71]

178. Though apparently sponsored by fewer authors, the opinion that baptized infants become converts to the Church upon the conversion of their parents seems to enjoy a greater intrinsic probability.[72] It is admitted even by the authors who deny this opinion that parents are competent to determine the intention of their infant children,—some even extend it to the early age of reason. Vermeersch, however, seems to limit this competence to the determination of the intention for Baptism: *"Dum baptismus recipitur etiam sine propria voluntate, in infantia, conversio dicit actum personalem. Quare, non ipsa parentum conversione conversi putandi sunt etiam filii, sed*

---

[68] Wernz, *Ius Decret.*, IV, Pars I, p. 306; Petrovits, *New Church Law on Matrimony*, n. 228; Augustine, *Commentary*, V, p. 299.

[69] Vermeersch, *De Forma Spons. ac Matr. post Decretum "Ne Temere"*, n. 87.

[70] "The parents' own reception into the Church does not *ipso facto* make their children Catholics, nor is the desire or intention of the parents sufficient to do so. Some external act is necessary to make one a member af the body of the Church."—Cronin, *The New Matrimonial Legislation*, p. 280.

[71] Vermeersch-Creusen, *Epitome*, II, n. 344; Chelodi, *Ius Matr.*, n. 138; Vlaming, *Prael. Iuris. Matr.*, n. 598b; Wernz-Vidal, *Ius Canonicum*, V, n. 551; Farrugia, *De Matr.*, n. 238.

[72] Augustine (*Commentary*, V, p. 300) draws an argument from an affirmative answer given by the Congregation of the Council to the following *dubium*: "Num in Imperio Germaniae catholici, quid ad sectam haercticam vel schismaticam transierunt, vel *conversi* ad fidem catholicam ab ea postea *defecerunt, eitam in iuvenili vel* INFANTILI aetate, ad valide cum persona catholica contrahendum adhibere debeant forman in decreto Ne Temerc statutam . . ."—S. C. Conc. 1 Feb. 1907, ad V,—*ASS*, XLI (1908), 108, 110. In the *dubium* both conversion and defection *in the age of infancy* are considered. The point raised by Augustine is, therefore, well taken.

oportet ut ipsi actu satis personali, fidem catholicam sint amplexi."[73] He seeks confirmation in the decree of the Holy Office of March 8, 1882,[74] which approves the rule established by Cardinal Albitius.[75] But the Cardinal's rule does not appear to treat of infants, but rather of those who have already arrived at the use of reason. It may well be admitted that a personal act is required for conversion after the use of reason,—it does not follow, however, that conversion before the use of reason is impossible on the ground that the act is not personal. Why cannot the parents interpret the intention of the infant for conversion as well as for Baptism?

179. Cronin, in postulating the insufficiency of the parents' intention to procure the conversion of the infant,[76] has recourse to the act of supplying the Catholic ceremonies of Baptism in cases where the validity of the infant's non-Catholic Baptism is established.[77] While it appears that such ceremonies may and ordinarily should be supplied,[78] the *strict obligation* to supply them is not so evident. When Cronin quotes the decision of April 2, 1879, he omits the third question asked, and the answer,[79] which, however, renders the absolute *obligatory* nature of the supplying of the ceremonies in the connection he demands, rather questionable. It may readily be admitted with Cronin that if the ceremonies of Baptism are supplied, the infant is to be considered a convert. The admission, however, militates against Vermeersch's opinion that the act of conversion cannot be ascribed to an infant since it is not personal.

---

[73] *De Forma Spons. ac Matr. post Decretum "Ne Temere"*, n. 87.

[74] *Fontes*, n. 1073.

[75] *De Inconstantia in Fide*, Cap XIV, n. 58 (quoted also in *Fontes*, IV, p. 389, not. 2.)

[76] See No. 177, note 70.

[77] *The New Matrimonial Legislation*, p. 282-283.

[78] S. C. S. Off. (Nottingham.), 2 Apr. 1879,—*Fontes*, n. 1061; Suffragia super Decreto S. Rit. Cong., n. 2743,—*Decreta Authentica Congregationis Sacrorum Rituum*, Romae, 1897-1912, Vol. IV (1900), p. 353. Vide etiam *Rituale Romanum*, Tit. II, cap. III, n. 12.

[79] 3. "Quatenus affirmative, quid faciendum de permultis huiusmodi qui fere passim iam per multos annos in pueritia sub conditione sine caeremoniis iam baptizati sunt?" R. "Dissimulandum; quod si quis petat *remittitur prudenti arbitrio R. P. D. Ordinarii.*"—*Fontes*, n. 1061. The whole decree, moreover, concerns conditional Baptism.

180. On the other hand, Cronin's demand of an external act seems to be satisfied by the conversion of the parents. The *external evidence* of the parents' conversion implies (if it is not expressed) the parents' intention for the children in infancy. If the ceremonies of Baptism are not supplied, how long are the infant children to be regarded as non-Catholics? Vermeersch says that the reception of the sacraments by the child, especially of First Holy Communion, would render the child a convert. Cronin takes exception to this: "But surely this personal act will not be the reception of the Sacraments of Penance, Confirmation, Holy Eucharist, nor the living of the ordinary life of a Catholic child, for this shows that the child is already a Catholic fully and completely, like any other member of the Church. We must go further back for the act which formally made this child a Catholic; and it is the profession of faith made in his formal reception into the Church."[80] He then refers to the rule of Cardinal Albitius for confirmation.

181. Attention has already been directed to the fact that the rule apparently applies only to those who become converts after the age of reason,—it does not appear to demand a profession of faith of a child arriving at the use of reason whose parents had already become converts during the child's infancy. Indeed, it does not appear in any way illicit to admit a child (after proper instruction) in such circumstances to the sacraments without exacting the formal profession of faith. The child is already a Catholic by the conversion of its parents.

182. What if only one of the parents becomes a convert? Even in this case infant children may, perhaps, be regarded as converts. The duties undertaken in conversion imply the Catholic education of the children, and the expressed or interpretative intention of complying with this obligation is sufficient to constitute infants as converts. The right of the convert parent is further a natural and a divine right which is above the right of opposition of the other parent. Infant children who cannot express their intention may perhaps have this intention supplied by the parent who has the right and obligation of direct-

---

[80] *The New Matrimonial Legislation*, p. 278.

ing it. Admittedly such cases would present serious difficulties, and the opinion is defended with due hesitancy.

183. If, on the other hand, infants on arriving at the use of reason must first receive a Catholic education before they will be regarded as converts,—how much education, it may be asked, is required to constitute evidence of conversion? At what period of Catholic instruction will the child become a Catholic? It appears intrinsically more probable, therefore, to maintain that baptized infant children become converts *ipso facto* upon the conversion of both parents, and perhaps of even one parent.[81]

184. By way of summary with regard to the conversion of children, the following may without hesitation be regarded as converts: 1) baptized infants who, at the will of one or both convert parents, have been received into the Church through the supplying of the Catholic ceremonies of Baptism; 2) children, who, enjoying the use of reason, have received any of the sacraments, or who have made a formal profession of faith with the motive of entering the Church. While, indeed, the opinion is defended which maintains that infant children become converts by the conversion of one or both parents,—a serious doubt obviously remains as to the positive will of the Church. The authors themselves disagree on the issue. Marriage cases involving the diriment impediment of Disparity of Cult, where no further evidence exists for the conversion of the baptized party, are to be sent to the Holy Office for solution. The question could become practical only after the marriage had already been contracted.

---

[81] Catholic parents who would knowingly dare to present their children to non-Catholic ministers for Baptism, would incur excommunication. Cf. canon 2319, § 1, n. 3. Such children in infancy who at the time of the reconciliation of their parents still remained in their custody, would seem to become converts by the very fact of their parents' reconciliation. The conditions of reconciliation would demand this duty, and the implied or expressed acquiescence to the obligation would be sufficient to constitute the infant children as converts. The same may, perhaps, be said of the reconciliation of one parent. If, on the other hand, the presentation for Baptism to a non-Catholic minister were made in ignorance or good faith, the censure would not be incurred. This would imply that the Baptism itself is to be regarded as Baptism in the Catholic Church.

CHAPTER X

DOUBTFUL BAPTISM

ART. I. MATTER AND FORM

Fundamental to the validity of Baptism is the adherence
to the required matter and form of the sacrament, and the
necessary intention of the minister of the sacrament.

185. The great scholastics, followed thereafter by all theologians, distinguished the matter of Baptism into remote and
proximate.[1] Natural water is the remote matter prescribed by
Christ Himself: "Unless a man be born again of *water* and the
Holy Ghost, he cannot enter into the kingdom of God."[2] The
proximate matter of Baptism is the washing or the ablution.
For validity, it may be either by infusion, immersion or asper-
sion.[3] The essential element seems to be the ablution,[4] which
takes place on the flowing of water upon the skin of the head
of the person to be baptized. The form of the sacrament necessary for validity is the expression of the baptismal action in the
name of the Three Divine Persons: "*Ego te baptizo in nomine
Patris, et Filii, et Spiritus Sancti.*" A moral unity must, moreover, exist between the ablution and the form.

186. Since these elements are essential, the omission of
any one of them will render the Baptism invalid. Doubt of the
validity of a Baptism may, therefore, arise with regard to the
matter and form of Baptism. But in addition there is required

---

[1] Cf. S. C. de Prop. F., instr. (ad Vic. Ap. Siam), 23 Iun. 1830,—
Coll., n. 814.

[2] John, III, 5. The Council of Trent (sess. VII, *de baptismo*, can.
2) gave the following definition: "Si quis dixerit, aquam veram et naturalem
non esse de necessitate baptismi, atque ideo verba illa Domini nostri Iesu
Christi: '*Nisi quis renatus fuerit ex aqua et Spiritu Sancto*' ad metaphoram aliquam detorserit: A. S."—Denz., n. 858. Vide *CIC*, canon 737, § 1.

[3] *CIC*, canon 758.

[4] On the 14th of December 1898 the Holy Office ordered the conditional
repetition of a Baptism that had been conferred by an unction instead of an
ablution.—*Fontes*, n. 1211.

the intention of the minister.[5] On this score in particular, recent discussions have arisen, especially with regard to the intention of ministers of certain non-Catholic sects.[6] In order to understand the mind of the Church on this issue, it may be to advantage to review briefly the historical controversies pertaining to the intention of the minister.

ART. II. THE INTENTION OF THE MINISTER

187. Beginning in the early centuries of Christianity, the problem of determining the validity of Baptism has engaged the mind of the Church, and of theologians and canonists. It has existed particularly with regard to Baptisms administered outside of the Catholic Church. Indeed, St. Cyprian was so swayed by the conviction that Baptism could not be administered validly outside of the Catholic Church that he vigorously defended the practice, adhered to in Northern Africa, of baptizing all who had been baptized by heretics. Starting with the principle that Christ established one Church and one Baptism, he was convinced that a Baptism conferred by a counterfeit church, an heretical sect, was nothing short of a forgery of the true Baptism. He reasoned, moreover, that no Baptism was efficacious without the Holy Ghost, and since the Holy Ghost dwells only in the Catholic Church, true Baptism must likewise belong to the Catholic Church alone.[7]

The Donatists carried St. Cyprian's argument to its logical conclusion and declared invalid not only a Baptism conferred by a heretic, but also that administered by anyone who had lost the Holy Ghost through sin. In combating their error, St. Augustine showed that the validity of Baptism did not depend on the dipositions of the minister; that Baptism was a means of grace objectively efficacious; that as long as the Christian[8]

---

[5] Cf. Conc. Trident., sess. VII, *de sacramentis in genere*, can 11,—Denz., n. 854.

[6] Cf. *AER*, LXXIV (1926), 158-180; LXXV (1926), 136-151; 358-370; LXXVI (1927), 155-165; 496-504; *Gregorianum*, VIII (1927), 41-54.

[7] Cf. Corblet, *Histoire du sacrament de Baptême*, I, 328-333.

[8] From the ninth century on, it was generally admitted that Baptism conferred by anyone, *whether baptized or unbaptized*, using the essential rite, was valid. Cf. Labauche, *The Three Sacraments of Initiation*, p. 75-76; Nicolaus I (ad consulta Bulgarorum), Nov. 866,—Denz., n. 335. The question

administered the ablution and pronounced the Trinitarian form, the Baptism was valid.[9]

At Rome, the practice of the Church conformed to its teaching that the efficacy of Baptism should be attributed especially to the Trinitarian invocation which accompanied the ablution, since Christ so wished it when He instituted the sacrament of Baptism and established its rite.[10]

188. It was no far step from the discussion regarding the dispositions or moral qualifications of the minister to that of his intention. St. Augustine was the first to turn to the question and he considered two cases, namely, "the fallacious administration of Baptism (either where the subject alone acts, 'fallaciously', or where he acts in concert with the minister) performed either in the Catholic Church or in an heretical sect, supposed in good faith to be the true Church; and Baptism conferred for the mere purpose of amusement . . ."[11] By a fallacious administration of Baptism he understood that which would take place upon the minister performing seriously all the sacred rites and the subject receiving them in the same manner, though both intend to act only in pretension.[12] For St. Augustine, the internal intention of deception did not apparently constitute an obstacle to the validity of the sacrament.[13] On the other hand, he would not commit himself upon the validity of a Baptism conferred in mockery or amusement.[14]

---

was no longer a matter of discussion after the thirteenth century, for the Church herself defined that Baptism could be administered validly outside of the Church. Cf. Conc. Lateran. IV, Cap. I *De fide catholica*,—Denz., n. 430: Eugenius IV (in Conc. Florentin.), const. *Exultate Deo*, 22 Nov. 1439 § 10,—*Fontes*, n. 52; Conc. Trident., sess. VII, *de baptismo*, can. 4,—Denz., n. 860.

[9] ". . . iam satis ostendimus ad Baptismum qui verbis evangelicis con-secratur, non pertinere cuiusquam vel dantis vel accipientis errorem, sive de Patre, sive de Filio, sive de Spiritu sancto aliter sentiat, quam coelestis doctrina insinuat."—*De Baptismo contra Donatistas*, Lib. IV, cap. XV, n. 22, —*MPL*, XLIII, 168.

[10] Cf. Labauche, *op. cit.*, p. 72-73. Vide etiam index systematicus, verbum, "Baptismus" apud Denz., p. [30].

[11] Pourrat, *Theology of the Sacraments*, p. 363.

[12] Pourrat, *op. cit.*, p. 366.
cit, p. 367. See No. 190.

[13] The opinion of St. Augustine (taken in its proper context) must not be confused with the opinion later defended by Catharinus. Cf. Pourrat, *op.*

[14] Cf. Pourrat, *op cit.*, p. 368.

The discussion was again resumed in the twelfth century. According to some, no intention was required in the minister,— it sufficed that the rite be performed according to the prescriptions of the Church.[15] Others again, among them Hugh of St. Victor and Peter Lombard, demanded the intention of conferring a sacrament.[16]

189. The great scholastics of the Middle Ages approached the final solution. They taught that the minister of Baptism is the rational instrument of Christ and the Church. He must, therefore, have the intention to do what they do.[17] But a difficulty still remained to be solved. If the intention, which is mental and hidden, be demanded for the validity of Baptism, in what might the faithful place their assurance that the intention was present in the minister? St. Thomas ventured the following solution: *"minister sacramenti agit in persona totius Ecclesiae, cuius est minister; in verba autem, quae profert, exprimitur intentio Ecclesiae; quae sufficit ad perfectionem sacramenti nisi contrarium exterius exprimatur ex parte ministri, vel recipientis sacramentum."*[18]

190. In the sixteenth century Catharinus, a Dominican theologian, arguing from the teaching of St. Thomas and other sources,[19] distinguished between an external and an internal intention of administering Baptism. According to Catharinus the external intention of doing what the Church does was present when the minister intended the correct administration of the sacramental rite, though inwardly he would have a positive

---

[15] Pourrat (*op. cit.*, p. 372) gives a quotation from Roland who defended this opinion. Vide etiam *op. cit.*, p. 374-375.

[16] Cf. Petrus Lombardus, *Sent.*, Lib. IV, Dist. VI, cap. V. With regard to marriage, however, he appears to depart somewhat from his teaching concerning the necessity of the intention. "Si autem verbis explicatur quod tamen corde non volunt, si non sit ibi coactio vel dolus, obligatio illa verborum, quibus consentiunt dicentes; Accipio te in virum, et ego te uxorem, matrimonium facit."—*Sent.*, Lib. IV, Dist. XXVII, cap. III.

[17] William of Auxerre (1223) was the first to use the formula that was to express the teaching of the Council of Trent: *"intentio faciendi quod facit Ecclesia."* The quotation is cited by Pourrat, *Theology of the Sacraments*, p. 376, *". . . et ideo requiritur eius intentio qua se subiiciat principali agenti, ut scilicet intendat facere, quod facit Christus et Ecclesia."*—Thomas Aq., *Summa Theol.*, IIIa, q. 64, art. 8, ad 1.

[18] *Summa Theol.*, IIIa, q. 64, art. 8, ad 2.

[19] Cf. Pourrat, *op. cit.*, p. 388.

intention of not conferring the sacrament. In his opinion the exterior intention as it manifested itself in the observance of the baptismal rite was sufficient for the validity of the sacrament. Opposed to this opinion were those who taught that the interior intention was likewise required for validity. This teaching ultimately prevailed, especially after the condemnation of a thesis defended by Francis Farvacques: *"Valet baptismus collatus a ministro, qui omnem ritum externum formamque baptizandi observat, intus vero in corde suo apud se resolvit: Non intendo, quod facit Ecclesia."*[20] The opinion of Catharinus, though not thereby directly condemned, did fall into discredit.[21]

The controversies among the theologians did not serve to give a satisfactory answer whereby the presence of the internal intention of the minister could be determined. To allay all disquietude and anxiety in this regard, the Church herself enunciated the principle that the intention of the minister was to be presumed if evidence was at hand of the proper administration of the matter and form of the sacrament.[22]

ART. III. THE VALIDITY OF NON-CATHOLIC BAPTISMS

191. It is of some significance, indeed, that the principle thus stated was given primarily as an answer to questions related to the validity of non-Catholic Baptisms. The Church at the Council of Trent,[23] in requiring of the minister the intention of doing what the Church does, did not demand for validity that this intention should be expressed or determined,—it re-

---

[20] S. C. S. Off., decr., 7 Dec. 1690, n. 28,—*Fontes*, n. 760.

[21] Cf. Benedictus XIV, *De Synodo Dioec.*, Lib. VII, cap. IV, n. 8.

[22] "In illa vero disquisitione facienda de validitate prioris baptismatis, antequam sub conditionata forma iteretur, debent animarum pastores inquirere praesertim super formam et materiam adhibitam in priore baptismate. Nam relate ad intentionem quae, ex superius expositis, necessaria est ad valorem baptismi, *nisi prudens de ea fuerit dubitatio*, PRAESUMENDA ILLA EST, ut recte observavit Cardinalis Petra: *Si materiam et forman adhibeant, praesumendum est habere intentionem baptizandi, alias non baptizarent; quod etiam satis est ut baptisma collatum a calvinistis sit validum, quamvis ipsi nullam efficaciam Baptismo tribuant.*"—S. C. de Prop. F., instr. (ad Vic. Ap. Siam), 23 Iun. 1830,—*Coll.*, n. 814. Cf. Petra, *Comment. ad Const. Apost.*, Const. II Gregorii XI, nn. 9-10.

[23] Sess. VII, *de sacramentis in genere*, can. 11,—*Denz.*, n. 854.

quired only the general intention of doing what the Church does, what Christ instituted, or what Christians do.[24]

192. Cardinal Bellarmine, whose teaching regarding the required intention for Baptism has on several occasions been quoted with approval by the Church,[25] clearly points out that it is not necessary to intend what the Roman Church does, but that it is sufficient to intend what Christ instituted, or what Christians do. Even the intention to do what the sect does, is sufficient to constitute a general intention of doing what the universal Church does.[26] Nor does the Council of Trent[27] require the intention of doing what the Church *intends*,[28]—it

---

[24] "Ad valorem tamen Sacramenti necessariam non esse eam intentionem quam vocant expressam seu determinatam, sed sufficere intentionem tantum *genericam* nimirum *faciendi quod facit Ecclesia seu faciendi quod Christus instituit vel quod christiani faciunt*, theologi passim docent. 'Ad valorem Sacramenti, ait P. Antoine, *de Sacr. in gen.*, Cap. II, non requiritur expressa, et distincta intentio faciendi Sacramentum, sed sufficit confusa et implicita, qua quis intendat facere id quod facit Ecclesia Christi, aut quod Christus instituit, aut quod vidit per parochum fieri, aut quod christiani faciunt. Constat ex praxi Ecclesiae, quae non rebaptizat eos qui baptizati sunt ab imperitis et rudibus, aut paganis, cum debita materia et forma, licet illi non noverint distincte quid sit Baptismus, aut Sacramentum. Praeterea tunc est intentio faciendi quod facit Ecclesia, quam solam requirunt. Concilium Florentinum et Tridentinum'."—S. C. S. Off., instr. (ad Custodem Terrae Sanctae), 30 Ian. 1833.—*Fontes*, n. 871. Cf. Bellarminus, Lib. I *de Sacram. in genere*, cap. XXVII,—*Op. Omnia*, Tom. III, 413.

[25] Cf. S. C. S. Off., instr. (ad Vic. Ap. Oceaniae Central.), 18 Dec. 1872, —*Fontes*, n. 1024; instr. (ad Ep. Nesquallien.), 24 Ian. 1877,—*Fontes*, n. 1050.

[26] "Petes, quid si quis intendat facere, quod facit Ecclesia aliqua particularis, et falsa, quam ipse putat veram, ut Genevensis, et intendat non facere, quod facit Ecclesia Romana? Respondeo, etiam id sufficere. Nam qui intendit facere, quod facit Ecclesia Genevensis, intendit facere, quod facit Ecclesia universalis. Ideo enim ille intendit facere, quod facit talis Ecclesia, qua putat illam esse membrum Ecclesiae verae universalis; licet fallatur in cognitione verae Ecclesiae. Non autem tollit efficaciam Sacramenti error minsitri circa Ecclesiam, sed defectus intentionis. Atque hinc est quod in Ecclesia Catholica non rebaptizantur baptizati a Genevensibus [but see Corblet, *Histoire du sacrement de Baptême*, I, 350-351.], qui tamen dum baptizant, intendunt facere quod facit Ecclesia Genevensis, et non quod facit Ecclesia Romana."—Lib. I *de Sacram. in genere*, cap. XXVII,—*Op. Omnia*, Tom. III, 413.

[27] Sess. VII, *de baptismo*, can. 4,—Denz., n. 860.

[28] ". . . Concilium enim in toto can. 11 [sess. VII, *de sacram. in genere*,— Denz., n. 854] non nominat finem Sacramenti, neque dicit Concilium, ut illi [Tilmannus et Kemitius] videntur accepisse, oportere ministrum intendere id facere, quod Ecclesia intendit, set quod Ecclesia facit. Porro, quod Ecclesia facit, non finem, sed actionem significat. Denique ex praxi id constat. Nam neque vetus Ecclesia rebaptizabat baptizatos parvulos a Pelagianis, neque nos rebaptizamus baptizatos a Zwinglianis et Calvinistis, et tamen scimus omnes istos baptizare sine intentione veri finis, qui est tollere peccatum

requires for validity only that intention of doing what the Church *does*. Errors, therefore, concerning the nature of Baptism, or of its efficacy, are not incompatible with the intention of doing what the Church *does*.[29] Even the express mention of the minister to the candidate that the rite will have no effect whatever on the soul, does not *per se* vitiate the validity of the intention.[30] The primary concern of the Church is centered upon

originale."—Bellarminus, *loc. cit.* Cf. Benedictus XIV, *De Synodo Dioec.*, Lib. VII, cap. VI. n. 9; S. C. S. Off., instr. (ad Vic. Ap. Oceaniae Central.), 18 Dec. 1872,—*Fontes*, n. 1024; instr. (ad Ep. Nesquallien.), 24 Ian. 1877,—*Fontes*, n. 1050.

[29] "Itaque circa Baptismum a ministris sectae methodistarum administratum refers, tot et tales esse horum haereticorum errores circa necessitatem virtutem et efficaciam eiusmodi sacramenti, ut pro certo retineri debeat eos illum habere tamquam ritum mere indifferentem, quem ideo in praeteritis temporibus penitus omittere consueverunt, et in posterioribus reassumpserunt sola prava voluntate homines infideles, vel etiam fideles fallendi, iisdem scilicet ostendendi falsam eorum religionem a nostra unice vera non differre . . . Etenim novit A. Tua dogma fidei esse Baptismum a quocumque sive schismatico, sive haeretico, sive etiam infideli administratum validum esse habendum, dummodo in eiusdem administratione singula concurrerint, quibus sacramentum perficitur, scilicet debita materia, praescripta forma, et persona ministri cum intentione faciendi quod facit Ecclesia. Hinc consequitur errores peculiares, quos ministrantes sive privatim, sive etiam publice profitentur nihil officere posse validitati baptismi, vel cuiuscumque sacramenti, quia ut loquitur S. Augustinus, sacramenta ubique integra sunt, etiamsi prave intelligantur, et discordiose tractentur (*S. August., de Bapt., lib. 3, cap. 15, N. 20*). Imo, quod praesertim in casu de quo agitur notandum est, peculiares errores ministrantium, per se et propria ratione, neque excludunt illam intentionem, quam minister sacramentorum debet habere, faciendi nempe quod facit Ecclesia . . . Videt igitur A. Tua quomodo in Ecclesia semper traditum inveniatur, errores quos haeretici sive privatim, sive etiam publice profitentur, non esse incompossibiles cum illa intentione, quam sacramentorum ministri de necessitate eorumdem tenentur habere, faciendi nempe quod facit Ecclesia, vel faciendi quod Christus voluit ut fieret; et eosdem errores per se non posse inducere generalem praesumptionem contra validitatem sacramentorum in genere, et Baptismi in specie ita ut ea ipsa sola statui possit practicum principium omnibus casibus applicandum, vi cuius quasi a priori, ut aiunt, baptismus sit iterum conferendus."—S. C. S. Off., instr. (ad Ep. Nesquallien.), 24 Ian. 1877,—*Fontes*, n. 1050. Vide etiam S. C. S. Off., instr. (ad Custodem Terrae Sanctae), 30 Ian. 1833,—*Fontes*, n. 871; instr. (ad Vic. Ap. Oceaniae Central.), 18 Dec. 1872,—*Fontes*, n. 1024; S. C. de Prop. F., instr. (ad Vic. Ap. Siam), 23 Iun. 1830,—*Coll.*, n. 814; instr. (ad Vic. Ap. Pondicher.), 26 Iul. 1845,—*Coll.*, n. 999; Benedictus XIV, *De Synodo Dioec.*, Lib. VII, cap. VI, n. 9.

[30] "Denique A. Tua quartum adiecit classem dubiorum circa baptismum, quae haec fuere: '*In quibusdam locis nonnulli (haeretici) baptizant cum materia et forma debitis, simultanee applicatis, sed expresse monent baptizandos, ne credant baptismum habere ullum effectum in animum: dicunt enim ipsum esse signum mere externum aggregationis illorum sectae. Itaque illi saepe catholicos in derisum vertunt circa eorum fidem de effectibus baptismi, quam vocant quidem superstitiosam. Quaeritur: 1. Utrum baptismus ab illis haereticis administratus sit dubius propter defectum intentionis faciendi quod*

the rite of Baptism, and when proof of its integrity is furnished, the intention is to be presumed. Since the intention is of its nature internal and hidden, the rule established by the Church is the only possible solution of avoiding constant anxieties and scruples.[31]

At first sight, the instance that follows may, perhaps, appear as a contradiction to this rule of the Church, yet on careful analysis it will be found to offer even further confirmation.

193. A synod held in 1844 in the vicariate of Pondicheri (in India) enacted the following statute: "*Iuxta usum generatim exceptum, omnes pueri qui a pseudo-ministris protestantibus, quidquid de istorum dotibus et opinionibus praedicetur, baptizati sunt, sub conditione rebaptizandi sunt. Hoc ita statuitur, ex eo quod merito et multis dubitatur de fidei capitibus et praxi diversarum sectarum, quae ex reformatione prodierunt.*"[32] The instruction of the Congregation of the Propaganda on turning to this statute of the synod approved it substantially but it did take exception on one score:

Baptizatos porro ab hodiernis haereticis, denuo a catholicis baptizari, non est imprudens nec insuetum, propter haereticorum incertam et suspectam praxim; NON TAMEN EO NOMINE QUOD DUBITETUR DE FIDEI BAPTIZANTIUM CAPITIBUS. Etenim si certo constaret praedictos haereticos legitimam adhibuisse formam, materiam atque

---

voluit Christus, si expresse declaratum fuerit a ministro, antequam baptizet, baptismum nullum habere effectum in animum. 2. Utrum dubius sit baptismus sic collatus, si praedicta declaratio non expresse facta fuerit immediate, antequam baptismus conferretur, sed illa saepe pronunciata fuerit a ministro, et illa doctrina aperte praedicetur in illa secta' . . . Itaque ad praefata dubia S. C. respondit: '*Ad primum, Negative: quia, non obstante errore quoad effectus baptismi, non excluditur intentio faciendi quod facit Ecclesia* . . . *Ad secundum, Provisum in primo*'."—S. C. S. Off., instr. (ad Vic. Ap. Oceaniae Central.), 18 Dec. 1872,—*Fontes*, n. 1024.

[31] "Hae autem cautelae ac diligentiae omnes in ferendo iudicio de baptismo iam collato, de cuius validitate dubitatur, ut adhibeantur, tum Sacramenti eiusdem dignitas et sanctitas, tum fidelium utilitas, et animarum quies, atque tranquillitas cui in primis consulendum est, omnio suadent. Quandoquidem si nimia, seu imprudenti quadam facilitate, dubia quae circa huius Sacramenti validitatem in dies nascuntur excipiantur, homines timidi et scrupulosi de suscepti baptismi valore semper dubitabunt, seque iterum baptizari requirent. Horum exemplum alii atque alii imitabuntur, ideoque multa eaque gravia in religionem orirentur incommoda et scandala, quae omnino evitari debent."— S. C. S. Off., instr. (ad Custodem Terrae Sanctae), 30 Ian. 1833,—*Fontes*, n. 871.

[32] Feije, *De Imped. et Dispens.*, n. 465.

intentionem, rebaptizare prorsus non liceret, ut omnes norunt, neque Synodi (Pondicheriensis) Patres certe ignoraverunt, qui illis decreti sui verbis aliud fortasse designant, quam hodiernos haereticos, socinianos, methodistas, quakeros, et forte alios, qui cum Baptismi necessitatem negant, ritum fere contemnunt, idcirco baptizare recte nullo modo creduntur.[33]

194. The line of reasoning and the points emphasized in the answer are deserving of close attention. Though the Congregation did not disapprove of the practice of baptizing conditionally those baptized by the heretics of that time, it did call attention to an error in the statute. The synod had justified its enactment on the basis of two leading reasons: *"ex eo quod merito et multis rationibus dubitatur de fidei capitibus* ET *praxi diversarum sectarum."* The Congregation rejected the first, but admitted the second, namely, the suspected practice. Again, when the Congregation named the Socinians, the Methodists, and the Quakers as sects whose Baptisms could be suspected, it admitted the suspicion on the ground that these sects, in denying the necessity of Baptism, usually rejected the rite,— *"idcirco baptizare recte nullo modo creduntur."*[34] The fundamental reason for suspicion alleged by the Congregation is, therefore, the suspected practice, the suspected rejection of the rite.

195. What, precisely, is meant by the clause *"cum Baptismi necessitatem negant"*? It cannot refer to a doctrinal error regarding the necessity of Baptism for salvation, nor to an error regarding the nature and efficacy of the sacrament. The Holy

---

[33] Instr. S. C. de Prop. F., (ad Vic. Ap. Pondicher.), 26 Iul. 1845,—
Coll., n. 999.

[34] Pope Benedict XIV (*De Synodo Dioec.*, Lib. VII, cap. VI, n. 8) also mentions an instance of a just suspicion *based on the corruption of the rite*: "Rationabiliter porro Patribus Concilii Provincialis Mechliniensis anni 1606, incertum saltem, et dubium visum est Baptisma collatum ab haereticis Hollandiae, finitimarumque regionum, apud quos mos invaluerat, ut uno aquam fundente, alter Sacramenti formam pronunciaret; ac propterea iuste illud iterandum decrevere . . . cuius quidem Concilii sanctionem tuto sectari possunt et debent aliarum Ecclesiarum Praesules, a quibus sint Ecclesiae reconciliandi haeretici, iis in locis baptizati, ubi eumdem erroneum Baptismi ritum plerumque adhiberi, non ex incerto rumore, sed ex fide dignis testimoniis acceperint, atque ideo merito suscipientur . . ." The complete quotation is cited also in S. C. de Prop. F., instr. (ad Vic. Ap. Siam), 23 Iun. 1830,— Coll., n. 814. Vide etiam S. C. de Sacram., 17 Nov. 1916,—*AAS*, VII (1916), 478-480.

See has constantly insisted that doctrinal errors do not constitute a ground of presuming a Baptism as doubtful or invalid.
The clause seems to refer rather to the rejection by certain sects
of the rite of Baptism.[35] Thus the Socinians and the Quakers
have always repudiated Baptism and do not administer it.[36]

196. With regard to the Methodists, the Bishop of Nesqually (Seattle) urged that the very fact of a *change* from the
former practice did not remove the doubt: *"ut pro certo retineri
debeat eos illum habere tamquam ritum mere indifferentem,
quem ideo in praeteritis temporibus penitus omittere consueverunt, et in posterioribus reassumpserunt sola prava voluntate
homines infideles, vel etiam fideles fallendi, iisdem scilicet ostendendi falsam eorum religionem a nostra unice vera non differre."*[37] When the Holy See in the instruction of July 26, 1845,
referred to the Baptisms of Methodists, it admitted the pre-
sumptive suspicion of a rejected rite or a suspected practice because at that time the Methodists *repudiated* Baptism. But in
the instruction sent to the Bishop of Nesqually, the Holy See
admitted no such presumption of suspicion for *de facto* they
were again administering Baptism. Even the additional abuses

---

[35] The presumption resting on the repudiation of Baptism by a sect in
the instruction of July 26, 1845 must not be confused with the presumption
in the decision of August 1, 1883 ([Savannah], ad II, *"Affirmative quoad
primum,"*—Fontes, n. 1083). In the instruction of July 26, 1845, the
presumption is that of doubtful Baptism on the supposition that some evidence exists for a Baptism having been conferred in a sect that rejects the
rite iteslf. It is doubtful because of the suspected practice or rejected rite.
The decision of August 1, 1883; *"Si pars vel partes acatholicae parentes
habuerint ad sectam pertinentes quae Baptismum respuit, hic non est prae-
sumendus"*, supposes the absence of any evidence for the fact of Baptism
and admits the presumption of its absence in accordance with the actual
and avowed policy of the sect. The difference of the evidence actually in pos-
session of the one making the investigation, gives rise to the difference in
the presumptions.

[36] *"Qua super re A. Tua ante oculos habeat regulam generalem iam
saepe traditam ab hac S. C. et praesertim in fer. IV, die 10 Martii 1824,
quam in pluribus aliis casibus similibus confirmavit, quaeque est tenoris se-
quentis: 'Quoad venientes a sectis, ex. gr. quakerorum, quas notum est vel
baptisma minime ministrare, vel. invalide conferre, ipsos, dum in sinu Ecclesiae recipiuntur, solemniter baptizandos esse . . ."*—S. C. S. Off., instr.
(ad Ep. Nesquallien.), 24 Ian. 1877,—*Fontes*, n. 1050. Cf. Perrone, *De
Matr.*, Tom. II, cap. VII, art. 2. Perrone includes also the Mennonites and
Swedenborgians.

[37] *Loc. cit.*

mentioned by the Bishop of Nesqually[38] were not admitted as existing presumptively, but required proof.[39]

197. Only those Baptisms, therefore, which are conferred in those sects that repudiate Baptism are under an initial presumption of doubt. On the other hand, those sects which prescribe Baptism must first be examined with regard to their ritual before forming any presumption. If the ritual prescribes a valid matter and form, the initial presumption will be for the validity of the Baptism. If the rite prescribed is of doubtful validity or of manifest invalidity, the initial presumption will bear the corresponding character of doubt or of invalidity.

198. The term "initial presumption" is used advisedly, for the Church does not permit the investigation to stop with a presumption regarding a sect. Each individual case must be examined to determine the value of the initial presumption. The norm of investigation prescribed by the Holy Office in the instruction sent to the Bishop of Nesqually centered on two points: "1. *Utrum ritus administrandi sacramentum Baptismi, ab ista secta in istis regionibus retentus, aliquid contineat quod illius nullitatem inducere valeat. 2. Utrum talis sectae ministri de facto sese conforment praescriptionibus in propria eorum secta sancitis.*" The ritual of the sect together with the actual administration of the minister represents the extent of the investigation, though an inquiry should also concern the intention of the minister:[40] The Holy See has constantly insisted that each individual case must be examined.[41]

---

[38] See No. 192, note 29.

[39] ". . . probe intelliges quod si in hac materia possibilis foret quaedam generalis praesumptio in principium practicum convertenda, haec non quidem ex defectibus et abusibus ministrorum differentium sectarum esset derivanda, sed praesertim ex indole, natura et consuetudine actuali earumdem sectarum." —S. C. S. Off., instr. (ad Ep. Nesquallien.), 24 Ian. 1877,—*Fontes*, n. 1050.

[40] S. C. S. Off. (Bulgariae), 5 Iul. 1853,—*Fontes*, n. 925. An investigation as to the intention of the minister may disclose a lack of the necessary intention or a positive indication of its doubtful validity. If no such evidence is brought to light, the intention of doing what the Church does, or what Christ instituted is presumed to exist provided that the required matter and form of the sacrament has been adhered to.

[41] Cf. S. C. S. Off. (Bulgariae), 5 Iul. 1853,—*Fontes*, n. 925; litt. (ad Ep. Harlemen.), 6 Apr. 1859,—*Fontes*, n. 950; instr. (ad Ep. Nesquallien.), 24 Ian. 1877,—*Fontes*, n. 1050; 20 Nov. 1878,—*Fontes*, n. 1058: 7 Iul. 1880, ad 6,—Gasparri, *De Matr.*, n. 691; (ad Vic. Ap. Iaponiae

199. As a summary of the discussion of non-Catholic Baptisms, the following conclusions seem to be fully warranted. A Baptism bearing the initial presumption of validity must continue to be regarded as valid until a *positive* reason is found for regarding it as doubtful or invalid. If nothing positive is found to upset this presumption, the intention of doing what the Church does must be presumed. An initial presumption of doubt concerning a Baptism retains its character of doubt until a positive reason demands that it cede to the presumption of certain validity or invalidity. A Baptism bearing the initial presumption of invalidity cedes to the presumption of doubt or validity only on the ground of positive reasons.[42] Those indivi-

Merid.), 4 Feb. 1891,—*Fontes*, n. 1130; 2 Aug. 1901,—*ASS*, XXXIV (1901-1902), 640; S. C. de Prop. F., instr. 17 Apr. 1777,—*Coll.*, n. 522; instr. (ad Vic. Ap. Myssur.), 31 Dec. 1851,—*Coll.*, n. 1069. The Church demands a thorough investigation also of the Baptisms of Catholics which have been conferred in extraordinary circumstances by others than her ordained ministers, or when a prudent doubt arises concerning the very fact of its administration. Cf. S. C. Conc. (Ripana), 12 Dec. 1733,—*Thes.*, VI, 178-180; (Tarvisina Baptismi), 28 Apr. 1736,—*Thes.*, VII, 210-213; 4 Maii 1737,—*Thes.*, VIII, 54-56; (Sutrina Baptismi), 12 Iul. 1794,—*Thes.*, LXIII, 165-171; (Brixien. Dubia Baptismi, et Matrimonii), 27 Aug. 1796,—*Thes.*, LXV, 209-220; 17 Dec. 1796,—*Thes.*, LXV, 296-297; (Brixien. Baptismi), 11 Feb. 1797,—*Thes.*, LXVI, 26-28; 16 Mart. 1897,—*Coll.*, n. 1962.

[42] It is not the purpose of this study to determine the status of individual sects of today regarding the question of Baptism. For the benefit of the reader a few decisions relative to particular sects are cited. These decisions are of value *primarily* as confirmations and reiterations of principles. They offer no guarantee that the sects in question have remained the same with regard to their rituals or with regard to their rejection or requirement of Baptism. The investigation of the ritual of the sect of a locality must be made with reference to the one *in use at the time of the Baptism*. The following decrees may be consulted: ANGLICANS—S. C. S. Off., 20 Iul. 1840,—*NRT*, XV (1883), 401-402; (Bombaay), 21 Feb. 1883,—*Fontes*, n. 1078; CALVINISTS—S. C. de Prop. F., instr. (ad Vic. Ap. Siam), 23 Iun. 1830, —*Coll.*, n. 814; S. C. S. Off., instr. (ad Custodem Terrae Sanctae), 30 Ian. 1833,—*Fontes*, n. 871; instr. (ad Vic. Ap. Oceaniae Central.), 18 Dec. 1872,—*Fontes*, n. 1024; instr. (ad Ep. Nesquallien.), 24 Ian. 1877,—*Fontes*, n. 1050. LUTHERANS—S. C. S. Off. (Bulgariae), 5 Iul. 1853,—*Fontes*, n. 925. METHODISTS—S. C. de Prop. F., instr. (ad Vic. Ap. Pondicher.), 26 Iul. 1845,—*Coll.*, n. 999; S. C. S. Off., instr. (ad Vic. Ap. Oceaniae Central.), 18 Dec. 1872,—*Fontes*, n. 1024; instr. (ad Ep. Nesquallien.), 24 Ian. 1877,—*Fontes*, n. 1050. QUAKERS—S. C. de Prop. F., instr. (ad Vic. Ap. Pondicher.), 26 Iul. 1845,—*Coll.*, n. 999; S. C. S. Off., instr. (ad Ep. Nesquallien.), 24 Ian. 1877,—*Fontes*, n. 1050. SOCINIANS— S. C. de Prop. F., instr. (ad Vic. Ap. Pondicher.), 26 Iul. 1845,—*Coll.*, n. 999. UNITARIANS—S. C. S. Off. (Bulgariae), 5 Iul. 1853,—*Fontes*, n. 925. ZWINGLIANS—S. C. S. Off., instr. (ad Vic. Ap. Oceaniae Central.), 18 Dec. 1872,—*Fontes*, n. 1024; instr. (ad Ep. Nesquallien.), 24 Ian. 1877,—*Fontes*, n. 1050.

dual cases that bear some evidence for the fact of Baptism, but which for various reasons cannot be examined in the light of an initial presumption, must be judged according to the evidence afforded by the individual investigation. As long as evidence is wanting to produce moral certainty either of the fact of its administration, or of the use of a valid rite, this lack of evidence forms a positive reason for regarding the Baptism as doubtful.

200. Baptisms of uncertain validity must be investigated, whether it be with reference to the existence of Baptism as it is required by the divine law for salvation, or with reference to the necessity of a valid Baptism required by the ecclesiastical law for the validity of a sacramental marriage. Yet the demands of the divine law and of the law of the Church, especially with reference to doubtful Baptism, will not impose the same norms of procedure consequent upon the investigation. A doubtful Baptism that cannot be proved to be certainly invalid will, *per se,* suffice for marriage, but no such norm is permissable in dealing with the matter of salvation. Here the safer course *must* be followed by the administration of conditional Baptism.[43]

ART. IV. PRE-CODE LEGISLATION WITH REFERENCE TO DOUBTFUL BAPTISM IN CONTRACTED MARRIAGES

201. In the law existing before the Code, a doubtful Baptism was presumed valid *in ordine ad validitatem matrimonii.* The principles in force were enunciated in a decision of the Holy Office of November 17, 1830[44]:

---

[43] "Duo alia dubia versantur circa baptizatos, sive eorum baptismus sit validus, sive de eius valore iuste dubitaretur, et circa hos S. Sanctitas iussit imprimis Vicario Apostolico communicari Instructionem Emorum datam fer. IV, 17 Nov. 1830 [*Fontes,* n. 869], prout S. C. de facto transmittit. *Advertendum est tamen, quamvis baptismus in casibus in decreto expressis, validus censendus sit in ordine ad matrimonium, tamen partem conversam, de cuius baptismi valore prudenter dubitaretur, rebaptizandum fore sub conditione quia Baptismus est Sacramentum necessitatis.*"—S. C. S. Off., instr. (ad Vic. Ap. Oceaniae), 6 Apr. 1843,—*Fontes,* n. 894.

[44] *Fontes,* n. 869. Later decisions constantly referred to this decree as best expressive of the law in force. Cf. S. C. S. Off., 20 Dec. 1837,—*Acta et Decreta Conc. Balt. II* (1866), Appendix, n. XVI; 20 Iul 1840,—*NRT,* XV (1883), 401-402; 29 Apr. 1842, ad 2,—*Fontes,* n. 888; instr. (ad Vic. Ap. Oceaniae), 6 Apr. 1843,—*Fontes,* n. 894; 5 Feb. 1851,—Feije, *De Imped. et Dispens.,* n. 467; 7 Mart. 1862,—*NRT,* XXIV (1892), 496-

An degentes in iis protestantium locis, ubi baptisma dubium est, tamquam infideles habendi sint, ita ut inter catholicos et eos disparitatis cultus impedimentum dirimens adesse censeatur.

R. 1.   Quoad haereticos quorum sectae ritualia praescribunt collationem Baptismi absque necessario usu materiae et formae essentialis, debet examinari casus particularis.   2. Quoad alios qui iuxta eorum rituale baptizant valide, validum censendum est Baptisma. Quod si dubium persistat, etiam in primo casu, censendum est validum Baptisma in ordine ad validitatem matrimonii.   3. Si autem certo cognoscatur nullum baptisma ex consuetudine actuali illius sectae, nullum est matrimonium.

The practical application of the principles will be sufficiently demonstrated by a brief discussion of the possible cases that could arise.

202. Since, in the law before the Code, the impediment of Disparity of Cult affected all the baptized (without distinction as to Catholic and non-Catholic), it will be evident that, on the score of this impediment, marriages of two baptized persons or of two unbaptized persons, were to be regarded as valid. Those marriages contracted between the certainly baptized and the certainly unbaptized were invalid on the ground of Disparity of Cult.[45] The rule that doubtful Baptism was to be presumed valid with reference to the validity of a marriage applied to the marriages of the doubtfully baptized with the unbaptized. Such marriages were regarded as invalid on the ground of Disparity of Cult.[46] In conformity with this prin-

---

497; instr. (ad Ep. Nesquallien.), 24 Ian. 1877,—*Fontes*, n. 1050; 3 Apr. 1878,—Aichner, *Compend. Juris* Eccles., § 173, not. 4; 18 Sept. 1890,—*NRT*, XXIII (1891), 522-523; 3 Apr. 1893,—Blat, *Comment.*, Vol. III, P. I, n. 467.

[45] The certainty predicated of the validity or invalidity of Baptism is to be understood in the sense of *moral* certainty derived either from direct proof, or through the legitimate use of presumptions.

[46] S. C. S. Off., 20 Iul. 1840,—*NRT*, XV (1883), 401-402; 3 Apr. 1878,—Aichner, *Compend. Juris* Eccles., § 173, not. 4; 7 Iul. 1880,—Gasparri, *De Matr.*, n. 691; (ad Vic. Ap. Iaponiae Merid.), 4 Feb. 1891, —*Fontes*, n. 1130. Arendt is of the opinion that the application of the principle did not rest on a mere *praesumptio iuris humani*, otherwise it would have been in flagrant opposition to the favor constantly extended to the validity of a marriage,—"Necessario igitur requirenda aliunde est ratio qua fundaretur illa praxis . . . Adverteram, nimirum, factum suscepti baptismi non fundare *per impressum characterem*, certam subiectionem legibus Ecclesiae, nisi, ut docet etiam S. Thomas, *in quantum hic per signum sensi-*

ciple of regarding doubtful Baptism[47] as valid in the matter of determining the validity of a marriage, it followed that the marriages of those doubtfully baptized with the certainly baptized or with the doubtfully baptized, were valid.

203. Cardinal Gasparri[48] went even further in his conclusions, defending the opinion that marriages which had been contracted between two certainly or doubtfully baptized persons would continue to remain valid even if it were later discovered that one of the parties was not baptized.[49] The principal grounds

---

bile innotescit. Iamvero Christus D., instituendo sacramenta quae consistant in actione ministri humana cum *interna* intentione debite posita, . . . contentus fuit illa certitudine morali, aut magna coniecturali probabilitate quae sufficit in ordinario consortio humano, ut tuto firmare nostram praxim possimus. Haec itaque, utut in se praesumptiva et probabilis tantum, non ex sola praesumptione iuris humani, sed ex praesumptione iuris de iure *divino* quoties in signo sacramentali exterius adest iuxta communiter contigentia, debet sufficere ad fundanda *certam* subiectionis obligationem."—*Jus Pont.*, V (1925), 136. Vide etiam *NRT*, LI (1924), 385-399; Lehmkuhl, *Theol. Mor.*, II, n. 322.

[47] The doubt could be one of law or fact: *"Utrum sive dubium sit iuris sive facti* (scilicet de baptismo recepto) *conclusiones debeant esse eaedem respectu matrimonium?* Resp.: *praevio diligenti examine in singulis casibus, et persistente adhuc dubio sive iuris, sive facti, eaedem debent conclusiones respectu matrimonium."*—S. C. S. Off., 7 Iul. 1880, ad 6,—Gasparri, *De Matr.*, n. 691. The explanatory clause *"scilicet de baptismo recepto"* appears to be an insertion made by Gasparri,—at least it is not clear that it existed in the *dubium* proposed. The same insertion in parentheses is given by Wernz, *Ius Decret.*, IV, n. 508, not. 33. The Holy See seems to have admitted the principle that a doubtful Baptism was to be presumed valid *"in ordine ad validitatem matrimonii"* only in those cases where moral certainty existed as to the administration of the rite of Baptism,—"denique si post diligens et accuratum examen dubium de valide *suscepto baptismate* tolli nequeat, et constet *de facto suscepti baptismatis,* huiusmodi validum censendum esse in ordine ad validitatem matrimonii iuxta decretum d. 17 Nov. 1830."—S. C. S. Off., 3 Apr. 1878,—Aichner, *op. cit.*, § 173, not. 4. Vide etiam S. C. S. Off., 3 Apr. 1893,—Blat, *op. cit.*, Vol. III, P. I, n. 467. Moreover, the instruction sent by the Holy Office to the Bishop of Savannah (1 Aug. 1883, ad secundum partem, n. 5,—*Fontes*, n. 1083) did not admit the application of the principle in the case of an insoluble *dubium facti* of the administration of Baptism, but demanded that such cases with all their circumstances be sent to the Holy See. It appears, therefore, that the *dubium facti* mentioned in the decision of July 7, 1880 is not to be interpreted by what appears to be merely an explanatory note (*"scilicet de baptismo recepto"*) inserted by Gasparri and Wernz, but is to be construed as concerning a *dubium facti* arising on some point in the administration of the rite. Doubts of this kind might arise on several grounds: e. g., with regard to the moral unity of the matter and form, or upon the external ministerial actions of the minister in reference to the *ablutio.*

[48] *De Matr.*, n. 689-691.

[49] The opinion was defended likewise by Konings-Putzer (*Comment. in Facult.*, p. 391-392) though in another instance he admits an objection

of his argument for the limitation of the impediment may be summarized as follows: 1) The custom introducing the impediment did not contemplate such cases. 2) In reference to a number of cases of doubtful Baptism, the Holy See replied that the Baptism was to be administered conditionally *"secreto, et sine praeiudicio validitatis matrimonii."*[50]

Ex his clarum est matrimonium in casu valere non solum prae-sumptione fori externi, quatenus in dubio praesumitur baptismus rite datus, ideoque validum matrimonium, sed etiam in foro interno, licet reapse baptismus datus non sit, aut nulliter datus; secus S. C. respon-dere non potuisset baptismum esse conferendum sub conditione et se-creto *sine praeiudicio validitatis matrimonii*, sed potius his casibus pro-videndum foret per baptismi collationem sub conditione, et simul per consensus renovationem ad cautelam aut per sanationem in radice. Exinde sequitur matrimonium valere, etsi post matrimonium certitudo acquiratur de baptismi defectu in alterutra parte, valere, inquam, usque ab initio ita ut, baptismo absolute collato, consensus renovari non debeat.[51]

3) The Holy See seemed to appear altogether unwilling to grant the dispensation *"mixtae religionis et ad cautelam dispa-ritatis cultus."*

204. With regard to the argument drawn from the his-torical foundation of the impediment, it may be said that the custom introducing the impediment in the twelfth century (which Cardinal Gasparri,[52] in referring to the opinion of Car-dinal Bellarmine, appears to accept as a probable date) did not, in all likelihood, contemplate such a case. The custom at this period represented, more or less, a popular reaction to all things alien to the Faith,—the diriment impediment affecting even the marriages of Catholics with heretics.[53] Yet, as early as the thir-

---

to it (*op. cit.*, p. 394). Wernz (*Ius Decret.*, IV, n. 507, not. 28) and Vlaming (*Prael. Iuris Matr.*, n. 291, not. 3) refer to Santi-Leitner as sub-scribing to Gasparri's opinion.

[50] Cf. S. C. Conc. (Tarvisina Baptismi), 4 Maii 1737,—*Thes.*, VIII. 54-55.

[51] Gasparri, *De Matr.*, n. 687. He also draws arguments from further de-cisions given by the Holy See with regard to doubtful Baptism: S. C. S. Off., 9 Sept. 1868 (n.688); 17 Nov. 1830 (n. 689); 5 Feb. 1851; 20 Iul. 1840 (n. 690).

[52] *Op. cit.*, n. 695.

[53] See No. 66, note 6.

teenth century, the impediment received a new foundation of a theological and canonical principle, and it is not altogether evident that cases involving the logical consequences of the principle were thereby excepted on the ground that the particular case in question was not mentioned explicitly. In like manner it might be said that ignorance of the existence of the impediment in a particular case was scarcely contemplated by the custom introducing the impediment. It does not follow, however, that the ambit of the impediment was thereby restricted. Apparently, therefore, the argument based on the historical foundation of the impediment can scarcely be ventured without the challenge of a serious doubt.

205. The prescription to administer Baptism "conditionally" without prejudice to the validity of the marriage does not of itself warrant the conclusion that even if the Baptism were to be administered "absolutely", the marriage would have to be regarded as valid *ab initio*.[54] In like manner, the argument based on the fact that the Congregation did not prescribe a conditional renewal of consent nor grant a *sanatio in radice*, seems to assume the identity of the norms of procedure with reference to Baptism as it is necessary for salvation, and as it is necessary for a valid sacramental marriage.[55]

206. On the other hand, a decision of the Holy Office of April 29, 1842 offers a striking confirmation of the probability of Cardinal Gasparri's opinion:

---

[54] "Nam ad declarandam *nullitatem* matrimonii requiritur *certa* probatio; hinc cum in suppositione facta dubius *maneat* baptismus unius coniugis, actio contra valorem matrimonii in possessione constituti necessario repellenda est per sententiam: *Non constare de nullitate matrimonii.* Quae sententia non aequivalet alteri: Certo constare de valore matrimonii ab initio."—Wernz. *Ius Decret.*, IV, n. 507, not. 28. Cf. Petrovits, *New Church Law on Matrimony*, n. 234.

[55] The Holy See has made a clear distinction regarding the two norms of procedure in the case of *doubtful* Baptism. See No. 200, note 43. The same answer, namely, to baptize *conditionally* without prejudice to the marriage could be given for a marriage of two Catholics contracted after the Code if a positive doubt would arise concerning the validity of the Baptism of one party. Nor would there be any necessity of renewing consent conditionally, nor of petitioning for a *sanatio in radice ad cautelam*. But it does not follow that the prescription to administer Baptism *absolutely* would likewise be without prejudice to the marriage. In fact this would be quite at variance with canon 1070, § 2.

1.   Utrum possessio publica nominis christiani, publicaque opinio qua quis creditur christianus sive quia ortum habuit ex parentibus christianis, sive quia constanter christianae alicui communioni fuit annumeratus, christianumque se profitetur, sufficiat ad validitatem matrimonii in casu, *in quo dictus homo revera non fuisset, aut invalide fuisset baptizatus*, et matrimonium iniisset cum baptizata, non petita dispensatione disparitatis cultus: Si praedictum matrimonium declaretur invalidum propter disparitatem cultus.

Resp.: Ad 1.   Iuxta exposita, Negative.[56]

While, indeed, manifest difficulties arise in applying the opinion to practice,[57] Scherer's dismissal[58] of the opinion, as being wholly improbable, is scarcely justified.[59]

207. The argument based on the unwillingness of the Church to grant the dispensation from Mixed Religion together with the dispensation *ad cautelam* for Disparity of Cult again appears to add further cogency to the opinion. The Holy Office, when asked on several occasions with regard to this kind of dispensation, replied in each case that the presumptions enunciated in the decree of November 17, 1830[60] were to be fol-

---

[56] *Fontes*, n. 888. Primarily, the answer seems to be given to the last sentence of the *dubium* proposed. Whether every phase of the *status quaestionis* preceding the ultimate question is contained in the answer is not so certain.

[57] "Ceterum, quamvis theoria haec—si solido in iure inniteretur fundamento—sua haberet commoda, ea tamen, pluribus laborare incommodis aeque certum est. Sane, diceturne Ecclesiam, in omni casu dubii, supplere seu removere impedimentum, etiam si nulla facta fuerit inquisitio praevia, vel ea valde negligenter fuerit peracta? Quodsi, id negetur, et retineatur Ecclesiam tunc tantum supplere cum seria adhibita fuerit inquisitio, et aeque libratis argumentis et praesumptionibus pro et contra baptismum, quis, tandem, determinabit in concreto utrum dispensasse censenda sit Ecclesia, unde tamen pendet valor ipsius matrimonii?"—De Becker, *De Spons. et Matr.*, p. 239.

[58] *Handb. des Kirchenrechtes*, II, p. 374, not. 12.

[59] No decisive argument can be drawn from the decision of the Congregation of the Sacraments given on November 17, 1916. Cf. *AAS*, VIII (1916), 478-480. The brief summary of the reason for presenting the case ("*Ad tribunal ecclesiasticum huius Dioeceseos inductus est quidam casus circa validitatem matrimonii, quae validitas dependet a validitate baptismatis*") offers no certain parallel to the cases posited by Cardinal Gasparri, though it may cast a grave shadow of doubt upon the Cardinal's opinion. Does it refer to a marriage contracted (*in facie Ecclesiae*) by two supposedly baptized Catholics, or to a marriage (*extra faciem Ecclesiae*) of one supposedly baptized to an unbaptized person? The decision as to the invalidity of the Baptism throws no light on the nature of the marriage, nor as to the decision that was pending in the diocesan tribunal.

[60] See No. 201.

lowed.[61] Though a letter of Cardinal Ledochowski to the Bishop of Helena (May, 11, 1900) seems to suggest the possibility of exceptions,[62] and though De Becker[63] and De Smet[64] advised the asking of the dispensation *"ad cautelam"* in those cases where the doubt of the validity of the Baptism persevered, there is more than ordinary significance in the fact that no author consulted in the preparation of this study has pointed to a single instance of such a dispensation having been granted directly by the *Holy See* before the Code.[65]

208. Lehmkuhl sought to solve the difficulty by venturing the opinion that the Church in granting the dispensation from Mixed Religion implicitly granted a dispensation from Disparity of Cult.[66] The opinion was manifestly at variance with a decision of the Holy Office to which Lehmkuhl does not refer:

2. Utrum intendat Sancta Sedes dispensare etiam super impedimento disparitatis cultus quando dispensat partem catholicam ad contrahendum cum parte acatholica. Si intendat S. Sedes talem dispensationem concedere, quae validitati matrimonii sufficiat, quando dispensat super mixtae religionis impedimento, ita ut valeat matrimonium partis catholicae cum parte haeretica aut schismatica, etiamsi haec forte non fuerit baptizata.

3. Utrum Ordinarius dispensando virtute Indulti Apostolici super impedimento mixtae religionis, talem dispensationem concedat quae sufficiat ad validitatem matrimonii, etiamsi forte non fuerit, aut rite non fuerit baptizata pars acatholica.

Resp.: Ad 2. Negative; Sedes enim Apostolica super impedimento disparitatis cultus nonnisi expressa, et gravissima de causa dis-

---

[61] Cf. S. C. S. Off., 7 Mart. 1862,—*NRT*, XXIV (1892), 496-497; 3 Aug. 1873,—*NRT*, XV (1883), 399-400; 18 Sept. 1890,—*NRT*, XXIII (1891), 522-523.

[62] "Quoad alterum dubium, an, scilicet, parochus in dubio an adsit in aliquo casu matrimoniali impedimentum disparitatis cultus debeat, ad cautelam, dispensationem petere, S. haec Congregatio respondet *in singulis casibus ad ipsam recurrendum esse, exponendo particularem casum de quo agitur."* —De Becker, *De Spons. et Matr.*, p. 240.

[63] *Op. cit.*, p. 240-241.

[64] *De Spons. et Matr.*, (ed. 1909), n. 290.

[65] De Becker (*loc. cit.*), however, is sponsor for the statement that such dispensations were frequently granted by Diocesan Curiae. The Curial records of at least some American dioceses will confirm this.

[66] *Theol. Mor.*, II, n. 752. Vide etiam Göpfert, *Moraltheologie*, III, n. 243.

pensat. In reliquis detur decretum feriae IV, 17 Nov. 1830 super precibus R. P. D. Episcopi Anicien.

Ad 3.   Provisum in secundo.[67]

Lehmkuhl's opinion appears, therefore, to enjoy no further probability.[68]

209. On the other hand, the very decision which apparently removes the probability of Lehmkuhl's opinion is but a continuation of the decree cited to demonstrate the probability of Cardinal Gasparri's opinion.[69] The line of demarcation is not as clear as it may appear at first sight. Moreover, the answer favoring Cardinal Gasparri's opinion was given as a negation to the *dubium* as it was proposed (*"iuxta exposita"*),—at least the answer is scarcely stated in the form of the general principle proposed by Cardinal Gasparri. Again, the answer to the second part of the second *dubium* by its reference to the decree of November 17, 1830, casts some difficulties in the way of the absolute acceptance of the opinion. The decree of 1830 appears to serve for both contemplated and contracted marriages.

210. Yet the probability of Cardinal Gasparri's opinion is not wholly destroyed and due cognizance should be taken of it. It has no value, however, in determining the validity of marriages contracted after the Code.[70] For the purpose of determining the validity of Pre-Code marriages, an account of the opinion need be taken only with regard to the marriages of two supposedly baptized Catholics. The opinion need not be heeded with reference to the marriages of two non-Catholics for their Baptisms were not submitted to the Church's investigation before marriage to establish the presumption of validity. If the marriage *post contractum* is thereupon brought to the attention

---

[67] S. C. S. Off., 29 Apr. 1842,—*Fontes*, n. 888.

[68] Cf. Cappello, *De Sacram.*, III, n. 423; Petrovits, *New Church Law on Matrimony*, n. 241; De Smet, *De Spons. et Matr.*, p. 516, not. 4; Ayrinhac, *Marriage Legislation*, p. 151; Durieux,*The Busy Pastor's Book on Matrimony*, p. 95, note 124; Vlaming, *Prael. Iuris Matr.*, n. 296. Pighi's opinion (*De Matr.*, n. 50): "Baptismus enim dubius relate ad matrimonium praesumitur collatus, et collatus valide; quod si objective collatus valide non fuerit, *Ecclesia pro matrimonio dispensationem supplere censetur"*, seems to lack both intrinsic and extrinsic probability, especially after the Code. See infra No. 251, note 85.

[69] See No. 206.

[70] Cf. canon 1070, § 2.

of the Church, the result of this investigation must determine the validity of the marriage *ab initio*.[71] On the basis of the decision of April 29, 1842, the marriage of a Catholic to an unbaptized non-Catholic, contracted with but a dispensation from the impediment of Mixed Religion, would apparently be invalid *ab initio*.[72] But in the event of a marriage (*before the Code*) of two supposedly baptized Catholics, if proof is furnished that one of the parties was not baptized, a declaration of nullity should not be given without consulting the Holy Office.[73]

ART. V. DOUBTFUL BAPTISM IN MARRIAGES CONTRACTED AFTER THE CODE

211. The general principle that doubtful Baptism is presumed to be valid *"in ordine ad validitatem matrimonii"* is in force also after the Code but it is conditioned by the principle *"in dubio standum est pro valore matrimonii."* With reference to the impediment of Disparity of Cult, the principle of the legislation in the Code is stated as follows:

CANON 1070, § 2

Si pars tempore contracti matrimonii tanquam baptizata communiter habebatur aut eius baptismus erat dubius, standum est, ad normam can. 1014, pro valore matrimonii, donec certo probetur alteram partem baptizatam esse, alteram vero non baptizatam.

§ I. RESTRICTED REFERENCE OF CANON 1070, § 2

212. The prescriptions of canon 1070, § 2, do not propose a general norm to be applied without exception in judging of the validity of any marriage whatever, contracted without dispensation.[74] If canon 1070 be examined contextually, both with

---

[71] Cf. Wernz, *Ius Decret.*, IV, n. 508, not. 33.

[72] This conclusion receives added confirmation from the argument presented in the Reid-Parkhust case. Cf. *AAS*, II (1910), 584-600.

[73] Cf. Wernz, *Ius Decret.*, IV, n. 507, not. 30; Cappello, *De Sacram.*, III, n. 419, d; Chelodi, *Ius Matr.*, n. 80, 2, c; Wernz-Vidal, *Ius Canonicum*, V, n. 270.

[74] Arendt ("Brevis Animadversio circa Interpretationem Doctrinalem § 2ae Canonis 1070", *Jus Pont.*, V [1925], 134) takes exception with sound logic to the affirmation of Wernz-Vidal (*Ius Canonicum*, V, n. 268).

reference to its component parts, and with reference to its position among the canons in the Chapter *"De impedimentis dirimentibus"*, it will be manifest that the entire canon deals exclusively with the impediment of Disparity of Cult. Since the ambit of the impediment is defined in canon 1070, § 1, and since the entire canon deals with the impediment of Disparity of Cult, the extension and restriction of canon 1070, § 1, must be kept in mind when determining the provisions of canon 1070, § 2. The marriages of baptized non-Catholics (who have never been converted to the Catholic Church) with the unbaptized, are not included in the terms of canon 1070, § 2. Only those marriages are comprehended, therefore, in which at least one of the parties at the time of the contracting of the marriage was bound by the impediment of Disparity of Cult *as it is defined in the Code.*[75]

§ II. *"Standum est pro valore matrimonii"*

213. Canon 1070, § 2, in establishing the norms of determining the validity of a marriage with reference to the impediment of Disparity of Cult, has ushered in a change regarding the interrelation of two principles. In the law before the Code, the principle *"standum est pro valore matrimonii"* yielded to the principle *"standum est pro valore baptismi"*. After the Code, the principle favoring the validity of a marriage takes precedence over the principle favoring the validity of Baptism where the latter would be prejudicial to the validity of the marriage. The general norm contained in canon 1014[76] is given a specific application with regard to the impediment of Disparity of Cult.

---

[75] Cf. Vlaming, *Prael. Iuris Matr.*, n. 291 bis; Hilling, *Das Eherecht des C. I. C.*, p. 30, not. 1; Linneborn, *Grundriss des Eherechts*, p. 200, not. 2; Leitner, *Lehrb. des kath. Eherechts*, p. 185; Blat, *Comment.*, Vol. III, P. I, n. 467; Genicot-Salsmans, *Theol. Mor.*, II, n. 594; Arendt, *loc. cit.* While the authors cited all agree as to the restriction of canon 1070, § 2, their phrasing is not always apt. There is need of care in stating the restriction correctly. It is not altogether accurate to say that canon 1070, § 2 refers only to the marriages of a Catholic with a non-Catholic, or, that at least one of the parties must be a Catholic. The term "Catholic" needs some qualifying phrase to bring out the proper designation. It is not necessary that the party bound by the impediment of Disparity of Cult, as it is defined in the Code, be a Catholic by profession of faith at the time of the marriage.

[76] "Matrimonium gaudet favore iuris; quare in dubio standum est pro valore matrimonii, donec contrarium probetur, salvo praescripto can. 1127." —Canon 1014.

§ III. *"Donec certo probetur"*

214. The presence of the impediment of Disparity of Cult is not admitted to exist in a marriage contracted after the Code until it is *proved with certainty* that at the time of the contracting of the marriage, one of the parties was baptized, and the other was not baptized. The certainty required is a moral certainty for obviously it is impossible to arrive at a physical certainty regarding the validity of a Baptism. Where positive doubts arise after the contracting of the marriage as to the validity of the Baptism of one of the parties, a serious investigation must be made to resolve the doubt of the Baptism into moral certainty of its validity or invalidity.

215. This moral certitude may be acquired either through direct proof or through the legitimate use of presumptions. If the doubt remains unsolved,—*"standum est pro valore matrimonii"*. With reference to the marriage of two Catholics, if an insoluble doubt of the Baptism of either, or of both parties arises, the safer course must be followed in providing a moral certainty of the presence of a valid Baptism necessary for salvation. Conditional Baptism must, therefore, be administered *without prejudice to the validity of the marriage,* i. e., no conditional renewal of consent is required, nor the application of a *sanatio in radice ad cautelam.*[77] The same manner of procedure is to be observed with regard to a doubtful Baptism of a Catholic in a mixed marriage. But conditional Baptism is not to be administered to the non-Catholic party whose Baptism is doubtful, unless he becomes a convert to the Catholic Church.[78]

216. A direct proof of Baptism may be acquired through witnesses,[79] or through documents.[80] If direct proof cannot be

---

[77] Cf. Cerato, *Matr.*, n. 65; Chelodi, *Ius Matr.*, n. 80, 2, a; Petrovits, *New Church Law on Matrimony*, n. 240; Wernz-Vidal, *Ius Canonicum*, V, n. 269; Linneborn, *Grundriss des Eherechts*, p. 200, not. 4; Cappello, *De Sacram.*, III, n. 419, a, cum not. 12.

[78] "Reprobandum atque illicitam omnino esse praxim administrandi a parochis baptismum sub conditione parti *acatholicae*, quae in haeresi permanere declarat, quando dubium circa eiusdem sacramenti validitatem exoritur. Tunc enim tantummodo licite id fieri potest, cum pars heterodoxa paratam se praebeat abiurandi errores ac redeundi ad gremium Ecclesiae catholicae."—S. C. S. Off., 13 Apr. 1878.—Wernz, *Ius Decret.*, IV, n. 507, not. 29.

[79] Cf. canons 742, § 1; 779.

[80] Cf. canons 1813-1816; 1990. Vide etiam Cappello, *op. cit.*, III, n. 420; Vlaming, *Prael. Iuris Matr.*, n. 293; De Smet, *De Spons. et Matr.*, p. 515, not. 4; Hilling, *Das Eherecht des C. I. C.*, p. 31.

had, recourse is left to indirect proof through presumptions.[81] If there is evidence for the fact of the administration of Baptism, the decree of the Holy Office of November 17, 1830,[82] will serve as a guide in attaining moral certainty of the validity or invalidity of the Baptism. If a doubt arises as to the very fact of its administration, the decision of the Holy Office of August 1, 1883,[83] sent to Bishop Gross of Savannah will serve as a reliable guide. Bishop Gross had proposed the following questions:

"*I*. May ignorance as to the fact of the administration or non-administration of Baptism be solved on the principle of presumption when the validity or invalidity of a contracted marriage depends on the solution?[84]

"*II*. In this ignorance as to the administration of Baptism, is the principle of presumption in relation to the validity of a contracted marriage correctly applied in the following cases:

"1. Baptism is not to be presumed if the parents of the non-Catholic party or parties are members of a sect that rejects Baptism.

"2. The same conclusion holds for those whose parents are members of a sect that does not admit infant Baptism, namely, in which Baptism is not conferred except to adults,—for instance, at the age of thirty, as is the custom of the Baptists.

"3. The same is to be said of those whose parents, while living, professed their unwillingness to join a sect, preferring, as they say, to worship a supreme Being by an honest and upright life, rather than by any special worship.

"4. If the parents were zealous members of a sect that regards Baptism as necessary, or, at least, in which it is ordinarily administered, the Baptism of the children is to be presumed. But what if their parents were indifferent or negligent members of such a sect, or adhered to a sect, which, though not rejecting Baptism, does not regard it as necessary, and ordinarily does not administer it? Is Baptism to be presumed in both instances or in either of them?

---

[81] See No. 198, note 41; S. C. de Prop. F., 2 Aug. 1901,—*ASS*, XXXIV (1901-1902), 640.

[82] See No. 201, with note 44.

[83] *Fontes*, n. 1083.

[84] Bishop Gross quotes the affirmative opinion of Kenrick, *Theol. Mor.*, Tract. XXI, n. 48.

"5. If only one parent is a zealous member of a sect that regards Baptism as necessary and ordinarily administers it, and if this parent has the unquestioned ascendancy over the child's education, the child's Baptism is to be presumed.

"The same is to be said if, after investigation, ignorance or doubt still remains as to whether such a parent exercised the predominant control over the child's education. But what if neither the sect, nor the disposition of mind of the parent, having the principal control over the child's education, favors Baptism, while the disposition of the less influential parent and his sect are favorably inclined towards Baptism?

"6. Cases in which no presumption favors Baptism should be governed by the rule: *factum non praesumitur, sed probandum est.*"

217. To these questions the Holy Office replied:

"In answer to *I*,—Affirmatively, provided that each case has first been investigated.

"In answer to *II*,—Affirmatively with regard to the first, second and third article, and the first part of the fourth[85] and fifth article, but in the latter article, after the words 'predominant control over the child's education', are to be inserted the words 'and the other parent is not known to be positively opposed to Baptism, then Baptism is to be presumed'. With regard to the other cases noted in the second part of the fifth article, recourse must be had to the Holy See with a complete exposition of all the circumstances calculated to shed light on the case presented. The sixth inquiry is provided for in the preceding answers."[86]

218. By way of summary, the following solutions of the possible hypotheses arising in marriages contracted after the Code, may be of some assistance. When the modifying expression of "certainly unbaptized" is predicated of the term "Catholic" the word "Catholic" is to be understood in the sense of "reputed Catholic". The word "certainly" is used by way of

---

[85] The answer to the second part of the fourth article is not given. It seems that such cases should be sent to the Holy Office for decision.

[86] With few modifications, the translation is that of Petrovits, *New Church Law on Matrimony*, n. 238.

contrast to the word "doubtfully". "Doubtfully" is employed in the sense of doubt insoluble after due investigation. The invalidity or validity predicated of the marriage is only with reference to the prescriptions of canon 1070, § 2.

1. A certainly baptized Catholic marrired to a certainly baptized Catholic or non-Catholic—marriage is valid.

2. A certainly baptized Catholic married to a doubtfully baptized Catholic or non-Catholic—marriage is valid.

3. A certainly baptized Catholic married to a certainly unbaptized Catholic or non-Catholic (both conditions verified to have existed at the time of the contracting of the marriage)—marriage is to be considered invalid.

4. A doubtfully baptized Catholic married to a doubtfully baptized Catholic or non-Catholic—marriage is valid.

5. A doubtfully baptized Catholic married to a certainly unbaptized Catholic or non-Catholic—marriage cannot be declared invalid.[87]

6. A certainly unbaptized Catholic married to a certainly baptized non-Catholic—marriage is valid.[88]

7. A certainly unbaptized Catholic married to a doubtfully baptized non-Catholic—marriage is valid.[89]

8. A certainly unbaptized Catholic married to a certainly unbaptized Catholic or non-Catholic—marriage is valid.[90]

§ IV. Canon 1070, § 2, in Relation to Marriages Contracted before the Code

219. It has already been demonstrated that canon 1070, § 2, must be interpreted in the light of canon 1070, § 1,—that it establishes norms of determining the presence in contracted marriages of the impediment of Disparity of Cult *as it*

---

[87] With regard to this conclusion the following authors may well be consulted: Cappello, *De Sacram.*, III, n. 419, b; Cerato, *Matr.*, n. 65, 3; Chelodi, *Ius Matr.*, n. 80, 2; De Smet, *De Spons. et Matr.*, n. 587; Farrugia, *De Matr.*, n: 170; Vermeersch-Creusen, *Epitome*, II, n. 345; Ayrinhac, "Disparity of Worship in the New Code", *AER*, LXI (1919), 696; Wernz-Vidal, *Ius Canonicum*, V, n. 269. See infra No. 167, note 50.

[88] Canon 1070, § 1.

[89] Canon 1070, § 1.

[90] It is a *matrimonium simpliciter legitimum.*

is defined in the Code.[91] It seems but a reasonable deduction,
therefore, to say that canon 1070, § 2, applies only to marriages contracted after the Code. De Smet, on the other hand,
does not admit this conclusion and ventures the opinion that
since canon 1070, § 2 gives precedence to the principle *"standum est pro valore matrimonii ad normam can. 1014"*, this
precedence must be observed also in judging of the presence of
the impediment of Disparity of Cult in marriages contracted before the Code.[92]

220. With regard to the law before the Code favoring the
validity of Baptism even to the prejudice of the validity of a
marriage, it may be said that this was not a mere human conjecture of validity enunciated solely for a practical service in determining the validity of a marriage. The presumption of the
validity of a doubtful Baptism was and *is* a presumption based
on the divine law itself.[93] Given the evidence of the conferring
of the baptism rite,[94] there is a *"praesumptio iuris* ET DE IURE
DIVINO" that the person to whom the rite has been administered
is subject to the laws of the Church. This presumption will not
admit a direct proof of the contrary but only an indirect proof.
To destroy the force of the presumption it must be shown either
that the rite was not conferred, or that it was invalidly conferred. The presence of the character of Baptism is judged
from the presence of the rite and not *vice versa*. If the rite has
been administered the character is presumed to be present by a
presumption founded on the divine law,—for Christ in instituting the sacrament of Baptism instituted an *external rite* having
the divine efficacy of imprinting a character on the soul. The
presumption that a doubtfully baptized person is subject to the

---

[91] See No. 212.

[92] ". . . praesumptio, canone 1070, § 2, statuta, de favore praestando, iuxta
normam canonis 1014, matrimonii valori, applicanda videtur matrimoniis de
quorum validitate nunc est iudicandum, licet contracta sint sub disciplina Codici anteriori, sub qua disciplina vigebat praesumptio in favorem Baptismi."—
De Spons. et Matr., n. 475. Vide etiam *op cit.*, n. 587.

[93] See No. 201, note 46.

[94] See No. 201, note 47. Vide etiam S. C. S. Off., 8 Maii 1924,—*AER,*
LXXI (1924), 405-406. In this latter case there was question of a total ignorance as to whether Baptism had been received by one party.

laws of the Church holds, therefore, both for the internal and external forum.

221. When, therefore, the impediment of Disparity of Cult, as it existed before the Code, bound all the baptized, it did not distinguish between those who had been doubtfully or certainly baptized,—rather it included all who had been admitted to the Church's jurisdiction through the sacrament of Baptism as it is recognizable by the administration of the Baptismal rite. The marriage of a doubtfully baptized person with an unbaptized person was, consequently, invalid *ab initio* by a *praesumptio iuris* ET DE IURE DIVINO for the very reason that the doubtfully baptized were bound by the impediment *ante contractum*. They were included in the very law of the impediment.

222. Canon 1070, § 2 does not destroy this presumption but rather releases from the *consequences* of the presumption where they would be prejudicial to the validity of a marriage on the basis of the impediment of Disparity of Cult. It does not follow, however, that this release is retroactive.[95] The marriages of those baptized in the Catholic Church with the unbaptized, *if contracted before the Code*, are not declared invalid on the basis of canon 1070, § 1 but on the basis of the law that bound *all* the baptized. According to canon 1070 § 2, the marriages of the doubtfully baptized (the term "baptized" to be understood in the light of canon 1070, § 1) with the unbaptized cannot be declared invalid since the canon has released the doubtfully baptized from the consequences of this subjection to the law regarding the impediment of Disparity of Cult. But since canon 1070, § 2 in no way implies the granting of a *sanatio*

---

[95] "Vis novi Codicis estne retroactiva in his, quae modificantur circa sponsalia et impedimenta tum impedientia quam dirimentia matrimonium, ita ut quodlibet ius acquisitum vigore sponsalium validorum, nullimode possit reclamari, nisi in quantum novus Codex concedit, et contracta impedimenta modificata a novo Codice, nulla dispensatione indigeant?" *Resp.* "Codici, etiam quoad sponsalia et impedimenta, non esse vim retroactivam, sponsalia autem et matrimonia regi iure vigenti quando contracta sunt vel contrahentur, salvo tamen, quoad actionem ex sponsalibus, canone 1017, § 3."—Pont. Comm., 2-3 Iun. 1918, *Dubia* (IV) *De Matr.*, n. 6.—*AAS*, X (1918), 346.

in radice[96] to marriages contracted *before the Code* by the doubt-fully baptized with the unbaptized, it may be asked: when did such marriages (invalid *ab initio* according to the law before the Code) become valid? In other words, why are such pre-Code marriages to be judged by canon 1070, § 2 the prescriptions of which are to be interpreted in the light of canon 1070, § 1? Canon 1070, § 2 seems, therefore, to apply only to marriages contracted *after the Code*. The determination of the presence of the impediment of Disparity of Cult is to be governed by the *law* under which the marriage was contracted.

---

[96] Cf. Pont. Comm., 2-3 Iun. 1918, *Dubia* (IV) *De Matr.*, n. 7,—*AAS*, X (1918), 346.

CHAPTER XI

CESSATION AND DISPENSATION

ART. I. CESSATION OF THE IMPEDIMENT OF MIXED RELIGION AND OF THE PROHIBITIONS OF CANONS 1065 AND 1066

223. With reference to both the divine and ecclesiastical law, the impediment of Mixed Religion ceases *ipso facto* if, antecedent to the marriage, the non-Catholic party becomes a convert to the Catholic Church. Where conversion does not take place the prohibition derived from the divine and natural law could, indeed, cease, yet the prohibition of the Church still remains.[1] Much the same may be said with reference to the prohibitions contained in canons 1065 and 1066. As soon as those who have notoriously left the Faith or joined condemned societies return to the Church or renounce their membership in such societies, the pastor may assist at their marriages, whether they be with Catholics who have never fallen into such delinquencies, or with those who like themselves have again been reconciled to the Church. The prohibition to assist at the marriages of Catholics with public sinners or those notoriously under censure ceases likewise upon the delinquents' reconciliation with the Church.[2]

---

[1] Cf. Benedictus XIV, *De Synodo Dioec.*, Lib. IX, cap. III, n. 4. The prohibition of the divine law may well have ceased at the time when all the conditions required for dispensation are realized, yet the marriage would be illicit until the Church has removed the impediment. Cf. Wernz, *Ius Decret.*, IV, n. 582; Benedictus XIV, *op. cit.*, Lib. VI, cap. V, n. 4; Feije, *De Imped. et Dispens.*, n. 567; Cappello, *De Sacram.*, III, n. 307; Cerato, *Matr.*, n. 54; Vlaming, *Prael. Iuris Matr.*, n. 211.

[2] Cf. S. Poenit. 10 Dec. 1860,—Feije, *op. cit.*, n. 277. In the case of a public sinner it is sufficient that he go to confession, but if possible this should be in a public place such as in a Church. If, on the other hand, it is made in a private place, the fact of the confession should generally be made known in order that the assistance of the pastor at his marriage will not be an occasion of scandal. The giving or refusal of absolution will not affect the procedure in the external forum. Cf. Cappello, *op. cit.*, III, n. 332; Cerato, *Matr.*, n. 60; Chelodi, *Ius Matr.*, n. 67; Wernz-Vidal, *Ius Canonicum*, V, n. 202. If there is question of an absolution from censure, canon 2251 must be taken into consideration.

Art. II. Cessation of the Impediment of Disparity of Cult

224. The divine law forbidding the marriages of Catholics with the unbaptized is, generally speaking, fundamentally the same as that for mixed marriages, provided that the unbaptized party adheres to a non-Catholic profession of faith.[3] The diriment element of the impediment of Disparity of Cult, which through the law of the Church rests upon a foundation quite distinct from that of the impediment of Mixed Religion, ceases upon the Baptism of the unbaptized party.[4] On the other hand, a marriage laboring under the impediment of Disparity of Cult does not become valid *ipso facto* upon the Baptism of the infidel party.[5] True marital consent must be renewed or a *sanatio in radice* applied. The liceity and validity of the renewal of consent must be judged in accordance with the requirements of the law of the Church in the time and place of the renewal.

§ I. Cessation through Urgent and Common Necessity

225. The authors are somewhat divided in their opinions with reference to the cessation of impediments because of extraordinary circumstances. Some deny absolutely any cessation whatever unless it be through dispensation. Others distinguish between diriment and prohibitive impediments and affirm that neither cease for mere particular instances.[6] In the case of common necessity, some authors maintain that only prohibitive im-

---

[3] In this respect the natural and divine law contemplates only the marriages of *Catholics* with the unbaptized (who are also non-Catholics in their religious beliefs). The diriment element of the impediment, which before the Code bound all the baptized, is of ecclesiastical origin. It would be somewhat farfetched to urge the presence of a divine prohibition to all marriages of baptized non-Catholics with the unbaptized.

[4] For the cessation of the impediment of Disparity of Cult it is not necessary that the infidel receive Baptism in the Catholic Church. The fact of the valid reception of Baptism is sufficient to suppress the impediment. Cappello (*De Sacram.*, III, n. 425) and Wernz-Vidal (*Ius Canonicum*, V, n. 272) refer, however, to the requirement of Baptism in the Catholic Church.

[5] S. C. S. Off., 12 Ian. 1769,—*Fontes*, n. 822; 8 Mart. 1899,—*Fontes*, n. 1217; Sylvius, *Comment. in Tertiam Part. S. Thomae*, Suppl., Q. LIX. art. I, concl. 3.

[6] See Cappello (*De Sacram.*, III, n. 199) who cites the various opinions sponsored by the authors.

pediments cease, while others urge this cessation also for diriment impediments.[7] As a general rule, laws that bind under pain of invalidity urge their force in both common and particular necessity unless exception may, perhaps, be made for particular regional circumstances which would be such that persons would be forced either to marry with an impediment or to abstain from marriage entirely.[8] The authors are wont to apply this principle of the superiority of the natural right to marriage over the obstacle of the ecclesiastical impediment of Disparity of Cult. The following case upon which the Holy Office gave a favorable decision is urged by some[9] in support of their opinion.

226. It had often happened in Manchuria that Chinese Christians in order to escape persecution or to procure a better livelihood, or for other reasons, moved with their family to totally pagan places that were a forty or fifty day's journey from Christian localities. Since it was impossible for children of such families to go to Christian communities, they were forced in these circumstances either to marry pagans or to remain unmarried. Accordingly it was asked whether these children were bound by the impediment of Disparity of Cult, and what was to be done where those so married were unmolested as to their religion, and were in good faith as to the validity of the marriage. To this inquiry the Holy Office replied: "*In propositis circumstantiis non esse inquietandos, facto verbo cum SSmo. SSmus approbavit.*"[10] Other authors, though they admit of a

---

[7] Cf. Cappello, *loc. cit.* St. Alphonsus (*Theol. Mor.*, Lib. VI, n. 613) does not introduce the distinction between diriment and prohibitive impediments but does invoke the argument based on a benign interpretation of the mind of the legislator. Yet the cases he postulates are not the same as those contemplated in the present discussion. St. Alphonsus with Sanchez (*De Matr.*, Lib. II, Disp. 40, nn. 7-12) and most of the older authors refers only to the presumed faculty of a Bishop or a confessor (especially for occult impediments) to dispense in urgent necessity from an impediment reserved to the Holy See. The cases here under consideration refer rather to those circumstances where neither the Bishop, the pastor, nor a confessor can be approached to petition for a dispensation.

[8] Vlaming, *Prael. Iuris Matr.*, n. 198; Cappello, *loc. cit.*; De Smet, *De Spons. et Matr.*, n. 469; Ballerini-Palmieri, *Op. Theol. Mor.*, Tract. III, nn. 318-321; Gasparri, *De Matr.*, n. 311; Tanquery, *Theol. Mor.*, I, n. 926.

[9] Farrugia, *De Matr.*, n. 169; De Becker, *De Spons. et Matr.*, p. 230-231; Vlaming, *loc. cit.*; Petrovits, *New Church Law on Matrimony*, n. 241; Genicot-Salsmans, *Theol. Mor.*, II, n. 491.

[10] S. C. S. Off. (Mandciuriae), 4 Iunii 1851,—*Coll.*, n. 1062.

cessation of the impediment on the intrinsic value of the argument based on the superiority of the natural right to marriage, deny any conclusive force to arguments drawn from this answer of the Holy Office.[11]

227. On the other hand there are decisions which cast a serious doubt even upon the theoretical value of the principle of cessation. Rather than declare the cessation of the impediment in circumstances similar to those mentioned in the inquiry of 1851, the Holy Office in one instance gave a faculty for three particular cases to an Apostolic Vicar to grant dispensations by way of anticipation from the impediment of Disparity of Cult[12] The same Congregation, moreover, denied that entire ignorance of the Church's impediments,[13] or that persecution of the Christians by the Japanese Government offered a sufficient reason for supposing that the impediment had ceased.[14] If, then, the impedi-

---

[11] Wernz (*Ius Decret.*, IV, n. 510; n. 66, Scholion) seriously questions the objective value of the intrinsic argument and with reference to the answer of the Holy Office of June 4, 1851 remarks (n. 510 not. 37) : "Nam ex ipsis verbis: *'Facto verbo etc.'* patet R. Pontificem non dedisse aliquam *declarationem* de impedimento iam sublato, sed potius aliquam *gratiam.* Porro *'approbatio'* R. Pontificis parum iuvat adversarios; etenim omnia responsa S. C. Inq. etiam tolerantiae vel dissimultationis solent a R. Pontifice in forma *communi* approbari. Tandem ratio intrinseca non est ad rem; nam leges irritantes Ecclesiae in casibus particularibus et publicis adeo generaliter cessare non obstantibus rationibus mere theoreticis ob defectum consensus legislatoris non est doctrina undequaque practice tuta." Vide etiam Chelodi, *Ius Matr.*, n. 81; Cappello, *De Sacram.*, III, n. 199, not. 11; Wernz-Vidal, *Ius Canonicum*, V, n. 273, not. 41; Gasparri, *De Matr.*, n. 711.

[12] S. C. S. Off., instr. (ad Vic. Ap. Oceaniae Central.), 18 Dec. 1872,—*Fontes*, n. 1024.

[13] S. C. Off. (Iaponiae), 11 Mart. 1868,—*Fontes*, n. 1004.

[14] "1. Utrum in Iaponensi Imperio, perdurante saeculari persecutione, necnon Pastorum et doctrinae privatione perseverante, impedimenta ab Ecclesia instituta totam matrimonia dirimendi vim obtinuerit. Inde, utrum omnia matrimonia cum talibus impedimentis dirimentibus contracta invalida sint. Ratio dubii in eo est quod, cum ignorantia de matrimonii natura et impedimentis omnino universalis et invincibilis esset, forsan praesumitur Ecclesia de talibus impedimentis dispensasse, necon suas leges circa matrimonium in hoc casu totam vim obtinere noluisse. 2. In casu affirmative suppliciter ac humillime imploro ut SSmus dispensationem a radice, qua omnia matrimonia nulla ob impedimenta iure Ecclesiae dirimentia revalidentur, benigne concedere dignetur.

"R. Ad 1. Providebitur in sequenti.

"Ad 2. Quoad eos qui sunt in bona fide, R. P. D Vicarius Ap. sileat omnino. Quoad eos qui in bona fide non sunt, curet ut consensus renovetur, dispensationem concedendo iuxta facultates iam ipsi factas a S. C. de Prop. Fide . . . In casibus vero difficilioribus, recurrat, expositis omnibus cuiusque casus adiunctis."—S. C. S. Off. (Iaponiae), 11 Mart. 1868,—*Fontes*, n. 1004. Cf. S. C. S. Off., 12 Ian. 1769, n. II, 5,—*Fontes*, n. 822; (Coreae), 11 Sept. 1878,—*Fontes*, n. 1057.

ment is declared not to cease even in the dire times of persecution when Christians are dispersed among pagan communities through no fault of their own, it will be practically impossible for any local tribunal to give a declaration regarding the validity of marriages contracted with the impediment of Disparity of Cult in the extraordinary circumstances postulated by the authors without recourse to the Holy Office.[15]

ART. III. OBLIGATIONS OF ORDINARIES AND PASTORS

CANON 1064

Ordinarii aliique animarum pastores:
1° Fideles a mixtis nuptiis, quantum possunt, absterreant;
2° Si eas impedire non valeant, omni studio curent ne contra Dei et Ecclesiae leges contrahantur.

228. The Holy See has ever insisted that Ordinaries and pastors in charge of souls labor with all diligence to deter the faithful from contracting mixed or disparate marriages.[16] Scarcely a diocesan synod of this country has remained silent upon this all important duty. Admittedly, mixed and disparate marriages have been on the increase, but before becoming too sharp in criticism of this fact it is well to remember that the conditions in this country have been quite singular. The vast area of many parishes, the large non-Catholic population, and the problems of immigration and education have made truly arduous the task of preventing mixed and disparate marriages. Such conditions do not absolve from a continued vigilance, but they do, perhaps, account in large measure for the accentuated problem of mixed marriages in this country. While the Church has always protested against such unions, she has likewise been disposed to face situations as they actually exist and to recommend patience[17] rather than an unguided zeal. If, therefore, mixed and disparate

---

[15] Cf. S. C. S. Off. (Iaponiae), 11 Mart. 1868,—*Fontes,* n. 1004; De Becker, *De Spons. et Matr.,* p. 231.

[16] See also canons 1065, § 1; 1071.

[17] Cf. Pius VII, breve ad Archiep. Moguntin., 8 Oct. 1803, n. 5,—*Fontes,* n. 477; Pius VIII, litt. ap. *Litteris altero,* 25 Mart. 1830,—*Fontes.* n. 482; Gregorius XVI, litt. ap. *Quas vestro,* 30 Apr. 1841, n. 5,—*Fontes.* n. 497; Feije, *De Matr. Mixtis,* p. 227-230.

marriages cannot always be prevented, she will acknowledge the gravity of such situations and dispense rather than cause greater evils and even greater defections from the Faith. It is the duty of Ordinaries and pastors to see that when such marriages cannot be prevented, they will not be contracted against the laws of God and of the Church. The obligation implies more than a mere care to see that all the conditions requisite for dispensation are fulfilled,—it implies likewise a prudent zeal in preventing the clandestine entry into such unions.[18]

§ I. SHOULD DISPENSATIONS BE ABSOLUTELY ABOLISHED?

229. The growing number of mixed and disparate marriages has recently elicited a recommendation that dispensations be entirely abolished. The abuses connected with dispensations form the principle grounds of the argument as it is presented by Father Woywod.[19] It is contended that the present practice fosters a dangerous levity among Catholic people; that their mere will to contract a marriage with non-Catholics is often the only cause found for petitioning for a dispensation, and that dispensations granted for such causes render the law ineffectual; that the moral certainty of the sincerity of the "promises" may often be seriously questioned. The absolute refusal of dispensations, it is urged, will do more good than harm; it will stop many defections from the Faith that are now traceable to mixed marriages; it will give Catholics a more wholesome appreciation of their faith.

There is nothing really new in this attitude towards dispensations for mixed marriages,—in fact it was the attitude of the Church for centuries. But what is significant is that the Church herself has found it necessary to depart from the rigor of this absolute discipline.[20]

---

[18] Cf. Petrovits, *New Church Law on Matrimony*, n. 195.

[19] "Should Dispensations for Mixed Marriages be Altogether Abolished?"— *HPR*, XXVIII (1928), 701-711. The same volume of this Review (pages 954-959, 1066-1071, 1193-1197, 1315-1318) contains an open discusssion of the subject by correspondents. A last article by Father Woywod ("Dispensations for Mixed Marriages", *HPR*, XXIX [1928], 125-134) closes the discussion in this Review.

[20] Some European dioceses have attempted to enforce the discipline of refusing dispensations (cf. *HPR*, XXVIII [1928], 708; Linneborn, *Grundriss des Eherechts*, p. 166) yet the very diocese of Liverpool, to which Father Woywod refers, apparently permits exceptions to its rule.

230. Admittedly, the wish of the parties to marry is not of itself a sufficient cause for dispensation, and a dispensation granted on this ground alone would be invalid.[21] If the wish to marry is the only ground that can be urged on which to seek a dispensation from the impediment it is, indeed, a grave abuse to convert a mere wish into the canonical terminology of such a recognized cause as *"periculum matrimonii civilis"*. A salient issue, therefore, regards the objective existence of the cause or causes cited.

231. On the other hand, while the wish to marry is not of itself a sufficient cause for dispensation, it may be said that the danger of a civil marriage and other causes that are alleged with some frequency are, nevertheless, connected in some way with the wish to marry. Often, too, such causes imply grave sin. As a matter of fact, a large percentage of the causes recognized as canonical in the lists given by Cardinal Masella[22] and the Congregation of the Propaganda[23] have a connection with sin or are a direct outcome of it. It would be quite wrong, however, to accuse the Church of placing a premium on sin in order that those impeded from marrying may marry. Yet the Church does take cognizance of such and other situations as offering grave reasons why her law should be dispensed from in particular cases. The justified exceptions but emphasize the existence of the law.

232. The implication of sin or the connection of the cause with the will to marry does not necessarily, however, destroy the recognized gravity of the cause. The cause represents a situation or a reason *in addition* to the wish to marry; an evil that could not be averted, or a good that could not be realized unless a dispensation were given. It is these additional elements that move the Church to dispense. In order to avoid embarrassment there may be a temptation at times to allege such causes as *"periculum matrimonii civilis"*, *"spes conversionis"* and others as a last resort in the hope that at least one will fit the

---

[21] Cf. S. C. de Prop. F., encycl., 11 Mart. 1868,—*Coll.*, n. 1324; De Justis, *De Dispens. Matr.*, Lib. III, cap. I, n. 8; Giovine, *De Dispens. Matr.*, Tom. I, § LXV, n. 4; Linneborn, *loc. cit.*

[22] See No. 283, note 20.

[23] See No. 283, note 18.

case,—without determining carefully the reality of their existence. If such abuses do exist the imperative need of immediate correction is manifest, yet the existence of such abuses scarcely offers a convincing reason for the refusal of all dispensations. That the danger of civil marriage does exist in many instances, is a situation that may not be lightly dismissed nor cast aside altogether as an insufficient cause, even though it is intimately connected with the will of the parties to marry.[24] In addition to the correction of abuses (and it is well to remember on whom the accusation rests) a concern even more fundamental may well center on the factors responsible for the all too prevalent "nominal Catholicity" that gives rise to such causes.

233. The attention called to the questionable moral certainty of the fulfillment of the "promises" deserves serious consideration.[25] It is doubtful, however, whether the validity of many of the dispensations is to be challenged on this score. Too much stress must not be given an argument based on the statistics of the evil results attendant upon mixed or disparate marriages. While they confirm the warnings of the Church and vindicate, at least in part, the existence of the impediments, they do not necessarily imply insincerity or deception in the "promises" at the time when they were given. When the Church imposes the obligation upon Ordinaries and pastors to watch carefully that the "promises" will be faithfully fulfilled after the marriage has been contracted,[26] she does not thereby challenge the validity of her dispensations. She does seem to insinuate, however, that the neglect of this precept will spell ruin for the faith of many. May not a good number of defections be laid to the careless or injudicious fulfillment of this obligation? Is not the scarcity of priests in a missionary region a contributing factor?

234. Practically the entire argument for the absolute refusal of dispensations for mixed and disparate marriages rests on the assumption and line of reasoning that such a measure is the only possible safeguard that can be recommended to insure a respect for the law of the Church. Why not carry the argu-

---

[24] See No. 293, note 58.
[25] Nos. 355-364.
[26] Canon 1064, n. 3.

ment to its logical conclusion and upon the same line of reasoning urge the discontinuance of all matrimonial dispensations? Abuses in connection with dispensations will, indeed, foster a levity among Catholics regarding marriages with non-Catholics yet in the light of the abuses cited, the entire blame for the situation should not be laid too hastily upon the people themselves. If many of our Catholics have so little consciousness of the treasure of their faith that they have no hesitaton in continuing their courtship with non-Catholics; if many of them leave the matter of the "promises" to the pastor and defer it to the time when they seek hurried dispensations; if many of them regard dispensations as a mere matter of "red tape", it hardly supports Father Woywod's assumption that they have been sufficiently instructed, or that the methods of instilling Catholic principles of life have been altogether adequate.[27]

235. Granting, then, the existence of a certain indifference among altogether too many Catholics, may a remedy be reasonably sought in the absolute refusal of dispensations? The test appears to be too severe and hardly warranted by the practice of the Church within the last century.[28] While the Church *severely forbids* mixed and disparate marriages, she is not now disposed, as in bygone centuries, to refuse dispensations altogether. Ever since the Church has strictly enforced her discipline regarding the necessity of dispensations for mixed marriages among the common people, she has likewise been disposed to grant them for grave causes. Rather than lose many of her members entirely and deny legitimacy to their children she faces situations as they exist. Though reluctant to grant dispensations, she does dispense when grave causes demand it and when the divine and natural law are not in proximate danger of violation. Her norm of procedure is one of firmness yet tempered with mercy and with the recommendation that Ordinaries be not too severe and rigorous lest graver evils result. While she exhorts the Ordinaries and pastors to deter the faithful from such unions as far as possible, she does admit that it is not always possible, and rather than cause greater evils by an ab-

---

[27] Cf. *HPR*, XXVIII (1928), 705.
[28] This opinion implies no brief whatever for mixed marriages.

solute refusal of dispensations, she dispenses.[29] To the Bishops of the United States and of other countries she has granted faculties that are more extensive than ever,—including even the *sanatio in radice* for mixed and disparate marriages contracted civilly or before a non-Catholic minister, in cases where the consent perseveres but where the non-Catholic refuses to renew it or to give the "promises". This does not indicate a disposition of the Church to refuse dispensations altogether.

236. Does the recommendation for the absolute refusal of dispensations include also those cases where a marriage has already been contracted civilly, and where the Catholic party has given signs of repentance, but where a separation is practically impossible? The rigor manifested in an affirmative answer hardly finds justification in the attitude of the Church.[30] Yet if exceptions be made for such cases would it not be advisable to permit antecedent exceptions that are recognized as justified in the Code itself? Does the Church prefer to dispense for grave reasons antecedently to a marriage or does she prefer to validate an invalid marriage whose invalidity and consequent sinfulness could have been prevented by an antecedent dispensation?

ART. IV. NECESSITY OF DISPENSATION

237. Before a person who is an actual professed member of the Catholic Church may lawfully marry one who is a member of an heretical or schismatic sect, he must obtain a dispensation from the impediment of Mixed Religion. The necessity of dispensation follows from what has already been said regarding the fundamental elements of the Church's law on mixed and disparate marriages.[31] Apart from the prohibitions of the divine and natural law to such marriages, the Church has reasons of her own that determine her legislation. The Church must, therefore, first dispense from her law before a Catholic may contract a mixed marriage. Moreover, with reference to the divine and natural law, the Church alone has the right of giving an authentic declaration as to the absence of the prohibition in a particular

---

[29] Cf. canon 1064, nn. 1-2; Pius VIII, litt ap. *Litteris altero,* 25 Mart. 1830,—*Fontes,* n. 482; Vlaming, *Prael, Iuris Matr.,* n. 231 bis.

[30] See No. 284, note 26. Cf. *HPR,* XXVIII (1928), 1217-1218.

[31] See Chapter VII.

case.[32] The necessity of dispensation from the impediment of Disparity of Cult scarcely needs explanation for, since the impediment is diriment by the law of the Church, a dispensation is clearly necessary for the very validity of a marriage between a person bound by the impediment and one who is not baptized.[33]

§ I. Necessity of the Ordinary's Permission for the Pastor to Assist at Marriages Prohibited by Canons 1065 and 1066

238. A pastor may not assist at the marriages of Catholics with those who have notoriously left the Faith or joined condemned societies unless he has first consulted the Ordinary.[34] Again if a public sinner or one notoriously under censure refuses to go to confession beforehand, or to be reconciled with the Church, the pastor may not assist at his marriage unless a grave cause urges, about which he shall if possible consult the Ordinary.[35] Both canons 1065, § 2, and 1066 require a *permission* of the Ordinary, not a dispensation. The obligation of recourse, moreover, rests primarily upon the pastor, not upon the contracting parties, though the given or refused permission does, indeed, affect the parties themselves.

---

[32] Cf. canons 1038; 21; Reiffenstuel, *Jus Can. Univ.*, Lib. IV, Tit. I, n. 362; Laemmer, *Instit. des kath. Kirchenrechts*, p. 517, not. 4; De Smet. *De Spons. et Matr.*, nn. 502-503; Cappello, *De Sacram.*, III, nn. 307, 425; Farrugia, *De Matr.*, n. 131.

[33] Though the impediment *per se* does not directly bind the unbaptized, indirectly it does, for those who are bound by the impediment are prevented from contracting a valid marriage with the unbaptized. The contract of marriage cannot limp.—". . . cum matrimonium sit quaedam relatio, et non possit innasci relatio in uno extremorum, sine hoc quod fiat in alio, ideo quidquid impedit matrimonium in uno, impedit ipsum in altero . . . et ideo dicitur communiter, quod 'matrimonium non claudicat'."—Thomas Aq., *Summa Theol.*, IIIa, suppl., q. 47, art. 4. Since the very terms and nature of the impediment forbid that the direct exemption of the unbaptized pass to those bound by the impediment, it follows that a dispensation is necessary for the validity of the marriage.

[34] Cf. Canon 1065, § 2; S. C. S. Off. (Portus Aloisii), 1 Aug. 1855, —*Fontes*, n. 932; (Leodien.), 30 Ian. 1867,—*Fontes*, n. 998; 17 Sept. 1871,—*AkKR*, XXVII (1872), CLXXI; (S. Bonifacii), 23 Apr. 1873,— *Fontes*, n. 1026; instr. (ad Ordinarios Imperii Brasil.), 2 Iul. 1878,— *Fontes*, n.1056; 25 Maii 1897,—*Fontes*, n. 1186; 11 Ian. 1899,—*Fontes*, n. 1215; S. C. Conc., 27 Nov. 1896,—*AkKR*, LXXVIII (1898), 523-524; S. Poenit., 10 Dec. 1860,—Feije, *De Imped. et Dispens.*, n. 277.

[35] Canon 1066.

239. The duty of recourse to the Ordinary is apparently of graver moment in canon 1065, § 2, than in canon 1066. Canon 1065, § 2, directs that a pastor may not assist at the marriages of those who have notoriously rejected the Faith or joined condemned societies except after consulting the Ordinary to whom is reserved the ultimate decision, whereas canon 1066 states that a pastor may not assist at the marriage of a public sinner or one notoriously under censure unless for a grave cause, concerning which he should if possible consult the Ordinary. It is altogether reasonable to assume that the obligation of recourse would be graver in canon 1065, § 2, than in canon 1066, for in the former case the Ordinary must regard not only the gravity of the cause but also all the attendant circumstances, and especially the sufficiency of provision regarding the Catholic education of the children and the absence of a danger of perversion for the Catholic party.[36] Whatever proportions of gravity may be recognized between the prohibitions of canon 1065 and those of canon 1066, or in reference to the actual wording of these canons, or in the gravity of the matter requiring decision, it is the Ordinary and not the pastor who is to give the ultimate decision or permission.[37]

---

[36] A decision of the Holy Office of August 21, 1861 (*Fontes*, n. 967) did not seem, however, to recognize a proportion of gravity when it directed: "Quoad assistentiam matrimoniis eorum qui pertinent ad societatem *liberorum muratorum* parochi et missionarii se gerant uti cum agitur de praestanda assistentia matrimoniis eorum qui tamquam publici peccatores habentur." But see S. C. S. Off. (Leodien.), 30 Ian. 1867,—*Fontes*, n. 998. Yet the decisions of the latter half of the nineteenth century continually refer to the fact that the Holy See had not yet established a fixed discipline for such cases. In two decisions the pastor appears to be given the libery of forming his own judgment. Cf. S. C. S. Off. (Marysville), 21 Aug. 1861,—*Fontes*, n. 967; (Bombay), 21 Feb. 1883,—*Fontes*, n. 1079. A decision of the Holy Office of January 11, 1899 (*Fontes*, n. 1215) extended the faculty given to a particular Ordinary in an earlier decision of January 30, 1867 (*Fontes*, n. 998) to all Ordinaries. Indirectly, at least, this decision implied the consequent necessity of the pastor's recourse to the Ordinary before assisting at the marriages of Catholics with those who had fallen away from the Faith, or who had joined condemned societies.

[37] Excepion is to be made, of course, for situations such as those postulated in canons 1044 and 1045. If by virtue of these canons a pastor may dispense from impediments, *a fortiori* he may, when all the required conditions are fulfilled, assist at such marriages as are prohibited in canons 1065 and 1066. He should, however, inform the Ordinary of the contracted marriage. Cf. Cappello, *De Sacram.*, III, n. 331.

§ II. VINDICTIVE PUNISHMENT OF CANON 2375

CANON 2375

Catholici qui matrimonium mixtum, etsi validum, sine Ecclesiae dispensatione inire ausi fuerint, ipso facto ab actibus legitimis ecclesiasticis et Sacramentalibus exclusi manent, donec ab Ordinario dispensationem obtinuerint.

240. This vindictive punishment, as it is evident from the wording of the canon, falls upon the Catholic party alone. The primary purpose of every vindictive punishment is the expiation of the crime committed.[38] In this it differs from a censure which is a medicinal punishment intended for the reformation of the delinquent.[39]

The words *"ausi fuerint"* imply that in order to incur the punishment, the *delictum* must be committed with a full knowledge of both the law requiring the dispensation from the impediment, and of the punishment inflicted *ipso facto* upon its violation. Such elements as grave fear, ignorance (even crass and supine) that is not affected, and any lessening of imputability will grant exemption from the punishment.[40] Catholics incur the penalty who dare to enter a *matrimonium mixtum* without a dispensation even though the marriage be valid. There is some disagreement among the authors as to whether the term *"matrimonium mixtum"* is generic, including both mixed and disparate marriages, or whether it is specific, designating only marriages contracted with the impediment of Mixed Religion. Blat,[41] Vermeersch-Creusen,[42] Augustine,[43] Ayrinhac,[44] and Murphy,[45]

---

[38] Cf. canon 2286. With reference to the punishment of canon 2375, Cerato suggests a special reason: "Et haec suspensio sancita est profecto etiam ut facilius valeat Ordinarius cautiones de iure statuta exigere ad bonum sive prolis sive ipsius coniugis."—*Matr.*, n. 54, adn. e.

[39] See canons 2241, § 1; 2248, § 2.

[40] Cf. canon 2229; Cappello, *De Sacram.*, III, n. 321; Cocchi, *Comment.*, Vol. 8, n. 249; Cerato, *Censurae*, nn. 135, 30; Leitner, *Lehrb. des kath. Eherechts*, p. 243-244.

[41] *Comment.*, Vol. V, n. 217.

[42] *Epitome*, III, n. 578.

[43] *Commentary*, VIII, p. 452.

[44] *Penal Legislation*, p. 337.

[45] *Delinquencies and Penalties*, p. 107-108.

limit the term to strictly mixed marriages, whereas Chelodi[46] and Leitner[47] extend it likewise to disparate marriages.

241. The historical use of the term *"matrimonium mixtum"* offers no apparent clue to the solution.[48] Reasons drawn from the purpose of the canon would seem to favor the inclusion of disparate marriages, for why should a Catholic attempting a disparate marriage be dealt with less severely than a Catholic attempting to enter without dispensation either a valid or an invalid mixed marriage?[49] There is a positive element of doubt, however, and accordingly the strict interpretation of the term *"matrimonium mixtum"*, as referring only to mixed marriages, may be followed. This opinion, moreover, has found favor among the greater number of canonists.

242. The punishment in its form of an exclusion from legitimate ecclesiastical acts and the sacramentals is new.[50] The

---

[46] *Ius Poenale,* n. 96.

[47] *Lehrb. des kath. Eherechts,* p. 243-244.

[48] See No. 26. In the index to Cardinal Gasparri's edition of the Code, the term seems to refer to the marriages of Catholics with baptized members of non-Catholic sects.

[49] If Cerato's opinion may be accepted as a partial reason for the punishment (see No. 240, note 38), the inclusion of disparate marriages receives added confirmation. Murphy (*loc. cit.*) argues that since the canon is under the title treating of the crimes committed in the administration and reception of the sacraments, and since the punishment is limited to those mixed marriages that are validly [?] contracted, the inclusion of disparate marriages contracted without dispensation must be rejected. But the words *"etsi validum"* seem to insinuate that both valid and invalid *"matrimonia mixta"* are included.

[50] Cf. Chelodi, *Ius Poenale,* n. 96. The same author adds that in the pre-Code law such offenders were regarded as public sinners. Cardinal Albitius (*De Inconstantia in Fide,* Cap. XXXVI, nn. 185-197) dwells at considerable length upon the grounds whereby such delinquents would incur censures. Heiner (*Grundriss des kath. Eherechts,* Teil III, absch. I, cap. V, n. 7) likewise regarded them as public sinners under excommunication. Cf. Feije, *De Imped. et Dispens.,* n. 573. The opinion more clearly supported by the sources is given by Wernz (*Ius Decret.,* IV, n. 581 [ee also n. 587]) : "Catholici quamvis in contrahendis matrimoniis mixtis sine legitima dispensatione obtenta *grave delictum* committant, *tamen ex iure communi* ob solam matrimonii mixti celebrationem non subiiciuntur *poenis* ecclesiasticis sive ipso facto incurrendis sive per sententiam infligendis. At Episcopus pro sua iure decernere potest poenas latae vel ferendae sententiae, dummodo prudenti utatur moderatione. Nam compluries Sedes Apostolica censuit in huiusmodi casibus 'potius per exhortationes quam edictis poenalibus praesertim excommunicationibus' esse procedendum." Cf. Urbanus VIII., 14 Mart. 1630,—Ballerini-Palmieri, *Op. Theol. Mor.,* Tract. X, Sect. VIII, n. 712; Pius VIII, litt. ap. *Litteris altero,* 25 Mart. 1830,—*Fontes,* n. 482; S. C. S. Off., litt., 23 Aug. 1877,—*Fontes,* n. 1052; (Engolismen.), 27 Mart. 1878,—*Coll.,* n. 1490; S. C. de

list of legitimate ecclesiastical acts is given in canon 2256, n. 2, of which sponsorship at Baptism and Confirmation will be of more usual concern. Murphy[51] apparently accepts Blat's[52] observation that the exclusion from the sacramentals refers only to those sacramentals which consist of actions and not those which are things (*res*), e. g., holy water.[53] Does this exclusion refer to validity or liceity? Concerning sponsorship at Baptism and Confirmation, canons 765, n. 2,[54] and 795, n. 2,[55] prescribe that those who can validly act as sponsors must not be excluded from legitimate acts by a condemnatory or declaratory sentence. For liceity or lawfulness, canons 766, n. 2, and 796, n. 3, demand that sponsors be not excluded from legitimate acts. With reference to the punishment of canon 2375, it may be said that unless the exclusion from legitimate ecclesiastical acts has been incurred by a declaratory sentence, those laboring under the *ipso facto* exclusion will act illicitly but validly in the capacity of sponsors at Baptism and Confirmation. As to the exclusion from the Sacramentals, since there is no mention of the invalidity of their reception,[56] the reception seems to be valid though illicit.[57]

Prop. F., an. 1638,—Ballerini-Palmieri, *loc. cit.* A later decree of the Holy Office admonishes the Apostolic Vicar of Bombay to instruct his priests: ". . . ne coniuges, que de suo matrimonio mixto clandestine inito dolentes et poenitentes reconciliari Deo desiderant, monere omittant de necessitate obtinendi ab Episcopo dispensationem, ut matrimonio suo, valide quidem sed illicite contracto, in posterum uti licite valeant."—S. C. S. Off., 12 Mart. 1881,—NRT, XV (1883), 121-122. It is not said what is to be dispensed from though there is a suggestion as to the necessity of a dispensation from the impediment itself.

[51] *Delinquencies and Penalties,* p. 108.

[52] *Comment.,* Vol. V, n. 217.

[53] "Privatio Sacramentalium—citari possint benedictio domus; benedictio mulieris gravidae vel matris post tempus purgationis; benedictio agrorum [?]: aspersio aquae lustralis [?]."—Vermeersch-Creusen, *Epitome,* III, n. 492.

[54] "Ut quis sit patrinus, oportet:—Ad nullam pertineat haereticam aut schismaticam sectam, nec sententia condemnatoria vel declaratoria sit excommunicatus aut infamis infamia iuris aut exclusus ab actibus legitimis, nec sit clericus depositus vel degredatus."—Canon 765, n. 2.

[55] "Ut quis sit patrinus, oportet:—Nulli haereticae aut schismaticae sectae adscriptus, nec ulla ex poenis de quibus in can. 765, n. 2 per sententiam declaratoriam aut condemnatoriam notatus."—Canon 795, n. 2.

[56] See canon 2291, n. 6.

[57] An argument analogous to that employed by Pashang (*The Sacramentals according to the Code of Canon Law,* Washington, 1925, p. 74) may be used here. His argument centers on canon 2260 which excludes those excommunicated by a condemnatory or declaratory sentence from their reception. He urges that even in this instance the favorable interpretation may be employed.

243. Though the penalty is incurred only by those who *dared* to contract the *matrimonium mixtum* without a dispensation, the remission of the penalty is not dependent upon the cessation of the contumacy.[58] Moreover, a *dispensation* from the penalty is required, not an absolution.[59] The dispensation is to be sought from the Ordinary and since it implies an act of jurisdiction the norms of canon 94 should be followed.[60] The dispensation is from the *penalty,* not from the impediment. It should not be given until the scandal has been repaired, and the *cautiones* given at least by the Catholic party.[61] Once the marriage has been contracted validly, though without dispensation (this can refer only to mixed marriages), there is no further need of the dispensation from the impediment of Mixed Religion.[62]

ART. V. CONDITIONS REQUIRED FOR DISPENSATION

244. The Church is, indeed, reluctant to dispense from the impediments of Mixed Religion and Disparity of Cult.[63] Before she consents to dispense from her law in a particular case, she demands that certain conditions be fulfilled.[64] These conditions may be summarized under two principal headings: 1) the existence of just and grave causes;[65] 2) the absence of

---

[58] Cf. canons 2286; 2248, § 2.

[59] Cf. canon 2236, § 1.

[60] Blat, *Comment.,* Vol. V, n. 217.

[61] Cf. Wernz, *Ius Decret.,* IV, n. 587; Chelodi, *Ius Matr.,* n. 63; Wernz-Vidal, *Ius Canonicum,* V, n. 180; Urbanus VIII, 14 Mart. 1630,—Ballerini-Palmieri, *Op. Theol. Mor.,* Tract. X, Sect. VIII, n. 712; Pius VIII, litt. ap. *Litteris altero,* 25 Mart. 1830,—*Fontes,* n. 482; S. C. S. Off., litt., 23 Aug. 1877,—*Fontes,* n. 1052.

[62] See the preceding note.

[63] The Church is more disposed to dispense from other impediments such as consanguinity and affinity in order that a Catholic may marry a Catholic. Cf. S. C. S. Off., 12 Ian. 1769, n. I,—*Fontes,* n. 822; Gasparri, *De Matr.,* n. 707; Petrovits, *New Church Law on Matrimony,* n. 253. See infra No. 86, note 22.

[64] The conditions for dispensation are practically the same for both impediments. Cf. Cerato, *Matr.,* n. 17; Ayrinhac, *Marriage Legislation,* p. 153.

[65] Clement IX, 23 Ian. 1669,—Perrone, *De Matr.,* Tom II, cap. VII, art. 2 (quoted in No. 77, note 1); Pius VIII, litt. ap. *Litteris altero,* 25 Mart. 1830,—*Fontes,* n. 482; Gregorius XVI, ep. encyl. *Summo iugiter,* 27 Maii 1832, § 1,—*Fontes,* n. 484; litt. ap. *Quas vestro,* 30 Apr. 1841, n. 2, —*Fontes,* n. 497; Instr. Secret. Stat. iussu Pii PP. IX, 15 Nov. 1858,—*Coll.,* n. 1169; S. C. S. Off., instr. (ad Archiep. Quebecen.), 16 Sept. 1824, ad 5,—*Fontes,* n. 866; instr. (ad Archiep. Corcyren.), 3 Ian. 1871, nn. 3, 6,—*Fontes,* n. 1013; S. C. de Prop. F., instr. (ad Vic. Ap. Fokien.), 13 Sept. 1760,—*Coll.,* n. 435; (C. P. pro Sin.—Sutchuen), 31 Ian. 1796,—*Coll.,* n. 629; litt. encycl. 11 Mart. 1868,—*Coll.,* n. 1324.

the proximate danger to the faith of the Catholic spouse and the assurance of the Catholic education of the children.[66] To this latter end the Church demands that certain *"cautiones"* or *"promises"* be given to establish this assurance.

ART. VI. WHO CAN DISPENSE?

245. No one except the Roman Pontiff has the power to dispense from ecclesiastical impediments unless it has been granted him by common law or by special Apostolic Indult.[67] The repeated insistence of the Holy See that dispensations from the impediments of Mixed Religion and Disparity of Cult are reserved to itself, leaves no room for doubt on this score.[68] The right to dispense from either of the impediments is reserved to the Congregation of the Holy Office, over which the Holy Father presides as Prefect.[69] This rule must be observed even for regions subject to the Congregation of the Propaganda[70] and for those subject to the Congregation for the Oriental Church.[71]

---

[66] Clement IX, 23 Ian. 1669,—Perrone, *loc. cit.*; Benedictus XIV, 15 Feb. 1756,—Ballerini-Palmieri, *Op. Theol. Mor.*, Tract. X, Sect. VIII, n. 707; S. C. S. Off., 29 Ian. 1767,—*NRT*, XV (1883), 423-424; (Sutchuen), 15 Dec. 1769,—*Fontes*, n. 826; instr. (ad Archiep. Corcyren.), 3 Ian. 1871, nn. 3, 6,—*Fontes*, n. 1013; S. C. de Prop F., instr. (ad Vic. Ap. Fokien.), 13 Sept. 1760,—*Coll.*, n. 435; (C. P. pro Sin.—Sutchuen), 31 Ian. 1769,—*Coll.*, n. 629. These references represent only a few of the earlier instructions and decisions. Most of the decisions to which reference will be made in connection with the discussion on the *cautiones* (Chapter XIII) contain the same prescription. When the condition of the absence of danger to the faith of the Catholic party (especially for women) was insisted upon for dispensation from the impediment of Disparity of Cult, it was often expressed by the clause *"si contumelia Creatoris abest."* Cf. Clement IX, 23 Ian. 1669,—Perrone, *loc. cit.*; Benedictus XIV, 15 Feb. 1756,—Ballerini-Palmieri, *loc. cit.*; S. C. S. Off. (Sutchuen.), 15 Feb. 1780,—*Fontes*, n. 840; S. C. de Prop. F., instr. (ad Vic. Ap. Fokien.), 13 Sept. 1760,—*Coll.*, n. 435; (C. P. pro Sin.—Sutchuen), 31 Ian. 1796,—*Coll.*, n. 629; Gasparri, *De Matr.*, nn. 698, 700. The present faculties to dispense from this impediment, given to the Bishops of the United States, also have this clause. The terminology and connotation were evidently borrowed from a usage in connection with the Pauline Privilege. The term appears likewise to have comprised the freedom from the danger of polygamy. Cf. Wernz, *Ius Decret.*, IV, n. 510, not. 40; De Smet, *De Spons. et Matr.*, p. 517, not. 1; Konings-Putzer, *Comment. in Facult.*, p. 380.

[67] Cf. canons 1040; 80-81.

[68] See No. 80, note 11; No. 81, note 14; No. 104, notes 52-54.

[69] Cf. canon 247, § 3.

[70] Canon 252, § 2.

[71] Cf. canon 257, § 2. "In practice if Latin Ordinaries require faculties to issue dispensations in favor of their Oriental subjects they must apply to

246. By common law, Ordinaries can dispense from these impediments in particular cases if recourse to the Holy Office is difficult and if there be danger of grave impending evil in the delay.[72] Ordinaries may likewise dispense from these impediments when urgent danger of death necessitates the adjustment of matters of conscience, and should the case call for it, the legitimation of offspring.[73] In the same circumstances, pastors and those assisting at marriages by virtue of canon 1098, n. 2, who cannot approach the Ordinary, also enjoy this faculty by common law. The opinion that confessors in the same circumstances can validly dispense from these impediments in question for the internal forum and *"in actu sacramentalis confessionis tantum"* may, it appears, be accepted as probable.[74]

247. Having due regard for the "clausulae" at the end of canon 1043, Ordinaries can dispense also in cases where one of these impediments would be discovered after everything is ready for the marriage and the ceremony cannot be delayed without probable danger of grave evil until a dispensation is obtained from the Holy Office.[75] A probable opinion also holds that in like circumstances all those who are given the faculty to dispense in canon 1044 (the confessor only within the conditions postulated) may also dispense from such impediments as Mixed Religion and Disparity of Cult, provided that *the case is occult.*[76]

---

the Oriental Congregation . . . Even for dispensations reserved to the Holy Office, proper procedure sems to demand the intervention of the Oriental Congregation which will obtain the required faculty from the Holy Office or the concession of the requested dispensation."—Duskie, *The Canonical Status of the Orientals in the United States,* p. 179.

[72] See canon 81. These two impediments are among those from which the Holy See is wont to dispense.

[73] Canon 1043. It is scarcely within the scope of the present study to discuss all the requirements of canons 1043-1045. The requirement of the *cautiones* will be discussed in Chapter XIII.

[74] Cf. O'Keeffe, *Matrimonial Dispensations,* p. 118-124; Kelly, *The Jurisdiction of the Simple Confessor,* p. 84-85. "In practice he need not, and should not dispense from them [impediments public in nature and in fact] *qua confessor.* He should urge or even *command* the penitent to manifest the public impediment to him *qua sacerdos* outside the tribunal of penance, and then dispense by virtue of canon 1098, n. 2 . . ."—O'Keeffe, *op. cit.,* p. 124.

[75] Canon 1045, § 1.

[76] Though the impediments of Mixed Religion and Disparity of Cult are by their nature public impediments, they are, nevertheless, comprised in the

248. Those who have received the delegated faculties to dispense must abide by all the conditions enumerated in these faculties. The validity or liceity of dispensations will depend on the observance of the conditions imposed either for validity or liceity. Those who grant dispensations by virtue of a delegated faculty from the Holy Office must make express mention of the Indult in the dispensation.[77] This prescription regards rather the liceity than the validity of procedure.[78]

§ I. Faculties Delegated to the Bishops of the United States

249. The faculty to dispense from the impediment of Mixed Religion is as follows:

Dispensandi, iustis gravibusque accedentibus causis, cum subditis etiam extra territorium aut non subditis intra limites proprii territorii, super impedimento mixtae religionis, et, si casus ferat, etiam super disparitate cultus, ad cautelam; quatenus ante nuptias pars acatholica ad veram religionem adduci aut catholica ab ipsis nuptiis absterreri nequiverit, dummodo prius regulariter, ad praescriptum *Cod. I. C.* can 1061, § 2, cautum omnio sit conditionibus ab Ecclesia requisitis, et *Ipse R. P. D. Ordinarius moraliter certus sit easdem impletum iri,* scilicet: ex parte nupturientis acatholici, de amovendo a parte catholica perversionis periculo, et ab utroque contrahente, de universa prole utriusque sexus in catholicae religionis sanctitate omnino baptizanda

---

phrase *"pro casibus occultis"*. That point was apparently made clear by the Pontifical Commission for the Authentic Interpretation of the Code in the answer of December 28, 1927 to the following *dubium*: *"An verba* PRO CASIBUS OCCULTIS *canonis 1045 § 3 intelligenda sint tantum de impedimentis matrimonialibus natura sua et facto occultis, an etiam natura sua publicis et facto occultis.* R. *Negative ad primam partem, affirmative ad secundam."*—*AAS*, XX (1928), 61, ad III. For a discussion among the authors as to the meaning of *"pro casibus occultis"* see D'Angelo, "In can. 1045 Codicis I. C. excursus", *Apollinaris*, I (1928), 245-262; Noldin, *Theol. Mor.*, III, n. 607; De Smet, *De Spons. et Matr.*, nn. 793-794; Cerato, *Matr.*, n. 38; Cappello, *De Sacram.*, III, n. 236, d; Farrugia, *De Matr.*, n. 87, b; Chelodi, *Ius Matr.*, n. 44; Blat, *Comment.*, Vol. III, P. I, n. 437; Wernz-Vidal, *Ius Canonicum*, V, n. 428; Hilling, *Das Eherecht des C. I. C.*, p. 68; "Studien zum Eherecht des Codex Juris Canonici", *AkKR*, CII (1922), 3-17; O'Keeffe, *Matrimonial Dispensations*, p. 161-184; Kelly, *The Jurisdiction of the Simple Confessor*, p. 179-183. It seems to be a probable opinion that the "occultness" of a case required by canon 1045, § 3 may be determined according to the norms accepted by the Sacred Penetentiaria.

[77] Canon 1057.

[78] S. C. S. Off. (S. Ludovici), 15 Iun. 1875,—*Fontes*, n. 1042.

et educanda: declarata insuper parti catholicae obligatione, qua tenetur, prudenter curandi conversionem coniugis ad fidem catholicam.

Nupturientes autem moneantur se, ante vel post matrimonium
coram Ecclesia initum, ministrum quoque acatholicum ad matrimonialem consensum praestandum vel renovandum adire non posse, ad
mentem *Cod. I. C.*, can. 1063, § 1, sub poena excommunicationis latae
sententiae Ordinario reservatae a parte catholica incurrendae, iuxta
can. 2319, § 1, n. 1,—stricte caeteroquin servatis quae de parochi in
casu agendi ratione statuta sunt in can. 1063, § 2.

Quod si partes actu in concubinatu vivant, provideatur opportunis modis ut scandalum, si adsit, removeatur, et pars catholica ad
gratiam Dei recipiendam rite disponatur, *praevia eius absolutione ab
excommunicatione contracta, si forte matrimonium attentatum fuerit
coram ministro acatholico, eique impositis congruis poenitentiis salutaribus.*

The American Bishops also enjoy the faculty to dispense from
the impediment of Disparity of Cult.

Dispensandi iustis gravibusque accedentibus causis cum subditis
etiam extra territorium, aut non subditis intra limites proprii territorii super impedimento disparitatis cultus (excepto tamen casu matrimonii cum parte iudaica aut mahumetana); quatenus sine contumelia Creatoris id fieri possit et ante nuptias pars non baptizata ad
veram religionem adduci aut catholica ab ipsis nuptiis absterreri nequiverit, dummodo etc.[79]

A. "Cum subditis etiam extra territorium aut non subditis intra limites proprii territorii"

250. The former restrictions expressed in such clauses as
"*exceptis Italis de quibus non constat Italicum domicilium omnino deseruisse*" and that the one dispensing his subjects by
delegated power might dispense only "*intra fines dioecesis*" have
been abrogated.[80] The jurisdiction which the Ordinary enjoys
over his subjects is personal and he can, therefore, dispense in
their favor wherever they are. To those who are not his subjects
he can issue dispensations only while they are actually within
the limits of his diocese, since the jurisdiction in such cases is

---

[79] Vermeersch-Creusen, *Epitome*, II, n. 871.
[80] See No. 103, note 50.

territorial.[81] In this connection it appears that the term "subjects" must be understood in the sense of "Catholic subjects" for dispensations are not given in favor of the non-Catholic party.[82] The presence of non-subjects within the territory of the Ordinary dispensing seems, therefore, to be demanded only of the Catholic party to the marriage.[83]

B. THE DISPENSATION *"mixtae religionis et ad cautelam disparitatis cultus"*

251. The questions relative to the validity of non-Catholic Baptisms have already been discussed in Chapter X.[84] The conclusions that terminated the discussion will serve also as a guide in dealing with the dispensation from the impediment of Disparity of Cult *ad cautelam*. These conclusions suppose the careful investigation (unless this becomes impossible through the circumstances of a particular case) that the Church has always demanded of Baptisms conferred in non-Catholic sects when there is question of a proposed mixed marriage.[85]

252. The faculty given to Ordinaries to dispense from the impediment of Mixed Religion and *ad cautelam* from the impe-

---

[81] Cf. Maroto, *Institutiones*, n. 309, B, b; O'Keeffe, *Matrimonial Dispensations*, p. 94, 147; Motry, *Diocesan Faculties*, p. 133. Augustine (*Rights and Duties of Ordinaries*, p. 275) writes that non-subjects must be actually *residing* in the territory under the jurisdiction of the one dispensing. It is well to note that no canonical residence is required, nor any specified length of residence. Mere physical presence in the territory is sufficient, though necessary, for the validity of dispensations granted in favor of non-subjects.

[82] See No. 289, note 46.

[83] Chelodi (*Ius Matr.*, n. 59) and Cappello (*De Sacram.*, III, n. 313) state that the Ordinary of the Catholic party is the one competent to dispense. Should the Catholic party, however, be within the territorial limits of another diocese, either the Ordinary of that diocese (on the supposition that he has the faculty to dispense non-subjects) or the Catholic party's own Ordinary are competent to dispense.

[84] See Nos. 191-200.

[85] "Fertur insuper saepe non recte applicari principium, vi cuius baptismus dubius habendus est ut validus in ordine ad validitatem matrimonii. Contingit enim sacerdotem, cui incumbit inquirere utrum pars acatholica fuerit baptizata necne, totam suam inquisitionem limitare interrogationi factae parti acatholicae, utrum ipsa fuerit baptizata. Si haec respondit affirmative, nullo requisito documento aut probatione, habetur ut baptizata, et petita tantum dispensatione ab impedimento mixtae religionis, celebrantur nuptiae. Unde fit plura matrimonia sic contracta esse irrita propter impedimentum disparitatis cultus, quia pars acatholica non fuit baptizata, licet id affirmaverit."—Extract from a letter sent by Cardinal Ledochowski to Cardinal Gibbons on August 2, 1901,—*ASS*, XXXIV (1901-1902), 640.

diment of Disparity of Cult, is an apparent departure from the discipline established by the Holy See in the law before the Code.[86] Perhaps the underlying reason for the change is not yet clearly discernible. A very probable reason, however, is the fact that it is becoming increasingly difficult to arrive at the presumptions recognized by the Holy See, especially in those cases where there is only indirect evidence for the very fact of Baptism. This difficulty does not absolve from the necessity of making those investigations that are possible, but the faculty given to the Bishops to dispense *ad cautelam* from the impediment of Disparity of Cult, does seem to take cognizance of the fact that the results of such investigations are often quite unsatisfactory, and that at best they result in leaving the fact of the administration, or of its validity, in a very doubtful state.

253. Whenever, therefore, after due investigation, the fact of a Baptism or its validity conferred in a non-Catholic sect remains doubtful, the dispensation *"mixtae religionis et ad cautelam disparitatis cultus"* should be given rather than that of Mixed Religion alone. Whether the Baptism be doubtful on the score of a *dubium facti* or of a *dubium iuris* is immaterial, for in either event it will resolve itself into a *dubium facti* of the impediment of Disparity of Cult. The faculty to dispense *ad cautelam* may be employed only *"si casus ferat"*, thus forbidding its indiscriminate use. It is reasonable to assume, however, that where the case demands it (*"si casus ferat"*) the Holy See wishes the Ordinary to dispense from the impediment of Disparity of Cult *ad cautelam*, in addition to the dispensation from the impediment of Mixed Religion. This norm of procedure has the support of many canonists.[87]

A case may readily arise where a pastor may petition for permission to assist at the marriage of a Catholic with a non-

---

[86] The rule of refusing to dispense *ad cautelam* from the impediment of Disparity of Cult does not appear, however, to have been absolute. See infra No. 207.

[87] Cappello, *De Sacram.*, III, n. 419, d; Wernz-Vidal, *Ius Canonicum*, V, n. 268; De Smet, *De Spons. et Matr.*, n. 588; Farrugia, *De Matr.*, n. 171; Augustine, *Commentary*, V, p. 186; Durieux, *The Busy Pastor's Book on Matrimony*, p. 79, note 101; Woywod, *A Practical Commentary*, I, n. 1054; Genicot-Salsmans, *Theol. Mor.*, II, nn. 481, 492; Vermeersch, *Theol. Mor.*, III, n. 779; Petrovits, *New Church Law on Matrimony*, n. 239; Ojetti, *Commentarium*, I, p. 126.

Catholic who has formally renounced his membership in the sect in which his Baptism was of doubtful validty. If the non-Catholic has joined no other sect, permission may be given to the priest to assist (provided the requisite conditions have been fulfilled), and a dispensation given from the impediment of Disparity of Cult by virtue of canon 15. It is quite evident that on no condition shall a non-Catholic, whose Baptism is doubtful, receive conditional Baptism in the Catholic Church unless there be a conversion to the Catholic Faith.[88]

C. *"Excepto tamen casu matrimonii cum parte iudaica aut mahumetana"*

254. The Church has always been more severe in her attitude towards the marriages of Catholics with Jews and Mohammedans, than with those of other non-Catholic or pagan sects, and this discipline is based largely upon a presumption of a greater danger to the faith of the Catholic party and of the children. In fact, this presumption appears to have served as the primary impetus in the development of a diriment impediment to the marriages of Catholics with aliens to the Faith. In all probability the impediment of Disparity of Cult began as an impediment to the marriages of Catholics with Jews.[89] Even in modern times the presumption of a greater danger to the Faith in marriages of Catholics with Jews still prevails, for the Jews are more tenacious of their beliefs than most other non-Catholic denominations. The same may be said of Mohammedans. The history of Mohammedanism is that of greatest antagonism to everything Christian. Conversions from Mohammedanism are of the rarest occurrence. Moreover there is a grave danger of polygamous unions. The accentuated severity of the Church is, therefore, clearly justified.

255. The restriction of the faculty to dispense for marriages of Catholics with Jews existed also in former faculties given to the Bishops of the United States, as, for example in formulae "D" and "T". Formula "D", art. III, in granting the faculty to dispense from the impediment of Disparity of

---

[88] See No. 215, note 78.
[89] See Nos. 58-59.

Cult, stated the restriction in much the same way as in the present faculty: *"excepto tamen casu matrimonii cum viro vel muliere iudaeis nisi adsit periculum in mora."*[90]

256. A controversy exists among the authors on the point as to who is to be considered a Jew. Some[91] are of the opinion that a distinction is to be made between Orthodox and Reformed Jews, and that the Reformed Jews are not included in the restriction *"cum parte iudaica"* (or as it appears in the older faculties,—*"cum viro vel muliere iudaeis"*), since they no longer adhere to the practice of circumcision, and to many of the beliefs of Orthodox Judaism.[92] Others[93] refuse to accept the distinction and insist that even those professing Reformed Judaism must be included in the restriction,—*"cum parte iudaica"*. Strangely enough, the same decisions are used to support both contentions. It will be well, therefore, to examine them anew. The one most frequently employed is as follows:

Nella Congregazione di feria V. 3 corrente, proposto il quesito di N. N., in qual conto, trattandosi di dispense matrimoniali, debbano tenersi quegli ebrei che non osservano punto le pratiche della loro religione, anzi i più non sono neppure circoncisi, gli Eminentissimi Cardinali Inquisitori Generali hanno decretato:

Respondeatur in usu Formulae D. n. 3 de Propaganda Fide: Hebraeos de quibus agitur non ese excipiendos.[94]

257. The neglect of circumcision and the non-observance of the practice of the Jewish religion mentioned in the *dubium*, is the line of demarcation urged by the authors between Orthodox and Reformed Judaism. The answer *"Hebraeos de quibus*

---

[90] Konings-Putzer, *Comment. in Facult.*, p. 379.

[91] Wernz, *Ius Decret.*, IV, n. 510, not. 36; Sabetti-Barrett, *Theol. Mor.*, n. 881; Rock, "Disparity of Worship", *Catholic Encyclopedia*, V, 40.

[92] For a summary of the principal beliefs of both Orthodox and Reformed Judaism, see Gigot, "Jews and Judaism", *Catholic Encyclopedia*, VIII, 402-403.

[93] Konings-Putzer, *op. cit.*, p. 380; *AER*, IV (1891), 88-90; Nilles, "Exceptis Italis et Hebraeis", *ZkT*, XV (1891), 390. The language of the latter author is a bit vague, though he seems to follow the stricter interpretation.

[94] S. C. S. Off., 5 Apr. 1889,—*AER*, IV (1891), 90. The same decision was given by the Holy Office on August 3, 1889,—*ZkT*, XV (1891), 390.

agitur non esse excipiendos" is interesting in that it may lend itself to two entirely opposite interpretations. It may mean that those Jews who come under the description in the *dubium* are not to be excepted from the term *"iudaeis"* in formula *D*, n. 3, or it may mean that they are not to be an exception to the normal use of the faculty in dispensing from the impediment of Disparity of Cult.

258. Another decision of the Holy Office given on July 12, 1882, is to the following effect:

In facultate extraordinaria *D* sic legitur: *Dispensandi cum suis subditis . . ., excepto . . . casu matrimonii cum viro vel muliere iudaeis, super impedimento disparitatis cultus.*

Nunc: 1. Si quis ex familia iudaica ortus qui non circumcisus neque umquam iudaismum professus est, cupiat cum catholica matrimonium inire, subiicitur ne hic illi clausulae *excepto insuper casu matrimonii cum viro vel mulieri iudaeis?* Aliis verbis: an dispensatio super impedimento disparitatis cultus contrahentibus potest concedi iuxta hunc n. 3 Extra *D*. In casu negativo supliciter rogo dispensationem super impedimento disparitatis cultus inter catholicam et virum ex parentibus iudaeis natum.—2. Si quis e patre iudaeo et matre infideli vel haeretica natus, qui incircumcisus et nunquam iudaismum professus est desideret in matrimonium ducere catholicam, possuntne contrahentes in hoc casu dispensari super impedimento disparitatis cultus sine respectu interpositionis *excepto insuper casu matrimonii cum viro vel mulieri iudaeis?* Si in hoc casu dispensatio super iudaeismo opus sit, petam suppliciter hanc dispensationem.

R. Vi numeri III Facultatum concedi posse dispensationem super impedimento disparitatis cultus in casibus superius expositis, facto verbo cum SSmo.—SSmus benigne annuit pro praefata declaratione et extensione facultatum, durante indulto iam obtento.[95]

Wernz[96] argues that this decision is to be understood in the sense that Reformed Jews are not to be excepted from the faculty of dispensing from the impediment of Disparity of Cult, and his interpretation seems to be justified. It is well to note, however, that the reply is particular in its nature and cannot be urged as a general principle of interpretation for the present faculties. The limitation is clearly expressed in the last sentence:

---

[95] *Coll.*, n. 1572.
[96] *Ius Decret.*, IV, n. 510, note 36.

"SSmus benigne annuit pro praefata declaratione et extensione facultatum, DURANTE INDULTO IAM OBTENTO." Moreover, even at the time the last edition of Wernz was printed (1912), formula *D* was supplanted by formula *T* (in 1907) and his interpretation can scarcely be accepted as a general principle.[97]

259. Whatever limitations or extensions the foregoing decisions represent, it is but reasonable to assume that the restriction of the faculty is directed rather at the Jewish religion than at the nationality. It would be absurd to maintain that a Catholic could not marry a Catholic who is a Jew by nationality, or that in the term *"cum parte iudaica"* are to be included those who have become members of Christian religious denominations, even such as do not administer Baptism (e. g., the Quakers). On the other hand the distinction between Orthodox and Reformed Judaism is not decisively warranted by the decisions in the use of the faculty for the Reformed Jews, nor is it a safe guide to follow in practice. Reformed Judaism may, indeed, have departed in many respects from the tenets and practices of Orthodox Judaism,—still it is Judaism and a professed adherent is apparently comprised in the term *"cum parte iudaica"*. The faculty, therefore, to dispense from the impediment of Disparity of Cult excludes those cases where the unbaptized party is a professed member of Orthdox Judaism, Reformed Judaism, or Mohammedanism.

260. Having in mind the basis of the limitation of the faculty to dispense from the impediment of Disparity of Cult, it seems but a logical conclusion to urge the same restriction upon the faculty to dispense from the impediment of Mixed Religion should the baptized non-Catholic be a professed member of Judaism or Mohammedanism. The restriction, as it is inserted in the faculty, to dispense from the impediment of

---

[97] The doubtful value of Wernz's interpretation to serve as a general norm is exemplified in the following decision sent to Archibishop Elder of Cincinnati: ". . . Alterum dubium erat num non obstante speciali clausula de iudaeis in facultatibus quas habes, recte dispensaveris nonnumquam cum mulieribus catholicis ut inire possent matrimonium cum iudaeis, qui cupientes huiusmodi nuptias contrahere in scriptis Iudaeismo renuntiaverint. R. Quod ad praeteritum, *supplicandum Sanctissimo pro Sanatione in radice,* quatenus opus sit (quibus precibus Summus Pontifex annuit). Quod ad futurum, recurrat (Ordinarius) in singulis casibus, expositis omnibus circumstantiis."— S. C. S. Off., 20 Iun. 1892, ad II,—*ASS,* XXX (1897-1898), 383-384.

Disparity of Cult does not turn on the fact of the absence of Baptism, but on the presumption of a greater danger to the Faith. The same presumption would, therefore, seem to urge in either case.

261. The former modification *"nisi adsit periculum in mora"* is not explicitly mentioned in the present faculties; nevertheless, if there were danger of grave evil in delay, and time would not permit recourse to the Holy See or the Apostolic Delegate,[98] the Ordinary could dispense by virtue of canon 81. If he does dispense in such circumstances he must have regard for the following conditions: 1) that there be no danger of polygamy; 2) that there will be no danger that the offspring will have to undergo the *rite* of circumcision;[99] 3) that in those places where a civil ceremony must take place it must be of a strictly civil nature, without any invocations to Allah, and without the least semblance of superstition.

D. The *Sanatio in Radice*

262. Recourse to the *sanatio in radice* is the last resort at the disposal of American Bishops in validating mixed or disparate marriages attempted before a civil magistrate or a non-Catholic minister. If the parties living in an invalid union cannot be induced to separate, or if this will bring about even greater evils, the normal resort it to simple convalidation in which the following manner of procedure must be observed: 1) The *cautiones* are to be given by both the Catholic and the non-Catholic party. 2) If the Catholic party has incurred the censure of excommunication (reserved to the Ordinary) because of an attempted marriage before a non-Catholic minister (*"uti sacris addictum"*), the absolution from this censure must be obtained. 3) The dispensation from the impediment of Mixed Religion or Disparity of Cult must be obtained before the pastor can witness the necessary renewal of consent in the

---

[98] The Apostolic Delegate apparently enjoys the faculty. Cf. Vermeersch-Creusen, *Epitome*, I, n. 813.

[99] The reference is to circumcision as a *religious rite* and not as a prophylactic measure. Cf. Winslow, *Vicars and Prefects Apostolic*, p. 107-108; Vermeersch; *De Form. Facult. S. C. de Prop. F.*, n. 92.

form demanded by the Church.[100] When, however, the matrimonial consent (which must continue to persevere) cannot be renewed, either because the non-Catholic party cannot be advised of the invalidity of the marriage without grave danger to the Catholic party, or because the non-Catholic party cannot be induced to renew his consent in the form prescribed by the Church, or because he refuses to give the *cautiones*, there can be no question of simple convalidation, and the only recourse remains in the *sanatio in radice*.[101]

263. The faculty given to the Bishops of the United States is as follows:

Sanandi in radice matrimonia attentata coram officiali civili vel ministro acatholico a suis subditis, etiam extra territorium, aut non subditis, intra limites proprii territorii, cum impedimento mixtae relgionis aut disparitatis cultus, dummodo consensus in utroque coniuge perseveret, isque legitime renovari non possit, sive quia pars acatholica de invaliditate matrimonii moneri nequeat sine periculo gravis damni aut incommodi a catholico coniuge subeundi; sive quia pars acatholica ad renovandum coram Ecclesia matrimonialem consensum, aut ad cautiones praestandas, ad praescriptum *Cod. I. C.*, can. 1061, § 2, ullo modo induci nequeat; dummodo aliud non obstet canonicum impedimentum dirimens, super quo ipse dispensandi aut sanandi facultate non polleat.

Ipse autem R. P. D. Ordinarius serio moneat partem catholicam de gravissimo patrato scelere, salutares ei poenitentias imponat, et si casus ferat, eum ab excommunicatione absolvat iuxta *Cod. I. C.*, can. 2319, § 1, n. 1, simulque declaret ob sanationis gratiam a se acceptatam, matrimonium effectum esse validum, legitimum et indissolubile iure divino et prolem forte susceptam vel suscipiendam legitimam esse; eique insuper gravibus verbis in mentem revocet obligationem, qua semper tenetur, pro viribus tutandi baptismum et educationem universae prolis utriusque sexus, tam forte natae quam forsitan nasci-

---

[100] Cf. Benedictus XIV, instr. (per organum S. C. de Prop. F.), 15 Feb. 1756,—Giovine, *De Dispens. Matr.*, Tom. I, § CCXXXVI, n. 2; S. C. de Prop. F., instr. (ad Vic. Ap. Fokien.), 13 Sept. 1760,—*Coll.*, n. 435; S. C. S. Off., 12 Ian. 1769,—*Fontes*, n. 822; litt. 23 Aug. 1877,—*Fontes*, n. 1052; Chelodi, *Ius Matr.*, n. 63, b; Wernz-Vidal, *Ius Canonicum*, V, n. 181; De Smet, *De Spons. et Matr.*, n. 515; Farrugia, *De Matr.*, n. 138; Petrovits, *New Church Law on Matrimony*, nn. 249-252.

[101] Cf. S. C. S. Off., 6 Iun. 1860,—*AkKR*, VII (1862), 278-279; instr. (ad Ep. S. Alberti), 9 Dec. 1874,—*Fontes*, n. 1036; 22 Aug. 1875,—*NRT*, XV (1883), 579-580; 20 Iun. 1892,—*ASS*, XXX (1897-1898), 383-384; 12 Apr. 1899,—*Fontes*, n. 1219; 22 Aug. 1906,—*Fontes*, n. 1278; 22 Dec. 1916,—*AAS*, IX (1917), 13-14.

turae, in catholicae religionis sanctitate, et prudenter curandi conversionem coniugis ad fidem catholicam.

  Cum autem de matrimonii validitate et prolis legitimatione in foro
externo constare debeat, R. P. D. Ordinarius mandet ut in singulis vicibus documentum sanationis cum attestatione peractae executionis diligenter custodiatur in curia locali, nec non curet, nisi pro sua prudentia
aliter iudicaverit, ut in libro baptizatorum paroeciae, ubi pars catholica
baptismum recepit, transcribatur notitia sanationis matrimonii, de quo
actum est, cum adnotatione diei et anni.[102]

The faculty apparently excludes the granting of a *sanatio in
radice* for a clandistine union of two Catholics since their
union does not labor under the impediments of Mixed Religion or Disparity of Cult. Again, this faculty would not serve
to grant a *sanatio in radice* for a marriage of two reputed Catholics contracted in the form prescribed by the Church if later
it should be discovered that one of the parties was *de facto* unbaptized, for the faculty supposes a clandestine attempt at marriage.[103] Nor can a *sanatio in radice* be applied to a marriage if
the consent of one or both parties is wanting, whether this consent be absent from the beginning, or, if given in the beginning, it be afterwards withdrawn. If the consent was wanting
in the beginning but given later, the *sanatio in radice* can be
granted from the moment the consent was given, provided, of
course it perseveres to the time of the granting of the *sanatio in
radice*. It is sufficient that the consent exist at the moment the
sanatio in radice is given.[104] ___

---

[102] Vermersch-Creusen, *Epitome*, II, n. 871.

[103] In support of this strict interpretation see S. C. S. Off., 22 Dec. 1916,
—*AAS*, IX (1917), 13-14. The clause of the faculty,—"*matrimonia attentata coram officiali civili vel ministro acatholico a suis subditis, etiam extra
territorium, aut non subditis, intra limites proprii territorii*", might, perhaps,
be construed to mean that the clandestine mixed or disparate marriages of
non-subjects should have been attempted in the diocese of the Bishop dispensing. The wording and entire arrangement of this clause, however, so
closely follows that of the clauses referring to subjects and non-subjects in
connection with the faculty to dispense from the impediments of Mixed
Religion and Disparity of Cult (see infra No. 249) that the meaning is in
all probability the same. The slight difference in the construction of the
clause scarcely represents a sufficient variation to demand a change of purpose and meaning. It seems quite probable, therefore, that a Bishop possessing this faculty could grant a *sanatio in radice* in favor of non-subjects (even
though the marriage had been contracted elsewhere) provided that the Catholic party is actually within the limits of his diocese at the time the *sanatio in
radice* is granted. See No. 250.

[104] Cf. Canon 1140.

264. Careful investigation will at times lead to a moral certainty of the existence of a true matrimonial consent although given clandestinely and even with the knowledge of the consequent invalidity of the union. This will more readily be realized in cases where through religious indifference faith has become greatly weakened with the natural result that even the Catholic party will not be greatly concerned about the efficacy of the Church's law.[105] Knowledge or opinion regarding the nullity of a marriage does not necessarily exclude matrimonial consent.[106] As for the non-Catholic party, it will often be found that he will regard with indifference and even with contempt and manifest antagonism any effort on the part of the Catholic spouse or a priest to cast a shadow of doubt upon the validity of his marriage.[107]

265. Antecedent to the attempt at marriage, the Church will give no dispensation to a Catholic to marry a non-Catholic until both parties give the *cautiones*. This is the Church's method of safeguarding the divine law.[108] Additional elements do, however, demand consideration in such cases where a marriage has already been contracted and the parties continue to live together, and for various grave reasons cannot be induced to separate. As long as the Catholic party continues to live in that state, he cannot return to the sacraments, yet sincere repentance

---

[105] Cf. Vermeersch, *De Form. Facult. S. C. de Prop. F.*, n. 94; Wernz, *Ius Decret.*, IV, n. 658, note 30.

[106] Canon 1085.

[107] It does not seem at all improbable that many marriages in which the non-Catholic party manifests such an attitude, will come under the heading of a "putative marriage". Canon 1015, § 4 does not require that both parties be Catholics, but merely gives this descriptive definition: "*si in bona fide ab una saltem parte celebratum fuerit, donec utraque pars de eiusdem nullitate certa evadat.*" The existence of the good faith of the non-Catholic party is not to be assumed in every case, but where there is moral certainty of its existence, there seems to be no cogent reason why individual cases of invalid mixed and disparate marriages may not be regarded as "putative marriages". Those children born of a putative mixed or disparate marriage would be legitimate. Cf. canon 1114. It does not appear to be necessary for the putative quality of a marriage that it be contracted *in facie Ecclesiae* as it was required in the law before the Code. Cf. Wernz, *Ius Decret.*, IV, n. 682. Chelodi (*Ius Matr.*, n. 150) favors this opinion, though Cappello (*De Sacram.*, III, n. 746) does not accept it.

[108] Even subsequent to the attempt at marriage, the Church will not give a simple dispensation from either impediment if the *cautiones* are refused. Cf. S. C. S. Off., 12 Apr. 1899,—*Fontes*, n. 1219.

is not always incompatible with the reluctance to separate from the invalid marriage when grave evils are foreseen to follow this procedure. Weak as may have been the Catholic's faith in spurning the authority of the Church, it is possible for him sincerely to desire a reconciliation. Yet he finds his way blocked by a marriage invalid by the law of the Church. Can, and will the Church remove the obstacle to make his reconciliation possible?

266. The Church is here faced with two evils. If she refuses to dispense from her own law, there is an imminent danger of the loss of the soul of the Catholic party now desiring reconciliation. If she dispenses with the knowledge of the non-Catholic's refusal of the *cautiones*, she dispenses with the normal safeguard against the perversion of the faith of that family. Upon the Catholic party's manifest signs of repentance, the Church seems to turn her attention largely to the good to be accomplished, and apparently choosing the lesser of two evils,[109] she removes the invalidity of the marriage which stands as an obstacle. The imminent danger of the loss of the Catholic's soul is of graver concern than the maintenance of the normal safeguard against his perversion. The sincerity of his repentance may be accepted as an assurance of the remote danger of his perversion. As a kind of substitute for the non-Catholic's giving of the *cautiones* the full obligation is placed upon the Catholic party to do his utmost to procure the Catholic Baptism and education of the children that have been born or will be born. Grave obstacles may at times stand in the way of completely fulfilling this obligation, yet the Catholic party is saved from sin in this regard by the acceptance of the obligation and the honest attempt to fulfill it. Even if the Catholic education of the children would be quite defective, due to the interference of the non-Catholic party, there is reasonable assurance that they will receive some instruction. Moreover, after the age of reason,

---

[109] "Ecclesia igitur *ex sua parte* non raro rationem habere potest et habet relaxandae legis *suae*, etiam quando lex divina-naturalis vel non, vel non plene cessaverit, permittens quaedam mala, ut maiora praecaveantur."—Lehmkuhl, *Casus Consc.*, II, n. 910. Cf. Albitius, *De Inconstantia in Fide*, Cap. XVIII, n. 45; De Lugo, *Tract. de Virt. Fidei Div.*, Disp. XXII, n. 22; Pontius, *De Sacram. Matr.*, Append., cap. VI, n. 5; Leurenius, *Jus Can. Univ.*, Lib. IV, quaest. 117.

and especially in later years, they become personally responsible for their own salvation, and, *caeteris paribus*, the Church places no obstacle to their reception of the sacraments. Such a procedure does not place any premium on the sin of the Catholic attempting the marriage for the entire supposition is that the Catholic *hic et nunc* is truly repentant. The danger of the violation of the divine law is removed to as remote a degree as possible. Whatever danger may remain may be tolerated for the sake of the immediate good of the sinner's conversion. In all other instances, not comprehended by the faculty to grant a *sanatio in radice*, the *cautiones* must be given by both parties. The Holy Office has repeatedly insisted that no dispensations can be given without the *cautiones*.[110] The Church has recourse to the *sanatio in radice* only as a last and final resort to save the soul of the Catholic party. The very recourse to this extraordinary dispensation exemplifies the Church's unwillingness to dispense without the *cautiones*.

267. The question as to when, and in what circumstances, the *sanatio in radice* is to be applied is left largely to the prudence and good judgment of the Bishop possessing the faculty, provided, of course, that he observes the required conditions of the faculty itself. No definite and absolute rule can be given.[111]

ART. VII. *De Individuitate Contractus*

268. In an instruction of the Holy Office sent to the Archbishop of Quebec on September 16, 1824, the principle was enunciated that the Church in dispensing from the impediment of Disparity of Cult, in order that a Catholic might marry an infidel, was to be understood at the same time (and by this one dispensation) as dispensing likewise from those impediments from which the infidel was exempt, and this on the ground that the exemption of the infidel was communicated to the Catholic *"propter individuitatem contractus"*.[112] A further

---

[110] See No. 314, notes 32-33.

[111] The extremities to which the Church is at times willing to go in applying the *sanatio in radice* for such marriages is well exemplified in the following decisions: S. C. S. Off., 22 Aug. 1875,—*NRT*, XV (1883), 579-580; 20 Iun. 1892, ad I,—*ASS*, XXX (1897-1898), 383-384.

[112] "Si praevia Apostolica dispensatione Paulus Balbinam duxit, etiamsi praecessisset Demetrii copula cum eadem Balbina, iam pro valido habendum est matrimonium; quippe impedimentum affinitatis, praesertim ex copula illicita,

decision of the Holy Office of April 23, 1913, stated that this principle was effective also when a dispensation from the impediment of Disparity of Cult was given by delegated authority, —even when given by the delegate dispensing who had not the faculty to dispense from the impediment by which the Catholic party was bound.[113]

269. Does this principle retain its force after the Code? The authors who favor its retention[114] contend that on the basis of canon 20[115] the Roman *"Stylus Curiae"* is to be followed since there is no expressed prescription of the Code that covers the case.[116] On the other hand the authors who deny the

---

ut in casu, cum non habeatur ut iuris divini, aut naturalis, sed tantum ecclesiastici, infideles ex mente Ecclesiae non afficit, quia Ecclesiae non subditos: *et Ecclesia dispensando cum parte catholica super disparitate cultus ut cum infideli contrahat, dispensare intelligitur ab iis etiam impedimentis a quibus exempta est pars infidelis,* ut inde huius exemptio, propter contractus individuitatem, communicata remaneat et alteri."—*Fontes*, n. 866 (ad 2).

[113] "1. Utrum illa dispensatio impedimentorum ecclesiasticorum locum habeat non solum quando dispensatio a disparitate cultus impertitur a S. Sede, sed etiam quando datur a delegato. 2. Utrum dicta dispensatio locum habeat, quando dato a missionario, qui habet facultatem "cumulandi", vel non habet facultatem dispensandi ab impedimento, quo ligatur pars catholica e. g. secundus gradus collateralis. *R.* Ad utrumque affirmative."—*LQS*, LXIX (1916), 151-152.

[114] Cappello, *Da Sacram.*, III, n. 422; Wernz-Vidal, *Ius Canonicum*, V, n. 274; Vermeersch-Creusen, *Epitome*, II, n. 346; Chelodi, *Ius Matr.*, n. 81; Ayrinhac, *Marriage Legislation*, p. 155; Blat. *Comment.*, Vol. III, P. I, n. 468.

[115] "Si certa de re desit expressum praescriptum legis sive generalis sive particularis, norma summenda est, nisi agatur de poenis applicandis, a generalibus iuris principiis cum aequitate canonica servatis; a stylo et praxi Curiae Romanae; a communi constantique sententia doctorum."—Canon 20.

[116] Cappello (*loc. cit.*) seems to stand alone in his opinion that the principle covered also those impediments binding only the Catholic party. While it is true, as he says, that all impediments of the ecclesiastical law bind only the Catholic party in a disparate marriage, his argument limps somewhat by the fact that he uses the example of the impediment of affinity, which is an impediment implying a relation. He does not mention impediments such as age or solemn vows which imply no relation but bind one party alone. Notwithstanding the inapt example it is not so evident that the conclusion is wrong. It was recognized in the Old Law, and for precisely the same reason (*"propter individuitatem contractus"*), that those exempt from the Tridentine law regarding the form of marriage, communicated this exemption to those who were bound, when contracting marriage with them, (See No. 96, note 34). While clandestinity is not to be regarded as an impediment, the law which bound to the form is directly analogous in its comprehension to the impediments of age or solemn vows. Cappello's conclusion does not, therefore, deserve the summary dismissal that it apparently receives from some authors. Cf. De Smet, *De Spons. et Matr.*, p. 519, not. 4.

retention of this principle after the Code[117] lay stress on the point that since there is no mention in the Code of such an implication adhering to a dispensation from the impediment of Disparity of Cult, it must be regarded as abrogated. Canons 1051 and 1053 treat of extended implications of certain dispensations, a fact, which they say, indicates a taxative enumeration. Canon 1036, § 3, rules that though an impediment binds only one party, it nevertheless renders the marriage either illicit or invalid. Finally, though baptized non-Catholics (who have never been baptized in or converted to the Catholic Church) and the unbaptized are exempt from the Catholic form of marriage when marrying among themselves, they no longer communicate this exemption to Catholics even though they contract with them after the impediment has been dispensed from.[118]

270. The apparent weakness of all the arguments, whether they be urged for or against the retention of the principle of the communication of exemption enunciated in the two decisions of the Holy Office,[119] leaves the question largely *in statu quo*. The force of an appeal to canon 20 is somewhat dubious when canon 6, n. 6, is considered.[120] By virtue of canon 6, n. 6, the principle seems to be abrogated. But how reconcile this with canon 20? Does canon 20 take cognizance also of the Old Law or is it restricted to the law of the Code? Is only that *Stylus Curiae* to be regarded which exists after the Code, or may not the *Stylus Curiae* of the past be invoked? The position of canon 20 in the Code and the avowed purpose of canon 6 may indicate that canon 20 is to refer only to the law of the Code, but this is far from certain.[121] Canons 1051 and 1053 may or may

---

[117] De Smet, *op. cit.*, n. 591; Genicot-Salsmans, *Casus Consc.*, n. 1080; Leitner, *Lehrb. des kath. Eherechts*, p. 187; Petrovits, *New Church Law on Matrimony*, n. 256. Woywod (*A Practical Commentary*, I, n. 1057) is in doubt as to whether such force can be attributed to the *Stylus Curiae* as the authors favoring thte retention of the principle suppose.

[118] Canon 1099, § 1, n. 1.

[119] See No. 268, notes 112-113.

[120] "Si qua ex ceteris disciplinaribus legibus, quae usque adhuc viguerunt, nec explicite nec implicite in Codice contineatur, ea vim omnem amisisse dicenda est, nisi in probatis liturgicis libris reperiatur, aut lex sit iuris divini sive positivi sive naturals."—Canon 6, n. 6.

[121] "Whenever there is a gap in the legislation, be it general or particular, the canonist may appeal to laws enacted in similar circumstances. In such a case the old law may serve as a norm for supplying the deficient legislation.

not represent a taxative enumeration of effects beyond the explicit comprehension of dispensations. That is precisely the question. Canon 1036, § 3, states a principle in acceptance also at the time the decisions of the Holy Office were given. It is centuries old. Upon the very foundation of this principle a dispensation was and is required from the impediment of Disparity of Cult.[122] The appeal to canon 1099, § 1, n. 2, is of little avail for it is but a substantial repetition of Article XI, § 2, of the decree *"Ne Temere"*. The decision of the Holy Office of April 23, 1913, was given after the decree *"Ne Temere"*.[123]

271. *In practice*, it seems advisable for those who dispense by a delegated faculty to proceed as though the communication of exemption were no longer recognized.[124] Those enjoying a cumulative faculty to dispense from several impediments existing in one case[125] should, it appears, dispense from all the existing impediments, provided, of course, they have the faculty to dispense from each individual impediment. Those who have not this faculty should submit such cases to the Holy Office.[126] *Post factum* a marriage contracted with a dispensation from the impediment of Disparity of Cult, yet laboring under a diriment ecclesiastical impediment from which no dispensation was given, and from which the unbaptized party is exempt, may not be declared invalid without recourse to the Holy Office.

272. The sacrament of Baptism renders its recipient subject to the laws of the Church, and it is by reason of the subjec-

---

[The reference is to canon 20]. With this one exception the legislator passes a final sentence on antecedent laws which have been abrogated."—Neuberger, *Canon 6*, p. 63.

[122] See No. 237, note 33.

[123] If the communication of exemption still exists in the case of marriages with the unbaptized, it seems likewise to affect the post-Code marriages of the unbaptized with those whose Baptism has not been received in the Catholic Church or who have never been converted to the Catholic Church. Their liberation from the impediment of Disparity of Cult may be regarded as a kind of *quasi* dispensation in a very general sense, and should another diriment impediment of ecclesiastical law, to which the baptized non-Catholic party is bound, exist for a marriage with an unbaptized person, the exemption of the unbaptized party is in all probability communicated to the baptized party.

[124] The opinion favoring its retention seems, however, to be probable.

[125] Since the American Bishops dispense by virtue of a general indult, they possess the cumulative faculty. Cf. canon 1049, § 2.

[126] Cf. canons 1050; 247, § 3.

tion of one of the parties that the Church has exclusive jurisdiction over disparate marriages. The Church alone is competent to dispense from the impediment of Disparity of Cult and those impediments that imply a relation such as consanguinity and affinity,— regardless of their concomitant existence by virtue of the civil law for the unbaptized party.[127] While, indeed, the Church does not claim a direct jurisdiction over the unbaptized, the exemption cedes to an indirect jurisdiction over the unbaptized in reference to any marriage they may contract with the baptized.[128] It appears, therefore, that even if the unbaptized party were bound by an impediment of the civil law such as age, the *habilitas* given the baptized party by the Church would be communicated to the unbaptized party. Vlaming,[129] on the other hand, urges that in such cases the unbaptized remain *inhabiles* through the civil law, and that the Church could not render them *habiles*.

273. Vlaming's opinion supposes that the jurisdiction of the State over the marriages of the unbaptized extends likewise indirectly over marriages between the baptized and the unbaptized. The assumption seems to be somewhat gratuitous. Whether the State has jurisdiction over marriages *between the unbaptized* in its own right or *per accidens*, i. e., by virtue of necessity, is not a vital issue in the present discussion. It does seem apparent, however, that the State possesses such jurisdiction by neither title in disparate marriages, which are clearly under the jurisdiction of the Church.[130] The Roman civil law had its impediment to the marriages of Christians with Jews,[131] yet Pope Benedict XIV clearly draws attention to the fact that (in either capacity, whether it affected the Jew or the Christian) it in no way bound the Church.[132]

274. When Pope Leo XIII writes that marriage by reason

---

[127] Cf. Benedictus XIV, ep. *Singulari*, 9 Feb. 1749, § 7,—*Fontes*, n. 394.

[128] The restricted form of the impediment of Disparity of Cult as it is established in canon 1070, § 1, is not under consideration here.

[129] *Prael. Iuris Matr.*, n. 195. Vide etiam De Becker, *De Spons. et Matr.*, p. 44.

[130] Cf. canons 247, § 3; 1099, § 1, n. 2; 1964. ". . . exclusiva potestas iudicialis supponit exclusivam potestatem legiferam; nam ius fori sequitur ius condendi leges."—Wernz-Vidal, *Ius Canonicum*, V. n. 52.

[131] See No. 56, notes 26-27.

[132] Ep. *Singulari*, 9 Feb. 1749, § 7,—*Fontes*, n. 394.

of its divine origin is *"sua vi, sua natura, sua sponte"*, sacred, belonging *exclusively* to the authority of the Church,[133] a difficulty arises even as to the absolute acceptance of the opinion giving the State jurisdiction over marriages between the unbaptized. There can scarcely, therefore, be question of an indirect jurisdiction of the State over disparate marriages. It would be impossible, according to De Smet,[134] to have one and the same marriage (which is a *"contractus individuus"*) regulated independently by two distinct jurisdictions. De Smet,[135] Wernz,[136] Gasparri,[137] Chelodi,[138] Wernz-Vidal,[139] and Cappello[140] are, therefore, of the opinion that the unbaptized are not bound by the impediments of the civil law when contracting with the baptized who are rendered *habiles* by the Church.

275. As a practical measure, however, pastors should not, as a general rule, assist at the marriages of those impeded by the civil law. The civil law in the United States does not provide for dispensations from civil impediments. While in theory the State has no right to impede marriages under the jurisdiction of the Church, yet the practical consequences of disregarding the civil law must be kept in mind. Those who would contract marriage in spite of the civil law render themselves liable to civil prosecution, which would bring dire consequences upon themselves and their children. In many States also, the official witness of the marriage (such as the pastor) would be subject to prosecution. It is contrary to the mind and wish of the Church for pastors to assist at marriages which render them and the parties subject to severe civil penalties.

---

[133] "Etenim cum matrimonium habeat Deum auctorem, fueritque vel a principio quaedam Incarnationis Verbi Dei adumbratio, idcirco inest in eo sacrum et religiosum quiddam, non adventitium, sed ingenitum, non ab hominibus acceptum, sed natura insitum . . . Igitur cum matrimonium sit sua vi, sua natura, sua sponte sacrum, consentaneum est, ut regatur ac temperetur non principum imperio, sed divina auctoritate Ecclesiae, quae rerum sacrarum *sola* habet magisterium."—ep. encyl. *Arcanum*, 10 Feb. 1880, n. 11,—*Fontes*, n. 580.

[134] *De Spons. et Matr.*, n. 438.

[135] *Loc. cit.*

[136] *Ius Decret.*, n. 60, Scholion.

[137] *De Matr.*, n. 306. Here he recedes from the opposite position he had defended in the second edition (Parisiis, 1900), n. 297.

[138] *Ius Matr.*, n. 12.

[139] *Ius Canonicum*, V, n. 52.

[140] *De Sacram.*, III, n. 67.

ART. VIII. IMPLICATIONS OF DISPENSATION

276. The Church in dispensing either from the impediment of Mixed Religion or Disparity of Cult,[141] dispenses only from her own law, i. e., she removes those obstacles impeding or invalidating a marriage which have been erected through ecclesiastical legislation. The dispensation does imply, however, that, in the judgment of the Church, the divine and natural law are not in a proximate danger of violation. It is not permissible for anyone to condemn indiscriminately those mixed and disparate marriages contracted in conformity with all the conditions prescribed by the Church.[142]

277. A separation from bed and board may be permitted the Catholic party by the Ordinary if, after a mixed or disparate marriage contracted with a dispensation (*et coram Ecclesia*), the non-Catholic party violates the obligations assumed in the *cautiones*.[143] This separation is to take place only on the authority of the Ordinary, unless the danger of perversion is so imminent that delay would be perilous, in which case the Catholic party has the right to separate on his own authority.[144] There can, however, be no dissolution of the bond itself on the ground of a contumely of the Creator.[145] A disparate marriage contracted *coram Ecclesia* with a dispensation from the impediment of Disparity of Cult, cannot be dissolved *in favorem fidei*.[146]

---

[141] A dispensation from the impediment of Mixed Religion does not imply an implicit dispensation from the impediment of Disparity of Cult. See No. 208; No. 251, note 85.

[142] "Quum autem matrimonium mixtum debitis cautionibus superius indicatis et dispensatione obtenta contrahitur, illud tamquam legitimum, ut patet, haberi debet, utpote inter personas initum, quas Ecclesia agnovit in illis adiunctis habiles ad valide et licite matrimonium contrahendum. Nemo igitur hoc matrimonium damnare multoque minus sacrilegii notam illi inuere audeat."— Conc. Plen. Balt. III (1884), n. 132. But see Lehmkuhl, *Casus Consc,.* II, n. 910; No. 36, note 25; No. 115, note 4.

[143] An example of a declaration of nullity given on the ground of the non-observance of the *cautiones* whose fulfillment had been placed as a *sine qua non* condition of the Catholic party's matrimonial consent, may be found in S. R. Rota, 11 Aug. 1921,—*AAS,* XIV (1922), 512-523. Cf. *Apollinaris,* I (1928), 120-121.

[144]. Cf. canon 1131; S. C. S. Off. (Cochinchin.), 1 Aug. 1759, ad. 4,—*Fontes,* n. 810.

[145] Conc. Trident., sess. XXIV, *de Sacram. Matr.,* can. 5,—Denz., n. 975.

[146] Cf. canon 1120, § 2; S. C. S. Off., 14 Iun. 1708,—Ballerini-Palmieri, *Op. Theol. Mor.,* Tract. X, Sect. VIII, n. 704; (Cochinchin.), 1 Aug. 1759, ad 4,—*Fontes,* n. 810; (Nankin.), 5 Mart. 1852,—*Fontes,* n. 918; instr. (ad Ep. S. Alberti), 9 Dec. 1874, ad dub. 2,—*Fontes,* n. 1036; (ad Vic. Ap. Iaponiae Merid.), 4 Feb. 1891,—*Fontes,* n. 1130.

CHAPTER XII

CAUSES FOR DISPENSATION

ART. I. MODIFICATION OF EARLIER DISCIPLINE

278. The severe discipline of the Middle Ages regarding the association of Catholics with aliens to the Faith did not contemplate the possibility of dispensation for mixed and disparate marriages,—in fact the question was not even discussed by mediaeval canonists and theologians. When Pope Clement VIII, in 1604, granted the first recorded dispensation for a mixed marriage he explicitly called attention to the novelty and difficulty of the entire procedure.[1] The Church was apparently willing to grant certain exceptions for disparate marriages in the new fields of missionary activity, yet from the very beginning of the religious revolt of the sixteenth century the Church seemed to appear almost at a loss as to how dispensations for *mixed marriages* could be justified in the very places where the Catholic Faith had flourished for centuries. While she might tolerate for a time the contracting of mixed marriages among the common people without her express permission,[2] she was altogether reluctant to grant dispensations which might in any way be construed as a positive approval of such unions.[3] She would make only one exception, namely, for reasons of a manifest public concern to the Church or to the State, in other words for the *causa publica*.[4] For at least a century and a half the Church's dispensations for mixed marriages were confined to those of the Catholic nobility.[5] Yet, when mixed marriages contracted among the common people without the Church's permission continued to grow in number; when the Church could no longer tolerate such an abuse and sought to enforce

---

[1] See No. 86, note 23.
[2] See No. 97, note 37; No. 104, notes 53-54.
[3] See No. 97, note 37.
[4] See No. 95, notes 31-32.
[5] See No. 95, note 30.

strictly the necessity of dispensation for the mixed marriages of the common people,—it was then that the requirement of the *causa publica* was necessarily modified.[6] The *causa gravis*[7] came, therefore, to receive recognition and accordingly among modern authors, who commit themselves on the question of the necessary quality of the causes, it is acknowledged that the Church will admit also grave causes that regard the *bonum privatum*.

ART. II. NECESSITY OF JUST AND GRAVE CAUSES

279. The severity with which the Church has always forbidden mixed and disparate marriages would be but an idle gesture if, on the other hand, she freely and indiscriminately permitted such unions. The very reasons for the impediments, —the prohibition of a *"communicatio in sacris"* with non-Catholics, the profanation of a sacrament, the deformity of such marriages, proceeding either from a modal or radical difference existing between the parties, demand truly grave causes to justify a dispensation from the Church's law.[8] Moreover, though a dispensation is tantamount to a declaration that the divine and natural law is in no proximate danger of violation, there remains in most instances at least a remote danger to the faith of the Catholic spouse and the children. The Church will not permit her members to run risks that are more or less inherent to all such marriages unless there be just and grave causes for so doing.[9] If all the impediments demand just and grave

---

[6] In a certain sense a notable private good, i. e., one affecting only one person or a very small number (such as the contracting parties themselves) will redound to the public good (cf. Perez, *De Matr.*, Disp. XLV, Sect. V, n. 3), but this was not the sense in which the *bonum publicum* was demanded as a cause for dispensation from the impediment of Mixed Religion. It was rather in the sense of a public good for the Church or for the State.

[7] See No. 105 with note 55.

[8] Cf. Cappello, *De Sacram.*, III, n. 314; Ballerini-Palmieri, *Op. Theol. Mor.*, Tract. X, Sect. VIII, n. 712; De Smet, *De Spons. et Matr.*, n. 506; Bonacina, *Op. Omnia*, Tom. I, Disp. IX, Quaest. III, Punct. VII, n. 2.

[9] ". . . ad matrimonium mixtum permittendum minime sufficit ut sponsi cautiones . . . admittere parati sint, nec non ceteras clausulas in rescriptis Apostolicae Sedis adhiberi solitas, sed omnino iustae gravesque requiruntur causae, ut facultas dispensandi super mixtae communionis impedimento licite executioni mandetur. Cautiones enim illae ideo naturali divinoque iure exiguntur atque exigi debent, ut pericula intrinseca quae mixtis insunt matrimoniis removeantur; at vero ut gravibus fidei ac morum periculis etiam sub opportunis

causes for dispensation,[10] how much more so those which derive a part of their prohibitive force from the very natural and divine law. It is of no little significance that the Code in its legislation on the matrimonial impediments *specifically* mentions the necessity of just and grave causes only for the impediments of Mixed Religion and Disparity of Cult.

CANON 1061

§ 1. *Ecclesia super impedimento mixtae religionis non dispensat, nisi:*
1° *Urgeant iustae ac graves causae.*[11]

§ I. DISPENSATIONS GRANTED WITHOUT JUST AND GRAVE CAUSES

280. The authors are unanimous in their agreement that if the Pope were to dispense from the impediments, especially those of Mixed Religion and Disparity of Cult, without a just and grave reason, the dispensation would be gravely illicit. Others carry their conclusions even further with regard to the two impediments in question, insisting that under such circumstances the dispensation would be invalid. The Pope, they argue, is responsible to God for the proper administration of the divine law and he cannot, therefore, act validly in dispensing without a just cause.[12]

281. It is to be freely admitted that those who have received a delegated faculty to dispense would act invalidly if they dispensed without a just and grave cause.[13] In all likeli-

---

cautionibus fideles se exponere permittantur, grave aliquod incommodum ceteroquin haud devitandum immineat necesse est."—S. C. de Prop F., litt. encycl., 11 Mart. 1868,—*Coll.*, n. 1324. Cf. Albitius, *De Inconstantia in Fide*, Cap. XXXVI, n. 198.

[10] Cf. canon 84, § 1; Benedictus XIV, const. *Ad Apostolicae*, 25 Feb. 1742, §§ 1, 4, 6,—*Fontes*, n. 325; S. C. de Prop. F., instr., 9 Maii 1877,—*Coll.*, n. 1470.

[11] Canon 1071 establishes the same norms for the impediment of Disparity of Cult.

[12] Cf. De Justis, *De Dispens. Matr.*, Lib. III, cap. I, nn. 18-23; Giovine, *De Dispens. Matr.*, Tom. I, § LXIV, nn. 2-4.

[13] Canon 84, § 1. Cf. S. C. de Prop. F., litt. encycl., 11 Mart. 1868,—*Coll.*, n. 1324; Giovine, *op. cit.*, Tom. I, § LXVI, n. 4; Cappello, *De Sacram.*, III, n. 314; Cerato, *Matr.*, n. 55; Wernz-Vidal, *Ius Canonicum*, V, n. 178; De Smet, *De Spons. et Matr.*, n. 506.

hood, a dispensation is also invalid (at least in the external forum) if it is granted without a just and grave cause being known to the one dispensing by a delegated faculty,—even though a just and grave cause did exist objectively.[14] It does not appear, however, that invalidity may be predicated of dispensations granted by the Pope without cause from the impediments of Mixed Religion and Disparity of Cult. With reference to these impediments, the Church does not pretend to dispense from the divine or natural law, but rather exercises this power only over her own law. In such contemplated marriages where the divine prohibition may be judged to cease, but which from the point of view of the Church would not possess justifying reasons for dispensation, it is by no means manifest that a dispensation granted by the Pope without a cause would be invalid.[15] Even on the supposition that the divine law were in danger of being violated, such dispensations, though gravely illicit, appear to be valid. The dispensation is from the law of the Church, not from the divine law.[16] At best, the discussion has merely an academic interest for *de facto* the Pope will not dispense from these impediments unless just and grave causes do exist, and where the divine law is not in proximate danger of violation.[17]

ART. III. WHAT ARE JUST AND GRAVE CAUSES?

282. What, then, are just and grave causes for dispensing from the impediments of Mixed Religion and Disparity of Cult? While the Code specifically demands just and grave causes for dispensation, it does not indicate what causes are to be

---

[14] Cf. S. C. de Prop. F., 2 Aug. 1901,—*ASS*, XXXIV (1901-1902), 640; De Justis, *op. cit.*, Lib. III, cap. I, n. 28. Konings-Putzer (*Comment. in Facult.*, p. 80-81) is of the opinion that a dispensation would be valid if a sufficient cause existed objectively, even though unknown to the one dispensing. Maroto (*Institutiones*, n. 306, B) inclines to the same opinon though he admits the probability of the opposite opinion that the dispensation would be invalid.

[15] Cf. Augustine, *Rights and Duties of Ordinaries*, p. 121.

[16] Cf. Petrovits, *New Church Law on Matrimony*, n. 244. See infra No. 334.

[17] "Inutilis videtur esse ulterior inquisitio, num in ista hypothesi saltem valida sit dispensatio R. Pontificis super lege ecclesiastica, qua idem impedimentum nititur. Nam R. Pontifices manente prohibitione divina nunquam dispensant ab hoc impedimento canonico."—Wernz, *Ius Decret.*, IV, n. 583, not. 24.

regarded as just and grave. To aid in the solution of this question recourse will be had to those lists of causes recognized as canonical by the Holy See, and to those causes having a more particular reference to the impediments in question and generally accepted by approved authors.

283. There are two lists of causes that are recognized by the Holy See, though in most respects they are largely identical. One is a list of sixteen causes[18] contained in an instruction of the Sacred Congregation of the Propaganda;[19] the other is a list of twenty-eight causes[20] drawn up by Cardinal Masella as rep-

---

[18] 1. Angustia loci; 2. Aetas foeminae superadulta; 3. Deficientia aut incompetentia dotis; 4. Lites super successione bonorum iam exortae, vel earumdem grave aut imminens periculum; 5. Paupertas viduae; 6. Bonum pacis; 7. Nimia, suspecta, periculosa familiaritas, nec non cohabitatio sub eodem tecto, quae facile impediri non possit; 8. Copula cum consanguinea vel affini vel alia persona impedimento laborante praehabita, et praegnantia, ideoque legitimatio prolis; 9. Infamia mulieris, ex suspicione orta, quod illa suo consanguineo aut affini nimis familiaris, cognita sit ab eodem, licet suspicio sit falsa; 10. Revalidatio matrimonii; 11. Periculum matrimonii mixti, vel coram acatholico ministro celebrandi; 12. Periculum incestuosi concubinatus; 13. Periculum matrimonii civilis. Ex dictis consequitur, probabile periculum quod illi, qui dispensationem petunt, ea non obtenta, matrimonium dumtaxat *civile*, ut aiunt, celebraturi sint, esse legitimam dispensandi causam; 14. Remotio gravium scandalorum; 15. Cessatio publici concubinatus; 16. Excellentia meritorum, cum aliquis aut contra fidei catholicae hostes dimicatione aut liberalitate erga Ecclesiam, aut doctrina, virtute, aliove modo de Religione sit optime meritus.

[19] 8 Maii 1877,—*Coll.*, n. 1470.

[20] 1. Propter angustiam loci; 2. Propter angustiam locorum; 3. Propter angusutiam, cum clausula, *et si extra*, dos non esset competens; 4. Propter incompetentiam dotis Oratricis; 5. Propter dotem cum augmento; 6. Pro indotata; 7. Quando alius auget dotem; 8. Propter inimicitias; 9. Pro confirmatione pacis; et propter foedera inter Principes et Regna; 10. Propter lites super successione bonorum; 11. Propter dotem litibus involutam; 12. Propter lites super rebus magni momenti; 13. Pro Oratrice filiis gravata; vel parentibus orbata; 14. Pro Oratrice excedente 24 annum aetatis; 15. Propter difficultatem virorum accedendi ad locum, contrahendum cum loci habitatoribus, e. g., quia expositi pyratarum invasionibus. Propter virorum paucum numerum, e. g., ratione belli; 16. Propter catholicam religionem contrahentis in tuto ponendam; et periculum matrimonii mixti; 17. Propter spem conversionis compartis ad catholicam religionem; 18. Ut Bona conserventur in familia; 19. Pro. illustris familiae conservatione. Pro conservatione regiae stirpis; 20. Ob. excellentiam meritorum; 21. Ob familiarum honestatem conservandam.—Quod ipsi, qui ex honestis familiis sunt, ad eandem conservandam familiarùm honestatem; 22. Ob infamiam; et Scandalum; 23. Ob copulam. Ob raptum; 24. Ob marimonium civile; 25. Ob matrimonium coram ministro protestante; 26. Ob matrimonium nulliter contractum; 27. *Ex certis rationibilibus causis.*—Scilicet, *ob copiosiorum Compositionem* in gradibus aliquantulum remotis; vel in gradibus remotioribus ob causam boni publici Pontificis animum moventem; 28. *Ex certis specialibus rationabilibus causis, Oratorum animos moventibus et Sanctitati Vestrae* expositis.—Scilicet ob copulam, vel actus inhonestos, quos ob honorem Oratorum, attenta eorum qualitate, non expedit explicare.

resentative of those recognized by the Holy See.[21] The list of causes given by the Sacred Congregation of the Propaganda is preceded by an admonition that is to be examined carefully. It begins by reminding those who have delegated faculties of dispensing, that dispensations are not to be granted *"nisi legitima et gravis causa interveniat"*, and that the graver the impediment, the graver should be the cause for dispensing.[22] Certain abuses had arisen that prompted the necessity of an instruction:

Idcirco opportunum visum est in praesenti Instructione paucis perstringere praecipuas illas causas, quae ad matrimoniales dispensationes obtinendas iuxta canonicas sanctiones et prudens ecclesiasticae provisionis arbitrium, pro sufficientibus haberi consueverunt . . .

Atque ut a causis dispensationum exordium ducatur, operae pretium imprimis animadvertere, unam aliquando causam seorsim acceptam insufficientem esse, sed alteri adiunctam sufficientem existimari . . . Huiusmodi autem causae sunt quae sequuntur.

§ I. The Graver the Impediment, the Graver the Cause Required for Dispensation

284. With reference to the admonition that the graver the impediment, the graver should be the cause for dispensation, it is well to note that the special insistence of canon 1061, § 1, n. 1, that just and grave causes must exist before the Church will dispense, indicates clearly that the two impediments of Mixed Religion and Disparity of Cult are to be regarded as grave impediments.[23] And between these two impediments themselves there appears to be a difference of gravity that renders Disparity of Cult, because of its constituent elements and diriment nature, an impediment of greater concern than that of Mixed Religion.

---

[21] Ex S. Dataria Apostolica,—*ASS*, XXXIV (1901-1902), 34-35.

[22] "Cum dispensatio sit iuris communis relaxatio cum causae cognitione, ab eo facta, qui habet potestatem, exploratum omnibus est dispensationes ab impedimentis matrimonialibus non esse indulgendas, nisi legitima et gravis causa interveniat. Quin imo facile quisque intelligit, tanto graviorem causam requiri, quanto gravius est impedimentum, quod nuptiis celebrandis opponitur."—S. C. de Prop F., instr., 8 Maii 1877,—*Coll.*, n. 1470. Cf. canon 84, § 1.

[23] Even though Mixed Religion be but a prohibitive impediment, it must be regarded as a major impediment and can in no way be assimilated to the list of minor impediments given in canon 1042. The entire history of the Church's attitude towards the marriages of Catholics with heretics and schismatics quite destroys the probability of any opinion to the contrary. Cf. Augustine, *Rights and Duties of Ordinaries*, p. 274.

Indeed, some authors are of the opinion that a graver cause should exist for dispensing from the former than from the latter.[24] The Code, however, indicates no necessity of a graver cause for dispensation from the impediment of Disparity of Cult, nor can such a distinction be traced in the history of the Church's attitude in dispensing from these two impediments,—if anything, she appears to have had the graver concern for mixed marriages. Others call attention to the fact that a graver cause should exist in Christian communities than in missionary regions,[25] and that the Church is more disposed to dispense for cases of validation than for contemplated marriage.[26]

225. Some discussion has also turned upon the required gravity of a cause depending on whether the woman or the man be a Catholic. On the ground that the danger of perversion is more remote, Petrovits argues that the Church is more disposed to dispense in the case of a Catholic man marrying an infidel than *vice versa*.[27] It is to be noted, however, that the majority of the decisions of the Holy See that may be referred to in confirmation of this opinion are those concerned with the pagan countries of the Orient where the laws and customs grant the husband a complete *potestas* over his wife.[28] For this reason

---

[24] Cf. De Smet, *De Spons. et Matr.*, n. 590. Augustine (*Commentary*, V, p. 185) says that the causes should be as grave if not graver. Petrovits (*New Church Law on Matrimony*, nn. 190, 245) cites the same causes for both impediments. There is a real doubt, on the other hand, whether, *de facto*, the Church has always regarded the impediment of Disparity of Cult with graver concern than that of Mixed Religion. By virtue of the faculty granted by Pope Leo XIII in 1888, Ordinaries could dispense from the impediment of Disparity of Cult but not from the impediment of Mixed Religion. See No. 103, note 49.

[25] Chelodi, *Ius Matr.*, n. 81; Wernz-Vidal, *Ius Canonicum*, V, n. 273, not. 47.

[26] Chelodi, *loc. cit.*; Wernz-Vidal, *loc. cit.* Cf. S. C. de Prop F., instr. (ad Vic. Ap. Fokien.), 13 Sept. 1760,—*Coll.*, n. 435; litt. (ad Vic. Ap. Tunk. Orient.), 3 Maii 1828,—*Coll.*, n. 804.

[27] *New Church Law on Matrimony*, n. 248.

[28] "Quae duo quidem eo faciliora debent esse viris catholicis quod per leges sinenses maxima est virorum potestas super proprios uxores; itaque ea potestate uti possunt ut prolem, nullo metu, in fide catholica educent, atque ut persuasione, exemplo ceterisque modis charitatis et prudentiae propriis, uxorem ad fidem convertant."—S. C. de Prop. F., instr. (pro Miss. Sin.), 16 Feb. 1795,—*Coll.*, n. 623. The *dubia* proposed for the following two decisions of the Holy Office are witnesses to the observance of this practice: S. C. S. Off. (Sutchuen.), 15 Feb. 1780,—*Fontes*, n. 840; (Pekin.), 29 Apr. 1891,—*Fontes*, n. 1134. Vlaming (*Prael. Iuris Matr.*, n. 240) likewise favors this opinion for his country because of the prescriptions of the civil law.

the opinion has due limitations and scarcely enjoys the status of
a general principle. On the contrary Pope Pius VI seemed to be
quite inclined to the opposite opinion when he warned against
Catholic men marrying heretical women.[29] The authors such as
De Lugo,[30] Ballerini-Palmieri,[31] Gasparri,[32] and Cappello[33] merely
discuss both sides of the question[34] without arriving at any definite conclusions. They call attention to the apparent greater
danger of perversion if the woman be a Catholic (especially if
the civil law grants the husband almost a complete *potestas*
over his wife), yet admit that in many instances the Catholic
education of the children will be better safeguarded if the
mother be a Catholic.

Since in this country the *potestas* of the husband over the
religious matters of his household is scarcely recognized by the
civil law, it seems that the lesser of two evils would, as a general rule, be represented by the fact that the mother in a mixed
or disparate marriage be the Catholic, though the necessity of
demanding a graver cause if the husband be a Catholic is by no
means obvious.

286. But again, while it is to be admitted, as a general
principle, that the graver the impediment, the graver should be
the cause for dispensation, many difficulties will arise in putting this principle into practice. As a matter of principle, it is
thoroughly logical to contend, for example, that normally a
graver cause should exist to dispense from the second degree of

---

[29] In his opinion the danger of perversion would be greater if the woman
were a heretic and by way of confirmation he cites Biblical instances. He quotes
also from Cardinal Bellarmine: "ea siquidem est natura foeminarum, ut multo
facilius sit ut ipsae viros pertrahant ad errorem, quam ut viri eas perducant ad
veritatem."—rescript. ad Card. Archiep. Mechlinien., 13 Iul. 1782, n. 2,—
Fontes, n. 471. Cf. S. C. S. Off. (Helvetiae), 21 Ian. 1863, n. 2,—
Fontes, n. 973. Nevertheless, Pius VIII (litt. ap. *Litteris altero,* 25 Mart.
1830,—*Fontes,* n. 482) and Gregory XVI (ep. *Non sine gravi,* 23 Maii
1846, n. 2,—*Fontes,* n. 503) center their concern on Catholic women
marrying heretics. Cf. Albitius, *De Inconstantia in Fide,* Cap. XVIII, n. 45.

[30] *Tract de Virt. Fidei Div.,* Disp. XXVII, Sect. II, n. 90. De Lugo dwells
with some detail upon hypothetical cases of mixed marriages among the nobility.

[31] *Op. Theol. Mor.,* Tract. X, Sect. VIII, n. 719.

[32] *De Matr.,* n. 504.

[33] *De Sacram.,* III, n. 314.

[34] Vide etiam Clemens XIII, ep. *Quantopere,* 16 Nov. 1763, §§ 2-3,—
Fontes, n. 460.

consanguinity than from the third degree. There are, indeed, some causes, especially those of a public or a quasi public nature, that are obviously of greater import than others of a private kind, but at certain points the distinction among the causes between grave and graver is quite obscure. What is the precise difference in gravity, for example, between such causes as: the validation of an invalid union; the cessation of concubinage; the removal of grave scandals? Individual instances might emphasize a distinction but the point at issue is scarcely clarified by such a recourse. The principle seems to rest rather on the supposition that there is an objective degree of gravity among the causes irrespective of particular circumstances and that some causes will suffice for some impediments but not for others.[35] But to what degree in this scale of gravity can one point as a line of demarcation between those causes sufficient for the impediment of Mixed Religion but insufficient for the impediment of Disparity of Cult, or for any of the hypothetical situations postulated by the authors? Obviously, it will be difficult to apply the principle in practice and it may be stated at once that as long as there is a presence of a grave cause or causes, which requirement is the only one demanded by canon 1061, § 1, n. 1[36] for these impediments, the dispensation may be granted, whether the cause be graver or less grave than other grave causes.

§ II. The Sufficiency of Causes Taken Singly

287. There is yet another point in the introduction to the list of causes given by the Sacred Congregation of the Propaganda that deserves careful examination. It is stated that at times a certain cause may not suffice of itself but when taken conjointly with another or others it will suffice. Immediately following this is the last sentence: *"Huiusmodi autem causae sunt quae sequuntur."* Does this sentence refer to the preceding paragraph where the introduction states that a list of the principal canonical causes sufficient for matrimonial dispensations will be

---

[35] Cf. Vermeersch, *De Form. Facult. S C. de Prop. F.*, p. 90-91.

[36] The clause in canon 1061, § 1, n. 1, *"Urgeant iustate ac graves causae"*, does not necessarily imply that in every petition there must be more than one cause. The salient point seems to be that the cause or causes urged must be just and grave.

given, or does it refer rather to the paragraph of which it is the last sentence?[37]

Unless it is quite misplaced, the sentence refers to the paragraph of which it is a part and its meaning would, therefore, seem to be, that none of the causes listed, even though they be canonical and the principal causes recognized by the Holy See, are sufficient for dispensation when taken singly, but must be taken conjointly with at least one other, or be given this sufficiency through the circumstances of a particular case. Is there not perhaps some difficulty in reconciling this sentence with the preceding paragraph of the introduction and with a sentence immediately following the list of causes: *"Hae sunt communiores potioresque causae, quae ad matrimoniales dispensationes impetrandas adduci solent . . ."*? Are there no causes, apart from the *causae publicae*, that will suffice singly?

288. The question becomes more confused upon turning to the authors, for when they comment upon the causes sufficient for dispensation from the impediments of Mixed Religion and Disparity of Cult and admit that private causes will also be recognized, they call attention at the same time to the principle that the cause or causes must be proportionate to such grave impediments. They conclude, therefore, that such causes as *aetas superadulta, angustia loci, paupertas viduae, incompetentia dotis,* and *bonum pacis,* which may be urged for other impediments, will not readily suffice, when taken singly, for the impediments of Mixed Religion and Disparity of Cult.[38] The direct implication is that there are causes in the list given by the Congregation of the Propaganda that will suffice when taken singly. But why single out these causes that are to be regarded as insufficient when the last sentence of the introduction to the list in which they appear suggests that none of the causes in the entire list, when taken singly, have this sufficiency? And again, why do the authors number among the causes, appar-

---

[37] See No. 283.

[38] Cf. De Smet, *De Spons. et Matr.,* n. 506; Farrugia, *De Matr.,* n. 133; Cappello, *De Sacram.,* III, n. 314; Cerato, *Matr.,* n. 55; Vlaming, *Prael. Iuris Matr.,* n. 217; Winslow, *Vicars and Prefects Apostolic,* p. 106; Petrovits, *New Church Law on Matrimony,* nn. 190, 245; Wernz, *Ius Decret.,* IV, n. 586, not. 31; Wernz-Vidal, *Ius Canonicum,* V, n. 178, not. 30; Vermeersch, *De Form. Facult. S. C. de Prop. F.,* p. 91.

ently sufficient when taken singly, such a cause as *"periculum matrimonii civilis"* which appears in the list given by the Congregation of the Propaganda?[39]

289. In the attempt to offer a kind of solution of this difficulty, the opinion is ventured that, *post factum*, a dispensation granted by virtue of a delegated faculty from either of the two impediments in question, for any one of the causes enumerated in either of the two recognized lists as being canonical and legitimate,[40] is not to be presumed or to be declared invalid without referring the matter to the Holy Office.[41] *Ante factum*, those who dispense by a delegated faculty must follow the *Stylus Curiae* of Rome.[42] This *stylus* may be unknown to many in its more intricate details, yet a fair guide, as a substitute, may be offered in the lists of causes given by approved authors as sufficient for these two impediments.[43] Cognizance must be taken of the approved authors' opinions with reference to the insufficiency of certain causes taken singly. This is demanded at least for the liceity of the dispensation. Unless the cause urged for dispensation be of a public or at least a quasi public nature, more than one cause should normally be given in the petition. If there is a doubt about the sufficiency of a cause, canon 84, § 2[44] may be employed to solve the doubt. Attention is also to be

---

[39] See No. 283, note 18 (cause n. 13).

[40] See No. 283, notes 18, 20. Obviously, a cause such as *"periculum matrimonii mixit"* is not included in the comprehension of this statement.

[41] The presumption is for the validity of the act of dispensing until it is clearly proved to be invalid. Knecht (*Grundriss des Eherechts*, p. 108, not. 1) maintains that any of the causes given in Cardinal Masella's list (See No. 283, not 20), whether taken singly or collectively. is sufficient for matrimonial dispensations. Speaking of the causes required for the impediment of mixed Religion, Augustine (*Commentary*, V, p. 147 [also on p. 185]) writes: "Concerning the reasons we refer to canon 1054 [where he gives the list published by the Congregation of the Propaganda]. Any of the reasons there stated will suffice for obtaining a dispensation." Joseph Palica (*Analecta Ecclesiastica*, Romae, X [1902], 361) is of the same opinion: *"Hodie vero sufficiunt pro dispensatione largienda etiam ceterae causae canonicae quae pro reliquis impedimentis valeant, dummodo adsint semper cautiones."* Vide etiam Blat. *Comment.*, Vol. III, P. I, n. 456. The prescription of canon 84, § 2 likewise strengthens the presumption for the validity of the dispensation.

[42] Cf. Wernz, *Ius Decret.*, IV, n. 586; Konings-Putzer, *Comment. in Facult.*, p. 15.

[43] See also canon 29.

[44] "Dispensatio in dubio de sufficientia causae licite petitur et potest licite et valide concedi."—Canon 84, § 2.

called to the fact that such causes as *aetas superadulta*, and *angustia loci* must exist in the Catholic party,[45] since the dispensation is given only to the Catholic party.[46]

A. Causes Regarded as Sufficient by Approved Authors

290. Lists of causes that have a particular reference to the impediments of Mixed Religion and Disparity of Cult are found especially among the more recent authors. All agree, of course, that any cause representing the welfare of a Christian State or of the Church will be quite sufficient, but in addition the authors cite other causes that apparently possess this sufficiency.[47] Among them may be enumerated the following:

1. A grave scandal arising from diffamation, pregnancy, or from some other source, that cannot be prevented except through a mixed or disparate marriage.[48]

2. The predominance of heretics or schismatics (or infidels)

---

[45] Wernz, *Ius Decret.*, IV, nn. 510, 586;; Wernz-Vidal, *Ius Canonicum*, V, n. 178; De Smet, *De Spons. et Matr.*, p. 443, not. 4; Chelodi, *Ius Matr.*, n. 81; Durieux, *The Busy Pastor's Book on Matrimony*, p. 81, note 104.

[46] S. C. S. Off., 12 Ian. 1769, n. II, 1.—*Fontes*, n. 822; (Southwark), 22 Nov. 1865,—*Fontes*, n. 989; Pius VI. rescript. ad Card. Archiep. Mechlinien., 13 Iul. 1782, n. 3,—*Fontes*, n. 471; Wernz, *op. cit.*, n. 510.

[47] With reference to the sufficiency of a cause, Cerato (*Matr.*, n. 55) says: "*In periculo mortis, vel in casu urgentiore, causa iusta et gravis ad validitatem dispensationis habetur in ipsis rerum adiunctis.*" It appears, however, that the danger of death is postulated in canons 1043 and 1044 rather as one condition of the exercise of the faculty of dispensing than as a cause sufficient of itself for dispensation. The further condition demanded in canon 1043: "*ad consulendum conscientiae et, si casus ferat, legitimationi prolis*", may, in conjunction with the danger of death, be regarded as both a condition of, and as a grave and just cause for, dispensation. If by the term "*in casu urgentiori*" is included all that canon 1045 demands for the different situations enumerated, it may be regarded as a sufficient cause for dispensation.

[48] Bangen, *De Spons. et Matr.*, Tit. IV, p. 21; Vlaming, *Prael. Iuris Matr.*, n. 216; Petrovits, *New Church Law on Matrimony*, nn. 190, 245; Gasparri, *De Matr.*, n. 504; Cappello, *De Sacram.*, III, n. 314; Winslow, *Vicars and Prefects Apostolic*, p. 105; Augustine, *Commentary*, V, p. 147; Farrugia, *De Matr.*, n. 133; Leitner, *Lehrb. des kath. Eherechts*, p. 238; De Smet, *De Spons. et Matr.*, n. 506; Cerato, *Matr.*, n. 55; Konings-Putzer, *Comment. in Facult.*, p. 382. Vlaming (*loc. cit.*) cites two other causes which may, however, be grouped with the cause cited above. They are: 1. "*Si matrimonium mixtum finem imponet turpi concubinatui nubere cupientium; 2. si per matrimonium mixtum obtineri poterit, quod proles, ex partium fornicatione sive iam nata, sive nascitura, catholice baptizetur et educetur.*"

in a given region, provided that Catholics are secure and free in professing their religion.[49]

3. If a mixed (or disparate) marriage is the only means whereby children born of another mixed or disparate marriage will be educated in the Catholic Faith.[50]

4. Danger of apostasy of the Catholic party if the dispensation is denied.[51]

5. Danger of civil marriage, or of contracting before a non-Catholic minister.[52]

6. The cause of conversion:

a) A probable hope that a favorably disposed non-Catholic family will come into the Church through a mixed or disparate marriage.[53]

b) A written promise, or an oral promise before

------

[49] The delegated faculty of dispensing from the impediment of Disparity of Cult was given in the past to Ordinaries of missionary regions on the condition that it could be used only in those regions where infidels outnumbered Catholics. (See No. 77, note 1). Cf. Gasparri, *op. cit.*, n. 699; Petrovits, *op. cit.*, n. 243. On the other hand it is not altogether clear that this condition of itself was regarded as a canonical cause for dispensation even in missionary regions. Modern authors, however, apparently regard it as a canonical cause. Cf. Vlaming, Cappello, Winslow, Leitner (isti auctores *loc. cit.*); Zitelli, *De Dispens. Matr.*, p. 60; Petrovits, *op. cit.*, nn. 190, 245; Gasparri, *op. cit.*, n. 504; Giovine, *De Dispens. Matr.*, Tom. 1, § CLXXIII. n. 4; Wernz, *Ius Decret.*, IV, n. 586, not. 31; Vermeersch-Creusen, *Epitome*, II, n. 331; Konings-Putzer, *op. cit.*, p. 383. Vide etiam S. C. S. Off., 12 Ian. 1769, n. I,—*Fontes*, n. 822.

[50] Bangen, Vlaming, Petrovits, Gasparri, Cappello, Winslow, Augustine, Farrugia, Leitner, De Smet (isti auctores *loc. cit.*); Lehmkuhl, *Casus Consc.*, II, n. 911; Konings-Putzer, *op. cit.*, p. 382. With reference to the *cautiones* in such cases see Nos. 344-352.

[51] Cf. Leitner, Augustine, Vermeersch-Creusen, Vlaming (isti auctores *loc. cit.*). These authors seem to suggest an intimate relation between this cause and the cause, "*Periculum matrimonii civilis, vel coram ministro acatholico celebrandi.*" There may be a close relation in some specific instances, yet it is quite manifest that the two causes are not synonymous. Feije (*De Imped. et Dispens.*, n. 666) calls attention to one significant point in connection with the cause under discussion: "*Affirmat Kutschker, t. 5, p. 222, Greg. XVI constanter denegasse dispensationem iis qui minabantur se defecturos a fide nisi concederetur.*"

[52] See No. 283, notes 18 (causes n. 11, 13), and 20 (causes n. 24-25), and also the authors mentioned in the preceding note (No. 290, not. 51). Cf. Konings-Putzer, *loc. cit.*; Conc. Plen. Balt. III (1884), n. 131.

[53] Vlaming, Petrovits, Gasparri, Cappello (isti auctores *loc. cit.*). Cf. Bangen, *De Spons. et Matr.*, Tit. IV, p. 20-21; Farrugia, *De Matr.*, n. 133; De Smet, *De Spons. et Matr.*, n. 506; Konings-Putzer,*Comment. in Facult.*, p. 382.

witnesses, made by the non-Catholic party to embrace the Catholic Faith after the marriage.[54]

c) Hope of the conversion of the non-Catholic party.[55]

The last two causes, namely, the danger of civil marriage, and the cause of conversion, deserve special consideration since they are so frequently cited as a cause for dispensation for mixed and disparate marriages.

1. DANGER OF CIVIL MARRIAGE

291. On the ground that in almost every case the moral certainty of the fulfillment of the promises would have to be seriously questioned, Vlaming[56] draws attention to what he deems an inconsistency in citing for dispensation for mixed or disparate marriages the cause "danger of civil marriage, or of contracting before a non-Catholic minister." The objection he raises seems to draw its force from an assumption that the danger of contracting civilly or before a non-Catholic minister is so intimately connected with the *cautiones* that the presence of such a danger would offer almost an invariable obstacle to the moral certainty of their fulfillment. While this assumption may be substantiated in specific instances or particular localities, it may readily be challenged with reference to its sweeping generality. The existence of this cause is not necssarily accompanied by a reluctance to sign the promises; by any indication of in-

---

[54] Zitelli, *De Dispens. Matr.*, p. 60; Vlaming, *Prael. Iuris Matr.*, n. 216; Petrovits, *New Church Law on Matrimony*, nn. 190, 245; Gasparri, *De Matr.*, n. 504; Cappello, *De Sacram.*, III, n. 314; Giovine, *De Dispens. Matr.*, Tom. I, § CLXXIII, n. 5; Winslow, *Vicars and Prefects Apostolic*, p. 105; Wernz, *Ius Decret.*, IV, n. 586, not. 31; Wernz-Vidal, *Ius Canonicum*, V, n. 178, not. 30; Leitner, *Lehrb. des kath. Eherechts*, p. 237.

[55] Among the authors the subheadings of *a*, *b*, and *c* have appeared as separate causes though no one author consulted has listed all three as distinct causes. Each author, while accepting one or two of these subheadings, invariably remains silent as to a third possibility, though each individual subheading seems to be sponsored by a sufficient number of approved authors who urge it as a sufficient cause. In the present study, these three grounds, though apparently sufficient of themselves, are grouped under the one general heading "The cause of conversion". The relation between them is intimate enough to justify this grouping, and, on the other hand, the differences are sufficiently marked to warrant a separate discussion. See Nos. 296-300.

[56] *Prael. Iuris Matr.*, n. 216.

sincerity, or by a manifest desire of a civil or non-Catholic ceremony. More often the cause will spring from a determination to
contract the marriage. True, if the Catholic party is an accom-
plice to the existence of this cause, or if his faith is so weak as
to be easily the prey of the non-Catholic's insistence to contract
the marriage at all costs, it does not redound to the character of
the Catholic. Yet it is precisely the avoidance of a danger of civil
marriage or one to be attempted before a non-Catholic minister
that the Church will recognize as a cause for dispensation.

292. The existence of a danger of contracting before a non-
Catholic minister will in many instances give rise to a graver
suspicion of the insincerity of the promises, but its connection
with the moral certainty of their fulfillment is not necessarily
as intimate as the opinion of Vlaming would postulate. Primarily, the prohibition of canon 1063 rests upon an additional
communicatio in sacris with heretics, not upon its connection
with the promise. Nay more, by virtue of canon 1063, § 2, a
double ceremony may even be tolerated for the gravest of reasons that are to be determined by the Ordinary.[57] Nor do canons
1063, § 2, and 1064, n. 3, in any way imply the invalidity of
the dispensation upon a want of moral certainty regarding the
fulfillment of the promises. On the other hand, the presence of a
danger of a clandestine marriage upon the refusal of a dispensation should be carefully considered in relation to the moral certainty of the fulfillment of the promises in each particular case.

293. A more vital issue regards the very determination of
the existence of this cause in particular cases. The cause may,
indeed, arise in several ways. A certain locality may have this
danger emphasized because of the small number of Catholics.
Again, in a particular case, the parties may give such indica-
tions of their determination to marry that the danger of a
clandestine marriage may be prudently judged to be present. It
is a lamentable confession to be forced to admit that in this
country the present cause is altogether too prevalent in many
contemplated mixed and disparate marriages, but it does not
on that account force the conclusion that it is, therefore, to be
disregarded as a legitimate cause. *A fortiori* it does not support

---

[57] See No. 383.

the contention that because of its presence all dispensations should be denied.[58]

294. No hard and fast rule can be laid down for determining the presence of this cause in a particular instance. A few general guides may, however, be given. If the parties explicitly manifest their determination to contract a marriage even if a dispensation were to be denied, and from a knowledge of the persons and the circumstances it is foreseen that they cannot be deterred from their purpose, the danger of a clandestine marriage is quite obvious. It is not necessary, moreover, that it exist in this marked degree. De Becker gives a sound warning to priests who wish to arrive at some certainty as to the objective existence of this cause, cautioning them not to provoke the parties to formal sin in this regard when they have not explicitly expressed this determination, but rather to form a prudent judgment as to its existence, mentioning in the petition that its existence is urged upon the judgment of the priest presenting the petition rather than upon the basis of any explicit statement of the parties.[59]

295. Such is the nature of the cause that an absolute moral certainty of its existence is not necesary. A prudent suspicion or judgment as to its existence is sufficient.[60] The priest who pre-

---

[58] The Third Plenary Council of Baltimore (n. 131) in repeating the constant insistence of the Church that just and grave causes must exist for dispensation for mixed marriages, continues: "*Hac in re attendenda etiam sunt locorum, rerum et personarum adiuncta, praesertim ubi periculum est gravioris mali, ne videlicet denegata dispensatione matrimonia mixta nihilominus, idque sine cautionibus clandestine contrahantur.*" Cf. Linneborn, *Grundriss des Eherechts*, p. 286. At the time the Baltimore decree was enacted, mixed marriages could be contracted validly without the observance of the Tridentine form in most parts of this country. Now, that Catholics are strictly bound to the form, the Baltimore decree has, perhaps, lost some of its significance, yet it may still be accepted as a sound norm of advice. It is of far greater importance to center a real concern upon the present factors responsible for the existence of the cause than to speculate upon the effectiveness of a policy ignoring its existence. See infra Nos. 229-235.

[59] "*Vix etiam advertere opus est prudentem sufficere suspicionem de contrahentium intentione neque, ullo modo, provocandum esse, ex parte parochi, manifestationem huius malae intentionis: utiliter tamen, in libello supplici, adderetur periculum allegatum inniti personali parochi existimationi, si ita res se haberet.*"—De Becker, *De Spons. et Matr.*, p. 330.

[60] The Congregation of the Propaganda cites the danger of a civil marriage as a legitimate cause and indicates that a complete moral certainty of its existence is not required: "*Ex dictis consequitur, PROBABILE periculum quod illi, qui dispensationem petunt, ea non obtenta, matrimonium dumtaxat CIVILE, ut aiunt, celebraturi sint, esse legitiman dispensandi causam.*"—S. C. de Prop. F., instr., 8 Maii 1877,—*Coll.*, n. 1470. Chelodi (*Ius Matr.*, n.

sents the petition should state the reason for his judgment as to
the presence of this danger, if this cause is cited merely as a result
of his judgment. Though this cause, when taken singly, seems
to possess a sufficient gravity upon which to grant a dispensation, it appears that in this latter case, where its existence is determined only upon the judgment of the priest and not on the
confession of the parties, it should be supplemented by another
or other causes to make up for a probable deficiency. The manifestation by the parties of this perverse intention would seem,
indeeed, to make the Catholic party quite unworthy of receiving
a dispensation, yet in this matter the Church regards rather the
possible and ultimate salvation of souls than the present bad
dispostion of the Catholic, and will grant a dispensation even
in such circumstances.[61]

2. THE CAUSE OF CONVERSION

296. The first phase of the cause of conversion, the probable hope of the conversion of a non-Catholic family, partakes
of the nature of a public cause. The family is the natural and
fundamental unit of society. Any factor that will affect a family
must be estimated to be of at least a quasi public concern. A
hope of the conversion of a non-Catholic family through a
mixed or disparate marriage is consequently to be regarded as a
public or at least a quasi public cause. It is the only phase of the
cause of conversion that bears this public character.[62] It follows,
of course, that the larger the group for which the hope of conversion exists, the greater the cogency of this cause.

---

46) has this to say: "*Probabile debet esse periculum, non certum, at non im-
aginarium. S. C.* [Sacra Congregatio de Disciplina Sacramentorum] *in simili
casu adduxit: 'mala praevenienda ob firmitatem in proposito!*" Cf. De Becker,
loc. cit.

[61] "Quid si partes ultro et spontanee pessimam suam intentionem manifes-
tarent contrahendi matrimonium mixtum vel coram ministro acatholico, nisi
dispensatio eis concedatur? Haec sane dispositio efficit, ut tales catholici favorem
dispensationis nullatenus mereantur: nihilominus, cum suprema semper urgeat
ratio salutis animarum, praedicta circumstantia non impedit necessario, quominus gratia adhuc concedatur."—De Becker, *op. cit.*, p. 330. "Nec obstat
mala dispositio dispensationem sollicitantium, sed potius complet."—De Smet,
De Spons. et Matr., n. 826. There is a distinct difference between the threat
of apostasy and the threat of a clandestine marriage, and it is not to be assumed that the Church's policy in refusing to dispense for the former (see
No. 290, note 51), will likewise be maintained in the latter.

[62] Vermeersch (*De Form. Facult. S. C. de Prop. F.*, p. 91) lists also "*spes
conversionis partis acatholicae*" as a public cause.

297. The written promise, or oral promise of conversion made before witnesses, is well recognized by canonists as a just and grave cause. This phase of the cause of conversion is definite enough to preclude the necessity of further discussion. The hope of the conversion of the non-Catholic party as a factor or cause inclining the Church to dispense for mixed marriages, has apparently been recognized since the beginning of the seventeenth century. Early diocesan statutes of this period warned pastors not to join Catholics in marriages with heretics unless there existed some hope of conversion.[63] A hope of the conversion of the non-Catholic, and a remote danger of the Catholic's defection, were among the causes urged for a dispensation granted by Pope Urban VIII on March 8, 1633.[64] In this case, however, this cause was really of a public nature since it turned upon the conversion of a member of the royalty, Catherine Charlotte of Zweibrücken. The same Pontiff decreed that Catholics who had married heretical women might, at the judgment of the Ordinary, continue cohabitation as long as there was some hope of conversion and an absence of the danger of perversion.[65] On the other hand, a decision of the Congregation of the Holy Office of February 15, 1780, seems to regard the hope of conversion as a *condition* of dispensation rather than as a cause.[66] There seems

----

[63] "Die Statuta quatuor Dekanatuum Juliae v. J. 1602 haben 'Pastores diligenter moneant suos, ne contrahant cum haereticis, nec coniungant aut copulent catholicas personas cum haereticis, nisi sit aliqua spes conversionis'."— Binterim, *Denkwürdigkeiten*, VII, II, p. 33. The statute does not seem to imply the necessity of formal dispensation,—a silence or an omission more readily understood if the prevalent opinion of many canonists and theologians, of that, and a later period, be considered. See infra No. 81, notes 13-14; No. 82.

[64] "Et primum eius, quae proponitur, educate rationis ab unanimi Principum, et Praelatorum, quibus carum Regionum explorati mores esse debent, asseveratione, nullum ex hoc Matrimonio rite permisso Fidei Catholicae in iis locis fieri praeiudicium; nullum in ipso Wolfango, eiusque liberis, aut subditis subversionis periculum subesse, quin potius magnam effulgere spem conversionis ipsius Catherinae ad Avitam Romanam Fidem . . ." Urbanus VIII, 8 Mart. 1633,—Albitius, *De Inconstantia in Fide*, Cap. XXXVI, n. 210. According to Schulte (*Handb. des kath. Eherechts*, p. 252) these were the principal causes of this dispensation.

[65] Urbanus VIII, 14 Mart. 1630,—Ballerini-Palmieri, *Op. Theol. Mor.*, Tract. X, Sect. VIII, n. 712. This instance represents more a toleration of an already existing valid mixed marriage than a cause for dispensation.

[66] ". . . Erit proinde e munere ipsius Vicarii Ap. facultatem, quae sibi adesse ac perdurare supponitur, dispensandi super disparitate cultus, iis tantum prudentibus ac piis in sua Missione laborantibus sacerdotibus subdele-

to be little question, however, that the hope of conversion may be regarded as a sufficient cause. Cardinal Masella's list of causes for matrimonial dispensations includes the cause: "*Propter spem conversionis compartis ad catholicam religionem.*"[67] There are several well known authors who apparently regard it as a sufficiently just and grave cause so that it may be accepted.[68]

298. What, then, is a hope of conversion? In a certain sense, the Church has a hope of converting the world, but obviously so large a comprehension of the term will be unacceptable as a cause for dispensation. Again a hope of conversion is not to be confused with a *wish* that the non-Catholic be converted. A mere wish for the non-Catholic's conversion is a purely subjective element and cannot be urged as an objective cause for dispensation. Nor can a hope of conversion be said to rest in the non-Catholic's signing of the "promises" and the attendant moral certainty of their fulfillment. The Church will not regard the *cautiones* as a cause for dispensation but demands them rather as a *conditio sine qua non.*[69]

gare, qui neminem fidelium permittant matrimonium contrahere cum infideli, ni viderint antea graves illas causas concurrere in singulis plane casibus expetendas, quas accurate inspici iubet Apostolica Sedes, atque illud maxime caverint quod pars infidelis, *nisi spem suae conversionis praebuerit,* saltem sine contumelia Creatoris et christiani nominis iniuria sit cum parte fideli cohabitatura, nec ullatenus impeditura educationem prolis utriusque sexus in sancta religione."—S. C. S. Off. (Sutchuen.), 15 Feb. 1780,—*Fontes,* n. 840. In this decision the causes seem to be distinguished from the hope of conversion or the absence of any contumely of the Creator.

[67] See No. 283, note 20 (cause n. 17).

[68] Pirhing (*Jus Can.*, Tom. IV, Tit. I, Sect. VI, n. 166) regards the hope of conversion as a grave cause. Ballerini-Palmieri (*Op. Theol. Mor.,* Tract. X, Sect. VIII, n. 721) lists it among three of the gravest causes. Wernz (*Ius Decret.*, IV, n. 586, not. 31) and Wernz-Vidal (*Ius Canonicum,* V, n. 178, not. 30) demand the existence of a well-founded hope ("*spes fundata*"), and seem to classify it among the causes of lesser importance which, when added to other causes, move the Holy See to dispense more readily. Konings-Putzer (*Comment. in Facult.,* p. 382) regards it as a private cause and demands a "*magna spes conversionis*". Vermeersch (see infra No. 296, note 62) regards it as a public cause. Hilling (*Das Eherecht des C. I. C.,* p. 70) classifies "*spes conversionis*" (which he selects from Cardinal Masella's list) as a *causa honesta.* Other authors recognizing the hope of conversion as a cause, but offering little or no commentary, are: Lehmkuhl, *Theol. Mor.,* II, n. 715; Göpfert, *Moraltheologie,* III, n. 243 (who recognizes it in connection with the impediment of Disparity of Cult); Perathoner, *Das kirch. Gesetzb.,* p. 319, not. 1; Cerato, *Matr.,* n. 55. Vide etiam *AkKR,* XIV (1865), 324.

[69] Cf. S. C. de Prop. F., litt. encyl., 11 Mart. 1868,—*Coll.,* n. 1324 (see infra No. 279, note 9); Conc. Plen. Balt. III (1884), n. 131; Wernz,

299. No hard and fast rules can be laid down for determining the presence of this cause in a particular instance though a number of leading considerations can be indicated which may serve as a guide. A careful estimation of the character and disposition of the non-Catholic party is of primary importance, though the influence of the Catholic party over the non-Catholic must likewise be weighed. Some consideration should dwell also upon the influence that the relatives and close associates of either party will have after the marriage has been contracted. Such factors as a willingness to take instructions before the marriage, or in some instances a promise to take instructions after the marriage, a genuine interest in Catholic beliefs and practices, a decided absence of bigotry, which can at times be determined by the type of questions asked about Catholic beliefs and practices, or from a general attitude toward the Church,—may contribute to the determination of the presence or absence of the cause of conversion. It is to be remembered that in this study the hope of conversion of the non-Catholic party is distinguished from the formal or solemn promise of conversion. Ultimately, therefore, the priest who has charge of the case must weigh the elements that he finds present, and, if he deems the cause of conversion to exist, he must present in sufficient detail the grounds upon which he urges the cause of a hope of conversion, so that the one dispensing may judge of its existence.

300. Must the hope of conversion of the non-Catholic be "well-founded" or is it sufficient that the hope be merely a probable hope? While, indeed, a probable hope of the conversion of a non-Catholic *family* suffices, because of the quasi public nature of the cause, it appears that more should be required than a mere probability of the conversion of the non-Catholic party alone. A "well-founded" hope of the conversion of the non-Catholic party seems to be demanded if the distinction between a hope of the conversion of a non-Catholic family and the non-Catholic party is to be fully justified. It is the one who dispenses who is to judge of this quality and this judgment can be formed from the details that should be presented in the petition.

Ius Decret., IV, n. 510, not. 42; Wernz-Vidal, *Ius Canonicum,* V, n. 273, not. 47; Bangen, *De Spons. et Matr.,* Tit. IV, p. 20; Chelodi, *Ius Matr.,* n. 59.

ART. IV. CAUSES REQUIRED FOR PASTOR'S ASSISTANCE AT
MARRIAGES PROHIBITED BY CANONS 1065 AND 1066

301. A grave cause is explicitly demanded that an Ordinary may permit a pastor to assist at the marriage of a Catholic with anyone of the following: those who notoriously have left the Faith; those who are members of a society condemned by the Church;[70] those who are public sinners, or those notoriously under censure.[71] Most of the causes that are commonly cited by the authors as having a more immediate reference to such cases, and possessing a sufficient gravity for the removal of the prohibition, have already been discusesd in connection with the impediments of Mixed Religion and Disparity of Cult. The causes that are usually cited as sufficient are: to save the Catholic party from some great evil;[72] to prevent scandals that would follow upon the refusal of this permission;[73] to avoid the danger of concubinage;[74] or to prevent a civil marriage. Since these prohibitions are not in the form of a canonical impediment, other causes that are not always recognized as canonical may also be urged, though several will have to concur to possess a sufficient gravity.[75]

302. A cause of lesser gravity may be admitted to permit the assistance of the pastor at marriages forbidden in canon

---

[70] Canon 1065, § 2. Here are included also those baptized non-Catholics who have never professed the Catholic Faith but who, having been baptized or having attained membership in a non-Catholic religious sect, have formally renounced their membership in that sect and have become members of no other religious sect.

[71] Canon 1066.

[72] If the marriage will prevent a grave evil from falling upon the pastor or the parish, it may likewise be urged as a cause. Cf. Chelodi, *Ius Matr.*, n. 67; Cappello, *De Sacram.*, III, n. 332; Wernz-Vidal, *Ius Canonicum*, V, n. 203; Vlaming, *Prael. Iuris Matr.*, n. 249; S. Poenit., 10 Dec. 1860,—Feije, *De Imped. et Dispens.*, n. 277; S. C. S. Off. (Leodien.), 30 Ian. 1867,—*Fontes*, n. 998; 17 Sept. 1871,—*AkKR*, XXVII (1872), CLXXI; instr. (ad Ordinarios Imperii Brasil.), 2 Iul. 1878,—*Fontes*, n. 1056.

[73] See the preceding note.

[74] De Smet, *De Spons. et Matr.*, n. 196; Chelodi, *loc. cit.*; S. C. S. Off. (Portus Aloisii), 1 Aug. 1855,—*Fontes*, n. 932; (Marysville), 21 Aug. 1861,—*Fontes*,n. 967.

[75] The following selection, with certain modifications, is made from a list given by Farrugia, *De Matr.*, n. 106: *Ex parte oratricis catholicae*: ex natalibus illegitimis orta; infirmitate, deformitate aliove defectu detenta; iam ab alio deflorata est. *Ex parte oratoris catholici*: si infirmitate detentus; si viduus prole oneratus; si adiutorio huius mulieris indigens est, e. g. ad gerendam rem domesticam. *Ex parte matrimonii*: omnia ad nuptias iam parata; oratoris catholici vel oratricis catholicae munificentia erga bonum publicum.

1066[76] than those prohibited in canon 1065[77] for the presumption of danger to the faith of the Catholic party and the children is normally less grave in the former than in the latter case. A graver cause is required if both of the parties be public sinners.[78] Whatever proportions of gravity may be recognized as existing between the prohibitions of canons 1065 and 1066, either with reference to their wording and context, or with reference to the gravity of the matter determining the prohibition, it is the Ordinary and not the pastor who is to judge of the gravity of the causes as they exist in the particular circumstances of each case. Regardless of the gravity of the cause, if both parties to the proposed marriage have notoriously fallen away from the Faith, or are sectless non-Catholics, or if both of the parties are notorious members of condemned societies and refuse to be reconciled with the Church, the Ordinary is to refuse permission for the pastor's assistance. Canon 1065, § 2, presupposes that one of the parties be a professed Catholic at the time of the marriage when it prescribes: *"dummodo . . . pro suo prudenti arbitrio Ordinarius iudicet satis cautum esse catholicae educationi universae prolis* ET REMOTIONI PERICULI PERVERSIONIS ALTERIUS CONIUGIS.*"*[79]

---

[76] The gravity of the required cause is increased, however, if the person notoriously excommunicated be a *vitandus*.

[77] The difficulties of observing this norm in practice have already been indicated in No. 286.

[78] Cf. Wernz-Vidal, *Ius Canonicum*, V, n. 202.

[79] Vide etiam S. C. S. Off. (Leodien.), 30 Iun. 1867,—*Fontes*, n. 998; 17 Sept. 1871,—*AkKR*, XXVII (1872), CLXXI; (Bombay), 21 Feb. 1883,—*Fontes*, n. 1079; S. C. Conc., 27 Nov. 1896,—*AkKR*, LXXVIII (1898), 523-524.

CHAPTER XIII

THE *CAUTIONES*

ART. I. CATHOLIC EDUCATION OF THE CHILDREN AND THE
PRIMARY END OF MARRIAGE

303. A few of the older canonists were of the opinion that
if a marriage were contracted with an agreement (given as a
very condition of matrimonial consent) to rear the children in
a non-Catholic religion, the marriage itself would be invalid
because of the opposition of the agreement to the *bonum prolis*.[1]
It has, however, been the teaching of the great majority of the
authors that no such effect can be attributed to an agreement of
this kind, even though it be placed as an essential condition of
the matrimonial consent.[2]

304. Although both procreation and education of children
constitute the primary end of marriage,[3] it does not follow that
a pact (even when entered upon as a formal condition of matrimonial consent) to frustrate or to hinder the Catholic education of the children will render the marriage itself invalid. If
both procreation and education are considered in relation to each
other, it will be evident that education is contingent upon and
subordinate in relation to procreation, for the education of a
child is consequent upon and contingent to its procreation.
Again, while procreation does not in a logical sense admit of

---

[1] Schmalzgrueber, *Jus Eccl. Univ.*, Tom. IV, P. II, Tit. VI, n. 150;
Mazzei, *De Matr. personarum div. Relig.*, cap. II, § XX.

[2] Perez, *De Matr.*, Disp. XXXVI, Sect. I, n. 2; Frassen, *Scotus Academicus*, Tom. XII, Tract. III, Disp. ult., art. III, § VIII; Gury, *Theol. Mor.*,
Pars II, n. 828; Feije, *De Matr. Mixtis*, p. 161-169; Blieck, *Theol. Univ.*,
IV, p. 245; Gasparri, *De Matr.*, n. 498; Wernz, *Ius Decret.*, n. 577, not.
16; n. 587; Cappello, *De Sacram.*, III, n. 315, not. 28; Farrugia, *De
Matr.*, n. 52. Pichler (*Jus Can.*, Tom. I, Lib. IV, Tit. I, n. 131) uses an
unusual argument based, as he says, upon the tolerance of the Church of such
pacts: ". . . reclamat insuper communis Doctorum, imo *et Ecclesiae tolerantia*,
dum videbimus, saltem in Germania nostra, saepius iam fuisse contracta, et
hodiedum, quamvis impie, sub dicta conditione contrahi Matrimonia, imo or-
dinarie sub tali conditione tacita."

[3] Cf. canon 1013, § 1.

degrees of perfection, since by the marriage contract it is based upon the *ius coniugale* which is absolute and unlimited,—education, on the other hand, does admit of many degrees of perfection. Thus for example, the physical, intellectual, and moral elements constitutive of education admit of a great scale of gradation. In the moral and intellectual order, religious education normally represents a higher perfection than a mere natural morality. Catholic religious education, which again admits of many degrees of perfection, represents, indeed, the ideal of perfection, yet its frustration does not of itself preclude all moral and intellectual development, but rather its perfection.[4] But this degree of perfection is not of itself, and *per se*, the sole and only constitutive element of education. A violation of a perfection does not, therefore, destroy that of which it is not the sole constitutive element. Since, moreover, education in its entirety is in itself only one of two elements constituting the primary end of marriage, and again, since it is contingent upon the element of procreation,—a violation of a perfection of a contingent element of the primary end of marriage does not destroy the primary end of marriage, and hence an agreement to violate this perfection does not invalidate the marriage.

ART. II. OBLIGATION UPON CATHOLICS TO EDUCATE THEIR CHILDREN AS CATHOLICS

305. The obligation upon Catholics to raise their children as Catholics is, indeed, one that they cannot renounce. Any agreement entered into by a Catholic to raise any or all of the children as non-Catohlics is a clear violation of the divine and natural law and possesses no binding force whatever.[5] Catholics

---

[4] ". . . nam ad matrimonii substantiam pertinet bonum prolis *naturale*, non vero bonum spirituale: bonum naturale curare tenentur qua coniuges, bonum vero spirituale, qua christiani . . ."—Blieck, *Theol. Univ.*, IV, p. 245.

[5] The authors are agreed that such pacts are devoid of validity. Cf. Sanchez, *De Matr.*, Lib. VII, Disp. 72, n. 6; Navarrus, Lib. I *Consiliorum*, consil. 1, nn. 62-63,—*Op. Omnia*, Tom. V; Reiffenstuel, *Jus Can. Univ.*, Lib. IV, Tit. I, n. 371; Blieck, *Theol. Univ.*, IV, p. 245; Cappello, *De Sacram.*, III, n. 315. Schmalzgrueber (*Jus Eccl. Univ.*, Tom. IV, P. II, Tit. VI, n. 151), however, concedes a rather strange exception: "Excipiatur, si aliunde huiusmodi matrimonium licitum fiat, eo quod v. gr. per illud speretur promovendum bonum publicum; tunc enim si spes non sit, ut maritus haeret-

who contract marriage with either an explicit or an implicit pact that all or any of their children will be educated outside of the Catholic Church incur *latae sententiae* an excommunication reserved to the Ordinary.[6] In order to incur the censure, however, an agreement must be entered into either before or at the time of the marriage.[7] The censure is incurred, not when the pact is made, but when the marriage is contracted, either with the perseverance of the agreement or its concomitant entry at the time of the marriage,—otherwise the condition mentioned in canon 2319, § 1, n. 2, *"Qui matrimonio uniuntur cum pacto explicito vel implicito"*, would not be verified.[8]

306. Petrovits is of the opinion that the term *"matrimonium"* in canon 2319, § 1, n. 2 must be taken in its strict canonical sense, implying a valid contract.

Therefore, the Catholic who would attempt marriage before a non-Catholic clergyman incurs only one excommunication. He would not incur another censure because the marriage was attempted with an explicit understanding that one or all of the children should be brought up outside of the Church . . . In the case given, the mar-

---

icus permittat omnes liberos in catholica religione educari, hoc casu non videtur esse illicitum in pactis coniugalibus talem conditionem adiicere, ut saltem aliqua pars liberorum in fide catholica educetur, et instruatur; salvo tamen iure matris catholicae, ut etiam ceteros liberos, quantum fieri poterit, in vera religione instruere, ut tenetur, non praetermittat." Vide etiam Pirhing, *Jus Can.*, Tom. IV, Tit. I, Sect. VI, n. 167.

[6] Canon 2319, § 1, n. 2.

[7] Cappello, *De Censuris*, n. 370. Cerato, *Censurae*, n. 47, e; Farrugia, *Comment. in Censuras*, n. 47; Cipollini, *De Censuris*, Lib. II, n. 71.

[8] Cipollini, *loc. cit.*; Ayrinhac, *Penal Legislation*, p. 208; Pighi, *Censurae*, n. 103; Vermeersch-Creusen, *Epitome*, III, n. 518. Cerato (*Censurae*, n. 47, e) is the author of the following statement:*"Procul dubio tollitur censura, si tollatur ipsum pactum antequam matrimonium fiat"*, to which Cappello (*De Censuris*, n. 370) takes exception in the following words: *"Quod minus recte affirmatur. Sane vel censura est incursa, vel non; si est incursa, cessare nequit nisi per absolutionem; si non est incursa, non potest tolli. Eo ipso quod nupturientes huiusmodi pactum inierunt, censuram contraxere, quae pacto revocato, non cessat, sed more ordinario i. e. absolutione auferri debet."* While the wording employed by Cerato is subject to criticism, Cappello's conclusion seems likewise to be somewhat of an overstatement. When he says that the censure is incurred at the moment the pact is made, he does not seem to provide for the event of the marriage never taking place, a condition apparently demanded by the clause *"qui matrimonio uniuntur"*, —not merely the agreement without the marriage. The pact does not entail a censure unless it is completed with the actual contracting of the marriage. Cf. Leech, *The Constitution "Apostolicae Sedis" and the "Codex Juris Canonici."*, p. 94.

riage being invalid, the understanding with which it is attempted
does not occasion another censure. If in such a marriage the consent
was given before a priest and subsequently renewed in presence of a
non-Catholic minister, the Catholic party incurs a double excommunication.[9]

307. While it is true that the censure deals *in odiosis* and
should, therefore, be strictly interpreted, it is doubtful whether
the interpretation given by Petrovits can be sustained. There is
no clear evidence that the clause *"qui matrimonio uniuntur"* is
to be understood as referring to a valid marriage. Number one
of the first paragraph of the same canon has the clause, *"Qui
matrimonium ineunt coram ministro acatholico"*, which in no
sense implies a valid marriage. Neither the wording of the section of the canon under consideration, nor the context of the
entire canon manifests a patent transition from the term *"matrimonium"* used in the sense of a *"matrimonium attentatum"* to
the same term understood in the sense of a *"matrimonium
verum"*. On what ground is a putative marriage excluded, or a
union bearing the *"species matrimonii"*? It does not appear in
any way obvious that a marriage attempted before a priest without a dispensation from a diriment impediment (for example,
either because it was not disclosed, or because it was unknown
to the parties) would on the score of its objective invalidity
render the parties immune from the censure.[10] Neither is it evident, therefore, that such an agreement made in connection with
an attempted marriage before a non-Catholic minister or civil
official does not bring upon the Catholic party the censure of
canon 2319, § 1, n. 2.[11]

---

[9] *New Church Law on Matrimony*, n. 270, Cappello (*loc cit.*) is of the
same opinion: *"Intelligitur matrimonium verum seu religiosi, sive mixtum
sit sive non."*

[10] The supposition is, of course, that the impediment is later discovered
before the question concerning the censure is to be disposed of.

[11] A further doubt regarding the benign interpretation may, perhaps, be
derived from the answer of the Holy Office of August 29, 1888 (*NRT*,
XXII [1890], 137) to the following *dubia*: "1. *Utrum absolutio a censuris omnibus catholicis, qui coram haeretico ministro nuptias contraxerunt,
necessaria sit, an potius in eo tantum casu impertienda sit, quo in huiusmodi
celebrationem ab Antistite censurae promulgati sint? Et quatenus negative ad
primam partem, quaeritur: 2. Utrum absolutio a censuris necessaria sit eis
saltem, qui, in huiusmodi nuptiis, consenserunt acatholicae prolium educationi?*"

308. An implicit agreement is quite sufficient to contract the censure. Such an agreement may readily be present in a Catholic's promise, for example, not to oppose the wishes of the other with regard to the education of the children outside of the Catholic religion, or in an agreement to conform to the custom of a region where the boys follow the religion of the father and the girls that of the mother.[12] The clause *"ut omnes vel aliqua proles educetur extra catholicam Ecclesiam"* has, perhaps, more of the connotation of an education in a non-Catholic religion, though it seems to include also an agreement to deprive the child of a Catholic education.[13]

309. There are further censures incurred by Catholic parents who are responsible for the non-Catholic Baptism or non-Catholic religious education of their children. Catholics who knowingly presume to present their children to non-Catholic ministers for Baptism incur *latae sententiae* an excommunication reserved to the Ordinary.[14] One or both parents, if both are Catholics, can incur this censure if it concerns their own children (*"liberos suos"*). Full knowledge of the law, the censure, and the fact that the person to whom the child is presented is a non-Catholic minister in the strict sense of the term[15] is implied to incur the censure. The question of the validity of the Baptism is not the one of primary concern as far as there is question of incurring the censure, but rather the *communicatio in sacris* with non-Catholic ministers.[16] A censure incurred *latae senten-*

R. Ad 1. *Affirmative ad primam partem, negative ad secundam.*
    Ad 11. *Provisum in primo."*
Vide etiam S. C. S. Off., 8 Maii 1907,—*Fontes*, n. 1282. Does the answer to the second *dubium* imply that only one censure is incurred by reason of the fact of the attempted marriage before a non-Catholic minister, or does it not perhaps imply that the agreement to bring up the children as non-Catholics in such attempted marriages has entailed a censure that must be absolved? Frankly, the answer scarcely permits a definite solution, but it may readily indicate the doubtful value of the benign interpretation which would restrict the term *"matrimonium"* to valid marriages contracted before a priest.
    [12] Ayrinhac, *Penal Legislation*, p. 208; Augustine, *Commentary*, VIII, p. 298.
    [13] Cf. Augustine, *op. cit.*, VIII, p. 299. Cappello (*De Censuris*, n. 370) and Vermeersch-Creusen (*Epitome*, III, n. 518) seem to restrict the interpretation to education in a non-Catholic religion.
    [14] Canon 2319, § 1, n. 3.
    [15] Cf. Cappello, *op. cit.*, n. 372; Ayrinhac, *op. cit.*, p. 208.
    [16] Leech, *op. cit.*, p. 95.

tiae and reserved to the Ordinary is contracted also by Catholic parents, or Catholics holding their place, who knowingly offer their children to be educated or brought up in a non-Catholic religion.[17] Ignorance, either crass or supine, whether of the law, the censure, or the nature, for example, of the instruction the children are to receive in a school or from a tutor, will again excuse from incurring the censure.

310. The violations of parental obligations that have been referred to, not only subject the Catholic party to the censures incurred *latae sententiae* and reserved to the Ordinary, but also render such Catholics *"suspecti de haeresi"*,[18] which makes them subject to the rulings of canon 2315. To the end, therefore, that she will have an assurance of the absence of the danger of the non-Catholic education of the children, the Church demands for mixed and disparate marriages a promise on the part of both the Catholic and the non-Catholic party that the children will be baptized only in the Catholic Church and that they will receive their religious education exclusively in the Catholic Faith.[19]

ART. III. SUMMARY HISTORY OF THE *Cautiones*

311. From time immemorial, the Church has repeated again and again the need of vigilance lest Catholics contract marriages with aliens to the Faith in violation of the divine and natural law. The enactments of early councils[20] to the effect that Catholics were not to marry heretics, infidels, and Jews unless these became converts to the Catholic Faith, represented a measure adapted for that period to ward off the imminent danger of perversion.[21]

312. When the exigencies of missionary conditions, that arose in the sixteenth century and after, forced the necessity of dispensations from the impediment of Disparity of Cult, the

---

[17] Canon 2319, § 1, n. 4.

[18] Canon 2319, § 2.

[19] Canon 1061, § 1, n. 2. Regarding the additional promise of the non-Catholic party, see No. 341.

[20] Elvira (306), can. 16,—Mansi, II, 8; Laodicacea (343-381), can. 31,—Mansi, II, 569; Chalcedon (451), can. 14,—Mansi, VII, 388.

[21] It is not certain whether this conversion was always demanded as a condition to be fulfilled antecedently to the marriage. In many instances, perhaps, the promise of a future conversion was accepted as a sufficient surety.

Church again insisted that such dispensations could not be given unless the conditions required by the divine law were fulfilled.[22] In Europe, dispensations from impediments existing between Catholics and heretics were refused by the Holy See unless the abjuration of heresy preceded.[23] For a long time the only admitted exception to this rule concerned the mixed marriages of the Catholic nobility, and for these, formal guarantees and sureties were strictly demanded.[24] When at last the *Stylus Curiae* of Rome was urged as a medium of reform for the laxities of discipline existing in many regions, definite and formal guarantees known as *cautiones* were exacted also for the mixed marriages of the common people.[25] Once these *cautiones* or formal guarantees providing against a danger of the perversion of the faith of the Catholic party and the children had become a part of the universal discipline of the Church, they were given such an emphasis that one might almost gather that they were of divine obligation.

ART. IV. RELATION OF THE *Cautiones* TO THE DIVINE AND NATURAL LAW

313. While the *cautiones* are founded on the conditions prescribed by the divine and natural law, they are, nevertheless, an ecclesiastical measure adopted to safeguard the divine law rather than a formal prescription of the divine law itself.[26] When, therefore, it is said that the *cautiones*, because of their foundation in the divine and natural law, cannot be dispensed from,[27] the term

---

[22] See No. 77, note 1.

[23] See No. 79.

[24] See Nos. 84-95.

[25] See Nos. 99-101.

[26] "Quae *cautiones* licet quandoque cum *conditionibus confundantur,* tamen evidenter ab iisdem distinguuntur, sicuti *media* ad obtinendum triplicem *finem* scl. avertendi periculum perversionis in coniuge catholico, obtinendi educationem catholicam universae prolis, procurandi conversionem partis acatholicae, quae ex lege caritatis a coniuge catholico serio et prudenter promovenda est."—Wernz, *Ius Decret.,* IV, n. 587, not. 32. Cf. Wernz-Vidal, *Ius Canonicum,* V, n. 179, not. 31; Cappello, *De Sacram.,* III, n. 309; De Smet, *De Spons. et Matr.,* p. 441, not. 3; O'Keeffe, *Matrimonial Dispensations,* p. 85; Kelly, *The Jurisdiction of the Simple Confessor,* p. 93.

[27] "Quae quidem cautiones remitti seu dispensari numquam possunt, cum in ipsa naturali ac Divina lege fundentur, quam Ecclesia et haec Sancta Sedes

"*cautiones*" must be understood rather in the sense of "*conditiones*" or "*cautelae*" demanded by the divine and natural law than the actual formalities of the promises themselves.[28] To maintain that the Church *cannot* dispense from the exacted formalities of the guarantees, the "*cautiones opportunae*", is to overlook the fact of their ecclesiastical origin,[29] and to forget that by an extraordinary dispensation granted through a *sanatio in radice* the Church does at times dispense from the normal means which she has established to safeguard the divine and natural law.[30]

ART. V. NECESSITY OF THE *Cautiones* FOR DISPENSATION

314. In her normal discipline, however, i. e., outside of the recourse to the *sanatio in radice*, the Church will grant no dispensation from the impediments of Mixed Religion and Disparity of Cult unless the *cautiones* or formal promises are given.[31] These *cautiones* have become the *conditio sine qua non* of dis-

---

sartam tectamque tueri omni studio contendit, et contra quam sine ullo dubio gravissime peccant, qui promiscuis hisce nuptiis temere contrahendis se ac prolem exinde suscipiendam perversionis periculo committunt. Insuper, in tribuendis huiusmodi dispensationibus, praeter enunciatas cautiones quae praemitti semper debent, et super quibus dispensari nullo modo umquam potest, adiectae quoque fuere conditiones, ut haec mixta coniugia extra ecclesiam . . . etc."—Instr. Secret. Stat. iussu Pii PP. IX, 15 Nov. 1858,—*Coll.*, n. 1169. Vide etiam Card. Rampolla, litt. (ad Card. Simor), 26 Sept. 1890, —*NRT*, XXIII (1891), 388-391.

[28] "*Conditiones* omnino necessariae, quae ideo in promiscuis nuptiis requiruntur, quia in naturali ac divino iure fundantur, huiusmodi sunt, quae remitti seu dispensari nunquam possunt. Iure igitur meritoque factum est, ut mixtae nuptiae in ista dioecesi nunquam sint permissae, uti refers, quin hisce *conditionibus* cautum prorsus fuerit."—S. C. S. Off., instr. (ad Archiep. Corcyren.), 3 Ian. 1871, n. 6,—*Fontes*, n. 1013. Vide etiam Pius VIII, litt. ap. *Litteris altero*, 25 Mart. 1830,—*Fontes*, n. 482; S. C. Off., instr. (ad omnes Ep. Ritus Orient.), 12 Dec. 1888, n. 5,—*Fontes*, n. 1112.

[29] "Quam sane legem [naturalem divinamque] sartem tectamque tueri contendit Eccleisa et haec Apostolica Sedes, seu in generali ipsarum nuptiarum prohibitione, seu in cautionibus, *quas* IURE SUO *exigit*."— Gregorius XVI, ep. *Non sine gravi*, 23 Maii 1846, n. 1,—*Fontes*, n. 503. Cf. Wernz, *Ius Decret.*, IV, nn. 585, 587; Wernz-Vidal, *Ius Canonicum*, V, n. 177; De Smet, *De Spons. et Matr.*, n. 590.

[30] See Nos. 262-267.

[31] See No. 101, note 40 and in addition Aichner, *Compend. Juris Eccles.*, § 183, cum not. 10-11; Feije, *De Imped. et Dispens.*, n. 568; De Smet, *De Spons. et Matr.*, n. 590; (1909 ed.), n. 254; Blat. *Comment.*, Vol. III, P. I, n. 456; Genicot-Salsmans, *Theol. Mor.*, II, n. 514; *LQS*, LXXIX (1926), 806, 810.

pensation from either impediment[32] so that the very validity of
the dispensation depends upon the giving of the *cautiones.*[33]

§ I. In Danger of Death and Urgent Necessity

315. An exception, however, is urged by some canonists
and theologians in the case of danger of death. While all admit
that *per se* the *cautiones* must be given even in such an extrem-
ity, a considerable number do not regard the *cautiones* in such
cases as a *sine qua non* condition for the *validity* of the dispensation,[34] but hold it to be a solidly probable opinion that should
the *cautiones* be refused by the non-Catholic party, the Ordinary
can dispense validly and (*per accidens*) even licitly, as long as

---

[32] Cf. Pius VIII, instr., 27 Mart. 1830,—Ballerini-Palmieri, *Op. Theol.
Mor.*, Tract. X, Sect. VIII, n. 724; Instr. Secret. Stat. iussu Pii PP. IX,
15 Nov. 1858,—*Coll.*, n. 1169; Card. Rampolla, litt. (ad Card. Simor),
26 Sept. 1890,—*NRT*, XXIII (1891), 388-391; S. C. S. Off., 30 Iun.
1842, ad 4,—*Fontes*, n. 890; litt. (ad Card. Simor), 21 Iul. 1880,—*NRT*,
XIX (1887), 4-9; (Leopolien.), 18 Mart. 1891,—*Fontes*, n. 1132; 6
Iul. 1898,—*Fontes*, n. 1200; 12 Apr. 1899,—*Fontes*, n. 1219; 10 Dec.
1902,—*Fontes*, n. 1262; 21 Iun. 1912,—*AAS*, IV (1912), 442-444;
Conc. Plen. Balt. III (1884), n. 131. A knowledge or hope of the good
will of the parties, or good faith regarding the necessity of the *cautiones*, can
in no way be urged as a substitute for the *cautiones*. Cf. S. C. S. Off., 21
Iul. 1880,—*NRT*, XIX (1887), 4-9; Wernz, *Ius Decret*, IV, n. 587;
Wernz-Vidal, *Ius Canonicum*, V, n. 179; Cappello, *De Sacram.*, III, n. 310;
Blat, *Comment.*, Vol. III, P. I, n. 456; De Smet, *De Spons. et Matr.*, (ed.
1909), p. 309, not. 4; p. 310.

[33] Chelodi, *Ius Matr.*, n. 50; Vlaming, *Prael. Iuris Matr.*, n. 482; Wernz
Vidal, *op. cit.*, n. 273, not. 46; Linneborn, *Grundriss des Ererechts*, p. 202,
not. 3; Leitner, *Lehrb. des kath. Eherechts*, p. 307-308; Farrugia, *De Matr.*,
nn. 118-119; Ayrinhac, *Marriage Legislation*, p. 121-122, 153; Blat, *op.
cit.*, Vol. III, P. I, nn. 435, 468; Augustine, *Commentary*, V, p. 186;
Woywod, *A Practical Commentary*, I, nn. 1041, 1055; Noldin, *Theol.
Mor.*, III, n. 578; Genicot-Salsmans, *Theol. Mor.*, II, n. 493; Sabetti-Barrett, *Theol. Mor.*, n. 881; Winslow, *Vicars and Prefects Apostolic*, p. 106-
107; Kelly, *The Jurisdiction of the Simple Confessor*, p. 176, 184-186.

[34] De Becker, *De Spons. et Matr.*, p. 243-244; 278, not. 1; De Smet, *De
Spons. et Matr.* (1909 ed.), p. 309, not. 5; De Smedt, in *LQS*, LXVII
(1914), 384-385; O'Neill, in *IER*, XXVIII (1926), 633-635; Mahoney,
in *AER*, LXXII (1925), 510; Cerato, *Matr.*, nn. 35-36; Pighi, *De Matr.*,
n. 90; King, *The Administration of the Sacraments to Dying Non-Catho-
lics*, p. 123-131; Cappello, *De Sacram.*, III, nn. 232, 310, 312; Petrovits,
New Church Law on Matrimony, nn. 160, 192, 254-255; Farrugia, *De
Matr.*, n. 83, d; Genicot-Salsmans, *Theol. Mor.*, II, nn. 493, 514; Vermeersch-Creusen, *Epitome*, II, nn. 306, c. 331, b; Vermeersch, *Theol. Mor.*,
III, n. 759; O'Keeffe, *Matrimonial Dispensations*, p. 85-92, 144-145;
Kelly, *The Jurisdiction of the Simple Confessor*, p. 92-94, 185; Kubelbeck,
*The Sacred Penitentiaria and its Relations to the Faculties of Ordinaries and
Priests*, p. 64. Vide etiam Konings-Putzer *Comment. in Facult.*, p. 386-
387; Ayrinhac, *Marriage Legislation*, p. 154-155.

the Catholic party is well disposed and the conditions of the divine law are fulfilled.

316. The arguments employed to defend this opinion may be summarized under the following headings.

1. The Church has always shown a disposition to relinquish the full rigor of her law regarding the *cautiones* in cases where a marriage has already been attempted, as is evident from an instruction of the Holy Office sent to the Vicar Apostolic of Sutchuen on January 12, 1769.[85] Again in a letter of the Congregation of the Propaganda of May 3, 1828, sent to the Apostolic Vicar of Tonkin,[86] a certain limited *cautio* was permitted concerning the Catholic education of a first born child or of the first male child born, or to be born, provided that the Catholic woman be at the point of death and that she give a promise that in case of recovery she would endeavor to convert the infidel party and to educate all the children in the Catholic Faith. The Holy See has, moreover, expressed its willingness to grant a *sanatio in radice* for invalid mixed or disparate marriages upon the non-Catholic's refusal of the *cautiones*, provided that the union could not be broken, that the consent persevered, and that the Catholic party would assume definite obligations.[87]

2. The decision of the Holy Office of June 21, 1912,[88] which permits the Ordinary, without recourse to the Holy See, to declare invalid a disparate marriage contracted without the *cautiones* has limitations which do not permit of its extension to canon 1043. It regards a delegated faculty, whereas canon 1043 has reference to ordinary jurisdiction. The decision, moreover, refers only to normal cases of dispensation, whereas canon 1043 refers to the danger of death. Finally the decision was given *"prout exponitur"* which indicates that in different circumstances a different answer might be given. If there is any circumstance which would warrant a different answer, surely it is the danger of death.

------

[85] *Fontes*, n. 822, ad II, 4. Vide etiam S. C. de Prop. F., 30 Ian. 1807, —Ballerini-Palmieri, *Op. Theol. Mor.*, Tract. X, Sect. VIII, n. 710.

[86] *Coll.*, n. 804.

[87] Cf. S. C. S. Off., 22 Aug. 1875,—*NRT*, XV (1883), 579-580; 20 Iun. 1892,—*ASS*, XXX (1897-1898), 383-384; 12 Apr. 1899,—*Fontes*, n. 1219.

[88] *AAS*, IV (1912), 443.

3. While canon 1043 demands that the *cautiones* be given if a dispensation from the impediments of Mixed Religion or Disparity of Cult be granted,[39] this requirement is to be understood to mean,—*"in quantum fieri potest"*, instead of an absolute condition of validity. It will be sufficient for validity if those conditions demanded by the divine and natural law are adhered to absolutely.

4. The requirement of canon 1043 is put in the ablative absolute,—*"praestitis consuetis cautionibus"*, a fact, which, in view of the disagreement among the authors, does not necessarily involve a condition required for validity. In this connection, therefore, canons 11[40] and 15[41] must be kept in mind, and canon 39[42] by way of analogy.

5. The *cautiones* are merely an ecclesiastical provision to safeguard the divine law. If in danger of death the divine law can be safeguarded in some other way (for example, if the non-Catholic party is at death's door) surely the Church will not urge her law. *"In extremis pereat lex."* The opposite opinion would be entirely too rigorous.

6. Only a few authors who wrote before the Code discuss the issue in question, and these favored the more liberal opinion.

7. After the Code a sufficient number of authors subscribe to the opinion to make it solidly probable. Their number continues to grow. Vermeersch, who at first upheld the stricter view,[43] has now changed his opinion.[44]

8. Since it cannot be denied that there is at least a *dubium iuris* concerning this question, dispensations granted in danger

---

[39] ". . . si dispensatio concedatur super cultus disparitate aut mixta religione, praestitis consuetis cautionibus."—Canon 1043. Vide etiam S. C. S. Off. (Leopolien.), 18 Mart. 1891.—*Fontes*, n. 1132.

[40] "Irritantes aut inhabilitantes eae tantum leges habendae sunt, quibus aut actum esse nullum aut inhabilem esse personam expresse vel aequivalenter statuitur."—Canon 11.

[41] "Leges, etiam irritantes et inhabilitantes, in dubio iuris non urgent . . ."—Canon 15.

[42] "Conditiones in rescriptis tunc tantum essentiales pro eorundem validitate censentur, cum per particulas *si*, *dummodo*, vel aliam eiusdem significationis exprimuntur."—Canon 39.

[43] *Epitome Juris Canonici* (1922 ed.), II, n. 348, d. This reference is found in O'Keeffe, *Matrimonial Dispensations*, p. 91, note 132.

[44] Cf. No. 315, note 34.

of death upon the non-Catholic's refusal of the *cautiones* must be regarded as valid by virtue of canon 209.[45]

317. Notwithstanding the apparent cogency of these reasons, there are many authors who maintain that dispensations from the impediments of Mixed Religion or Disparity of Cult without the *cautiones* must always be regarded as invalid, and that the danger of death offers no exception to this rule.[46] Others, while apparently inclined to accept this opinion, state it with guarded phrase to the effect that such dispensations are either not certainly valid,[47] or that they are not certainly invalid.[48] In view of this division of opinion it will be well to re-examine the evidence that may be used to interpret the meaning of the clause of canon 1043,—"*praestitis consuetis cautionibus.*" Such evidence may be classified as follows:

1) Decisions and instructions determining the law before the Code;

2) The opinions of authors writing before the Code;

3) The law of the Code expressed in canons 1043 and 1061, § 1;

4) The intrinsic merits of the opinions expressed by authors writing after the Code.

318. Since some of the authors who favor the more liberal opinion invoke decisions and instructions that refer to the discipline of the eighteenth century, it is necessary again to recall

---

[45] "In errore communi aut in dubio positivo et probabili sive iuris sive facti, iurisdictionem supplet Ecclesia pro foro tum externo tum interno."—Canon 209.

[46] De Smet, *De Spons. et Matr.*, nn. 505, 590; p. 518, not. 2; p. 644, not. 6 (also in English translation of the third latin edition [St. Louis, 1925], II, p. 32, not 3; p. 196, not. 6); Augustine, *Commentary*, V, p. 101-102; *The Pastor*, p. 131; Noldin, *Theol. Mor.*, III, n. 608; Prümmer, *Theol. Mor.*, n. 825; HPR, XXVII (1926-1927), 195; Woywod, *A Practical Commentary*, I, n. 1011; HPR, XXIII (1923), 1059; Leitner, *Lehrb. des kath. Eherechts*, p. 243. Vlaming (*Prael. Iuris Matr.*, n. 218, p. 190, not. 2), Harrington (*AER*, LXV [1921], 259-260), and Linneborn (*Grundriss des Eherechts*, p. 203, not. 1) may also be regarded as favoring this opinion though they are not as explicit as the other authors. O'Keeffe (*Matrimonial Dispensations*, p. 85, note 105) refers also to Simon [*Faculties of Pastors and Confessors for Absolution and Dispensation*, p. 86] as holding this opinion.

[47] Chelodi, *Ius Matr.*, n. 41; Wernz-Vidal, *Ius Canonicum*, V, n. 413, Scholion, a.

[48] Motry, *Diocesan Faculties*, p. 133-134.

that such evidence can scarcely be used as a norm of interpretation for it is only with the advent of the nineteenth century that the full discipline of the Church regarding mixed marriages among the common people became in any manner universally established.[49] The earlier instructions sent to the Vicars Apostolic of missionary regions are likewise an unsafe guide for apparently they deal with a discipline not entirely fixed as to the observance of definite formalities.[50]

319. With due allowance for a period of transition that may have extended into the early part of the nineteenth century, it may be said without hesitation that the decisions and instructions of the Holy See in the nineteenth and twentieth centuries demonstrate beyond the shadow of a doubt that the *cautiones* became a *conditio sine qua non* of the very validity of dispensations for mixed and disparate marriages.[51] There is the constant insistence that dispensations for mixed marriages cannot be given without the *cautiones*. The well known instruction of November 15, 1858, sent to the Bishops and Archbishops of the entire world, uses such expressions as: *"Insuper in tribuendis huiusmodi dispensationibus, praeter enunciatas cautiones quae praemitti semper debent, et super quibus dispensari nullo modo umquam potest"*, and further on,—*"salvis firmisque semper ac perdiligenter servatis cautionibus."*[52] Again, the formality of an oath could be dispensed with since the only *essential condition* was the promise of the customary *cautiones*.[53] In regions where the giving of the *cautiones* was proscribed by the civil law, the Holy Office continued to insist that on no condition could a dispensation for mixed marriages be given without them.[54] On no condition was an exception to this rule to be countenanced.[55]

---

[49] See Nos. 104-106.

[50] See No. 77; No. 345, note 115.

[51] See No. 314, notes 31-32.

[52] *Coll.*, n. 1169.

[53] "Che per farsi luogo alla dispensa nei matrimonii misti, è essenziale solamente la promessa della solite cauzioni . . ." S. C. S. Off., litt. (S. Germani), 17 Feb. 1875,—*Fontes*, n. 1039.

[54] ". . . eas nullimode concedant nisi prius a partibus et praesertim a parte heterodoxa consuetae cautiones exhibitae fuerint."—S. C. S. Off., litt. (ad Card. Simor), 21 Iul. 1880,—*NRT*, XIX (1887), 8. Cf. Card. Rampolla, litt. (ad Card. Simor), 26 Sept. 1890,—*NRT*, XXIII (1891), 388-391.

[55] "I. An ab impedimento mixtae religionis dispensari possit, si pars

320. True, for strictly mixed marriages, there appears to be no decision which states the necessity of the *cautiones* for the *validity* of a dispensation in so many words, yet it is stated equivalently by placing the necessity of the *cautiones* on an equal basis with the necessity of just and grave causes,[56]— a fact which further exemplifies their relation to the validity of mixed marriage dispensations. Even canon 1061, § 1 of the Code does not state explicitly, i. e., in so many words, that they are required for the *validity* of dispensations, yet it does make it an implicit requirement in precisely the same way as did the decisions, namely, by placing the *cautiones* on an equal basis with just and grave causes as a *conditio sine qua non* of dispensation.

321. In the case of invalidly contracted mixed marriages (if in such circumstances the Catholic is well disposed) the Church has, indeed, shown a disposition to mitigate the full rigor of her discipline,—even though the non-Catholic refuses to give the *cautiones*. But rather than depart from her insistence that dispensations be granted only upon the giving of the *cautiones*, she has turned as a last resort to the dispensation given through the *sanatio in radice*. Even the faculty to grant a *sanatio in radice* for mixed marriages invalid because of clandestinity did not include the faculty to grant a *sanatio in radice* if the non-Catholic party refused to give the *cautiones*. The Holy Office decided that on no account was such a contingency to be provided for by a dispensation and the renewal of consent before a pastor assisting passively.[57]

---

acatholica (quaecumque est) cautiones requisitas per litteras reversales, sive per iuramentum, sive per promissionem saltem omnimode recuset. R. Ad I. Negative, et detur Instructio 15 Novembris 1858."—S. C. S. Off., 10 Dec. 1902,—*Fontes*, n. 1262.

[56] See No. 314, note 32.

[57] "Ordinarius dioecesis N., obtenta enim facultate sanandi in radice matrimonia mixta, nulla ex capite clandestinitatis quia non celebrata ad normam decreti *Ne Temere*, quando pars acatholica renuit se sistere coram parocho catholico, quaerit nunc: 1) Utrum quando pars acatholica non renuit se sistere coram parocho catholico, renuit tamen omnino praestare debitas cautiones, providendum sit per dispensationem ad renovationem consensus coram parocho catholico passive se habente, vel potius per sanationem in radice: et quatenus providendum sit per sanationem in radice. 2) Utrum facultas sanandi in radice in hoc secundo casu comprehensa censenda sit necne in facultate iam obtenta sanandi in radice matrimonia mixta, nulla ex capite clandestinitatis, vel. 3) Utrum peti debeat an non nova facultas a S. Sede.

322. In the law before the Code a dispensation from the impediment of Disparity of Cult could never be given without the *cautiones*.[58] In fact, disparate marriages contracted without the *cautiones* could be declared null and void by the Ordinary and without referring such cases to the Holy See.

1. Utrum dispensatio super impedimento disparitatis cultus ab habente a Sancta Sede potestatem, non requisitis vel denegatis praescriptis cautionibus impertita, valida habenda sit an non? Et quatenus negative:

2. Utrum hisce in casibus, cum scilicet de dispensatione sic invalide concessa evidenter constat, matrimonii ex hoc capite nullitatem per se ipse Ordinarius declarare valeat, vel opus sit, singulis vicibus, ad Sanctam Sedem pro sententia definitiva recurrere?

R. Ad 1. Dispensationem prout exponitur impertitam esse nullam.

Ad 2. Affirmative ad primam; negative ad secundam partem.[59]

The answer to the first *dubium* is given *"prout exponitur"*. The proponents of the more liberal opinion regarding the validity of a dispensation granted in danger of death without the *cautiones*, urge that since the decision refers only to ordinary cases and to a delegated faculty, it cannot, therefore, serve as an interpretation of the clause *"praestitis consuetis cautionibus"* of canon 1043.

323. It is well to note that the question proposed in the first *dubium* mentions no circumstance whatever in connection with the use of the faculty. There is no suggestion that it refers

---

R. Ad 1. Negative ad primam partem, affirmative ad secundam.
Ad 2. Non comprehendi.
Ad 3. Provisum in secundo. Et supplicandum SSmo ut sanare dignetur in radice matrimonia ex hoc capite nulla quae usque adhuc ab Episcopis sanata fuerint."—S. C. S. Off., 22 Dec. 1916,—*AAS*, IX (1917), 13-14. Cf. S. C. S. Off., 21 Iun. 1912,—*AAS*, IV (1912), 443-444.

[58] The following decision was given on April 16, 1890, but was published in 1912: " 'An in concedendis ab habente a Sancta Sede potestatem dispensationibus super impedimento disparitatis cultus praescriptae cautiones semper sint exigendae', Emi ac Rmi DD. Cardinales in rebus fidei et morum Inquisitores generales, re perdiligenti examine discussa, respondendum decreverunt: 'Dispensationem super impedimento disparitatis cultus nunquam concedi, nisi expressis omnibus conditionibus seu cautionibus'."—S. C. S. Off., 21 Iun. 1912,—*AAS*, IV (1912), 442.

[59] S. C. S. Off., 21 Iun. 1912,—*AAS*, IV (1912), 443.

only to "ordinary cases" and not to a danger of death. There is no reason to suppose that the faculty was limited to "ordinary cases", nor is there any reason why a Bishop may not or cannot use his delegated faculty in cases of danger of death even though he has the same faculty by common law in such cases. The question proposed merely asks whether a dispensation granted without the *cautiones* by any one who has the power to dispense from the Holy See, is valid or not. To say that only "ordinary" or "normal" cases are considered is to read into the *dubium* and the answer something that is neither explicitly nor implicitly stated.

324. But, it is urged, the danger of death is not mentioned, and the answer concerns a delegated faculty. Now since it is a probable opinion even among authors, who espouse the liberal view regarding the question at hand, that the faculties of February 20, 1888[60] can be understood as pertaining to ordinary jurisdiction,[61] the decision of the Holy Office of March 18, 1891, will be of special interest since it refers both to the faculty of 1888 and consequently to the danger of death.

Relate ad facultates Episcopis a Sanctitate sua concessa (quae etiam parochis subdelegari possunt) dispensandi in articulo mortis in impedimentis matrimonium dirimentibus, rogo (ego Archiepiscopus) quoad impedimenta mixtae religionis et disparitatis cultus benignissimam declarationem, an in istis etiam in articulo mortis non aliter dispensari possit nisi 1) ambo contrahentes promittant educationem omnis prolis in religione catholica; et quidem 2) non solum prolis forte adhuc suscipiendae, sed etiam antea (in concubinatu vel civili matrimonio) iam susceptae, in quantum scilicet hoc a parentibus adhuc dependet; atque nisi etiam 3) pars catholica (licet privatim tantum) promittat quod, in quantum poterit, conversionem partis non catholicae procurare sataget.

R. Cautiones etiam in articulo mortis esse exigendas; disparitatem cultus utpote impedimentum dirimens in Encyclica Sancti Officii 20 Februarii 1888 comprehendi: mixtum vero religionem, uti impedimentum impediens, non comprehendi.[62]

---

[60] See No. 103, note 49.

[61] De Becker, *De Spons. et Matr.*, p. 316; O'Keeffe, *Matrimonial Dispensations*, p. 99. Vide etiam Gasparri, *De Matr.*, n. 435. Wernz (*Ius Decret.*, IV, n. 617, not. 63), however, regarded the power as delegated.

[62] S. C. S. Off. (Leopolien.), 18 Mart. 1891,—*Fontes*, n. 1132.

325. Though the *dubia* and the answer do not state in so many words the question as to the necessity of the *cautiones* for the validity of the dispensation, yet the question *"an in istis etiam in articulo mortis non aliter dispensari possit etc."*, and the answer,—*"cautiones etiam in articulo mortis esse exigendas"*, must be interpreted in the light of the host of decisions that had already demanded the *cautiones* as a *conditio sine qua non* of the validity of dispensations. Everything in the answer, i. e., its wording and its contextual relation to the *dubium*, shows that the fixed discipline must be adhered to for validity even in danger of death, or as the present decision has it,—*"in articulo mortis"*. Those who favor the liberal opinion say that the clause *"cautiones . . . esse exigendas"* does not express formally a condition of validity. Yet such an interpretation scarcely takes into consideration the relation of this decision to the many already existing,—it seems rather to manifest an attempt to defend an *a priori* assumption.

326. In a decision of July 6, 1898 the question was again asked in relation to the danger of death. The first two *dubia* concern a Catholic *in articulo mortis* who had lost the use of his senses, and there is, therefore, no question of validating the marriage since consent cannot be renewed. But then is proposed the following *dubium: "Quid, si iste moribundus* [catholicus] *sit compos sui et adsint filii baptizati, quos lex civilis retinet uti legitimos?"* To this it was answered: *"Episcopus vel parochus in casu uti poterit facultate Ordinariis concessa sub die 20 Febr. 1888, renovato consensu et datis cautionibus."*[63] In the wording of this decision the use of the faculty does not, indeed, precede the renewal of consent, though manifestly the use of the faculty must precede the renewal of consent. What is significant is the fact that both the renewal of consent and the giving of the *cautiones* are equally required, a clear indication that the *cautiones* are necessary for the *validity* of the marriage.[64]

327. Once more the question was put by a Bishop concerning the Leonine faculty of 1888.

---

[63] S. C. S. Off., 6 Iul. 1898, ad 3,—*Fontes*, n. 1200.

[64] The *dubium* considered the case of a dying Catholic married civilly to an infidel. The question of the force of the ablative absolute will be discussed in No. 332.

Il Vescovo N. espone che nella sua diocesi insieme ai cattolici trovasi frammisto grande numero di eretici, il cui battesimo dà molto a dubitare della validità. Chiede perciò, per coloro che trovansi in articolo di morte ed in concubinato con tali eretici . . . la facoltà (delegabile anche ai parochi) di dispensare dagl'impedimenti di religione mista o di disparità di culto se esistono, quando amendue i contraenti, o almeno la parte cattolica promette di allevare la prole nella religione cattolica o almeno la nascitura, quando la nata oltrepassi i sette anni.

To this question the reply was given that though the faculty of 1888 did include the impediment of Disparity of Cult it did not include that of Mixd Religion and continues:

Quoad dispensationem super impedimento mixtae religionis, pro casibus in quibus *omnes dentur cautiones,* et Episcopus moraliter certus sit easdem impletum iri, supplicandum SSmo pro facultate dispensandi ad triennium. Pro casibus vero in quibus vel praehabito actu mere civili, vel contractu coram ministro haeretico, vel utroque simul, *non omnes praestantur cautiones,* vel Episcopus moraliter certus non sit easdem impletum iri, supplicandum pariter SSmo *pro facultate sanandi in radice* matrimonia itidem ad triennium . . ."[65]

The answer is equivalent to this, that any dispensation from the impediment of Mixed Religion without all of the *cautiones* would be invalid unless given through a *sanatio in radice* by one possessing this delegated faculty. The immediate implication exists likewise that the same ruling would apply to dispensations from the impediment of Disparity of Cult granted by virtue of the faculty of 1888. The requirements for dispensation were the same for both impediments.[66]

328. In the light of the decisions of March 18, 1891, of July 6, 1898, of April 12, 1899, and of the decisions preceding and folowing these, how must the decision of June 21, 1912 be interpreted? Whatever doubt may have existed in the minds of the Bishops proposing questions, or of authors who upheld a more liberal opinion, the decision of 1912 appears to solve them. Dispensations from either of these impediments without the *cautiones* are to be regarded as invalid. The clause *"prout exponitur"* contemplates no exception of *circumstances* regarding the refusal of the *cautiones,* but it does limit the decision to

---

[65] S. C. S. Off., 12 Apr. 1899,—*Fontes,* n. 1219.
[66] See No. 355, note 148.

one point, and the only one proposed in the first *dubium*, namely, with reference to their refusal. It does not pass on other questions such as a lack of moral certitude regarding the fulfillment of the *cautiones*, a requirement likewise demanded for the validity of a dispensation, but of its nature difficult to determine *post factum*. The answer to the second *dubium* confirms the interpretation that the clause *"prout exponitur"* has the function of limiting the competency of the Ordinary to those cases representing a refusal of the *cautiones* in connection with dispensations. It was only upon this issue, the refusal of the *cautiones*, that the Ordinary could give a declaration of the nullity of a disparate marriage contracted without the *cautiones*. There is no *circumstance* of the refusal of the *cautiones* mentioned in the *dubia;* neither is there any implied in the answer. The assertion, therefore, that the clause *"prout exponitur"* leaves room for cases of danger of death, is quite gratuitous. Nor is the objection that the *dubia* or the answers do not mention the danger of death, or that they regard a delegated faculty, one that can be sustained. That objection was answered in the decisions of March 18, 1891; July 6, 1898; and of April 12, 1899.

329. Some have expressed a regret that as a general rule the authors who wrote before the Code did not single out the circumstance of a danger of death to comment upon, yet call attention to the fact that those few who did deal with the question *"ex professo"* decided in favor of the more benign interpretation.[67] Is not this very dearth of evidence from the authors an indication that the circumstance of a danger of death was not regarded as an exception, and that it was unnecessary to treat of it *"ex professo"*? True, De Becker, De Smet, and De Smedt did favor the more benign interpretation,[68] yet it is of some significance that both De Becker and De Smet expressed this opinion before the decision of June 21, 1912. Apparently, De Becker has not since written upon this subject. De Smet has departed from his former opinion and now subscribes to the stricter interpretation.[69] De Smedt[70] urges the recourse to *epikeia* only for

---

[67] Cf. O'Keeffe, *Matrimonial Dispensations*, p. 88-89.
[68] See No. 315, note 34.
[69] See No. 317, note 46.
[70] *LQS*, LXVII (1914), 384-385.

mixed marriages, yet in his total disregard of the decision of
June 21, 1912, he may not have had this decision in mind when
he wrote. It is not one that may be dismissed with silence, and
the best proof of this is that the authors favoring the benign
opinion, who have written since the Code, deem it necessary to
minimize its force by introducing limitations and distinctions
which betray their realization of a real weakness in their position.

330. There is, therefore, little or no support for the more
benign interpretation in the decisions and among the authors
who wrote before the Code. The sudden favor that the opinion
received after the Code leads one to suspect that perhaps there
has been an attempt "to stretch a text". Certainly the law demanding the *cautiones* for the validity of dispensations has in
no way changed. Canon 1061, § 1 clearly states that the Church
will not dispense unless there be just and grave causes, and unless the *cautiones* are given. Beyond the fact that the *cautiones*
and the causes are demanded as a *sine qua non* condition of dispensation, there is no further indication that the *cautiones* are
demanded for the *validity* of ANY dispensation for mixed and
disparate marriages. Yet that indication is certainly sufficient
that they are demanded for the validity of such dispensations,
and no canonist will maintain that canon 1061, § 1, n. 2, has
reference only to the liceity of such dispensations.[71]

331. If the clause "*datis consuetis cautionibus*" of canon
1043 is to receive an interpretation from any canon in the Code,
surely it is canon 1061, §1, which treats formally of the necessity of the *cautiones*.[72] And if canon 1061, § 1, demands the
cautiones under pain of invalidity, is there any reason to suppose
that the clause "*datis consuetis cautionibus*" of canon 1043 refers, either *per se* or *per accidens*, only to the liceity of a dispensation given in danger of death? If the entire last clause of canon
1043 referring to dispensations from the impediments of Mixed
Religion and Disparity of Cult had been omitted, as it was in

---

[71] King (*The Administration of the Sacraments to Dying Non-Catholics*,
p. 129) does seem to entertain a doubt, but his argument is accepted by no
other canonist.

[72] It is not amiss to note that canons 1043 and canon 1061 are in the
same book of the Code (Book III) and under the same title (Title VII).

the faculty of 1888, canon 1061, § 1, and the decisions would, nevertheless, demand the *cautiones* for the validity of such dispensations. The very insertion of the clause is significant. Its obvious meaning is that there is to be no exception as to the necessity of the *cautiones* even in cases of danger of death. And this necessity is expressed as a requirement for validity in canon 1061, § 1.

332. But it is said that the clause is put in the ablative absolute, and since there is a disagreement among the authors as to the force of such a grammatical construction, it is not certain that it binds under pain of invalidity. While a condition of validity is more often expressed by such particles as "*si*" or "*dummodo*", canon 39 explicitly leaves room for expressions of equivalent significance. The ablative absolute is not a usual way of expressing such a condition yet Pope Benedict XIV could write on this point: ". . . *certissimum est inter Iurisperitos, quod vera conditio ex* ABLATIVO ABSOLUTO *consequitur: qua de re praetermitti nullo modo potest, licet gravissima incommoda iam exposita interponantur.*"[73] In this connection the decision of July 6, 1898[74] expressed the necessity of the *cautiones* in a like manner: "*renovato consensu et datis cautionibus.*" Both requirements—the renewal of consent and the giving of the *cautiones*. were expressed by an ablative absolute construction for the validity of the marriage.

333. Again it is urged that the strict opinion exemplifies too great a rigor, that the Church in such circumstances would not wish to urge a discipline merely of her own creation. "In *extremis pereat lex.*" But *de facto* the Church does explicitly demand the *cautiones* for precisely such circumstances ("*si dispensatio concedatur super cultus disparitate aut mixta religione, praestitis consuetis cautionibus*"),[75] and for the very validity of the dispensation. There is, indeed, a certain appeal in the arguments that elaborate upon the hardships that might often result from the enforcement of the law of the Church in danger of death, but they lose their value in the presence of a positive law

---

[73] *Institutiones Ecclesiasticae*, Inst. LXXXVII, n. LXVIII.—*Op. Omnia* (18 vols., Prati, 1839-1847), X, 386.
[74] See No. 326.
[75] Canon 1043.

that takes cognizance of the very circumstances postulated by the defenders of the liberal opinion. The popular axiom *"in extremis pereat lex"* has its obvious limitations. Will it not likewise be a hardship to the Catholic if the non-Catholic refuses to renew consent to validate a union invalid only because of the law of the Church? And is not this renewal merely an ecclesiastical requirement if only an ecclesiastical impediment is in question?[76] Then why, upon the argument from the axiom *"in extremis pereat lex"*, may not a *sanatio in radice* be granted,— the Church has in the past, and also in her faculties that she now grants to Bishops of many dioceses, manifested her disposition to grant a *sanatio in radice* as a last resort if the *cautiones* are refused? It is well to note, however, that this resort to a *sanatio in radice* is *de facto* the only exception to her discipline on the necessity of the *cautiones*, yet canonists are agreed that a *sanatio in radice* cannot be granted by virtue of canon 1043.[77]

334. True, the prohibitions of the divine law may cease in a particular case without the giving of the *cautiones*, but the very concern that a dispensation be not invalid because of the violation of the divine law is based solely on the positive law of the Church that has demanded this as a condition of the validity of dispensation. The divine law itself contains no such invalidating clause. Had Mixed Religion and Disparity of Cult never become canonical impediments. there would be no question either as to the validity or invalidity of dispensation but only a question as to the lawfulness of such marriages in particular instances.[78] Will any canonist say that the positive law of the Church, demanding under pain of invalidity that dispensations be not granted in violation of the divine law, may be submitted to the axiom *"in extremis pereat lex"*? But in addition to demanding this as a condition of validity by positive law; by the

---

[76] Cf. canon 1133, § 2.

[77] Cf. canon 1141; O'Keeffe, *Matrimonial Dispensations*, p. 92-93; Wernz, *Ius Decret.*, IV, n. 616, not. 67 (who refers to the faculty of 1888); Cappello, *De Sacram.*, III, n. 232, 1; De Smet, *De Spons. et Matr.*, n. 761; Ayrinhac. *Marriage Legislation*, p. 323; Motry, *Diocesan Faculties*, p. 134.

[78] For example, there is no question of the invalidity of the Ordinary's permission in canon 1065, § 2, but only of the *lawfulness* of his permission. Canons 1065 and 1066 regard a prohibition, not a canonical impediment.

same positive law the Church demands for validity the necessity of the *cautiones,* and even in danger of death,—"*praestitis consuetis cautionibus*". Her law remains in force, and as a condition of validity, regardless of this circumstance. Nor can an appeal to *epikeia* be sustained, for among canonists it is generally admitted that *epikeia* cannot be used where there is question of the *validity* of an act.[79] Exception is, indeed, admitted for common necessity[80] but the present question is not concerned with that kind of necessity. The lawgiver has, moreover, provided for the necessity of a danger of death, and hence the resort to *epikeia* is futile.

335. If it were true that the clause "*datis consuetis cautionibus*" referred only to the liceity of the dispensation, then this interpretation should apply also to canon 1045.[81] Since, as the proponents of the liberal opinion maintain, the decision of June 21, 1912[82] does not include the cases of a danger of death but only ordinary [?] cases, it might likewise be said that it does not include other cases of urgent necessity. Cerato,[83] and Pighi[84] do accept the logical consequences of the liberal opinion[85] and extend it to canon 1045. O'Keeffe,[86] Kelly,[87] Cappello,[88] and Vermeersch[89] protest against this extension and deny all probability to such an interpretation. They argue that the just cause, posited

---

[79] Cf. Schmalzgrueber, *Jus Eccl. Univ.,* Tom. I, P. I, Tit. II, n. 49; Pichler, *Jus Can.,* Lib. 1, Tit. II, n. 76; Zitelli, *De Dispens. Matr.,* p. 9; Maroto, *Institutiones,* I, n. 243.

[80] Cf. Maroto, *loc. cit.;* Cocchi, *Comment.,* Vol. 1, n. 80; Vlaming, *Prael. Iuris Matr.,* n 198. De Smet (*De Spons. et Matr.,* nn. 469, 716; p. 614, not. 2) and Hilling (*Die allgemeinen Normen des C. I. C.,* p. 88) appear also to admit it for grave necessity in particular cases, but the legitimate use of this principle is, indeed, very doubtful.

[81] "Possunt Ordinarii locorum, sub clausulis in fine can. 1043 statutis . . . etc."—Canon 1045, § 1.

[82] See No. 322.

[83] *Matr.,* n. 37.

[84] *De Matr.,* n. 90.

[85] The same conclusion seems also to be suggested by Vermeersch-Creusen, (*Epitome,* II, n. 331): "E causa gravissima et urgente possit concedi dispensatio super cautione ab acatholica parte praestanda, si pars catholica periculum perversionis non incurrat etc."

[86] *Matrimonial Dispensations,* p. 144-145.

[87] *The Jurisdiction of the Simple Confessor,* p. 185-186.

[88] *De Sacram.,* III, n. 233.

[89] *Theol. Mor.,* III, n. 759.

especially by Cerato as existing in the urgent necessity itself, represents a confusion of the causes and the *cautiones*. Canon 1061, they say, clearly requires both causes and *cautiones*. Granting the existence of a cause, the *cautiones* are still required for the validity of a dispensation. But may not the extremities of circumstances be urged both as a cause for dispensation from the impediment and as a cause for dispensation from the *cautiones?* Canon 1061, § 1, canon 1043, the decisions, and the authors upholding the stricter opinion are arrayed against it, and it may be regarded as enjoying no sound probability. But in rejecting it, it is well to note that the entire position of the liberal opinion becomes more and more precarious.

336. Furthermore, among the authors favoring the benign interpretation of the clause *"praestitis consuetis cautionibus"* of canon 1043, there is no unanimity as to what circumstance is really necessary to grant a valid dispensation without the *cautiones*. Then what precisely may be said to be the so-called solidly probable opinion among the authors regarding the validity of dispensations without the *cautiones?* Is it that such dispensations will be valid if granted not only in danger of death but also in other urgent necessity? There are four of the liberal authors who deny all probability to this opinion.[90] Nor is the danger of death accepted without reservation by the liberal authors, for O'Keeffe demands that *the non-Catholic party* be in extreme danger of death before the dispensation can be given validly.[91] Kelly demands that the non-Catholic party be not only in danger of death "but in actual *articulo mortis*, death being inevitable and proximate."[92] King concludes his discussion: "If there are no offspring it is hard to see how there could be a just and sufficient cause to exercise the faculty with the denial of the *cautiones* as the *urgente mortis periculo* removes danger of concubinage, etc., for the present."[93] Genicot-Salsmans

---

[90] See No. 335.

[91] *Matrimonial Dispensations*, p. 89-92. O'Keeffe refers to the decision of July 6, 1898, (see No. 326) to support his distinction. But see the decision of April 16, 1890, (No. 322, note 58) which makes no such distinction. Moreover, neither these two nor any other decisions support the liberal opinion.

[92] *The Jurisdiction of the Simple Confessor*, p. 94.

[93] *The Administration of the Sacraments to Dying Non-Catholics*, p. 131.

draws a distinction between a non-attempted marriage and one already attempted. In the first hypothesis the absolute necessity of the *cautiones* is upheld; in the second a *dubium iuris* is admitted with a recommendation that such cases be referred to the Holy See.[94] Much has been made of the fact that Vermeersch has changed his position from the strict to the liberal view. In answer, attention has already been called to the fact that De Smet has changed to the strict opinion.[95] Even Vermeersch denies the validity of an argument from canon 1043 and deduces it rather from canon 81.[96] But the recourse to canon 81 is of doubtful value, for again it may be repeated with emphasis that the Holy See grants a dispensation from the impediments of Mixed Religion and Disparity of Cult without the *cautiones* only through the *sanatio in radice*. It is not a probable opinion that the Ordinary can grant a *sanatio in radice* by virtue of canon 81. Moreover, canon 81 will be of little assistance to the pastor, priest, or confessor mentioned in canons 1044 and 1045.

337. Granted that some phase or other of the benign interpretation is accepted by many authors, what limitation or extension of it can be regarded as solidly probable? Is canon 209 to be invoked for its widest extension as it is proposed by Pighi and Cerato? Other and more limited phases are likewise subject to the very criticisms of the liberal authors themselves. Which of these is to be regarded as solidly probable, and upon what norm of discrimination? If neither the decisions nor the canons lend intrinsic support to any one of the limitations or extensions of the benign interpretation, what is the value of a recourse to authors disagreeing among themselves? And even if a sufficient number of authors can be marshalled to the support of one phase of the liberal opinion, it is to be remembered that an argument from mere external authority has little weight in the face of a positive law of the Church to the contrary. At one time a

---

[94] *Theol. Mor.*, II, nn. 493, 514.

[95] See No. 315, note 34; No. 317, note 46.

[96] "Si plene obtinere vel prudenter [cautiones] peti posse non videntur, Ordinarius probabilius valide agit qui, in his rebus extremis, condicionibus iure divino requisitis contentus sit. Id tamen minus ex praesenti facultate, quam ex can. 81 colligimus quo, ubi mora inducit periculum gravis damni, Ordinarius ad mentem S. Sedis dispensare permittitur."— *Theol. Mor.*, n. 759.

host of canonists and theologians of name subscribed to the opinion that a custom had developed in the northern countries of Europe which had abrogated the necessity of dispensation from the impediment of Mixed Religion.[97] Even their great number did not make the opinion solidly probable. It was contrary to the mind of the Church and it was, therefore, rejected by the Church.[98] It may, therefore, be said that the opinion which would uphold the validity of a dispensation from the impediments of Mixed Religion and Disparity of Cult, given without the *cautiones* in any other way but through a *sanatio in radice*, is not solidly probable. The *sanatio in radice* can be granted only by those who have the delegated faculty from the Holy See.

338. Nor does there appear to be sufficient justification for a recourse to passive assistance for strictly *mixed* marriages when a dispensation in danger of death (*"ad consulendum conscientiae et, si casus ferat, legitimationi prolis"*) cannot be validly given without the *cautiones.*[99] Passive assistance in the emergency postulated seems indeed to be valid for its abrogation,[100] with reference to its *validity,* can be understood as referring to those cases where the observance of the form is strictly required for the validity of a marriage. Canon 1043, on the other hand, confers upon the Ordinary the power to dispense from the form, which appears to include the power (in as far as validity is concerned) to dispense from the asking of the consent as it is prescribed in canon 1102, § 1. There seems to be no evident reason why canon 1102, § 1, should represent an exception from the general power of dispensing from the form conferred by canon 1043.

339. Though a recourse to passive assistance for mixed marriages would not be a violation of the clause of canon 1043,

---

[97] See No. 81, note 13.

[98] See No. 104, note 54.

[99] Whatever justification may be attributed to a recourse to passive assistance for mixed marriages in such an emergency, needless to say, it will be of no avail for *disparate* marriages since their validity will depend on the validity of the dispensation from the impediment of Disparity of Cult. The dispensation from this impediment without the *cautiones* can be granted only through the *sanatio in radice.*

[100] See Nos. 385-386.

("*si dispensatio concedatur super cultus disparitate aut mixta religione, praestitis consuetis cautionibus*"), since no dispensation from the impediment is given, it is, nevertheless, a violation of the law of the Church. The Catholic who would dare to contract a mixed marriage without dispensation incurs the penalty of canon 2375. The Church, moreover, has time and again forbidden priests to assist at mixed marriages for which no dispensation had been given. The former tolerance of passive assistance was restricted to very definite regions[101] and it is not to be readily supposed that even with the power to dispense from the form granted by canon 1043, the Church would be willing to tolerate a passive assistance at mixed marriages contracted without dispensation in danger of death, when she has explicitly withdrawn her former tolerance from the very regions where it was permitted.[102] Perhaps a certain *epikeia* might be permitted in extreme cases since the question of the validity of an act does not seem to arise.[103] The suggestion of the possibility of such a recourse is given with the greatest hesitation. The lawfulness of such a procedure is in gravest doubt. The legislator demands the *cautiones* even in danger of death,—"*praestitis consuetis cautionibus*". It is, therefore, difficult to see how a legitimate use could be made of the principle of *epikeia*.

Art. VI. Nature and Content of the *Cautiones*

340. In every mixed or disparate marriage there is a certain amount of danger to the faith of the Catholic party and of the children,—a danger that constitutes one of the very elements of the Church's prohibition to such marriages. It is only when this danger of the violation of the divine and natural law has been rendered remote, that the Church will consider the matter of a dispensation.[104] To this end, namely, that the proximate danger[105] may be regarded as absent, she demands

---

[101] See No. 106, notes 57-58.

[102] Cf. Maroto, "De Matrimoniis Mixtis Illicitis", *Apollinaris*, I (1928), 342.

[103] Cf. Petrovits, *New Church Law on Matrimony*, n. 269.

[104] The requirement of a just and grave cause is not under consideration for the present, though it is a *conditio sine qua non* of dispensation.

[105] "Dico 'quibus saltem periculum proximum perversionis removeatur'. Ordinario enim nisi pars haeretica ad fidem catholicam transeat, aliqua peri-

certain guarantees. These guarantees are under the form of explicit promises or *cautiones*. The non-Catholic party must promise to remove the danger of perversion from the Catholic party; both parties must promise that the children will be baptized only in the Catholic Church and that their religious education will be exclusively in the Catholic Faith. In addition there is required a moral certainty of the fulfillment of these promises, and normally these promises must be exacted in writing.[106]

CANON 1061

§ 1. *Ecclesia super impedimento mixtae religionis non dispensat, nisi*:

2° *Cautionem praestiterit coniux acatholicus de amovendo a coniuge catholico perversionis periculo, et uterque coniux de universa prole catholice tantum baptizanda et educanda*;

3° *Moralis habeatur certitudo de cautionum implemento.*

§ 2. *Cautiones regulariter in scriptis exigantur.*[107]

§ I. *"Cautionem praestiterit coniux acatholicus de amovendo a coniuge catholico perversionis periculo"*

341. The non-Catholic's promise is a personal obligation to remove all danger of perversion of which he or she would in any way be a source by word or action. It is a promise to remove every obstacle which through his or her agency would hinder the free exercise of the religious obligations and practices that should be the normal part of Catholic life. The obligation is stated in the form of a general principle involving a

---

cula, plus minusve remota parti catholicae et liberis suscipiendis remanebunt. At, quia huismodi pericula nondum sunt formaliter peccata, fieri potest, ut propter causam proportionate gravem prohibitio legis naturalis aut cesset aut iam non sit gravis."—Vlaming, *Prael. Iuris Matr.*, I, p. 186, not. 1. Cf. De Smet, *De Spons. et Matr.*, n. 503.

[106] Since the *cautiones* are a very condition of dispensation, it need scarcely be repeated that they must precede not only the mixed or disparate marriage, but the dispensation itself. Cf. Cappello, *De Sacram.*, III, n. 311; Blat, *Comment.*, Vol. III, P. I, n. 456; Koudelka, *Pastors*, p. 137. In the law of the Church the *cautiones* are not demanded, however, as a condition of matrimonial consent, but rather of dispensation. If the *cautiones* are exacted as a condition of consent, this is a condition placed by the Catholic party, not by the Church. Cf. *Apollinaris*, I (1928), 120; Sacra Romana Rota, 11 Aug. 1921,—*AAS*, XIV (1922), 512-523.

[107] Canon 1071 establishes the same norm for the impediment of Disparity of Cult.

host of particular details, only a few of which will be mentioned by way of example. It implies the removal of every obstacle to the observance of all the obligations of the marital state which the parties wish to enter; a removal of any inducement to immoral practices which in a certain sense would be equivalent to a contumely of the Creator. Every hindrance must be removed from the Catholic's fulfillment of such duties as the attendance at Holy Mass, especially on Sundays and Holy Days of obligation; the reception of the Sacraments; the observance of the laws of fast and abstinence; the Catholic's reasonable support of the Church. Many of the Catholic's obligations will often, either directly or indirectly, affect the non-Catholic, yet the promise to remove every danger of perversion must be given before the Church will dispense.

§ II. *"Et uterque coniux de universa prole catholice tantum*
baptizanda et educanda"

342. Ever since the *cautiones* have become fixed in the Church's discipline for the mixed marriages of the common people, the non-Catholic party has always been required to give the *cautio* for the Catholic education of the children. The letter of the Holy Office sent to Cardinal Simor on July 21, 1880, expressed the concern that the *cautio* for the children be given especially by the non-Catholic.[108] The *cautio* of the Catholic party as to the Catholic Baptism and education of the children is a new element of the *cautiones* introduced by the Code. Formerly this promise does not appear to have been demanded expressly,[109]—perhaps on the assumption that this

---

[108] "Ut partes, *et praesertim haeretica*, veras cautiones praestiterint, quibus se coram Ecclesia obligent ad ea, quae ab iisdem eadem Ecclesia exigit: inter quae praecipuum locum tenet catholica educatio universae omnino prolis absque exceptione sive restrictione."—*NRT*, XIX (1887), 7.

[109] Cf. Petrovits, *New Church Law on Matrimony*, n. 191. The concern as to the Catholic education of the children was emphasized as an obligation which was to be imposed on the Catholic (cf. Rescript. Poenitentiariae, 19 Ian. 1836,—Roskovány, *De Matr. Mixtis*, III, p. 156, not. *) rather than as a formal *cautio* to be given by the Catholic party. This was especially true in cases where the marriage had already been contracted. Cf. S. C. S. Off., instr. (ad Archiep. Corcyren.), 3 Ian. 1871, n. 7,—*Fontes*, n. 1013; 9 Oct. 1877,—*NRT*, XV (1883), 578; 12 Apr. 1899,—*Fontes*, n. 1219. The same practice seems to be suggested in the present faculty given to the American Bishops for the granting of the *sanatio in radice* where the non-Catholic refuses the *cautiones*. See infra. No. 263; Vermeersch-Creusen, *Epi-*

would be the Catholic's intention. On the other hand the
former *cautio* required by the Catholic party that he extend
every effort ("*pro viribus suis*") toward procuring the conversion of the non-Catholic party[110] does not appear in the Code
as a formal *cautio* but is placed in canon 1062 as an obligation in charity upon the Catholic, to which he must prudently
("*prudenter*") direct his efforts.[111]

A. *"Uterque coniux"*

343. Though the letter of the Holy Office sent to Cardinal
Simor on July 21, 1880, emphasized the special necessity of
the non-Catholic's *cautiones*,[112] the Code in canon 1061, § 1,
n. 2, suggests no such preponderance of emphasis, but apparently
demands the *cautio* of both parties with equal emphasis as a
conditio sine qua non of dispensation. Would a dispensation
given without the *cautio* of the Catholic party be invalid? It
would seem to be invalid, though a case involving a question
of this kind should be referred to the Holy Office. Canon 1061,
§ 1, n. 2, likewise demands that the *cautiones* be given by the
parties themselves. It will not suffice that the parents, in their
stead, give the *cautiones*.[113]

---

tome, II, n. 871. In one instance, however, it appears that both the Catholic and the non-Catholic party were to give the *cautiones* regarding the education of the children. Cf. S. C. S. Off., 12 Mart. 1881,—*NRT*, XV
(1883), 121-122. In another instance a promise seems to have been exacted
of the Catholic party, both with regard to the conversion of the non-Catholic and the Catholic education of the children. Cf. S. C. S. Off., 15 Mart.
1854,—*LQS*, XLVI (1893), 21-22.

[110] Cf. Gregorius XVI, litt. ap. *Quas vestro*, 30 Apr. 1841, n. 2,—
Fontes, n. 497; instr. (ad Archiep. et Ep. Austriacae ditionis), 22 Maii
1841,—Ballerini-Palmieri, *Op. Theol. Mor.*, Tract. X, Sect. VIII, n. 720;
Instr. Secret. Stat. iussu Pii PP. IX, 15 Nov. 1858,—*Coll.*, n. 1169. In
one instance, however, where the marriage had already been contracted, this
seems to have been exacted more as an obligation than as a formal *cautio*.
The case concerned the exercise of the faculty of a *sanatio in radice*. Cf.
S. C. S. Off., 12 Apr. 1899,—*Fontes*, n. 1219. See No. 366, note 172.

[111] Cf. Petrovits, *New Church Law on Matrimony*, n. 258; Linneborn,
Grundriss des Eherechts, p. 165, not. 2; Woywod, *A Practical Commentary*, I, n. 1040.

[112] ". . . eas [dispensationes] nullimode concedant nisi prius a partibus et
praesertim a parte heterodoxa consuetae cautiones exhibitae fuerint."—*NRT*,
XIX (1887), 8.

[113] This will have particular reference to such regions of the Orient where
parents make all the marriage engagements for their children. Even in such
cases the parties themselves will have to give the *cautions* unless the Ordinary
who dispenses by a delegated faculty has also the faculty to dispense from

B. *"De universa prole"*

344. The requirement of canon 1061, § 1, n. 2, that *all* the children be included in the *cautiones* is not a new prescription but one that has always been insisted upon by the Church, —regardless of the leeway allowed by some authors for the *causa publica.*[114] It does away with any such arrangement that by the custom of a community or the agreement of the parties would, for example, permit the boys to follow the religion of the father and the girls that of the mother, or all of the children to be educated in the religion of the father if he be a non-Catholic. There can be no doubt whatever that the *cautio* given by both parties for the Catholic Baptism and education of the children must include, for both the validity and liceity of the dispensation, every child that will be born of that union. A natural question arises, however, as to whether this promise looks only to the future or whether it regards also the past.

345. The question proposed in the decision of the Holy Office of March 18, 1891, as to whether (even *in articulo mortis*) a dispensation could be given only upon the promise of both parties that all the children, whether born already of

---

this prescription. Cf. Ione, "Die Kautelen bei dem Hinderniss der Religionsverschiedenheit", *LQS.* LXXIX (1926), 810-814. The answer given by the Holy Office to the following *dubium* is of particular interest: "*Quando parentes catechumeni aut neophyti ante conversionem a paganismo suae filiae sponsalia fecerunt cum viro infideli, nec est possibile contractum rescindere, quid agendum cum puella quae baptismum postulat? Equidem ius habet ad baptismum, sed propter periculum fundatum perversionis, iuxta S. Ligorium, non expedit baptizare; at infidelis sponsi parentes cum iuramento affirmant quod relinquent puellam sacros religionis suae actus peragere: an baptizanda ante matrimonium? Denegamus baptismum, ut, peracto matrimonio, possimus iudicare an sit contumelia Creatoris; si non apparet periculum perversionis, sponsam baptizamus solum post matrimonium, ut si post tempus indeterminatum exurgit animae periculum, possit deserere infidelem, et alias legitimas nuptias appetere, et suae saluti providere. An iste modus agendi sit securior in praxi?*

R. *Modum, de quo in dubio, non improbari, nisi baptismi necessitas urgeat, aut nisi baptismus sit diutius differendus, et nisi etiam* CAUTIONES DATAE FUERINT NON SOLUM A PARENTIBUS, SED ETIAM A FUTURO CONIUGE; *quo in casu, praevia dispensatione, matrimonium permitti poterit.*" —S. C. S. Off. (Pekin.), 29 Apr. 1891, ad 2.—*Fontes,* n. 1134. For another case of the deferring of Baptism see S. C. S. Off., instr. (pro Vic. Ap. ad Gallas), 20 Iun. 1866, ad 10,—*Fontes,* n. 994. Dispensations are likewise not to be granted upon the request of parents for their children who are still *impuberes.* Cf. S. C. S. Off., 12 Ian. 1769, n. III.,—*Fontes,* n. 822.

[114] See No. 303, note 2; No. 305, note 5.

concubinage or a civil union, or to be born in the future, should be educated in the Catholic religion, was answered: *"Cautiones etiam in articulo mortis esse exigendas."*[115] Just what is implied in the answer regarding the children already born of the invalid union is not altogether clear. There is an indication, however, in the unqualified answer as to the necessity of the *cautiones*, that they should likewise regard the children already born of the invalid union.

346. In this connection, Vlaming proposes the question with regard to the children of the non-Catholic party by a former marriage and quotes from a decision given on March 20, 1899, by the Congregation of the Propaganda to the Bishop of Harlem: *"licet pro viribus sit curandum ut . . . in catholica religione instituantur, tamen haud absolute hoc exigendum pro concedenda dispensatione, nisi iidem filii ex altero matrimonio mixto sint orti, et parens priores conditiones non observavit."*[116] While it is stated that the obligation to care for the Catholic education of the children need not be exacted absolutely for the non-Catholic's children by a former marriage, it is implied, nevertheless, that the necessity is absolute if such children were born of a former mixed marriage in which the non-Catholic party had not observed the *cautiones*. The first part of the deci-

---

[115] *Fontes*, n. 1132. On the third of May, 1828, the Vicar Apostolic of Tonkin asked whether a dispensation from the impediment of Disparity of Cult could be given in gravest necessity, such as in *periculo mortis*, if the infidel consort (invalidly married to a Catholic woman) consented to everything except the Catholic education of the first born, or the first male child already born, or to be born. The answer of the Congregation of the Propaganda was given in the affirmative with the proviso *"pro casu mortis"*, and that the Catholic woman would promise, in the event of recovery, to exert every effort to procure the conversion of the infidel party, and the Catholic education of all the children. (Cf. *Coll.*, n. 804). Just what force this decision still retains, even for the region for which it was given, is very doubtful. Attention has already been directed to the fact of its date, and particularly the place to which it was sent. (See No. 318). The fact that extraordinary conditions have existed and continue to exist in the Orient must constantly be kept in mind. Yet even such unusual circumstances do not in modern times, with the fully established discipline regarding the necessity of the *cautiones*, necessarily permit the liberties apparently suggested in older decisions. The Holy Office deemed it necessary to provide anew, at least in part, for precisely such extraordinary circumstances by granting special faculties with reference to the *cautiones*. Cf. Winslow, *Vicars and Prefects Apostolic*, p. 106-107. This decision can, therefore, scarcely serve as a guide for other regions, and especially for an interpretation of canon 1061, § 1, n. 2.

[116] *Prael. Iuris Matr.*, n. 218.

sion seems to speak more in the terms of an obligation than of a strict *cautio* yet, since it refers to a manner of procedure in granting a dispensation, it must refer to the *cautiones* since at that time they were a *conditio sine qua non* of dispensation. Though the decision does not use the term "*cautiones*" when referring to the non-Catholic's observance of former conditions, it does imply that an obligation had been placed on the non-Catholic, and again it must refer to the *cautiones*. The entire context of the decision, therefore, demands the conclusion that there is question of the *cautiones*.

347. De Smet considers the case of a valid mixed marriage contracted without the *cautiones* and permits the reception of the sacraments by a well disposed Catholic giving the *cautiones* although the non-Catholic is unwilling to give them.[117] By way of confirmation, he quotes from a reply of the Holy Office of June 2, 1910, sent to the Bishop of Bruges, who presented the case of a well-disposed Catholic wife whose husband refused to promise the Catholic education of a child already born. The reply was: "*oratrix acquiescat, curet tamen pro viribus prolis etiam iam natae catholicam educationem.*"[118]

348. Apparently, few authors have committed themselves on this question. Konings-Putzer demands that the *cautiones* regard also the children already born, whether from illicit intercourse (apparently referring to that of the parties wishing to contract a mixed or disparate marriage), or of a former marriage of the Catholic party.[119] Prümmer requires that they regard not only the children to be born but also those begotten illegitimately by the contracting parties before the marriage, though he does not appear to require the absolute necessity of formal *cautiones* for children born to the non-Catholic party of a former marriage.[120] An unnamed writer, discussing the question in the

---

[117] *De Spons. et Matr.*, n. 514, d. Vide etiam S. C. S. Off., 2 Mart. 1842, —Gasparri, *De Matr.*, n. 523; (Georgiae), 5 Aug. 1846,—*Coll.*, n. 1009. By reason of canon 1098 such valid mixed marriages are still possible.

[118] *Op. cit.*, p. 451, not. 1.

[119] *Comment. in Facult.*, p. 381.

[120] "Haec conditio valet pro omni prole non solum ex isto matrimonio nascitura, sed etiam ab ipsis contrahentibus ante matrimonium illegitime genita. Praeterea cum parochus tum pars catholica prudenter curare debent, ut proles forte ex altero sponso in praecedenti connubio nata ab haeresi abducatur et catholice educetur. Nam quando alter sponsus prolem ex alio connubio

Ecclesiastical Review,[121] seems to favor the opinion requiring the *cautiones* for children already born of the parties, yet concludes: "At the present time it seems an open question. A pronouncement from the Holy See would be welcome, but since there has been no definite decision, a pastor would seem to be free to exact promises only with regard to future children, always presupposing that in the individual case there is moral certitude that the promises will be fulfilled."[122] O'Neill,[123] likewise, is of the opinion that the *cautiones* should be exacted both for children already born of these parties as well as for those to be born in the future, though he does not state it with finality. "We should say that the circumstances of each individual case would require to be examined in order to determine whether the danger of perversion were still serious."[124]

349. The well known instruction of 1858 uses the term "*universa proles*" in a sense that seems to designate only those children that are to be born of the marriage: "*ut universa utriusque sexus proles, ex mixtis hisce matrimoniis procreanda, in sanctitate catholicae religionis educari omnino deberet.*"[125] On the

---

progenitam in haeresi obstinate educare vult, saepe inducitur vehemens timor, ne ipsa in novo matrimonio non sit adimpleturus condiciones praescriptas. Quapropter tunc dispensatio valde caute petenda et executioni mandanda est." —*Theol. Mor.*, III, n. 781.

[121] LXXIV (1926), 630-632.

[122] *Ibid.* The reason given by the writer for including such children in the *cautiones* is that, if the non-Catholic party were insistent upon the heretical education of these children, the requirement of canon 1061, § 1, n. 3, could with difficulty be verified.

[123] *IER*, XXIII (1924), 417.

[124] *Ibid.*

[125] Instr. Secret. Stat. iussu Pii PP. IX, 15 Nov. 1858,—*Coll.*, n. 1169. Pope Gregory XVI also uses the expression "*de prole universa*" but gives no further qualification to its meaning. Cf. ep. encycl. *Summo iugiter*, 27 Maii 1832, § 2,—*Fontes*, n. 484. In other instances, however, where the same Pontiff speaks of the *cautiones* for the children, he seems to refer to children to be born in the future. Cf. allocut. *Officii memores*, 5 Iul. 1839, —*Fontes*, n. 492; litt ap. *Quas vestro*, 30 Apr. 1841, n. 2,—*Fontes*, n. 497. Vide etiam Pius VI, rescript. ad Card. Archiep. Mechlinien., 13 Iul. 1782, n. 4,—*Fontes*, n. 471; Pius VIII, litt. ap. *Litteris altero*, 25 Mart. 1830,—*Fontes*, n. 482. The term "*universa proles*" is found also in the following sources but without qualification: S. C. S. Off. (ad Ep. Osnabrugen.), 17 Feb. 1864,—*Fontes*, n. 976; instr. (ad Archiep. Corcyren.), 3 Ian. 1871, n. 3,—*Fontes*, n. 1013; litt. (ad Card. Simor), 21 Iul. 1880, —*NRT*, XIX (1887), 7-8. In the letter of Cardinal Rampolla of September 26, 1890, to Cardinal Simor (*NRT*, XXIII [1891], 388-391) the term is modified by such expressions as: "*ex hisce coniugiis procreanda*" or "*ex iis nascitura*", yet from another passage of the same letter (see No. 351, note 133) it appears that the children already born are to be included.

other hand, a decision of the Holy Office of October 9, 1877, seems to interpret the term as referring also to those children already born, and even of a former marriage.[126] Again, while the answer of the Holy Office in the decision of March 18, 1891,[127] (*"Cautiones etiam in articulo mortis esse exigendas"*) does not necessarily give a clear decision upon the question as to the inclusion of children already born to the parties in an invalid union, the opinion favoring their inclusion does no violence either to the wording or context of the decision,—in fact it appears to be more in conformity with it. The Code in canon 1061, § 1, n. 2,[128] does not qualify the phrase. The question regarding the inclusion of children other than those to be born in the future of the proposed mixed or disparate marriages is open, however, to a score of hypotheses, and there is necessarily a distinct hesitation in committing oneself to definite opinions. They are ventured only upon a meager source of evidence available for interpretation.

350. From the earliest times, however, the Church has shown her solicitude regarding the Catholic Baptism and education of children already born of mixed and disparate marriages.[129] It may be well also to direct attention to the fact that what in the law before the Code was generally demanded as an *obligation* on the part of the Catholic with regard to the Catholic education of the children is now, for the most part, demanded as a formal *cautio* in canon 1061, § 1, n. 2.[130] In modern legislation there are apparently only two recognized excep-

---

[126] "Cum ex supplici libello constet Oratricem viduam superstitem ex priori connubio habere prolem, pro qua sub dominio viri heterodoxi magnum imminet perversionis periculum, mens est eiusdem Sanctitatis Suae urgere pastoralem sollicitudinem tuam, ut adhibita parochi opera, mulierem moneas ut sedulo invigilet super catholica educatione *prolis universae tam natae* quae ad matrem pertinet, quam in posterum nasciturae."—*NRT*, XV (1883), 578. Though the decision does not apparently deal with a dispensation and seems to suppose the second marriage to be valid, the interpretation of the term *"proles universa"* is one that should be noted. Vide etiam S. C. S. Off., 2 Mart. 1842,—Gasparri, *De Matr.*, n. 523 (quoted infra in No. 351, note 133).

[127] See infra No. 345.

[128] See also canon 1065, § 2.

[129] Cf. Conc. Chalcedonense (451), canon 14,—Mansi, VII, 388; Conc. Toletanum IV (633), canon 63,—Mansi, X, 634.

[130] See No. 342.

tions to the strict demand of formal *cautiones* for children already born to the parties as joint parents. One concerns the case of a valid mixed marriage already contracted without the *cautiones*; the other, the prescriptions governing the exercise of the faculty to grant a *sanatio in radice* where the non-Catholic party in an invalid mixed or disparate marriage refuses to give the *cautiones*,—prescriptions which seem to imply more of an *obligation* to be imposed on the Catholic party disposed to assume it, than the absolute necessity of giving a formal *cautio*. The first exception does not deal with a dispensation from the impediment; the second deals with an extraordinary dispensation. Again, the decision of March 20, 1899,[131] implies that the *cautiones* are of absolute necessity for the non-Catholic's children born of a former mixed (or disparate) marriage where the present non-Catholic party had not observed the *cautiones*. With this in mind, the following opinions are ventured *salvo meliori iudicio*.

351. Those children born of the non-Catholic party in a former mixed or disparate marriage,[132] where this party did not observe the *cautiones*, who are to be under the care of the parties in the proposed mixed or disparate marriage, are to be included in the phrase *"de universa prole"* of canon 1061, § 1, n. 2. If they were born of a strictly non-Catholic marriage (i. e., between two non-Catholics) they should normally be included in the *cautiones*, at least for the liceity of the dispensation. If both of the parties to a proposed mixed or disparate marriage are the joint parents of children already born to them outside of a valid marriage and these are to be under their care after the proposed mixed or disparate marriage, they must, it seems, give the *cautiones* for these children also, and this for the validity of the dispensation.[133] It would, moreover, be very diffi-

---

[131] See No. 346.

[132] The opinion would scarcely need to be modified in the event that the present non-Catholic party had been the Catholic party in a former mixed or disparate marriage. If he had been a Catholic in a former Catholic marriage, the same ruling seems to apply.

[133] "Quoad matrimonia valida, ad sacramenta percipienda posse admitti sine praevia renovatione consensus; sed ab iisdem percipiendis arcendos donec vera dederint resipiscentia signa, et promiserint executuros totis viribus tam conversionem partis haereticae quam educationem in religione catholica *prolis universae natae et forsan nasciturae*, . . . Quoad matrimonia vero invalida,

cult in practice to arrive at the moral certainty of the fulfillment of the *cautiones* for the children to be born in the future if they are obstinately refused for those already born.

352. Those children already born, especially those who have not yet been baptized and educated as Catholics, who have the Catholic party for their parent and who are to be under the care of the parties proposing to contract a mixed or disparate marriage, should be included in the *cautiones*, and, perhaps, for the validity of the dispensation.[134] This opinion may, at first sight, seem to express a certain rigor, yet it seems to be in keeping with the mind of the Church, who could scarcely be considered as willing to grant a dispensation to a Catholic presump-

---

cum sit nullum eorum matrimonium vitio clandestinitatis, non esse admittendos ad receptionem sacramentorum, nisi prius promiserint post impetratam dispensationem super impedimento mixtae religionis se fideliter executuros eas omnes conditiones, quae exiguntur in praefata dispensatione . . ."—S. C. S. Off., 2 Mart. 1842,—Gasparri, *De Matr.*, n. 523. While this decision does not say explicitly that the conditions of the dispensation will demand that the *cautiones* regard also the children already born, there is no implication that the demands of the first part of the decree for a mixed marriage validly contracted will in any way be mitigated for one invalidly contracted. In a letter sent by Cardinal Rampolla to Cardinal Simor on September 26, 1890, there is this direction: "*Quare cum agnitum esset in quadem regione necessitatem imponi, ut proles ex mixtis coniugiis* NATA *omnino educetur in religione schismatica, Sancta Sedes dispensationes denegavit.*"—*NRT*, XXIII (1891), 389. Cf. S. C. S. Off., 12 Mart. 1881,—*NRT*, XV (1883), 121-122. At present, the faculty to grant a *sanatio in radice* seems to offer the only exception to this rule of exacting formal *cautiones* for children *already born* or to be born.

[134] If the present Catholic party is a convert and formerly was the non-Catholic party to a mixed or disparate marriage, the same ruling appears to hold regarding the *cautio* for the children of this former marriage. The non-observance of the *cautiones* in the former marriage seems to require this by the decision of March 20, 1899, (see No. 346). The supposition is that up to the present they have not been brought up as Catholics. If the former marriage had been contracted without the *cautiones*, the *cautiones* should be exacted at least for the liceity, if not for the validity of the dispensation for the proposed marriage. What if the present Catholic party was formerly the non-Catholic party to a strictly non-Catholic marriage (i. e., between two non-Catholics)? Those baptized children who were infants at the time of the parent's conversion may, perhaps, be regarded as converts through the interpretative intention of their convert parent (see No. 182), but this is by no means certain. But what if these children who have reached the age of reason (and those who were at the age of reason at the time of the parent's conversion) have not been educated in the Catholic Faith (supposing their valid non-Catholic Baptism),—must they be included in the *cautiones* for the validity of a dispensation? Perhaps they should, though this is not certain. For the liceity of the dispensation, however, they should normally be included if they are to be under the care of the parties to the proposed mixed or disparate marriage.

tively under excommunication and a suspicion of heresy[135] for the very violation of the divine law regarding the Catholic education of the children, which the Church strives to her utmost to protect in the *cautiones*. Moreover, at least an implicit agreement forbidden under pain of excommunication in canon 2319, § 1, n. 2, would seem to be implied in the case under consideration. Normally, the *cautio* seems to be required (at least for the liceity of the dispensation) for those children of the Catholic party who have been baptized and educated in the Catholic Church. Ordinarily there is as much danger of their perversion from the non-Catholic foster parent as there is for the children to be born of the marriage, and it is the general presumption of danger that the Church considers. The Code, however, demands the *cautio* not only from the non-Catholic party, but from both parties. That such a *cautio* for the children already raised as Catholics is not clearly demanded for the validity of the dispensation may, perhaps, be deduced by analogy from the decision of the Congregation of the Propaganda of March 20, 1899.[136]

C. *"Catholice tantum baptizanda et educanda"*

353. The *cautiones* as to the exclusively Catholic Baptism and education of the children precludes any double program of Baptism or religious education. Any double ceremony of Baptism is forbidden whereby, for example, the children would first be baptized in the Catholic Church and then also presented for a non-Catholic Baptism. Nor may the children be educated successively in both the Catholic Faith and in non-Catholic belief. Any limitation as to the age up to which the children are to be educated as Catholics, in the sense that thereafter they will receive a non-Catholic religious education, is likewise prohibited. True, there appear to be instances in which the Holy See seemed to tolerate a limitation of age within which the children were to be under the exclusive training of the Catholic parent, as it was exemplified in the Spanish and French treaties of marriage with James and Charles of England.[137] Yet it is certainly doubt-

---

[135] Cf. canon 2319, § 1, n. 4; § 2.

[136] See No. 346.

[137] See No. 90, note 27; No. 92. Cappello (*De Sacram.*, III, n. 315)

ful whether the Church, in any particular cases of mixed or disparate marriages among the common people, could in any sense be considered tolerant of any limitation of age as to their exclusively Catholic education.[138] While the age of fourteen for children of both sexes may, perhaps, be accepted as an age when children are presumed to possess a sufficient responsibility of their own to incur censures,[139] yet the parents would be forbidden to become the agent of their receiving a non-Catholic education.[140] They may not be able to exercise a compelling force to have their children enjoying the use of reason baptized in the Catholic Church,[141] or to have them educated in the Catholic Faith after they have reached the age of twenty-one,[142] but they are positively forbidden to become the agents of their non-Catholic religious education.

354. The obligations in the *cautiones* assumed by the parties to a mixed or disparate marriage imply that they will have the children baptized as soon as possible in the Catholic Church;[143] that they will have their children approach the sacraments of Penance and the Eucharist when they have reached the required age;[144] that they will cooperate with the pastor in having the children confirmed;[145] that they will have their children instructed in the Catholic Faith.[146] Normally, this latter ob-

---

says that many authors (he does not refer to any) seriously doubt whether the Holy See really admitted a condition of this kind, since the Catholic education of the children up to the age of thirteen does not seem to remove sufficiently the danger of perversion.

[138] Cf. Gasparri, *De Matr.*, n. 498.

[139] See No. 176, note 65.

[140] The civil law of a certain region spurned any arrangement made for a mixed marriage regarding the religious status of the children and demanded that the children be educated in the father's religion. No option was given to the children below the age of 14 years. Mixed marriages, in which the father was the non-Catholic, gave rise, therefore, to distressing situations and accordingly the following *dubium* was proposed (cf. Feije, *De Imped. et Dispens.*, p. 446, not. 3): "Quidnam Episcopis et parochis faciendum, si forte pars catholica ante annum 14 aetatis liberorum moriatur, et proinde promissis suis stare non potuit? R. Episcopis et parochis huiusmodi filios remanere commendatos, qui satagere debent pro viribus, ut catholica doctrina imbuantur."—S. C. S. Off., 30 Iun. 1842, ad 3,—*Fontes*, n. 890.

[141] Cf. canon 752, § 1.

[142] Cf. canon 89.

[143] Canon 770.

[144] Canons 860; 906.

[145] Canon 787.

[146] Cf. canons 1113; 1335; 1372.

ligation will imply their education in a Catholic school, and only where attendance at a Catholic school is impossible through circumstances, can any other means of their education be tolerated.[147]

§ III. *"Moralis habeatur certitudo de cautionum implemento"*

355. The giving of the *cautiones* is not sufficient for the validity of a dispensation, for in addition is required a moral certainty of their fulfillment,—a requirement quite as necessary for the validity of a dispensation from the impediments of Mixed Religion and Disparity of Cult as the very giving of the *cautiones* and the existence of just and grave causes.[148] Though the canon does not specify who is to have the moral certainty of the fulfillment of the *cautiones*, it is readily gathered from the wording of the faculties given to the Bishops of the United States,[149] and from the sources existing in the law before the Code, that it pertains to the Bishop, or, as it is worded in one instance: *"Ut superior ecclesiasticus moralem certitudinem habeat sive de cautionum sinceritate pro praesenti, sive de eorumdem adimplemento pro futuro."*[150]

---

[147] Cf. canons 1373-1374.

[148] This same requirement in the Law before the Code is particularly manifested in a decision of the Holy Office of April 12, 1899, (*Fontes*, n. 1219). The question apparently assumed that the Leonine faculty of 1888 extended to both the impediments of Disparity of Cult and Mixed Religion and therefore proposed a *dubium* regarding the *cautiones in articulo mortis*. The reply stated that the impediment of Disparity of Cult was, indeed, provided for in the faculty of 1888 and then continues: *"Quoad dispensationem super impedimento mixtae religionis, pro casibus in quibus omnes dentur cautiones,* ET EPISCOPUS MORALITER CERTUS SIT EASDEM IMPLETUM IRI, *supplicandum SSmo pro facultate dispensandi ad triennium. Pro casibus vero, in quibus vel praehabito actu mere civili, vel contractu coram ministro haeretico, vel utroque simul, non omnes praestentur cautiones,* VEL EPISCOPUM MORALITER CERTUS NON SIT EASDEM IMPLETUM IRI, *supplicandum pariter SSmo pro facultate sanandi in radice matrimonia itidem ad triennium . . ."* The implication of the reply is that the same moral certainty of the fulfillment of the *cautiones* would be required for a dispensation from the impediment of Disparity of Cult to be granted by virtue of the Leonine faculty of 1888. Vide etiam S. C. S. Off. (Helvetiae), 21 Ian. 1863, n. 4,—*Fontes*, n. 973; litt. (S. Germani), 17 Feb. 1875,—*Fontes*, n. 1039; (ad Ep. Aurelianen.), 6 Iun. 1879,—*Fontes*, n. 1064; litt. (ad Card. Simor), 21 Iul. 1880,—*NRT*, XIX (1887), 7; 10 Dec. 1902,—*Fontes*, n. 1262; S. C. de Prop. F., litt. (ad Ep. Ottawien.), 17 Apr. 1879,—*Coll.*, n. 1517; Litt. Secret. Stat. (ad Archiep. Strigonien.), 7 Iul. 1890,—*NRT*, XXIII (1891), 387-388.

[149] See No. 249.

[150] S. C. S. Off., litt. (ad Card. Simor), 21 Iul. 1880,—*NRT*, XIX (1887), 7. See the references to the decrees in note 148.

356. What is really the implication of canon 1061, § 1, n. 3, when it demands: "*Moralis habeatur certitudo de cautionum implemento*"? Several authors require the good faith of the parties giving the *cautiones*, so that if they were given fraudently, i. e., with the intention to deceive, and this deception could be proved to have existed at the time the dispensation was granted, the dispensation would have to be regarded as invalid.[151] The argument for this position may be summarized as follows. Only those promises can be regarded as real promises which are given sincerely and in good faith. A distinction must be made between the good faith of the parties giving the *cautiones*, and the moral certitude on the part of the ecclesiastical superior demanding the promises. The objective truth of the sincerity of the promises is of prime importance. Bad faith would vitiate the promises even if the Bishop had moral certitude. If the Church demanded no more than the mere fact of the promises she would be putting a premium on dishonesty. It would be tantamount to encouraging fraud in order to procure a dispensation. The Church would not jeopardize the spiritual welfare of her children by sanctioning and legalizing bad faith in the *cautiones*.

357. De Smet, on the other hand, goes to quite the opposite extreme when he writes: "*Nimirum coniuges debent, pro parte ipsos spectante, promittere cautelarum iniunctarum observationem, et quidem serio et fidenter. Pro valore tamen dispensationis sufficit quod cautiones exigantur ac praestentur, licet datae fuerint ficte.*"[152] O'Donnell is of the opinion that the matter of insincerity would affect the validity of a dispensation only in so far as its presence or absence would be manifested to the Ordinary upon which he [the Ordinary] could judge of the moral certainty of their fulfillment. His argument turns particularly upon the requisite character of the *cautiones*, namely, that they be "*verae*" and "*opportunae*". The term "*verae*" he understands as referring to *cautiones* that are not based on vague, casual, or ambiguous statements, nor on the supposed character

---

[151] Woywod, *A Practical Commentary*, I, n. 1056; Harrington, "The Importance of the Cautiones in Disparity of Worship", *AER*, LXV (1921), 261-262; Petrovits, *New Church Law on Matrimony*, n. 257.

[152] *De Spons. et Matr.*, n. 505. Vide etiam *op. cit.*, nn. 590, 874, et p. 731, not. 3. In this last reference, De Smet refers to S. Romana Rota, 26 Nov. 1921,—*AAS*, XIV (1922), 515 s. in confirmation of his opinion.

of the parties, nor in fact on anything that gives rise to conjecture rather than moral certainty. For the term *"opportunae"* he turns to the definition given in the decision of the Holy Office of July 30, 1842 (ad 5).[153]

358. De Smet's opinion, that for the validity of a dispensation it suffices that the *cautiones* are demanded and given, scarcely seems to take sufficient cognizance of the distinction which the Code clearly makes between the giving of the *cautiones* and the moral certainty of their fulfillment. O'Donnell's opinion is more acceptable though it seems to give too great a proportion of emphasis on the formalities of the *cautiones* to the neglect of other elements. At the same time, the authors who urge that an absence of good faith in the parties giving the *cautiones* renders the dispensation invalid, seem to demand an element for validity not required by the Church. Canon 1061, § 1, n. 2, simply requires that the *cautiones* be given; there is no suggestion that an objective good faith must exist for the validity of the dispensation. The solution of the question seems, therefore, to turn largely upon the interpretation given to canon 1061, § 1, n. 3, and, perhaps, also upon the significance of canon 1061, § 2.

359. True, the Ordinary must have moral certainty *"sive de cautionum sinceritate pro praesenti, sive de eorumdem adimplemento pro futuro"*,[154] yet the very means the Ordinary must employ to determine this, imply that the validity of a dispensation depends rather on the judgment of the Ordinary upon the facts revealed to him, than upon a correspondence of these manifestations with the objective truth of an intention actually existing. Underlying the Ordinary's judgment that a moral certainty exists as to the sincerity of the *cautiones* for the present, or as to their fulfillment in the future, is, indeed, a supposition that *hic et nunc* the parties are actually acting in good faith and

---

[153] *Fontes*, n. 890. O'Donnell's article appeared in *IER*, XVIII (1921), 411-418.

[154] Canon 1061, § 1, n. 3 does not explicitly contain the requirement of a moral certainty as to the sincerity at the time they are given, yet, since the law in this regard appears to be the same as it was in the law before the Code, there seems to be no significance in the silence of the canon. By virtue of canon 6, nn. 2, 4, this requirement is to be regarded as still remaining in force.

that the *cautiones* will really be fulfilled, but it is not a supposition that must be verified also in the internal or occult forum, or in the contingencies of the future for the validity of a dispensation.

360. In determining the presence or absence of this moral certainty, the Ordinary depends, in most cases, upon the judgment of the pastor presenting the petition or upon the facts submitted therein for his own judgment. In this connection the authors,[155] supported by decisions of the Holy See,[156] agree that many elements must be considered, of which a fair indication is given in the following passage from Vlaming:

Ad huiusmodi certitudinem moralem tum sibi, tum praesertim superiori dispensaturo comparandam, parochus debet cuiuslibet casus concreti adiuncta ponderare et videre, cuiusnam indolis sit uterque promittens (e. g. utrum pars acatholica eiusmodi sit, ut merito sperari possit, fore ut promissa teneat; utrum pars catholica sit satis constans et sufficienter de officiis suae religionis instructa) et cuiusnam conditionis (e. g. utrum pars acatholica libere possit de se suisque prolibus disponere, an vero dependeat ab aliis, et a quibusnam; nam saepe evenit, ut serio promittens a sua familia protestanti zelosa, quominus promissa adimpleat, persuadeatur; utrum forte alterutra pars semel mixto matrimonio iuncta fuerit, et quomodo in tali matrimonio susceptae prolis educatio processerit, etc.). Quodsi parocho omnibus ponderatis, serium aliquod dubium maneat sive "de cautionum sinceritate pro praesenti, sive de earum implemento pro futuro", non omittat tum dubium ipsum, tum rationes dubitandi in dispensationis petitione exponere.[157]

The entire process points rather to the issue of the Ordinary's judgment upon the facts revealed to him or to the pastor, than

---

[155] Konings-Putzer, *Comment. in Facult.*, p. 385-386; Cerato, *Matr.*, n. 55; Chelodi, *Ius Matr.*, n. 60; Blat, *Comment.*, Vol. III, P. I, n. 456; Vermeersch-Creusen, *Epitome*, II, n. 331; Vlaming, *Prael. Iuris Matr.*, n. 219.

[156] Cf. S. C. S. Off., litt. (S. Germani), 17 Feb. 1875,—*Fontes*, n. 1039; 10 Dec. 1902,—*Fontes*, n. 1262.

[157] *Loc. cit.* In this connection it will be well for pastors to keep in mind the warning of the Second Plenary Council of Baltimore (n. 335): "Moneantur tamen animarum pastores, ut in hisce promissionibus exigendis fortiter quidem in re, in modo tamen suaviter se gerant, ne 'aemulationem quidem Dei habentes, sed non secundum scientiam', utrumque sponsum exasperant, indeque mala oriantur graviora; quod eo magis praecavendum, cum constet raro hisce in regionibus ab Episcopo vel sacerdote pro ineundis eiusmodi nuptiis dispensationem peti, donec res iam eo usque processerit, ut Matrimonium per Ecclesiae monita abrumpi posse vix sit sperandum."

upon the objective correspondence of the intentionn of one or both parties. The fundamental question concerning the validity of the dispensation is not whether fictitious promises are real promises or not, but whether the character of the parties, the circumstances of the case, and the very character of the promises given,[158] justifies the judgment as to the sincerity and fulfillment of the *cautiones*.

361. This opinion receives ample confirmation from an examination of the history of the *cautiones*, especially with regard to their attendant formalities. Attention has already been directed to the fact that the *cautiones*, as they are known today, in all probability trace their origin to a *Stylus Curiae* that for at least a century and a half dealt almost exclusively with the formalities of religious-political treaties accompanying the mixed marriages of the Catholic nobility.[159] As far as the Church was concerned, such formalities served but one purpose, namely, to give the Church a sufficient assurance that the stipulations and guarantees were definite and sincere, and that they would be fulfilled. The well known treaties involved in what is known in English History as the Spanish and French match, by which Charles was engaged to marry a Catholic princess, exemplifies well this purpose. The writing of the guarantees, the oaths and witnesses demanded with the signatures, served as a sufficient evidence for the Church to judge of the definiteness and sincerity of the *cautiones*,—especially when the oath of a king and a prince was given. The promise exacted of Louis XIII that he bind himself and his successors to employ the power of France to see to it that the stipulations and guarantees were fulfilled, had the effect of giving the Church moral certainty of their fulfillment. There is no suggestion in the entire history of the procedure[160] that if the promises of James and Charles were given in bad faith, as in all probability they were, or that if the surety pledged by Louis XIII was insincere, that the dispensation would be invalid. The Church looked to the content of the stip-

---

[158] The character of the promises themselves is usually provided for by printed forms of the "*cautiones*" issued by diocesan Chanceries.

[159] See Nos. 95, 101.

[160] The same may be said of the many other instances of mixed marriages among the Catholic nobility. See No. 95, note 30.

ulations and to the manifestations of sincerity and surety rather than to the occult intentions that may have prompted them. The formalities served as a guide upon which the Church could judge of the justification of a dispensation, rather than as a condition which implied that the objective intention of the parties had to correspond in every detail for the objective validity of the dispensation.

362. Now while some of the formalities of state treaties necessarily disappeared in the application of the *Stylus Curiae* to the mixed marriages of the common people, many were retained, especially in the beginning. Their very retention marks their origin and also their identity of purpose, and indicates that the Church still employs them for the very reason that she is bent rather upon a judgment acquired through external manifestations than upon an absolute verification of the correspondence of these manifestations with the truth of a real intention. The Church continued to demand a "*cautio opportuna*" which she herself defined as: "*Talem promissionem, quae in pactum deducta praebeat morale fundamentum de veritate executionis, ita ut prudenter eiusmodi executio expectari possit.*"[161] With reference to the formality of an oath, the Holy Office decided on February 17, 1875, that it could be omitted since it was only an ecclesiastical requirement, provided *circumstances* permitted the omission.

Chè per farsi luogo alla dispensa nei matrimonii misti, è essenziale solamente la promessa delle solite cauzioni, la quale dev'essere così seria, che il Vescovo riesca a formarsi la certezza morale che sarà dal coniuge eterodosso osservata ed adempiuta fedelmente; e dove egli o per le qualità del soggetto, o per altre circostanze non potesse acquistare simile certezza, può a buon diritto domandare che la promessa sia munita di giuramento.[162]

The very point of emphasis is not upon the objective intention but upon the means to be employed by the Bishop to attain moral certainty of their fulfillment.[163] This same emphasis is

---

[161] S. C. S. Off., 30 Iun. 1842, ad 5,—*Fontes*, n. 890.

[162] S. C. S. Off., litt. (S. Germani), 17 Feb. 1875,—*Fontes*, n. 1039.

[163] The decision of April 17, 1879 (*Coll.*, n. 1517) directing that Bishops on no pretext grant a dispensation if they were not convinced that the

again manifested in an answer to an inquiry whether the assertion of the Catholic party under oath could be accepted to the effect that the non-Catholic party had given the *cautiones.*

> Per se et generatim negative, et ad mentem. Mens est: Quod in aliquo casu extraordinario talia concurrant adiuncta, ut Episcopus valeat sibi comparare moralem certitudinem tam de huiusmodi cautionum sinceritate pro praesenti, quam de earum adimplemento pro futuro, specialesque omnino adsint rationes impedientes ne consueto modo cautiones praestantur, ipsius conscientiae et prudentiae. Caeteroquin non obstante decreto regio, opportunae exhibentur in scriptis cautiones, sicut hucusque factum est, neque detur dispensatio nisi Episcopus moraliter certus sit eas impletum iri.[104]

363. The very prescription of canon 1061, § 2, that the *cautiones* be normally given in writing, serves a much larger purpose than suggested by Petrovits when he states that their written form impresses more deeply on the contracting parties the importance of the obligations embraced, and serves as a proof in the external forum of their voluntary assumption.[105] True, this purpose is served, but the whole history of the *cautiones* shows that the formalities of oaths, witnesses, or writing, is to serve more immediately as evidence upon which the Ordinary can form his ultimate judgment.[106] It is not the only evidence to be considered, however, since all the circumstances which manifest themselves must be taken into account. But the decisions and instructions of the Holy See, and the history of

---

written *cautiones* were sincerely given elicits the following remarks from O'Donnell: ". . . the implication is strong that if they were convinced [of their sincerity] even though the document was fraudulent, they were empowered to grant a real dispensation, and in the ordinary course would grant it as a matter of fact."—*IER,* XVIII (1921), 414.

[104] S. C. S. Off., 10 Dec. 1902, ad 2,—*Fontes,* n. 1262. The *votum* in the *causa Parisiensis* (S. Romana Rota, 11 Aug. 1921,—*AAS,* XIV [1922], 516) offers further confirmation. Though the question deals primarily with the *cautiones* as a condition of matrimonial consent, the absolute character of the following sentence is to be noted. "*Quare, etiamsi pars acatholica* FICTE *promittat, peccat utique, sed quia consensus alterius partis his promissionibus non subiicitur tamquam conditioni sine qua non,* MATRIMONIUM VALIDUM NIHILOMINUS CENSENDUM ERIT."

[105] *New Church Law on Matrimony,* nn. 192, 247.

[106] Cf. Sabetti-Barrett, *Theol. Mor.,* n. 872; Cappello, *De Sacram.,* III, n. 310; Vlaming, *Prael. Iuris Matr.,* n. 220; Blat, *Comment.,* Vol. III, P. I, n. 456.

the *cautiones* do seem to show that the validity of a dispensation depends rather upon the evidence which governed the judgment of the Ordinary than upon the objective good faith of the parties. Even if it were proved later on that, *de facto*, the promises were given fictitiously, it appears that the validity of the dispensation must depend rather upon the validity of the Ordinary's judgment of the evidence presented to him. If the evidence manifestly did not warrant a moral certainty of the sincerity of the promises and their fulfillment, the dispensation will probably have to be regarded as invalid.[107] Certainly no dispensation should be declared null on the ground that one or both parties were in bad faith without referring the case to the Holy Office.

364. The opinion that a dispensation is not vitiated by the bad faith of the parties in giving the *cautiones*, as long as it was not manifested to the Ordinary, does not put a premium on vice any more than a recognition of the gravity of causes for dispensation which have their ultimate source in a grave sin of the parties. It does not sanction fraud any more than canon 1054, which upholds the validity of a dispensation from a minor impediment even though the causes alleged for dispensation were fraudulent. If the prescriptions of the Church with regard to the determination of the sincerity of the promises and their fulfillment are carefully observed, the number of dispensations granted on the bad faith of the parties will be reduced to a minimum. The exceptions are accidents that will not injure the law, nor render it ineffective.

§ IV. *"Cautiones regulariter in scriptis exigantur"*

365. This prescription of canon 1061, § 2, that the *cautiones* be normally given in writing does not make the demand absolute for the very reason that in extraordinary circumstances (e. g. in danger of death) the Bishop may employ a less formal method of exacting the *cautiones*. The very word *"regulariter"*

---

[107] Too much stress must not be laid upon the fact that the parties manifested their fictitious intention to others. The oath taken by James and Charles before Parliament (see No. 93) was certainly a manifestation of bad faith, yet the validity of the dispensation given by Pope Urban VIII has never been challenged.

implies that the written form is not necessary for the validity of the dispensation. Even in the law before the Code it was the accepted opinion of the authors that the written form was not necessary for validity.[168] The written *cautiones* are to accompany the petition for dispensation and are to be kept on file in the Episcopal Curia.[169]

ART. VII. ADDITIONAL OBLIGATION OF THE CATHOLIC PARTY

366. The Catholic's obligation to strive prudently for the conversion of the non-Catholic party[170] is a divine and natural obligation of charity. Its prudent fulfillment in no way implies inopportune invitations and persuasions,—much less the promotion of arguments and altercations over religious questions. The fulfillment of the obligation will be rather through prayer, good example, and a *prudent* direction of conversation at opportune times.[171] The promise of the observance of this obligation is no longer required as a *conditio sine qua non* of dispensation.[172]

ART. VIII. OBLIGATION OF ORDINARIES AND PASTORS

CANON 1064, N. 3

Ordinarii aliique animarum pastores:
Mixtis nuptiis celebratis sive in proprio sive in alieno territorio, sedulo invigilent ut coniuges promissiones factas fideliter impleant.

367. This obligation upon Ordinaries and pastors is not new with the Code, but existed likewise in the law before the

---

[168] Cf. Gasparri, *De Matr.*, n. 499; Wernz, *Ius Decret.*, IV, n. 510, not. 41; n. 587, not 42.

[169] Cf. Cappello, *De Sacram.*, III, n. 310; Cerato, *Matr.*, n. 55, b.

[170] "Coniux catholicus obligatione tenetur conversionem coniugis acatholici prudenter curandi."—Canon 1062. See infra No. 342, notes 109-110.

[171] Cf. Cerato, *Matr.*, n. 56; Vlaming, *Prael. Iuris Matr.*, n. 224; De Smet, *De Spons. et Matr.*, n. 507.

[172] See No. 342. Even in the period immediately preceding the Code exceptions to the demand of this obligation in the form of a formal *cautio* became more frequent. Cf. De Smet, *op. cit.*, p. 444, not. 2; Vermeersch-Creusen, *Epitome*, II, n. 332.

Code.[173] It is an obligation upon the Ordinary and the pastor over those actually residing within their territory, regardless of whether these marriages were contracted there or not. Such mixed and disparate marriages will be discovered especially through a careful census of the parish, and thereupon the pastor must use every effort at his command to see to it that the promises which were given are fulfilled.[174] The exercise of a prudent zeal will in many cases promote their fulfillment. The neglect of this grave obligation may often explain the defections from the Faith through mixed and disparate marriages.

ART. IX. PROVISION FOR MARRIAGES FORBIDDEN IN CANON 1065

368. Canon 1065, § 2, demands that the Ordinary give his permission for the pastor's assistance at marriages of Catholics with those who have left the Faith or who have joined condemned societies only upon the following condition: ". . . *dummodo urgeat gravis causa et pro suo prudenti arbitrio Ordinarius iudicet satis cautum esse catholicae educationi universae prolis et remotioni periculi perversionis alterius coniugis."* The wording of the canon and the accepted opinion among the authors is to the effect that the formal *cautiones* demanded for mixed and disparate marriages are not strictly required for these cases. The nature of the provision is left rather to the good judgment of the Ordinary.[175] Whenever the particular law of a diocese or of a province demands formal *cautiones*, this provision must be observed, and there is nothing in the canon which forbids such a requirement. It is rather to be recommended that the *cautiones* should be given.

---

[173] Cf. Gregorius XVI, allocut. *Officii memores*, 5 Iul. 1839,—*Fontes*, n. 492; S. C. S. Off., 21 Ian. 1863, n. 2,—*Fontes*, n. 973; 9 Oct. 1877,—*NRT*, XV (1883), 578; instr. (ad omnes Ep. Ritus Orient.), 12 Dec. 1888, n. 12,—*Fontes*, n. 1112; S. C. de Prop. F., instr. (ad Archiep. Baltimoren.), 25 Iun. 1884,—*Coll.*, n. 1621.

[174] Linneborn (*Grundriss des Eherechts*, p. 169) demands that if the parties move to another diocese or parish, their future pastor is to be informed.

[175] The necessity of the formal *cautiones* seems to be demanded by Vermeersch-Creusen (*Epitome*, II, n. 335) but clearly this is not strictly required by the Code. Cf. Quigley, *Condemned Societies*, p. 105; Wernz-Vidal, *Ius Canonicum*, V., n. 201; Ayrinhac, *Marriage Legislation*, p. 132; Cappello, *De Sacram.*, III, n. 331; Blat, *Comment.*, Vol. III, P. I, n. 460.

CHAPTER XIV

THE CELEBRATION OF MIXED AND DISPARATE MARRIAGES

Canon 1063

§ 1. *Etsi ab Ecclesia obtenta sit dispensatio super impedimento mixtae religionis, coniuges nequeunt, vel ante vel post matrimonium coram Ecclesia initum, adire quoque, sive per se sive per procuratorem, ministrum acatholicum uti sacris addictum, ad matrimonialem consensum praestandum vel renovandum.*

§ 2. *Si parochus certe noverit sponsos hanc legem violaturos esse vel iam violasse, eorum matrimonio ne assistat, nisi ex gravissimis causis, remoto scandalo et consulto prius Ordinario.*

§ 3. *Non improbatur tamen quod, lege civili iubente, coniuges se sistant etiam coram ministro acatholico, officialis civilis tantum munere fungente, idque ad actum civilem dumtaxat explendum, effectum civilium gratia.*

ART. I. MARRIAGES ATTEMPTED BEFORE A NON-CATHOLIC MINISTER *"uti sacris addictus"*

369. Even though the parties to a mixed or disparate[1] marriage have received a dispensation to marry, they are strictly forbidden to give or to renew their matrimonial consent before a non-Catholic minister acting in his ministerial capacity (*"uti sacris addictus"*).[2] It is a sacrilege for a Catholic thus to participate in non-Catholic rites and ceremonies,[3] a *communicatio in sacris* forbidden by the divine law itself, since it involves at

---

[1] Cf. canon 1071.

[2] Cf. S. C. S. Off., 27 Aug. 1658,—*Fontes*, n. 731; (Hiberniae), 29 Nov. 1672,—*Fontes*, n. 751; (Saxoniae), 29 Ian. 1817,—*Fontes*, n. 852; 21 Apr. 1847,—Roskovány, *De Matr. Mixtis*, III, p. 331; litt. (ad Vic. Ap. Myssurien.), 26 Nov. 1862,—*Fontes*, n. 971.

[3] "Illicitum porro ac sacrilegum est se sistere coram haeretico seu schismatico ministro ante vel post contractas mixtas nuptias, quoties ipse ut minister

least an implicit profession of heresy or schism.[4] In as far as this prohibition is concerned, it matters little whether a dispensation either from the impediment of Mixed Religion or Disparity of Cult had been given or not; whether the parties give their consent first before a non-Catholic minister and then *coram Eccelsia Catholica*, or whether this process is reversed; whether they appear in person or by proxy.[5] The prohibition is concerned with the Catholic's appearance before a non-Catholic minister who acts in his ministerial capacity to witness the Catholic's matrimonial consent. The giving or renewal of matrimonial consent before a non-Catholic minister acting in this capacity is forbidden even though the Catholic party would declare in writing that he would conduct himself merely in a passive manner, in no way wishing to adhere to a non-Catholic rite.[6]

370. By a non-Catholic minister is designated one who is a minister of any religious sect,——it is immaterial whether this sect be Christian, pagan, Jewish, heretical, or schismatic.[7] He

----

sacris addictus adsistat, et quasi parochi munere fungens; nam pars catholica ritui haeretico aut schismatico se consociaret, ex quo vetita omnibus haberetur cum haereticis in eorum sacris communicatio. Quare ita contrahentes mortaliter peccarent, ac monendi sunt."——S. C. S. Off., instr. (ad omnes Ep. Ritus Orient.), 12 Dec. 1888, n. 7,——*Fontes*, n. 1112.

[4] "Lessius . . . id, salva conscientia, neque fieri, neque tolerari posse, contendit: eiusque opinio verissima esset, si haereticus ministellus adhiberetur tamquam persona sacra, quae sacram caeremoniam intenderet exercere, ac per eam, sanctitatem tribuere contractui matrimoniali; tunc siquidem viderentur Catholici eum agnoscere tanquam legitimum Christi Ministrum, ritumque haereticum approbare, et profiteri."——Benedictus XIV, *De Synodo Dioec.*, Lib. VI, cap. VII, n. 2. Cf. S. C. S. Off. (ad Ep. Osnabrugen.), 17 Feb. 1864,——*Fontes*, n. 976; Cappello, *De Sacram.*, III, n. 317; Vlaming, *Prael. Iuris Matr.*, n. 228; Wernz-Vidal, *Ius Canonicum*, V, n. 182; Ayrinhac, *Marriage Legislation*, p. 125.

[5] Cf. Benedictus XIV, ep. encycl. *Inter omnigenas*, 2 Feb. 1744, §§ 9-11, ——*Fontes*, n. 339; *De Synodo Dioec.*, Lib. VI, cap. VII, n. 2; S. C. de Prop. F., 12 Mart. 1897,——*ASS*, XXX (1897-1898), 158-159.

[6] "An permitti possit, ut ante vel post matrimonium pars catholica etiam coram ministello acatholico ad praestandum consensum matrimonialem se sistat, si pars catholica in scriptis declaraverit mere passive se gerere et nullo modo ritui protestantico adhaerere velle. R. Negative, et detur Instructio 17 Februarii 1864."——S. C. S. Off., 10 Dec. 1902, ad 3,——*Fontes*, n. 1262. The Code does not require a formal *cautio*, however, to safeguard this prohibition (cf. Ayrinhac, *Marriage Legislation*, p. 120; De Smet, *De Spons. et Matr.*, n. 507), though there is nothing to prevent the Ordinary from exacting it if he so wishes.

[7] "Comprehenduntur igitur etiam ministri ecclesiae sese dicentis catholicae independentis, quae in hac regione (Foederatis Statibus Americae) coepit propagari, quaeque inter suos ministros plures numerat sacerdotes, qui a catholica hierarchia sese subduxerunt."——Cipollini, *De Censuris*, Lib. II, n. 70.

acts in the capacity of a minister *"uti sacris addictus"* if he assists at the marriage by virtue of the fact that he is a minister of religion, not as a civil official deputed by the State to assist at marriages. If he is at the same time deputed by the civil authority to witness marriages he acts in his ministerial capacity if he uses any vestment of his office,[8] or employs any religious rites or ceremonies.[9] Presumably he act also in this capacity by the mere fact that he witnesses the marriage in a non-Catholic place of worship.

§ I. EXCOMMUNICATION

371. Catholics who violate this prohibition of giving or renewing their matrimonial consent before a non-Catholic minister *"uti sacris addictus"* incur *ipso facto* an excommunication reserved to the Ordinary.

CANON 2319

§ 1. *Subsunt excommunicationi latae sententiae Ordinario reservatae catholici:*

1° *Qui matrimonium ineunt coram ministro acatholico contra praescriptum can.* 1063, § 1.

This censure, following the general norms of all censures, implies the contumacy of the Catholic party.[10] In the censure under consideration, ignorance of the law or of the penalty will excuse only if it is not affected, crass, or supine.[11] Absolution from the censure is normally to be given *in foro externo*, especially where

---

[8] This refers rather to vestments that are worn at religious functions than to ministerial apparel worn on the street or about the house, such as a roman collar or the equivalent of a cassock or a habit.

[9] Cf. S. C. S. Off., 27 Aug. 1658,—*Fontes*, n. 731; (Saxoniae), 29 Ian. 1817,—*Fontes*, n. 852; 2 Apr. 1847,— Roskovány, *De Matr. Mixtis*, III, p. 331. Words of congratulation, or even an exhortation, can perhaps be exempted from the designation of a rite or a ceremony if the minister acts as a civil official. Cf. Augustine, *Commentary*, V, p. 151-152. Ayrinhac (*Marriage Legislation*, p. 126) also seems to favor this opinion, but he demands that such words of advice have no confessional character. If the exhortation or words of advice were, however, addressed to them in a non-Catholic place of worship, there would be a strong presumption that they would be given as a part of a religious ceremony. Cf. Gasparri, *De Matr.*, n. 518; Cappello, *De Sacram.*, III, nn. 317-318; Wernz-Vidal, *Ius Canonicum*, V, n. 182.

[10] Canon 2242, § 1.

[11] Canon 2229, § 1 et § 3, n. 1. Cf. Dargin, *Reserved Cases*, p. 48-51.

it has been notoriously incurred.[12] An absolution given in the internal sacramental forum by a priest who has the faculty to absolve will frequently suffice, especially if no grave scandal has been given,[13] but canon 2251 must be kept in mind.[14]

372. Some authors stress the point that a double ceremony (i. e., before a non-Catholic minister and *coram Ecclesia*) is necessary that the censure be incurred.[15]

It seems to be quite certain from the wording of these two Canons [2319, § 1, n. 1 and 1063, § 1] that it is the double ceremony which is punished with excommunication by the Code. The reason for the censure may be the implied denial of the Church's exclusive jurisdiction over marriage. However it is not important to inquire into the reason of the law, because that does not affect the law one way or the other . . .

If there is question of one religious ceremony only, that before a non-Catholic minister, does the Catholic party incur the excommunication by the law of the Code? No, the former excommunication incurred by marriage before a non-Catholic minister, as minister of his religion, was inflicted on account of the forbidden communication in the sacred rites of a non-Catholic religion, as an Instruction of the S. Congregation of the Propaganda in 1858 states (*Collectanea S. C. de Prop. Fide, N. 1154*), Later declarations of the Holy See held that marriage before a non-Catholic minister was punished under the Bull *Apostolicae Sedis* with excommunication for the reason of communication in the sacred rites or as implied adherence to the non-Catholic faith. The Code does not retain that censure from the Bull *Apostolicae Sedis*, but holds the one who communicates in the religious rites of non-Catholics as suspected of heresy (cf. Canons 2316 and 1258), and such a one is to be admonished, according to Canon 2315, and if he does not amend within six months, he is to be considered a heretic.[16]

---

[12] Cf. Petrovits, *New Church Law on Matrimony*, n. 198; Dargin, *Reserved Cases*, p. 61.

[13] Cf. De Smet, *De Spons. et Matr.*, n. 514; p. 450, not. 7; Vlaming, *Prael. Iuris Matr.*, n. 228; Prümmer, *Theol. Mor.*, III, n. 783; Hyland, *Excommunication*, p. 101-102.

[14] "Si absolutio censurae detur in foro externo, utrumque forum afficit; si in interno, absolutus, remoto scandalo, potest uti talem se habere etiam in actibus fori externi; sed, nisi concessio absolutionis probetur aut saltem legitime praesumatur in foro externo, censura potest a Superioribus fori externi, quibus reus parere debet, urgeri, donec absolutio in eodem foro habita fuerit."—Canon 2251.

[15] Linneborn, *Grundriss des Eherechts*, p. 171; Neuberger, *Canon 6*, p. 52; Woywod, in *HPR*, XXIV (1924), 510-511.

[16] Woywod. *loc. cit.*

According to these authors, therefore, when canon 2319, § 1, n. 1, rules that Catholics who enter marriage before a non-Catholic minister contrary to the prescription of canon 1063, § 1, incur, *latae sententiae*, an excommunication reserved to the Ordinary, the conditions for the incurring of the censure must be interpreted in the light of canon 1063, § 1. But since canon 1063, § 1, refers to a double ceremony, the censure of canon 2319, § 1, n. 1, is incurred only when a double ceremony has taken place, namely, before a non-Catholic minister and *coram Ecclesia*.

373. The fact can, indeed, scarcely be questioned that in the law before the Code (and particularly after the constitution "*Apostolicae Sedis*") Catholics incurred an excommunication by daring to appear for a marriage ceremony solely before a non-Catholic minister, and, moreover, that this censure was in no way conditioned by a necessity of a double ceremony. Yet it is important to note how often the prohibition of appearing before a non-Catholic minister or the mention of the incurred censure is coupled with a reference to a double ceremony. The frequent reference to a double ceremony in the prohibitions of the Old Law offers a striking parallel to the same reference in canon 1063, § 1,—in fact, the expressions are so identical that the slight differences that exist may be regarded as totally irrelevant.[17]

---

[17] "Quoad dubium autem:—Num sacramenta dari possint catholicae parti mente paratae ad ineundum coram ministro protestante *sive ante sive post catholicum matrimonium?* Attendum erit, an sponsi adeant ministrum protestantem ut legi tantum civili satisfaciant, an vero ut in sacris communicent etc."—S. C. S. Off., litt. (ad Vic. Ap. Myssurien.), 26 Nov. 1862,—*Fontes*, n. 971. A short time after, the Holy Office again gave an instruction regarding marriages before non-Catholic ministers. It begins by speaking of those cases that are not forbidden: "Tunc vero urgentibus haereticis, aut lege civili imperante, non improbatur quod pars catholica una cum haeretica se sistant, *ante vel post contractum ad formam Tridentini matrimonium,* etiam coram ministro haeresi addicto ad actum civilem dumtaxat implendum." Then without any departure from the reference to the double ceremony it enunciates the prohibition of appearing before a non-Catholic minister "*veluti sacris addictus*" and concludes: "Quod si tandem consensus coram parocho velit renovari, postquam praestitus iam fuerit coram ministro haeretico, idque publice notum sit, vel ab ipsis sponsis parocho notificetur: parochus huic matrimonio non intererit, nisi servatis, uti supponitur, ceteroquin servandis, pars catholica facti poenitens, praeviis salutaribus poenitentiis, *absolutionem a contractis censuris rite prius obtinuerit.*"—S. C. S. Off. (ad Ep. Osnabrugen.), 17 Feb. 1864,—*Fontes*, n. 976. Though there was reference to a double ceremony (the very condition that prompted the in-

374. True, the censure of the constitution "Apostolicae *Sedis*"[18] has undergone some modification in the Code. Instead of an attempted marriage before a non-Catholic minister *"uti sacris addictus"* entailing a censure by virtue of the implied inclusion of this *delictum* in the generality of acts forbidden by the constitution *"Apostolicae Sedis"*, it now entails a censure dealing *specifically* with such a sin, and instead of being reserved to the Roman Pontiff it is now reserved to the Ordinary. But as far as the conditions required for the incurring of the censure are concerned, there has been no change whatever. If, then, in the Old Law the reference to a *doubleness* of ceremony was not a condition of incurring the censure, there is no reason why an identical reference to a double ceremony in canon 1063, § 1, should be construed as a condition of incurring the censure of canon 2319, § 1, n. 1. That the *doubleness* of ceremony is not required as a condition for incurring the censure of canon 2319, § 1, n. 1, is clearly indicated by the direction in the faculty given to American Bishops for the granting of a *sanatio in radice*. The entire faculty supposes a clandestine marriage already attempted before a civil official or a non-Catholic minister[19] and that the consent of the parties has not been renewed *coram Ecclesia*. But with reference to the censure of canon 2319, § 1, n. 1, it directs: *"Ipse autem R. P. D. Ordinarius serio moneat partem catholicam de gravissimo patrato scelere, salutares ei poenitentias imponat, et* SI CASUS FERAT, EUM AB EXCOMMUNICATIONE AB-SOLVAT IUXTA COD. I. C. 2319, § 1, n. 1, *simulque declaret ob sanationis gratiam a se acceptatam etc."* The reference to the

---

struction) it is significant that the incurring of the censure and its absolution was in no way dependent upon the doubleness of ceremony, but rather upon the single ceremony before a non-Catholic minister *"veluti sacris addictus"*. In another instance the Holy Office said: "Illicitum porro ac sacrilegum est se sistere coram haeretico seu schismatico ministro *ante vel post contractas mixtas nuptias,* quoties ipse ut minister sacris addictus adsistat . . ." and the instruction concludes with the same reference to the necessity of absolution from the censure incurred by the *one* ceremony, as in the instruction of 1864.—S. C. S. Off., instr. (ad omnes Ep. Ritus Orient.), 12 Dec. 1888, nn. 7-8,—*Fontes,* n. 1112. Vide etiam S. C. S. Off., 27 Aug. 1658,—*Fontes,* n. 731; (Hiberniae), 29 Nov. 1672,—*Fontes,* n. 751; 21 Apr. 1847,—Roskovány, *De Matr. Mixtis,* III, p. 331; 10 Dec. 1902, ad 3,—*Fontes,* n. 1262.

[18] Pius IX, 12 Oct. 1869, § 1, n. 1,—*Fontes,* n. 552.

[19] See No. 263.

absolution from the excommunication *"si casus ferat"* can refer only to the censure already entailed through a single ceremony before a non-Catholic minister *"uti sacris addictus."* If a double ceremony were necessary to entail the censure, what need of a *sanatio in radice* is referred to in the faculty for a marriage already contracted *coram Ecclesia?* The faculty itself, and its legitimate use, supposes that the marriage has been contracted clandestinely and that an obstacle exists to a renewal of consent *coram Ecclesia.*

375. When canon 1063, § 3, permits (where the civil law requires it) an appearance before a non-Catholic minister acting in his civil capacity, it uses the clause *"officialis civilis tantum munere fungente"* by direct contrast to the phrase *"uti sacris addictum"* of canon 1063, § 1. There is, moreover, a direct suggestion in canon 1063, § 3, that whatever might be the requirements of the civil law, the appearance before a non-Catholic minister *"uti sacris addictus"* would be prohibited by the prescription of canon 1063, § 1. Throughout the entire canon there is a reference to a *doubleness* of ceremony,—the question of prohibition or permission does not, however, hinge upon the *doubleness* of ceremony but on a far more vital issue, namely, the presence or absence of a *"communicatio in sacris"* with heretics. The basic reason of the prohibition in canon 1063, § 1, is, as in the Old Law, the *"communicatio in sacris"* with non-Catholic ministers,[20] nor is the prohibition conditioned any more by a *doubleness* of ceremony than it was in the Old Law. The reference to a *doubleness* of ceremony is in all likelihood a direct repetition of the same reference in so many decisions and instructions in the law before the Code. It has been the sad experience of the Church that a double ceremony takes place only too frequently, especially in connection with mixed or disparate marriages. In fact, many of the *dubia* formerly proposed, supposed this practice, and the answers in referring to this practice delineated only the norms of liceity and illiceity. That is all that canon 1063 proposes to do, and its very position among the canons pertaining to mixed marriages suggests the historic

---

[20] See No. 369, notes 1-4 and also S. C. S. Off., 29 Aug. 1888,—*NRT*, XXII (1890), 137; 11 Maii 1892,—*Fontes*, n. 1154.

reason for the reference to a double ceremony. There is, however, not the slightest suggestion in canon 1063, § 1, that if only a non-Catholic ceremony took place, the *delictum* would not be forbidden *by this very canon*. It may be repeated, therefore, that the prescription of canon 1063, § 1 (to which canon 2319, § 1, n. 1, refers), is concerned primarily with the *"communicatio in sacris"* with non-Catholic ministers in appearing before them to give or to renew matrimonial consent. It is the violation of this prohibition, quite independent of any condition of a *doubleness* of ceremony, that entails the censure of canon 2319, § 1, n. 1.

376. Authors disagree also upon the question as to whether two Catholics contracting before a non-Catholic minister incur the censure of canon 2319, § 1, n. 1. Those authors who urge that two Catholics do not incur the censure point to the fact that canon 2319, § 1, n. 1, refers to a violation of the prescription of canon 1063, § 1, which seems to be concerned with mixed marriages. On the basis of the principle that penal laws must be interpreted strictly,[21] two Catholics giving or renewing their consent before a non-Catholic minister would not, therefore, incur the censure of canon 2319, § 1, n. 1.[22] Other authors take quite the opposite position and maintain the opinion that the censure of canon 2319, § 1, n. 1, refers to every marriage attempted before a non-Catholic minister.[23]

377. If the decisions given after the constitution *"Apostolicae Sedis"* may serve as a guide of interpretation, their examination will reveal no distinction between mixed marriages, and marriages between Catholics. On the contrary, they appear rather to imply that any marriage attempted by a Catholic before a non-Catholic minister rendered the Catholic subject to

---

[21] Cf. canons 19; 2219, §§ 1, 3.

[22] Chelodi, *Ius Poenale*, p. 76, not. 1; Cappello, *De Censuris*, n. 369; Leech, *The Constitution "Apostolicae Sedis" and the "Codex Juris Canonici"*, p. 93.

[23] Petrovits, *New Church Law on Matrimony*, n. 270; Leitner, *Lehrb. des kath. Eherechts*, p. 241; Cocchi, *Comment.*, Vol. 8, n. 147; Cipollini, *De Censuris*, Lib. II, n. 70; Augustine, *Commentary*, VIII, p. 297; Neuberger, *Canon 6*, p. 52-53.

the censure reserved to the Holy See.[24] The fact that canon 1063, § 1, includes the contingency of a dispensation from the impediment of Mixed Religion must not be overemphasized in an attempt to force a strict interpretation of canon 2319, § 1, n. 1. The reason for placing the prohibition of canon 1063, § 1, among the canons referring to mixed marriages,[25] and of the reference of the canon to the event of a dispensation for a mixed marriage, in all likelihood lies in the fact that the *communicatio in sacris* in question most frequently occurs in connection with such marriages, and hence the wisdom of inserting the prohibition in the place it commands. Attention has already been called to the fact that the primary purpose of canon 1063, § 1, is the prohibition of a *communicatio in sacris* with non-Catholic ministers,[26] and that the prohibition is, therefore, in no way limited to mixed marriages alone. It is the violation of this prohibition that incurs the censure of canon 2319, § 1, n. 1. "The prescriptions of canon 1063, § 1, do not exclude an attempted marriage between two Catholics. Canon 1063, § 1, merely determines the law which must be violated to incur the censure of canon 2319."[27] It seems, therefore, that two Catholics attempting a marriage before a non-Catholic minister *"uti sacris addictus"* incur the censure of canon 2319, § 1, n. 1,[28] and in addition are rendered suspects of heresy by virtue of canon 2316.

---

[24] "Utrum absolutio a censuris *omnibus catholicis, qui coram haeretico ministro nuptias contraxerunt necessaria sit,* an potius in eo tantum casu impertienda sit, quo in huiusmodi celebrationem ab Antistite censurae promulgati sint? *R.* Affirmative ad primam partem, negative ad secundam."—S. C. S. Off., 29 Aug. 1888, ad I,—*NRT*, XXII (1890), 137. Vide etiam S. C. S. Off., 11 Maii 1892,—*Fontes*, n. 1154. The decision of the Holy Office of April 25, 1770 (Gasparri, *De Matr.*, n. 520), to the effect that two Catholics contracting before a non-Catholic minister did not incur censures, dates too far back to serve as a norm of interpretation. It may be classified in this respect with the decision of April 4, 1871 (see No. 377, note 30), which was later rejected.

[25] See also canon 1071. Cappello (*De Censuris*, n. 369) urges that disparate marriages by virtue of canon 1071 are subject likewise to the censure of canon 2319, § 1, n. 1, yet he grants the probability of the opinion excluding disparate marriages from the censure. Cf. Woywod in *HPR*, XXIV (1924), 510-511. It is hard to see how disparate marriages can in any way be excluded and how such an opinion can enjoy any probability.

[26] See No. 375.

[27] Neuberger, *Canon 6*, p. 53.

[28] Augustine (*Commentary*, V, p. 151, note 40) is of the opinion that the censure is not incurred by the proxy even though he be a Catholic. This opinion, however, seems to be in conflict with canon 2230.

A. Canon 2319, § 1, n. 1, and the Third Plenary Council of Baltimore

378. In this connection must also be considered the legislation of the Third Plenary Council of Baltimore which prescribed:

Item decernimus Catholicos, qui coram ministro cuiuscumque sectae acatholicae matrimonium contraxerint vel attentaverint, extra propriam dioecesim, in quolibet statu vel territorio sub ditione praesulum qui huic concilio adsunt vel adesse debent, excommunicationem incurrere Episcopo reservatam, a qua tamen quilibet dictorum Ordinariorum sive per se, sive per sacerdotem ad hoc delegatum absolvere poterit. Quod si in propria dioecesi ita deliquerint, statuimus eos ipso facto innodatos esse excommunicatione, quae, nisi absque fraude legis alium Episcopum adeant, eorum Ordinario reservatur.[29]

There are two special points of interest involved in this prescription: 1) Did the prescription have any legitimate force at the time it was enacted? 2) In the event that it was a valid enactment, does it still retain its force after the Code?

379. The earlier decisions referring to censures incurred by Catholics who had given their matrimonial consent in mixed marriages before a non-Catholic minister, and requiring the necessity of absolution and the imposition of salutary penances,[30] retain their value only in so far as they were at least implicitly contained in the recast list of censures in the constitution *"Apostolicae Sedis"*. In this constitution an excommunication, incurred *latae sententiae* and reserved to the Roman Pontiff, was incurred by the following: *"Omnes a christiana fide apostatas, et omnes ac singulos haereticos, quocumque nomine censeantur, et cuiuscumque sectae existant, eisque credentes, eorumque recepto-*

---

[29] Conc. Plen. Balt. III (1884), n. 127.

[30] Cf. S. C. S. Off., 2 Mart. 1842,—Gasparri, *De Matr.*, n. 523; (Georgiae), 5 Aug. 1846, ad 3,—*Coll.*, n. 1009. In the light of these decisions it is somewhat surprising to find that a Council of Philadelphia held in 1842 reserved the censure for such a *delictum* to the Ordinary. Cf. Roskovány, *De Matr. Mixtis*, III, p. 303. On the other hand the Second Provincial Council of New Orleans held in 1860 (Decretum n. V) and the Second Diocesan Synod of Natchez held in 1869 (Decretum n. LXIV) decreed that Catholics, whether marrying Catholics or non-Catholics, incurred a censure reserved to the *Holy See* if they gave their consent before a non-Catholic minister.

res, fautores, ac generaliter quoslibet illorum defensores.''[31] A doubt apparently existed for a short time as to whether mixed marriages attempted before a non-Catholic minister were comprehended in this constitution for, soon after, the Holy Office declared that an absolution from censures was not necessary.[32] In subsequent decisions, however, the Holy Office departed from this position and demanded the necessity of absolution.[33] The further implication that the censure was reserved to the Holy See was given in a decision of the Holy Office of May 11, 1892, which referred to the power of Ordinaries to absolve by virtue of their *quinquennial faculties.*[34]

380. It was within this latter period, after the constitution *"Apostolicae Sedis"*, that the Baltimore decree was enacted, —apparently in violation of the law which reserved the censure to the Holy See, for also in the law before the Code, it was forbidden to reserve censures to Ordinaries which had already been reserved to the Holy See.[35] On the other hand, the decrees of the Third Plenary Council of Baltimore were recognized and approved by the Holy See,[36] and in view of this approbation it appears that the enactment was recognized in spite of the apparent contradiction.

---

[31] Pius IX, const. *Apostolicae Sedis*, 12 Oct. 1869, § 1, n. 1,—*Fontes*, n. 552.

[32] To the *dubium*: *"Se sia regolare la prassi tenuta sin qui nei rescritti di dispensa nei casi in cui siasi contratto il matrimonio avanti il magistrato civile o il ministro protestante, di assolvere le parti contraenti dalle censure incorse"*, the Holy Office replied on April 4, 1871,—*"Omittendam esse absolutionem a censuris."*—Wernz, *Ius Decret.*, IV, n. 588, not. 42.

[33] The decision of the Holy Office of March 17, 1874 (*Fontes*, n. 1029) demanded this in contrast to the decision of April 4, 1871. Vide etiam S. C. S. Off., 29 Aug. 1888,—*NRT*, XXII (1890), 137.

[34] "Quid faciendum sit de iis catholicis qui secundum veterem dioecesium nostrarum (in Borussia) usum, licet coram ministro acatholico matrimonium contraxerint, a confessariis sine speciali facultate absolvendi ad ss. sacramenta admissi sunt.

R. Qui matrimonium coram ministro haeretico ineunt, censuram contrahere; Ordinarios autem vi facultatum quinquennalium nedum posse eos absolvere, sed alios etiam subdelegare ad eosdem absolvendos. Qui vero huc usque, nulla praevia a censuris absolutione, ab huiusmodi culpa absoluti sunt, iuxta exposita non esse inquietandos,"—*Fontes*, n. 1154.

[35] Cf. S. C. S. Off., instr. 13 Iul. 1916, n. 4,—*Fontes*, n. 1302; S. C. Ep. et Reg., litt. 26 Nov. 1602,—*Fontes*, n. 1615. The law in the Code is expressed in canon 2247, § 1.

[36] "Itaque Emi. Patres Sacro Consilio Christiano Nomini Propagando praepositi in generalibus comitiis habitis diebus 17, 24, 27, et 31 mensis Augusti, nec non die 5 Septembris anni 1885, diligenti inquisitione adhibita,

381. If it is true that Catholics attempting any marriage before a non-Catholic minister *"uti sacris addictus"* incur, *latae sententiae*, an excommunication reserved to the Ordinary by virtue of canon 2319, § 1, n. 1, the Baltimore legislation may be regarded as supplanted by the common law of the Code. Catholics in the United States who attempt such marriages will not, therefore, incur two censures,—one by virtue of the Council of Baltimore, and one by virtue of canon 2319, § 1, n. 1,[37] but only one censure by virtue of the common law of the Code.[38] The prescription of the Council of Baltimore that if Catholics contracted such a marriage within their own diocese, the absolution would be reserved to their proper Ordinary, has been abrogated by the Code in canon 2247, § 2.[39]

§ II. Duties of the Pastor

382. Canon 1063, § 2, directs that if the pastor knows for certain that the parties will violate the prohibition expressed

---

atque omnibus accurato studio debitoque iudicii maturitate pensatis, Decreta eiusdem Concilii expenderunt et nonnullis emendationibus ac modificationibus adiectis, eadem ut ab omnibus ad quos spectat inviolabiliter observentur recognoverunt. Hanc autem S. Congregationis sententiam Summo Pontifici Leoni XIII a R. P. D. Dominico Iacobini eiusdem S. Congregationis Secretario in Audientia diei 10 Septembris 1885 relatam, Sanctitas Sua benigne approbare dignata est, et super his praesens Decretum expediri mandavit."—S. C. de Prop. F., decret., 21 Sept. 1885,—*Acta et Decreta*, Conc. Plen. Balt. III (1884), p. XV-XVI. Whatever corrections were to be made, there is no suggestion that they concerned the decree in question for these decrees were published in 1886 in the form in which they are now known. Moreover, many other diocesan synods thereafter reserved this censure to the Ordinary, —with reference to the marriage of a Catholic (regardless of whether it be with another Catholic or a non-Catholic) before a non-Catholic minister. Cf. Synodus Dioecesana Natchetensis V (1886), n. XXXIX; Constitutiones Dioecesanae Bostoniensis (1886), n. 132; Synodus Dioecesana Manchesteriensis I (1886), n. 148; Albanensis IV (1887), n. 107; Providentiensis (1887), n. 83; Omahanensis (1887), n. 97; Sanctae Fidei I (1888), n. 9; Neo-Aurelianensis V (1889), n. LV; Wayne-Castrensis (1903), n. 174.

[37] Cf. Chelodi, *Ius Poenale*, p. 38, not. 2.

[38] This opinion is not in violation of canon 2244, § 2, n. 3, which says that censures incurred *latae sententiae* are multiplied: *"Si delictum, diversis censuris a distinctis Superioribus punitum, semel aut pluries committatur."* The phrase *"diversis censuris"* can readily be understood to mean censures specifically different. Cf. Dargin, *Reserved Cases*, p. 56.

[39] "Reservatio censurae in particulari territorio vim suam extra illius territorii fines non exserit, etiamsi censuratus ad absolutionem obtinendam e territorio egrediatur; censura vero ab homine est ubique locorum reservata ita ut censuratus nullibi absolvi sine debitis facultatibus possit."—Canon 2247, § 2. Cf. Dargin, *op. cit.*, p. 73-76. The latter part of this canon, with its reference to censures *ab homine*, has no reference to the censure established *a iure* by the Council of Baltimore.

in canon 1063, § 1, or have already violated it, he shall not assist at their marriage except for the gravest reasons, all danger of scandal having been removed, and the Ordinary having been consulted. The prohibition of this canon is concerned primarily with the pastor's assistance, and in this it is similar to canon 1065, § 2. If, therefore, the pastor is *certain*[40] that the parties, after the marriage *coram Ecclesia*, will go also before a non-Catholic minister to give their matrimonial consent, or if he is asked by the parties concerning this matter, he cannot remain silent but must warn the parties of the crime they will commit, and of the excommunication to be incurred.[41] If they still persist in their intention, the pastor is forbidden to assist at their marriage until he has consulted the Ordinary, who is to judge of the effectiveness of the removal of scandal and of the gravity of the causes. The pastor must follow the Ordinary's decision.

383. If, on the other hand, the pastor foresees (though he does not know for certain) that the parties will go before a non-Catholic minister, and if he also foresees that they will not heed his warning, he can, to avoid grave evils, remain silent and assist at their marriage, provided there is no danger of scandal, and that in the case of a mixed or disparate marriage, a dispensation has been given.[42] He is not always bound

---

[40] "*Certe noverit.* Darin liegt wohl stillschweigend eine Ausweisung an die Praxis, milde zu verfahren und wenn möglich die Dissimulation anzuwenden."—Schönsteiner, *Grundriss des kirchl. Eherechts,* p. 36.

[41] "Sciant insuper parochi, si interrogentur a contrahentibus, vel si certe noverint eos adituros ministrum haereticum sacris addictum ad consensum matrimonialem praestandum, se silere non posse; sed monere eosdem debere sponsos de gravissimo peccato quod patrant, et de censuris in quas incurrunt."—S. C. S. Off. (ad Ep. Osnabrugen.), 17 Feb. 1864,—*Fontes,* n. 976. Vide etiam S. C. S. Off. (Hiberniae), 29 Nov. 1672,—*Fontes,* n. 751; 17 Ian. 1872, ad II,—*Fontes,* n. 1020; instr. (ad omnes Ep. Ritus Orient.), 12 Dec. 1888, n. 8,—*Fontes,* n. 1112.

[42] "Verumtamen ad gravia praecavenda mala, si in aliquo peculiari casu parochus non fuerit interpellatus a sponsis, an liceat nec ne adire ministrum haereticum, et nulla fiat ab iisdem sponsis explicita declaratio de adeundo ministrum haereticum, praevideat tamen eos forsan adituros ad matrimonialem renovandum consensum, ac insuper ex adiunctis in casu concurrentibus praevideat monitionem certo non fore profuturam, immo nocituram, indeque peccatum materiale in formalem culpam vertendum, tunc sileat, remoto tamen scandalo, et dummodo aliae ab Ecclesia requisitae conditiones, atque cautiones rite positae sint . . ."—S. C. S. Off. (ad Ep. Osnabrugen.), 17 Feb. 1864,—*Fontes,* n. 976. Vide etiam S. C. S. Off., 17 Ian. 1872, ad II,—*Fontes,* n. 1020; (Engolismen.), 27 Mart. 1878, ad 2,—*Coll.,* n. 1490; instr. (ad omnes Ep. Ritus Orient.), 12 Dec. 1888, n. 8,—*Fontes,* n. 1112.

to inquire as to this intention of the parties, even if he foresees that they will go before a non-Catholic minister.[43] If a marriage has already been attempted before a non-Catholic minister *"uti sacris addictus"*, the pastor may not assist at the renewal of consent until he has first consulted the Ordinary who, with due consideration for the removal of scandal and the gravity of the causes urged, will either refuse or grant the permission for the pastor's assistance.[44] Catholics who have been guilty of this sin must first receive an absolution from the censure of canon 2319, § 1, n. 1, which is to be given only upon the manifest signs of repentance.[45] Where mixed or disparate marriages are concerned, a dispensation from the impediment[46] must likewise precede the pastor's assistance, and if it is a question of marriages prohibited by canons 1065 and 1066, the further permission of the Ordinary for the pastor's assistance.

Art. II. Before a Non-Catholic Minister in His Civil Capacity

384. When the civil law demands it, the parties are not forbidden to present themselves before a non-Catholic minister acting as a civil official, solely to comply with a civil formality and for the sake of civil effects.[47] Such an act does not involve the *communicatio in sacris* with non-Catholic ministers forbidden by canon 1063, § 1. If, however, a civil ceremony has taken place, the parties may not cohabit until they have contracted a *valid* marriage *coram Ecclesia*,[48] and under normal conditions

---

[43] "An parochus timens, vel praevidens partem catholicam etiam ministrum acatholicum esse adituram, teneatur circa hanc intentionem catholicae sponsae inquirere . . . R. Non teneri inquirere."—S. C. S. Off., 22 Ian. 1851,—Feije, *De Imped. et Dispens.*, p. 459, not. 1.

[44] If such marriages have been contracted validly before a non-Catholic minister *"uti sacris addictus"* by virtue of canon 1098, n. 1, Catholics are not to be admitted to the sacraments until they have first received an absolution from the censure of canon 2319, § 1, n. 1. Cf. S. C. S. Off., litt. (ad Vic. Ap. Myssurien.), 26 Nov. 1862.—*Fontes*, n. 971.

[45] Cf. S. C. S. Off. (ad Ep. Osnabrugen.), 17 Feb. 1864,—*Fontes*, n. 976; instr. (ad omnes Ep. Ritus Orient.), 12 Dec. 1888, n. 8,—*Fontes*, n. 1112.

[46] Canon 2375 must likewise be kept in mind.

[47] Canon 1063, § 3.

[48] A marriage (even before a non-Catholic minister) could be validly contracted if the conditions of canon 1098, n. 1 are realized, since the presence of a priest is not required for the *validity* of marriages contracted in such cir-

this should take place *quam primum.*[49] From the point of view
of the scandal arising, the parties are not permitted to present
themselves before a minister acting as a civil magistrate, where the
civil law does not demand it.[50] In urgent necessity, in order to
avoid grave evils, the Catholic party may, perhaps, be permitted
to present himself before a non-Catholic minister acting in his
civil capacity if the non-Catholic party absolutely insists upon
it,—even though the civil law would not demand it.[51] The absolute silence, however, of canon 1063, § 3, upon such a provision may render the former tolerance a very doubtful guide for
the present practice. Moreover, if in such a case the non-Catholic
party insists upon going before the minister of his sect in pref-
erence to others, there is a strong presumption that there will be
a *communicatio in sacris.*[52] Since the civil laws of the United
States of America do not demand a civil in addition to a religious ceremony, there can be little excuse for the parties approach-
ing a minister even though he acts as a civil magistrate.[53] Exception may, perhaps, be made for situations such as those contemplated in canon 1098, n. 1, where the minister would be the
only civil official in the locality, and when the parties would
present themselves before him merely to secure the civil effects
of their contract. This, of course, presupposes that no canonical
impediments exist, or if they exist, that they have been dispensed
from by the Church.

---

cumstances. See canon 1098, n. 2. If the parties approached the minister
acting in a civil capacity, they would incur no censure by the common law
of the Code.

[49] Cf. Benedictus XIV, ep. *Redditae sunt*, 17 Sept. 1746, § 4,—*Fontes*, n.
372; Wernz, *Ius Decret.*, IV, n. 208.

[50] Cf. Cerato, *Matr.*, n. 57; Cappello, *De Sacram.*, III, n. 318.

[51] "Utrum catholicus coram proprio catholico parocho cum haeretica contrahens licite possit, urgentibus haereticis, matrimonium hoc ratificare coram
ministro haeretico, si nulla hinc ritus haeretici professio habeatur aut colliga-
tur, et quidquid minister haereticus in casu peragit, civilis dumtaxat et politica
gratulatio sit ac censeatur. R. Affirmative."—S. C. S. Off., 14 Nov. 1748,—
Fontes, n. 799. Vide etiam S. C. S. Off. (ad Ep. Osnabrugen.), 17 Feb.
1864,—*Fontes*, n. 976; instr. (ad omnes Ep. Ritus Orient.), 12 Dec. 1888,
n. 7,—*Fontes*, n. 1112; Cappello, *op. cit.*, III, n. 318.

[52] S. C. de Prop. F., 12 Mart. 1897,—*ASS*, XXX (1897-1898), 158-
159. Cf. Augustine, *Commentary*, V, p. 152.

[53] Cf. Woywod, *A Practical Commentary*, I, n. 1042.

Art. III. The Apostolic Letter "*Provida*" and Passive Assistance.

385. After the decree "*Ne Temere*" there existed only two exemptions from the universal law of the Latin Church regarding the form of marriage. One existed for Germany by virtue of the apostolic letter "*Provida*", that was later also extended to Hungary;[54] the other in the form of a continued tolerance of passive assistance exclusively in those regions where it had formerly[55] been permitted by the Holy See.[56] The exemption granted by the apostolic letter "*Provida*" was abolished by canon 1099 of the Code.[57] Passive assistance was also abolished by the Code for canon 1102, § 1, directs: "*In matrimoniis inter partem catholicam et partem acatholicam interrogationes de consensu fieri debent secundum praescriptum can. 1095, § 1, n. 3.*"[58]

386. Some authors, who wrote after the Code, continued to subscribe to the opinion that passive assistance could still be employed in the regions where it was formerly tolerated.[59] The Pontifical Commission for the Authentic Interpretation of the

---

[54] See No. 113, note 87.

[55] See No. 106, notes 57-58.

[56] "Praescriptionem Decreti *Ne Temere*, n. IV, § 3, de requirendo per parochum excipiendoque, ad validitatem matrimonii, nupturientium consensu, in matrmoniis mixtis in quibus debitas cautiones exhibere pervicaciter partes renuant, locum posthac non habere; sed standum *taxative* praecedentibus Sanctae Sedis ac praesertim s. m. Gregorii PP. XVI (Litt. ap. diei 30 Aprilis 1841 ad episcopos Hungariae) ad rem concessionibus et instructionibus; facto verbo cum SSmo."—S. C. S. Off. 21 Iun. 1912,—*AAS*, IV (1912), 444. Vide etiam S. C. Concilii, 27 Iul. 1908,—*Apollinaris*, I (1928), 340; S. C. S. Off., 5 Aug. 1916,—*AAS*, VIII (1916), 316. In this connection, the Second Diocesan Synod of Kansas City held in 1912 decreed (Decretum n. 141, 4): "*In casu vero quo pars catholica receptionem poenitentiae sacramenti recusaverit, rector tali matrimonio passive assistere debet.*" What precisely was meant by "*passive assistere*" is not indicated.

[57] "Ad dubium autem utrum Consitutio ["*Provida*"] illa canone 1099 novi Codicis, ut *lex particularis*, abrogata esset (ad normam can. 6, n. 1), an potius ,ut *privilegium*, non obstante can. 1099, persisteret, Com. Pont. Codici interpretando praeposita die 9 Dec. 1917 respondit, esse abrogatam (Strassb. Dioezesanbl. 1918, S. 97), quod similiter ab Emin. Secretario Status die 30 Mart. responsum fuit clo. Schaepman, de consensu Illmi Archiepi Ultraiecten. idem sciscitanti."—Vlaming, *Prael. Iuris Matr.*, I, p. 200, not. 2.

[58] "Parochus et loci Ordinarius valide matrimonio assistunt: n. 3.—Dummodo neque vi neque metu gravi constricti requirant excipiantque contrahentium consensum."—Canon 1095, § 1, n. 3. See canon 1064, n. 4.

[59] A reference to some of these authors may be found in Schönsteiner, *Grundriss des kirchl. Eherechts*, p. 35, and Cappello, *De Sacram.*, III, n. 715, not. 4.

Code put an end to all doubts on this score when on March 10, 1928, it gave an affirmative answer to the following *dubium*: "*An canone* 1102, § 1, *revocata sit facultas, alicubi a S. Sede concessa, passive assistendi matrimoniis mixtis illicitis.*"[60] The reply indicates that the Church is quite unwilling that such a tolerated assistance shall again be permitted, and hence the opinion sponsored by De Smet[61] and Farrugia[62] that an Ordinary could have recourse to such assistance in cases of urgent necessity by virtue of canon 81, seems to be at variance with the mind of the Holy See.[63]

ART. IV. THE PROHIBITION OF ALL SACRED RITES

387. While passive assistance has thus been abolished, and the matrimonial consent of the parties must be asked in conformity with canon 1102, § 1, all sacred rites are, moreover, prohibited. If, however, greater evils are foreseen to follow from a strict adherence to this prohibition, the Ordinary may permit some of the usual ecclesiastical ceremonies, always to the exclusion of the celebration of Mass.

CANON 1102, § 2

Sed omnes sacri ritus prohibentur; quod si ex hac prohibitione graviora mala praevideantur, Ordinarius potest aliquam ex consuetis ecclesiasticis caeremoniis, exclusa semper Missae celebratione, permittere.[64]

The reason for the prohibition is manifest. If Ordinaries and pastors have the grave obligation to employ those means at their command in deterring the faithful from contracting mixed and disparate marriages, they must conduct themselves consistently. The sacred rites of the Church may not, therefore, be used at such marriages since they imply an approbation of the Church.

---

[60] *AAS*, XX (1928), 120. Vide etiam S. C. S. Off., 26 Nov. 1919,—*ArKR*, C (1920), 28.

[61] *De Spons. et Matr.*, p. 448, not. 4.

[62] *De Matr.*, n. 246.

[63] Maroto, "De Matrimoniis Mixtis Illicitis", *Apollinaris*, I (1928), 342.

[64] See also canons 1064, n. 4; 1071.

In employing such rites the Ordinaries and pastors would appear to approve what they have disapproved by their teaching.[65]

388. Ever since the Church has begun to grant dispensations for mixed and disparate marriages, the use of any blessing for such marriages has been constantly forbidden.[66] The prohibition contemplates all blessings[67] (even of the ring),[68] the use

---

[65] "Nunquam enim tolerari debet, ut sacrilegis hisce contractibus sacri ritus admisceantur, et sacerdotes Dei videntur suo facto probare, quod ore illicitum esse edocent et praedicant. Atque id probe sentiunt adversarii nostri, qui certe in huiusmodi nuptiis de catholici sacerdotis benedictione minime laborarent, nisi intelligerent illam conducere ad extenuendam, atque adeo ad obliterandam sensim in catholici populi animis memoriam canonum, qui haec detestantur connubia, et constantissimi studii, quo sancta mater Ecclesia filios suos avertere consuevit ab iisdem coniugiis in eorum futuraeque prolis perniciem contrahendis. [To this is added the following interesting observation]. Nostri scilicet contradictores cognoscunt, si res ex eorum votis succederet, facile inde futurum, ut catholicae potissimum foeminae aut licita aut non tam graviter illicita existimarent ea coniugia, quae sacris Ecclesiae ritibus et sacerdotali benedictione honestari viderent."—Gregorius XVI, ep. *Non sine gravi*, 23 Maii 1846, n. 2,—*Fontes*, n. 503. Vide etiam Instr. Secret. Stat. iussu Pii PP. IX, 15 Nov. 1858,—*Coll.*, n. 1169; S. C. S. Off., instr. (ad Ep. S. Alberti), 9 Dec. 1847,—*Coll.*, n. 1427.

[66] See No. 107, note 60. Already at the time of Pope Clement VIII blessings were forbidden to be imparted to mixed marriages. "*Matrimonia Catholicorum cum Acatholicis non sunt benedicenda. Plures enim summi Pontifices, praesertim Clemens VIII, expresse prohibuerunt, ne huiusmodi connubiis sacerdotalis benedictio impendatur.*"—*Rituale Romanum*, Suppl. pro Prov. Am. Septentr. Foed., p. 10. Cf. Benedictus XIV, *De Synodo Dioec.*, Lib. VII, cap. V, n. 5. Dom Chardon refers this prohibition of the blessing to the marriage of Henry of Bavaria and Catherine of Navarre (see No. 86): "Le pape Clément VIII usa de cette dispense envers le duc de Bar, qui l'avait longtemps sollocité de réhabiliter son marriage avec Catherine de Bourbon, soeur de Henri IV. Le pape . . . lui permit de se marier avec cette princesse en présence du curé de la paroisse et de deux témoins, sans aucune bénédiction nuptiale, en cas que le concile de Trent eût été publié en Lorraine, ou bien en se donnant de nouveau le consentement mutuel, s'il n'y était pas publié." —*Histoire du Sacrement de Mariage*, Chap. XIII,—Migne, *Theol. Curs. Complet.*, XX, 1119.

[67] It includes also the nuptial blessing given outside of the Mass by one having this permission by Apostolic Indult. Cf. *Rituale Romanum*, Appendix, *De Matr.*, I. At times there were some very unusual exceptions to the prohibition of sacred rites in the law before the Code. "*Attamen si agatur de matrimoniis mixtis coram haeretico ministro iam contractis* [the context of the decision supposes that they are validly contracted in places not subject to the decree "*Tametsi*"], *quatenus cautiones a iure necessariae praestitae fuerint, et pars catholica facti poenitens benedictionem petat, poterit ei, praevia absolutione a censuris, impositisque salutaribus poenitentiis, benedictio impertiri, exclusa tamen semper Missae celebratione.*"—S. C. S. Off., litt. (ad Vic. Ap. Myssurien.), 26 Nov. 1862,—*Fontes*, n. 971. Vide etiam S. C. S. Off., instr. (ad omnes Ep. Ritus Orient.), 12 Dec. 1888, n. 8,—*Fontes*, n. 1112.

[68] S. C. S. Off., 1 Aug. 1821,—*Fontes*, n. 863; 17 Ian. 1877, ad 3 et 4,—*NRT*, XX (1888), 463-464. Vlaming (*Prael. Iuris Matr.*, n. 225) is of the opinion that the pastor could bless the ring privately, though the opinion given by Petrovits (*New Church Law on Matrimony*, n. 197) and

of liturgical vestments,[69] prayers,[70] and sacred rites.[71] Above all is forbidden the celebration of Holy Mass which could in any way be construed as a complement of the celebration of the mixed or disparate marriage.[72] A formal sermon which would be the equivalent of any act of approbation is forbidden, though a short exhortation may be given if the Bishop permits it.[73] Ap-

Tanquery (*Theol. Mor.*, I, n. 914), allowing this upon the Ordinary's permission, is more in accord with the decisions. In the United States the unblessed ring is placed on the bride's finger. Cf. *Rituale Romanum, Suppl. pro. Prov. Am. Septentr. Foed.*, p. 12; *The Priest's New Ritual* (complied by Rev. P. Griffith), Baltimore, 1914, p. 199.

[69] Pius VI, rescript. ad Card. Archiep. Mechlinien., 12 Iul. 1782, n. 4,—*Fontes*, n. 471; S. C. S. Off., instr. (ad Ep. S. Alberti), 9 Dec. 1847,—*Coll.*, n. 1427; 17 Ian. 1877, ad 3 et 4,—*NRT*, XX (1888), 463-464; (Rosen.), 16 Iul. 1885,—*Fontes*, n. 1094. Such vestments as a surplice and stole are forbidden, but not such as a cassock, or the customary dress of prelates. Cappello, *De Sacram.*, III, n. 716; Rossi, *De Matr. Celebratione*, n. 99, not. 22.

[70] Pius VI, *loc. cit.*; instr. 19 Iun. 1793,—Migne, *Theol. Curs. Complet.*, XXV, 682; Pius VIII, litt. ap. *Litteris altero*, 25 Mart 1830,—*Fontes*, n. 482; S. C. S. Off., 1 Aug. 1821,—*Fontes*, n. 863; instr. (ad Ep. S. Alberti), 9 Dec. 1847,—*Coll.*, n. 1427. *The Priest's New Ritual* [(compiled by Rev. P. Griffith), Baltimore, 1914, p. 199-200] has a prayer in the vernacular that is apparently permitted though it is not contained in the supplement for the United States of the *Rituale Romanum*.

[71] Canon 1102, § 2. The Sixth Provincial Council of Baltimore (1846) determined to petition the Holy See to use some of the sacred rites in the following words (n. 1): "*Censuerunt Patres expedire ob specialia locorum adiuncta, ut preces porrigantur ad Sedem Apostolicum, ut liceat in Matrimoniis mixtis ritus in Rituali Romano praescriptos usque ad Annuli benedictionem et traditionem inclusive adhibere, servata semper conditione de Catholicae partis libero religionis exercitio, et prolis utriusque sexus in fide Catholica educatione, iuxta Decretum 1. concilii Provincialis IV.*" Cardinal Fransonius, in his letter of July 3, 1847, to Archbishop Eccleston, replied, however, that no religious rite could be employed. See infra No. 108.

[72] "*An canone 1102, § 2, in matrimoniis mixtis, praeter Missam pro sponsis, prohibeatur etiam alia Missa, licet privata. R. Affirmative, si haec Missa ex rerum adiuncta haberi possit uti complementum caeremoniae matrimonialis.*"—Pont. Comm., 10 Nov. 1925,—*AAS*, XVII (1925), 583. The same reply was given in a much earlier decision,—S. C. S. Off., 17 Ian. 1872, ad I,—*Fontes*, n. 1020. Vide etiam Instr. Secret. Stat. iussu Pii PP. IX, 15. Nov. 1858,—*Coll.*, n. 1169; S. C. S. Off., litt. (ad Vic. Ap. Myssurien.), 26 Nov. 1862,— *Fontes*, n. 971; instr. (ad Archiep. Corcyren.), 3 Ian. 1871, n. 5,—*Fontes*, n. 1013; 17 Ian. 1877, ad 5,—*NRT*, XX (1888), 463-464. There were, however, earlier exceptions to this rule. See No. 392, notes 86, 88.

[73] Cf. S. C. S. Off., 17 Ian. 1877, ad 4,—*NRT*, XX (1888). 463-464; (Rosen.), 16 Iul. 1885,—*Fontes*, n. 1094. The custom in the United States has been to give a short exhortation. Such a permission already appeared in earlier diocesan synods (e. g., S. Ludovici [1850], n. XVII; Natchitochensis II [1869], n. LXI), and in the Baltimore Ritual of 1873 (printed by John Murphy), p. 546. At present, examples of such exhortations are found in the supplement to the *Rituale Romanum* (p. 12-15)

parently the only cause recognized[74] (to the exclusion of others)
for any exception to the prohibition of canon 1102, § 2, is the
avoidance of graver evils, which may readily arise because of the
customs of a locality or because of the circumstances of a particular case.[75]

§ I. SACRED RITES IN CONNECTION WITH MARRIAGES FORBIDDEN BY CANONS 1065 AND 1066

389. A certain disagreement exists among the authors as to
the use of sacred rites in assisting at marriages prohibited by
canons 1065 and 1066. Some authors are of the opinion that
since canon 1102, § 2, does not explicitly or implicitly refer to
the marriages of Catholics with those who have notoriously left
the Faith or joined condemned societies, or with public sinners
or those notoriously under censure, it cannot, therefore, be used
as a norm for such marriages. Further attention is directed to
the point that nowhere else in the Code is there a canon referring
either explicitly or implicitly to the prohibition of sacred rites
or the celebration of Mass for such marriages. This silence of
the Code must, therefore, be construed as an abrogation of the
prescriptions of former decrees forbidding the celebration of Mass
or the use of sacred rites.[76] Other authors, however, hold that the

---

and in *The Priest's New Ritual* (p. 194-197). Cf. Konings-Putzer, *Comment. in Facult.*, p. 384; Petrovits, *New Church Law on Matrimony*, n. 511; Augustine, *Commentary*, V, p. 309; Tanquery, *Theol. Mor.*, I, n. 914.

[74] The following are exemplary causes recognized as sufficient: "a) quotiescumque, ob denegatam matrimoniis mixtis benedictionem, faciles exciterentur haereticorum quaeremoniae et odia adversus fideles legesque ecclesiasticas; b) quotiescumque (timendum esset ne), denegata a parocho catholico benedictione, sponsi . . . ministellum adeant . . .; c) quotiescumque insuper timendum esset quod, recusata ab ipsis expetita benedictione, aut non servarentur necessariae cautiones . . . aut, quod detestabilius foret, ne pars catholica ad haereticorum castra, in sui et futurae prolis aeternam perniciem, transiret."—S. C. de Prop. F., ep., 4 Dec. 1862,—De Smet, *De Spons. et Matr.*, p. 446, not. 1.

[75] Cf. instr. Secret. Stat. iussu Pii PP. IX, 15 Nov. 1858,—*Coll.*, n. 1169; S. C. S. Off., instr. (ad Archiep. Corcyren.), 3 Ian. 1871. n. 5,—*Fontes*, n. 1013; 17 Ian. 1877,—*NRT*, XX (1888), 462-464; S. C. de Prop. F., ep., 4 Dec. 1862,—De Smet, *loc. cit.*; litt. encycl., 11 Mart. 1868,—*Coll.*, n. 1324.

[76] Quigley (*Condemned Societies*, p. 106) is of the opinion that the celebration of Mass is permitted, but that the Ordinary for reasons of scandal may prohibit it. Cf. Vlaming, *Prael. Iuris Matr.*, n. 250; Cerato, *Matr.*, n. 59. Wernz-Vidal (*Ius Canonicum*, V, nn. 201, 203) states the opinion with more caution to the effect that the celebration of Mass or the use of

decisions before the Code may still be invoked as a norm and require the Ordinary's permission for the celebration of Mass or the use of sacred rites.[77]

390. While, indeed, no canon in the Code makes explicit reference to the prohibition of the celebration of Mass and the use of sacred rites for the marriages in question, canon 2260, § 1, states, nevertheless, that those excommunicated by a declaratory or a condemnatory sentence cannot receive the sacramentals. If, then, the bride is so excommunicated, she cannot receive the nuptial blessing since this is an invocative blessing.[78] Moreover, if either of the parties is excommunicated, the public prayers and sacrifice of the Nuptial Mass seem to be excluded by virtue of canon 2262, § 1.[79] If then, there is at least an implicit reference of the Code to a prohibition of the nuptial blessing in certain instances, and of the celebration of the Nuptial Mass, it is not at all certain that the decisions of the past have been abrogated. In the law before the Code the use of sacred rites was forbidden for marriages of Catholics with those under censure;[80] with Masons,[81] or those notoriously members of secret societies (*"in quo una contrahentium pars clandestinis aggregationibus notarie adhaeret"*).[82] It was left to the Ordinary to determine (*"quae magis in Domino expedire iudicaverit"*) in each particular case whether the sacred rites could be permitted. The celebration of

---

sacred rites do not appear to be absolutely excluded. Leitner (*Lehrb. des kath. Eherechts*, p. 251) permits the celebration of Mass if there is no question of a condemnatory or declaratory sentence of excommunication. Petrovits (*New Church Law on Matrimony*, nn. 200, 203) and Farrugia (*De Matr.*, n. 140) seem to require a recourse to the Ordinary, who in their opinion may, however, permit the full ritual and even the celebration of Mass. Petrovits (*ibid.*, n. 203) requires a *causa gravissima* if the excommunicated party be a *vitandus*.

[77] Chelodi, *Ius Matr.*, n. 67; Pighi, *De Matr.*, n. 34; Augustine, *Commentary*, V, p. 157. See also the preceding note and *AER*, LXXIV (1926), 310-311.

[78] Cf. Hyland, *Excommunication*, p. 78-80; Pashang, *The Sacramentals according to The Code of Canon Law*, Washington, 1925, p. 73.

[79] "Excommunicatus non fit particeps indulgentiarum, suffragiorum, publicarum Ecclesiae precum."—Canon 2262, § 1. The *private* character of the application of the ministerial fruits of the Mass (permitted by § 2, n. 2, of the same canon) is scarcely to be presumed for a Nuptial Mass.

[80] S. Poenit., 10 Dec. 1860,—Feije, *De Imped. et Dispens.*, n. 277.

[81] S. C. S. Off. (S. Bonifacii), 23 Apr. 1873,—*Fontes*, n. 1026; instr. (ad Ordinarios Imperii Brasil.), 2 Iul. 1878,—*Fontes*, n. 1056.

[82] S. C. S. Off. (Bombay), 21 Feb. 1883,—*Fontes*, n. 1079.

Mass was to be excluded unless the gravity of the circumstances demanded a relaxation of the prohibition.[83]

391. The character of the notoriety emphasized in canons 1065 and 1066 indicates clearly that the element of scandal demands careful consideration. The scandal of such marriages can arise not merely from the fact that they are contracted at all, but also from the fact that they are contracted with the solemn blessing and approbation of the Church. It seems, therefore, that the decisions antedating the Code must be used as a norm; that ordinarily the use of sacred rites and the celebration of Mass are prohibited unless the Ordinary sees fit to permit some or all of the rites, and even the celebration of Mass.[84] There seems to be no clear prohibition in the Code or in any of the decisions as to the celebration of such marriages in a Church. The Ordinary may, however, forbid their celebration in a Church if he foresees that grave scandal will arise if they do take place in a Church.

Art. V. The Place of Celebration

Canon 1109, § 3

Matrimonia vero inter partem catholicam et partem acatholicam extra ecclesiam celebrentur; quod si Ordinarius prudenter iudicet id servari non posse quin graviora oriantur mala, prudenti eius arbitrio committitur hac super re dispensare, firmo tamen praescripto can. 1102, § 2.

392. Though the celebration in a church of mixed and disparate marriages has been universally forbidden at least within the last century and a half, the exact time of the origin of this discipline is, perhaps, not altogether evident. In many sections of the Western Church, particularly in England and in France, marriages even among Catholics were contracted at the church-

---

[83] "Omnino vero excludatur celebratio Sacrificii Missae nisi quando gravia adiuncta aliter exigant."—S. C. S. Off. (Bombay), 21 Feb. 1883,—*Fontes,* n. 1079.

[84] The Church is less severe in her discipline regarding the marriages under consideration than with reference to mixed or disparate marriages for which the celebration of Mass is never permitted.

door. It was the nuptial blessing that was given before the altar within the church itself.[85] The fact that the marriage of Charles, the Prince of Wales, to Henrietta Maria of France, took place on a platform outside the portals of Notre Dame, scarcely affords any proof of a peculiarity of discipline for mixed marrages.[86] At times a certain significance is attached to the fact that the Catholic, who acted as proxy for the heretical prince Charles, conducted Henrietta Maria as far as the choir of the church, but did not remain in the church for the Mass.[87] What is of more striking significance is the fact that a Mass was actually celebrated as a complement of the ceremony at the church-door.[88] But whatever uncertainty may be connected with the discipline of earlier times, it became well established, especially in the nine-

---

[85] Dom Chardon quotes the prescriptions of two ancient rituals used in France, which show that the marriage itself took place at the church-door. —*Histoire du Sacrament de Mariage*, Chap. XIII,—Migne, *Theol. Curs. Complet.*, XX, 1026. "It was this 'marriage at the church door' which had to be established according to Bracton, in any question as to the legality or non-legality of the contract. After 'this taking to wife at the church door', the parties entered the church and completed the rite in the church itself."— Gasquet, *Parish Life in Mediaeval England*, New York, 1906, p. 78. (Cardinal Gasquet refers to the custom of the fifteenth century). *The New English* [Oxford] *Dictionary* (Vol. II, p. 406) refers the word "church-door" immediately to the contracting of marriage. Cf. Salzman, *English Life in the Middle Ages*, London, 1927, p. 254.

[86] Benedict XIV (*De Synodo Dioec.*, Lib. VI, cap. V, n. 5) gives an interesting description of the wedding.—"*quae nuptiae descriptae habentur etiam* [Pope Benedict had already referred to another source] *in Historia, seu Commentario, cui titulus* MERCURIUS GALLICUS, tom. 2. pag. 359. *Narrant itaque, matrimonium inter praedictam Catholicam Principem, et haeretici Regis Procuratorem, extra Ecclesiam contractum fuisse ad limina Ecclesiae Metropolitanae Parisiensis coram Cardinale magno Franciae Eleemosynario, a quo tamen benedictio nuptialis data non fuit: deinde Britannici Regis Procuratorem novam nuptam deduxisse usque ad ingressum Chori: ibi vero a praedicto Cardinale celebratam solemni ritu fuisse Missam, adstantibus Rege, et Regina Franciae, et nova Magnae Britanniae Regina, ac universa Regia Familia: sed praedictum Regis Angliae Procuratorem, quamvis ipse Catholicus esset, cum personam gereret Principis Anglicanae sectae addicti, in proximum Archiepiscopi Palatium interim accessisse, donec Missa terminaretur, qua demum expleta, ad reducendam ab Ecclesia Reginam accessit.*" In view of the fact that the Mass did take place as an immediate complement of the ceremony outside of the Church, Giovine's full approbation of this procedure must be rejected.—*De Dispens. Matr.*, Tom. I, § CLXXV, n. 8.

[87] See the preceding note.

[88] The marriage of Henry of Navarre (later King Henry IV of France) to the Princess Margaret (August 18, 1572) also took place on a platform outside of the church. At this time Henry was a Hugenot, yet a Mass immediately followed at which Henry, however, did not accompany his bride. No dispensation for this marriage had been given by the Holy See. Cf. Van Dyke, *Catherine De Médicis*, 2 vols., New York, 1923, Vol. II, p. 77-78.

teenth century, that mixed marriages were to be contracted outside the church.[89] Apparently, the Ordinary may permit exceptions to this prohibition for only one reason, namely, to avoid greater evils.[90] The phrase *"extra ecclesiam"* may be strictly interpreted so that a sacristy may be used for the celebration of mixed or disparate marriages.[91]

§ I. Celebration in Private Houses

393. Canon 1109, § 2, directs that the celebration of marriages in private houses may be permitted by the local Ordinary only in extraordinary cases and for a just cause. This prescription may be interpreted as referring only to marriages between Catholics. It does not follow, however, that because canon 1109, § 3, forbids the celebration of mixed and disparate marriages in a church, a tacit permission is thereby given to celebrate them in private houses. It would seem to be at variance with the mind of the Church utterly to disregard canon 1109, § 2, when attempting to discern a norm for canon 1109, § 3. What is even more fundamental is that the pastor conduct himself in no way which might normally be construed as implying a favor to the celebration of mixed and disparate marriages.[92] If a mar-

---

[89] Pius VI (rescript. ad Card. Archiep. Mechlinien., 13 Iul. 1782, n. 4, —*Fontes*, n. 471) uses the phrase *"non . . . in loco sacro"*. The later sources refer to the term *"ecclesia"*. Cf. instr. Secret. Stat. iussu Pii PP. IX, 15 Nov. 1858,—*Coll.*, n. 1169; S. C. S. Off., instr. (ad Archiep. Quebecen.), 16 Sept. 1824, ad 5,—*Fontes*, n. 866; (Vic. Ap. Sandwic.), 11 Dec. 1850, ad 22,—*Fontes*, n. 913; instr. (ad Archiep. Corcyren.), 3 Ian. 1871, n. 5,—*Fontes*, n. 1013; (Rosen.), 16 Iul. 1885,—*Fontes*, n. 1094; 29 Nov. 1899, ad 2,—*Fontes*, n. 1230.

[90] Through force of custom, mixed marriages are today celebrated in churches in many places in Germany and in at least one diocese of Poland. Cf. Hilling, *Das Eherecht des C. I. C.*, p. 125; Synodus Archidioecesana Varsaviensis (ad can. 1102), Stat. 122. In the United States such a custom has apparently never existed.

[91] Cf. S. C. S. Off., 17 Ian. 1877, ad 2,—*NRT*, XX (1888), 463-464; Chelodi, *Ius Matr.*, n. 141; Vlaming, *Prael. Iuris Matr.*, n. 225; *AkKR*, CV (1925), 112; Augustine, *Commentary*, V, p. 323. De Smet (*De Spons. et Matr.*, p. 447, not. 3) calls attention, nevertheless, to the danger of celebrating a mixed marriage in a sacristy: *". . . quod in sacristia contracturi sollicitent solemniter ingredi ecclesiam et per eam transire at sacristiam."* Cf. Genicot-Salsmans, *Theol. Mor.*, II, n. 516.

[92] *". . . sed alia ex parte abstinere etiam catholicus pastor debebit non solum a nuptiis, quae deinde fiant, sacro quocumque ritu honestandis, sed etiam a quovis actu, quo approbare illas videatur."*—Pius VIII, litt. ap. *Litteris altero*, 25 Mart. 1830,—*Fontes*, n. 482. Vide etiam Gregorius XVI,

riage between Catholics may not be celebrated in a private home, the pastor's assistance at the celebration of a mixed or disparate marriage in a private home will normally, therefore, be regarded as an act of favor.[93] On this principle, therefore, the celebration of mixed and disparate marriages in private houses is forbidden unless the Ordinary in an extraordinary case and for a just and reasonable cause permits it.

ART. VI. PUBLICATION OF THE BANNS

394. Whatever uncertainties may have existed in the law before the Code with reference to the publication of the banns for mixed and disparate marriages,[94] they have been solved by the Code in canon 1026: *"Publicationes ne fiant pro matrimoniis quae contrahuntur cum dispensatione ab impedimento disparitatis cultus aut mixtae religionis, nisi loci Ordinarius pro sua prudentia, remoto scandalo, eas permittere opportunum duxerit, dummodo apostolica dispensatio praecesserit et mentio omittatur religionis partis non catholicae."* The normal rule is, therefore, that the banns are not to be published for mixed and disparate marriages. If the Ordinary deems their publication necessary in a particular case, the permission is to be given only on the following conditions: 1) that all danger of scandal be removed; 2) that a dispensation from the impediment precede their publication; 3) that the religion of the non-Catholic party be not mentioned. If there is a doubt of the existence of other impediments, the pastor is to be guided by canon 1031, § 1, nn. 1, 3. For the examination of the witnesses referred to in canon 1031, § 1, n. 1, many questions are suggested in the instruction of the Holy Office of August 21, 1670.[95]

---

ep. encycl. *Summo iugiter,* 27 Maii 1832, § 7,—*Fontes,* n. 484; allocut, *Officii memores,* 5 Iul. 1839,—*Fontes,* n. 492; litt. ap. *Quas vestro,* 30 Apr. 1841, n. 5,—*Fontes,* n. 497; canon 1064, n. 1.

[93] "Aus diesem obersten Princip des Gesetzgebers [the concern of the Church that Catholics are to be deterred from mixed and disparate marriages] ist für eine sachgemässe Auslegung zu folgern, dass strengstens alle Handlungen verboten sind, die in ihrem Effekt auf eine Bevorzugung der gemischten Eheschliessungen hinauslaufen oder wenigstens als solche in den Augen des gläubigen Volkes aufgefasst werden können."—Hilling in *AkKR,* CV (1925), 113. Cf. De Smet, *De Spons. et Matr.,* p. 447, not. 3.

[94] See Nos. 107-111.

[95] *Fontes,* n. 742. Cf. S. C. S. Off., litt. 4 Iul. 1874,—*Fontes,* n. 1031.

§ I. Banns for Marriages between Catholics and Converts

395. The prohibition of canon 1026 must apparently be limited to strictly mixed and disparate marriages[96] so that if the non-Catholic party is to be received into the Church before the marriage, the normal rule of canon 1022[97] is to apply.[98] Augustine is of the opinion, however, that while such marriages seem to be governed by canon 1022, there is no need of a dispensation for the omission of the banns for marriages between Catholics and those recently converted to the Church.

However, the text [canon 1022] does not say that *all* Catholic marriages *must* be called, and can. 1028 allows the Ordinaries to dispense for any lawful reason. Neither is the law a perfect one, since it has no penal sanction attached to it. The purpose of the law is to discover impediments. This aim could be attained only in part, since the friends of the former non-Catholic party would hardly attend the service. Besides, the publication of the banns is not intended to arouse curiosity or ridicule or surprise. Finally the instruction will easily permit the pastor to find possible impediments.[99]

396. If, according to Augustine, the banns need not be published for *all* marriages between Catholics, it may be asked what line of demarcation is to be employed? The very fact that the Ordinary *can* dispense for a reasonable cause supposes that the law does extend to *all* marriages between Catholics *unless the Ordinary dispenses.* The statement that the friends of the former non-Catholic party will not attend the service to hear the publication of the banns seems to suppose that an extensive "friendship" is a condition of the effectiveness of the law prescribing the banns. Who were the non-Catholic's friends? Were

---

[96] The publication of the banns has evidently never been prohibited by the common law of the Church for marriages prohibited by canons 1065 and 1066. Yet the Ordinary in determining the effectiveness of the removal of scandal in order to permit the pastor's assistance, may likewise forbid the publication of the banns, provided that sufficient care has been taken to discover the possible existence of impediments.

[97] "Publice a parocho denuncietur inter quosnam matrimonium sit contrahendum."—Canon 1022.

[98] Cf. De Smet, *De Spons. et Matr.*, p. 447, not. 1; *AER*, LXXIX (1928), 648.

[99] *Rights and Duties of Ordinaries*, p. 289.

they all non-Catholics? The supposition, moreover, that the *knowledge of the free status* of the former non-Catholic party is confined to non-Catholic associates is quite gratuitous. There is no general presumption that the publication of the banns in such cases will expose the parties to ridicule,—rather, as the Ecclesiastical Review has it: "it is of some importance that the banns be published in this case that the faithful may know that this is not another mixed marriage."[100]

ART. VII. WHAT PASTOR IS TO ASSIST?

397. Canon 1097, § 2, states that in every case it is to be held as a rule that marriages are to be contracted before the pastor of the bride.[101] Does this prescription hold also for mixed and disparate marriages where the non-Catholic party is the bride? Apparently the majority of authors deny that the canon has reference to mixed or disparate marriages.[102] Hilling[103] draws attention to canon 1964 which rules that if one of the parties is a non-Catholic, the competent judge in a *causa matrimonialis* is that of the domicile or quasi-domicile of the Catholic party. But it is well to note that this prescription seems to apply only with reference to the question of domicile—it does not exclude the place in which the marriage was contracted. To say that on the basis of canon 1964 the marriage must be contracted before the pastor of the Catholic party seems to be begging the question. Moreover, canons 1097, § 2, and 1964 deal with entirely different questions. Woywod, who has receded from his former opinion upholding the reference of canon 1097, § 2, also to mixed marriages,[104] seems to draw the principal argument of his later

---

[100] *AER,* LXXIX (1928) 648.

[101] "In quolibet casu pro regula habeatur ut matrimonium coram sponsae parocho celebretur . . ."—Canon 1097, § 2.

[102] The same prescription was contained in the decree "Ne Temere" (Art. V, § 5) so that the interpretation of the first three authors will apply also to canon 1097, § 2. Cf. Wernz, *Ius Decret.,* IV, n. 188 in fin.; Cronin, *The New Matrimonial Legislation,* p. 287, note 1; McNicholas, "Difficulties on the New Marriage Legislation", *AER,* XXXIX (1908), 35-36; Ayrinhac, *Marriage Legislation,* p. 242; Fanfani, *De Iure Parochorum,* n. 309; Hilling, *Das Eherecht des C. I. C.,* p. 107; Woywod, in *HPR,* XXVIII (1928), 410.

[103] *Loc. cit.*

[104] *A Practical Commentary,* I, n. 1118.

opinion[105] from the fact that since the Church does not deal directly with non-Catholics in the matter of dispensation, the parties to a mixed or disparate marriage would have to approach the pastor of the Catholic party, since the pastor of the non-Catholic party cannot deal directly with her concerning the marriage. This opinion seems to imply either that the pastor of the Catholic party can deal directly with the non-Catholic bride or that the pastor of the non-Catholic bride cannot deal with the Catholic party if he does not belong to his parish. Neither supposition can be sustained. Why may not the pastor of the non-Catholic bride apply for a dispensation for the Catholic party from the Catholic party's Ordinary or from the pastor's own Ordinary (if he be other than that of the Catholic party) as long as the Catholic party is in the diocese at the time the dispensation is to be granted?[106]

398. Since the decree "Ne Temere" stated the prescription of canon 1097, § 2, in almost identical words,[107] it will be of interest to examine the decision of the Sacred Congregation of the Sacraments[108] with reference to the following case. A certain non-Catholic girl having a domicile in parish *B* wished to marry a Catholic having a domicile in parish *L* of the same archdiocese. Before the marriage, however, the girl took a month's vacation in parish *S* of the same archdiocese. Here she was *baptized* and received into the Catholic Church by the pastor of parish *S*. Only a small part of the month's vacation remained after her entry into the Church and upon its conclusion she returned to parish *B* where she stayed three weeks. Thereupon she went again to parish *S* and on her arrival contracted the marriage (April 28, 1915) before the pastor of parish *S* who did not receive the permission to assist from the pastor of parish *B*. The pastor of parish *B*, regarding himself the proper pastor of the girl, brought the case before the diocesan Matrimonial Tribunal. The diocesan decision was adverse to the claim of the pastor

---

[105] *HPR*, XXVIII (1928), 410.

[106] This has reference particularly to the faculties given to the Bishops of the United States who may give dispensations from these impediments to non-subjects within the limits of the diocese. See Nos. 249-250.

[107] See Art. V, § 5, of the decree "Ne Temere".

[108] *AAS*, VIII (1916), 64-66.

of parish *B*. The case was then submitted to the Congregation of the Sacraments. In the discussion, the following opinion was given by the consultor:

> Menstrua commoratio sponsae in paroecia *S* computanda ne est a die eius conversionis ad fidem catholicam, an vero ab eiusdem in paroeciam ingressu? Liquido patet sufficere, ad liceitatem, factum mere externum commorationis, praescindendo a facto conversionis sponsae in fidem catholicam. Porro voluntas legislatoris ex verbis legis petenda est iuxta illud effatum: *Legislator quod voluit expressit.* At in Decr. *Ne Temere* requiritur tantummodo menstrua commoratio alterutrius contrahentis, quin ullus sermo habeatur de eorumdem religione.[109]

The decision of the Congregation was to the following effect: "*Rectorem paroeciae* S *illicite adstitisse matrimonio in casu ob amissam a sponsa, per discessum trium hebdomadarum menstruam commorationem.*"[110]

399. The opinion expressed by the consultor and the decision itself imply two chief points of interest for the question under discussion, namely: 1) that the pastor of parish *S* had acquired a right to assist at the marriage by reason of the month's stay, even though the girl was *baptized* and received into the Church only during the latter part of the month's stay; 2) that the pastor of parish *B* was the proper pastor of the girl before her Baptism. By the common law of the Church, therefore, the pastor of the bride has the right to assist at the marriage regardless of the religious or baptismal status of the bride.[111] The question may, however, take on another aspect in many dioceses of this country where the custom seems to exist of giving the right of assisting at the marriage to the pastor of the Catholic party.[112] Many of the older diocesan synods granted this right to the pastor of the Catholic party.[113] It is not altogether certain

---

[109] *AAS*, VIII (1916), 65.

[110] *Ibid.*, p. 66.

[111] Cf. Durieux, *The Busy Pastor's Book on Matrimony*, p. 60; *AER*, LXIII (1920), 417-419; LXXVIII (1928), 523-524; LXXX (1929), 200.

[112] Cf. *HPR*, XXVIII (1928), 410.

[113] Statuta Dioecesis Pittsburgensis lata in synodo Dioecesana habita 1844 et in aliis synodis 1846 et 1854 emmendata, n. 16; Synodus Dioecesana

that the custom is universally observed in this country, but it may be said that in those dioceses in which it has existed for forty years or more[114] it may be regarded as a valid and legitimate custom retaining its force even after the decree *"Ne Temere"* and the Code. In many dioceses in this country there may be a distinct element of doubt, but this, in conjunction with the opinion of the majority of the authors who favor the pastor of the Catholic party, may, perhaps, be sufficient to constitute a *dubium iuris*, in which case the pastor of the Catholic party, even if the Catholic party be the groom, may assist licitly at mixed and disparate marriages.

Bostoniensis II (1868), n. 126; Wheelingensis IV (1882), n. 85; Albanensis (1884), n. 100; Constitutiones Dioecesana Bostoniensis (1886), n. 146; Synodus Dioecesana Manchesteriensis I (1886), n. 156; Providentiensis (1887), n. 81; S. Ludovici III (1896), Cap. III, n. 30; Wayne-Castrensis (1903), n. 174; Riverormensis I (1905), n. 97; Chicagiensis (1905), n. 195. A recent diocesan synod approved by Rome evidently prescribed something to this effect. Cf. *AER*, LXXX (1929), 200.

[114] See canon 27, § 1.

APPENDIX

THE SACRAMENTAL CHARACTER OF DISPARATE AND MIXED MARRIAGES

ART. I. DISPARATE MARRIAGES

400. For centuries the discussion of disparate marriages has turned to the question as to whether the baptized party in a valid disparate marriage receives the sacrament of Matrimony. There are eminent canonists and theologians who maintain that the baptized party does receive the sacrament[1] though they appear to be greatly outnumbered by those who are of the opposite opinion.[2] The intrinsic value of the arguments seems to favor the non-reception of the sacrament by the baptized party.

A disparate marriage contracted with a dispensation from

---

[1] Salmanticenses, *Curs. Theol. Mor.*, Lib. II, Tract. IX, n. 83; Bonacina, *Op. Omnia*, Tom. I, Disp. IX, Quaest. II, Punct. II, nn. 3-4; Frassen, *Scotus Academicus*, Tom. XII, Tract. III, Disp. II, art. I, quaest. II; Ferraris, *Bibliotheca Canonica*, Vol. V, v. "*Matrimonium*", art. I, n. 19; Perrone, *De Matr.*, Tom. II, cap. VII, art. I; Blieck, *Theol. Univ.*, IV, p. 258; Pesch, *Tract. Dogm.*, VII, n. 728; Sasse, *Instit. Theol. de Sacram.*, Vol. II, p. 390-391; Tanquery, *Theol. Mor.*, I, n. 808; Vlaming, *Prael. Iuris Matr.*, n. 37.

[2] Pontius, *De Matr.*, Lib. I, cap. 6, nn. 7-10; Lib. VII, cap. 47, n. 8; Sanchez, *De Matr.*, Lib. II, Disp. 8, n. 2; Castropalao, *Op. Mor.*, Pars V, disp. 2, punct. 2, nn. 10-12; Schmalzgrueber, *Jus Eccl. Univ.*, Tom. IV, P. II, Tit. I, nn. 307-308; Vasquez, *Comment. in Tertiam part. S. Thomae—De Matr.*, Disp. II, cap. X, nn. 113-115; Mastrius, *Disp. Theol. in IV Lib. Sent.*, Quaest. I, nn. 37-39; Perez, *De Matr.*, Disp. XIX, Sect. XII, nn. 3-4; Mercerus, *Comment. in Tertiam part. S. Thomae*, suppl., Quaest. 42, prop. II; Pirhing, *Jus Can.*, Tom. IV, Tit. I, Sect. III, n. 71; De Coninck, *De Sacram.*, Tom. II, Disp. 24, n. 24; Leurenius, *Jus Can. Univ.*, Lib. IV, quaest. 83; Schmier, *Jurisprudentia*, Lib. IV, Tract. II, cap. I, nn. 41-42; Pichler, *Jus Can.*, Tom. I, Lib. IV, Tit. I, n. 75; Pappiani, *De Sacram.*, Tract. VII, cap. I, § 13; Sporer, *Theol. Mor.*, Tom. III, pars IV, n. 348; De Justis, *De Dispens. Matr.*, Lib. II, cap. XV, nn. 2-3; Gury, *Theol. Mor.*, Pars II, n. 772; De Augustinis, *De Re Sacram. Prael.*, Lib. IV, p. 230-232; Tepe, *Instit. Theol.*, Vol. IV, n. 763; Heiss, *De Matr.*, p. 12; Pohle, *Lehrb. der Dogmatik*, III, p. 601; Billot, *De Eccl. Sacram.*, II, p. 357-359; Wernz, *Ius Decret.*, IV, n. 44; Cappello, *De Sacram.*, III, n. 36; Chelodi, *Ius Matr.*, n. 6; Petrovits, *New Church Law on Matrimony*, n. 17; De Smet, *De Spons. et Matr.*, n. 179; Leitner, *Lehrb. des kath. Eherechts*, p. 52.

the impediment of Disparity of Cult cannot, indeed, be dissolved *in favorem fidei* but this does not demonstrate that the bond of marriage is sacramental in the Catholic party. When Christ raised marriage to the dignity of a sacrament, He did not thereby add something accidental to the contract, but rather elevated the very contract to a sacrament. Those parties, therefore, who by Baptism are capable of entering a sacramental contract concur as one in positing the matter and form of the sacrament. The result of this action is one and indivisible. It is not a contract plus a sacrament, it is a sacramental contract. If, therefore, the bond exists in both parties, the sacrament must exist in both parties. The sacrament cannot exist in one party alone any more than the contract can exist in one party alone. It is no less illogical to say that the bond is a *vinculum sacramentale* incapable of sacramental efficacy in the unbaptized party than it is to say that the bond is a *vinculum naturale* capable of sacramental efficacy in the baptized party. As a matter of fact, the bond is not sacramental but natural. That is now beyond dispute for a decision of the Holy Office of November 5, 1924 dissolved *in favorem fidei* a valid disparate marriage contracted after the Code without dispensation by a baptized Anglican and an unbaptized party on the ground that it was a *vinculum naturale*.[3] It is a *vinculum naturale* for the very reason that the unbaptized party cannot receive the sacrament.[4] Nor is anythnig other effected than a *vinculum naturale* if a disparate marriage is contracted with a dispensation. The dispensation removes only the impediment, it does not remove the radical disparity existing between the parties. The unbaptized party is still incapable of receiving the sacrament and the result of the contract is a *vinculum naturale*. It is a natural bond binding both parties equally. It cannot bind the baptized party with greater force *ratione sacramenti*; for the contract cannot limp.[5] The bond is either natural or sacramental for both.

---

[3] *AER*, LXXII (1925), 188.

[4] A further confirmation of this, though less direct, is furnished by the fact that the marriage bond contracted by two infidel parties continues to be a *vinculum naturale* as long as only one of the parties to the bond receives Baptism. It may be dissolved by virtue of the Pauline Privilege,—given the conditions for the valid use of this privilege.

[5] Cf. Thomas Ap., *Summa Theol.*, III a, suppl., p. 47, art. 4.

401. While it is indeed possible to consider a marriage from two aspects, namely, *ratione sacramenti* and *ratione contractus*, yet the ability to prescind from the one, in the consideration of the other, is a process confined to the logical order. But the possibility of their separation in the logical order in no way posits the possibility of their objective separation in the ontological order. It cannot, therefore, be said that while a marriage cannot limp *quoad rationem contractus*, it can limp *quoad rationem sacramenti*. The bond and the sacrament are inseparable in the ontological order.

402. The fact that the Church does not dissolve *in favorem fidei a vinculum naturale* contracted with her dispensation is not based on the intrinsic nature of the bond (which is a natural bond for both parties) but on an extrinsic reason. It would be entirely against good morals for the Church, who had dispensed in order that a natural bond might be effected, to dissolve the bond *in favorem fidei* because of its natural character,—a bond given the full sanction of a dispensation from its beginning. It will not be necessary to call attention again to the fallacy in the argument of those who urge as proof for the Catholic's reception of the sacrament, the fact that the Church has jurisdiction over disparate marriages. The Church has jurisdiction over a disparate marriage by the very fact that one of the parties is baptized.[*] The argument that the Catholic's special need of sacramental grace in a disparate marriage shows it to be reasonable that he does receive it, is at best an argument *ex convenientia*. On a similar line of reasoning, the non-reception of the sacrament may likewise be one of the reasons why the Church has made a diriment impediment of Disparity of Cult. It is sometimes urged that Christ in instituting the sacrament of Matrimony would not wish the early Christians, who were often by force of circumstance drawn into disparate marriages, to be deprived of the sacrament. The same reason should logically apply to disparate marriages contracted with dispensation in the pagan countries of today, but it is well to call to mind again the constant protests of the Fathers and early councils to such marriages. The memorable words of St. Ambrose are par-

---

[*] See Nos. 272-274.

ticularly significant: *"Si Christiana sit, non est satis, nisi ambo initiati sitis sacramento baptismatis . . . Non possunt hoc dispares fide credere, ut ab eo quem non colit putet sibi impartitam gratiam."*[7]

ART. II. MIXED MARRIAGES

403. On the other hand, since both parties to a mixed marriage are baptized, and since the contract is inseparable from the sacrament, there can be no valid mixed marriage that is not at the same time a sacramental bond.[8] Christ, in raising to the dignity of a sacrament the contract of marriage established by God, made the very contract a sign efficacious of grace. Substantially, the sacramental rite is the same as that already existing for marriage before the time of Christ. Because of Christ's institution, the giving and receiving of marital consent between the baptized is now a sign of grace independently of man's wish, and including every marriage to be contracted between the baptized. What Christ has instituted as one, namely the contract and the sacrament, cannot be disassociated by the contracting parties. The baptized (in their marriages with the baptized) when positing the rite of marriage effect either a sacramental bond or no bond whatever. Just as the intention of the minister of Baptism is not vitiated by error or false belief concerning the nature or efficacy of the rite he is performing, so neither is the intention of one or both of two baptized parties to a matrimonial contract vitiated by an error or false belief regarding the sacramental efficacy of the rite they mutually perform.[9] If they

---

[7] *De Abraham,* Lib. I, cap. 9, n. 84,—*MPL,* XIV, 451.

[8] ". . . *inter fideles matrimonium dari non posse, quin uno eodemque tempore sit Sacramentum."*—Pius IX, allocut. *Acerbissimum,* 27 Sept. 1852, n. 3,—*Fontes,* n. 515. When Pope Urban VIII on March 8, 1633, granted a dispensation from the impediment of Mixed Religion he placed the obligation upon the Catholic party (Wolfangus, Dux Neoburgi) to warn his heretical spouse (Catherina Carlotta Principis Bipontini filia) that if she did not return to the Church *before she received the sacrament,* she would sin gravely: *"Coniugem suam commoneat, quatenus non resipiscat in Domino, sed in errore persistat, ipsam graviter peccaturam, si ad hoc unum ex Ecclesiae Sacramentis accedat, antequam Romanam Ecclesiam communem Fidelium Matrem agnoscat."*—Albitius, *De Inconstantia in Fide,* Cap. XXXVI, n. 210.

[9] Pope Pius X, through the Holy Office, condemned the following proposition: "Matrimonium non potuit evadere sacramentum novae legis nisi serius in Ecclesia; siquidem ut matrimonium pro sacramento haberetur necesse erat ut praecederet plena doctrinae de gratia et sacramentis theologica explicatio."

mutually exchange marital consent they implicitly intend what
Christ instituted as the rite of the sacrament, namely the external giving and receiving of the *ius coniugale*. If one or both of
the parties *de facto* formally and absolutely withholds the intention of conferring the sacrament the contract itself is void
since the contract and the sacrament are inseparable.[10]

—S. C. S. Off., decr. *Lamentabili*, 4 Iul. 1907,—Fontes, n. 1283. Cf.
Sasse, *Instit. Theol. de Sacram.*, Vol. II, p. 389.

[10] Cf. De Lugo, *Tract. de Virt. Fidei Div.*, Disp. XXII, n. 34; Schmalz-
grueber, *Jus Eccl. Univ.*, Tom. IV, P. I, Tit. I, nn. 303-304; Estius, *In
IV Lib. Sent. Comment.*, Dist. 39, § 4; Carriere, *Prael. Theol.*, I, n. 152;
Ballerini-Palmieri, *Op. Theol. Mor.*, Tract. X, Sect. VIII, n. 217; Scavini,
Theol. Mor., Lib. II, nn. 726-727; Gury, *Theol. Mor.*, Pars II, n. 772;
Sasse, *op. cit.*, Vol. II, p. 388-389; Cappello, *De Sacram.*, III, n. 33; Cerato,
Matr., n. 1.

BIBLIOGRAPHY

SOURCES

Acta Apostolicae Sedis, Romae, 1909————.

Acta Sanctae Sedis, 41 vols., Romae, 1865-1908.

Codex Iuris Canonici Pii X Pontificis Maximi iussu digestus Benedicti Papae XV auctoritate promulgatus, Romae, 1918.

Codiccis Iuris Canonici Fontes, cura Emi Petri Card. Gasparri editi, 4 vols., Romae, 1926————.

Collectanea S. Congregationis de Propaganda Fide, 2 vols., Romae, 1907.

Concilii Plenarii Baltimorensis I (1852), *Acta et Decreta*, Baltimorae, 1853.

Concilii Plenarii Baltimorensis II (1866), *Acta et Decreta*, Baltimorae, 1868.

Concilii Plenarii Baltimorensis III (1884), *Acta et Decreta*, Baltimorae, 1886.

Corpus Iuris Canonici, Editio Lipsiensis II (Richter-Friedberg), 2 vols., Lipsiae, 1922.

Corpus Scriptorum Ecclesiasticorum Latinorum, Vindobonae, 1866————.

Decretum Gratiani emendatum et notationibus illustratum, una cum glossis, Gregorii XIII Pont. Max. iussu editum, 2 vols., Romae, 1852.

Mansi, Joannes Dominicus, *Sacrorum Conciliorum Nova et Amplissima Collectio*, 51 vols., Florentiae, 1859————.

Migne, Jacques Paul, *Patrologiae Cursus Completus - Series Latina*, 221 vols., Parisiis, 1844-1855.

Rituale Romanum, Pauli V Pontificis Maximi iussu editum aliorumque Pontificum cura recognitum atque auctoritate SSmi D. N. Pii Papae XI ad normam Codicis Iuris Canonici accomodatum, prima ed., Ratisbonae, 1925.

Roskovány, Augustinus, *De Matrimoniis Mixtis inter Catholicos et Protestantes*, (Tomus III), Pestini, 1854.

Rushworth, John, *Historical Collections . . . Beginning the Sixteenth Year of King James, anno 1618 and Ending the Fifth Year of King Charles, anno 1629,* 8 vols., London, 1682.

Theodosiani Libri XVI cum Constitutionibus Sirmondianis, ed. Th. Mommsen, Berolini, 1905.

Thesaurus Resolutionum Sacrae Congregationis Concilii, 167 vols., Romae, 1718-1908.

AUTHORS

Aichner, Simon, *Compendium Juris Ecclesiastici,* 6 ed., Brixinae, 1887.

Albertus Magnus, *Commentarii in IV Sententiarum,* (*Opera Omnia,* Volumen XXX), cura ac labore Steph. Caes. Aug. Borgnet, Parisiis, 1894.

Albitius, Franciscus, *De Inconstantia in Iure Admittenda vel Non,* Amstelaedami, 1683. [Only one tract of this *opus* of Cardinal Albitius has any reference to the present study. It is the most widely known and by far the largest of the tracts. Any reference, therefore, to Albitius will bear only the designation of this tract, namely: *De Inconstantia in Fide*].

Alexander, Natalis, *Theologia Dogmatica et Moralis secundum Ordinem Catechismi Concilii Tridentini in Quinque Libros Distributa,* 2 vols., Venetiis, 1705.

Alphonsus, M. de Ligorio, *Theologia Moralis,* 5 vols., Taurini, 1872.

Antoine, Paulus Gabrielis, *Theologia Moralis Universa,* amplificata a R. P. Philippo de Carboneano, 4 ed., 2 vols., Romae, 1764.

Astesani de Asta, *Summa Astensis . . .* studio, atque industria Fr. Joannis Baptistae Lamberti . . . 2 vols., Romae, 1730.

Augustine (Rev. Charles), *A Commentary on the New Code of Canon Law,* 8 vols., St. Louis, 1921-1924.

——————, *Rights and Duties of Ordinaries according to the Code and Apostolic Faculties,* St. Louis, 1924.

——————, *The Pastor according to the New Code of Canon Law,* St. Louis, 1926.

Ayrinhac, H. A., *Marriage Legislation in the New Code of Canon Law*, New York, 1918.

——————, *Penal Legislation in the New Code of Canon Law*, New York, 1920.

Bailly, Louis, *Theologia Dogmatica et Moralis*, 3 ed., Parisiis, 1830.

Ballerini, Antonius, - Palmieri, Dominicus, *Opus Theologicum Morale*, 3 ed., 7 vols., Prati, 1898-1901.

Bangen, Ioannes Henricus, *Instructio Practica de Sponsalibus et Matrimonio*, Monasterii, 1858-1860.

Barbosa, Augustinus, *Collectanea Doctorum tam Veterum quam Recentiorum in Ius Pontificium Universum*, Lugduni, 1658.

Beda Venerabilis, *Opera Quae Supersunt Omnia*, editit J. A. Giles, 11 vols., Londoni, 1843.

Bellarminus, Card. Robertus, *Opera Omnia ex Editione Veneta*, iterum edidit Justinus Fèvre, 12 vols., Parisiis, 1870-1874.

Benedictus XIV, *De Synodo Dioecesana*, 2 Parmensis ed., 2 vols., Parmae, 1764.

——————, *Opera Inedita*, primum publicavit Franciscus Heiner, Friburgi Brisgoviae, 1904.

Berardi, Carolus Sebastianus, *Gratiani Canones Genuini ab Apocryphis Discreti, Corrupti ad emendatiorum Codicum Fidem Exacti, Difficiliores Commoda interpretatione illustrati*, 4 vols., Venetiis, 1777.

Bernardus Papiensis, *Summa Decretalium*, edidit Ern. Ad Theod. Laspeyres, Ratisbonae, 1860.

Billot, Ludovicus, *De Ecclesiae Sacramentis Commentarius in Tertiam Partem S. Thomae*, 2 ed., 2 vols., Romae, 1897.

Billuart, Carolus Renatus, *Cursus Theologiae Juxta Mentem Divi Thomae*, 20 vols., Parisiis, 1827-1831.

Binders, Matthaeus Joseph, *Praktisches Handbuch des katholischen Eherechtes*, 4 ed., Freiburg im Br., 1891.

Binterim, Anton Joseph, *Die vorzüglichsten Denkwürdigkeiten der Christ-Katholischen Kirche*, 17 vols., Mainz 1830.

Blat, Albertus, *Commentarium Textus Codicis Iuris Canonici*, 6 vols., Romae, 1921-1927.—*De Sacramentis*, 2 ed., Romae, 1924;—*De Delictis et Poenis*, Romae, 1924.

Blieck, Henricus, *Expositio Methodica et Elementaris Theologiae Universae*, 4 vols., Brugis, 1876.

Boich, Henricus, *In Quinque Decretalium Libros Commentaria*, Venetiis, 1576.

Bonacina, Martinus, *Opera Omnia in tres tomos distributa*, Venetiis, 1686.

Bonaventura, S., *Opera Omnia*, iussu et auctoritate Rmi P. Bernardini a Portu Romatino, 12 vols., Ad Claras Aquas (Quaracchi) prope Florentiam, 1882-1895.

Bouquillon, Thomas, *Institutiones Theologiae Moralis Specialis,—Tractatus de Virtutibus Theologicis*, Brugis, 1890.

Brouwer, Henricus, *De Jure Connubiorum libri duo*, 2 ed., Delphis, 1714.

Brys, J., *De Dispensatione in Iure Canonico praesertim apud Decretistas et Decretalistas usque ad Medium Saeculum Decimum Quartum*, Brugis, 1925.

Calmet, Augustinus, *Commentarius Literalis in Omnes Libros Veteris et Novi Testamenti*, ed. Latina a J. D. Mansi, 8 vols., Venetiis, 1754-1756.

Cappello, Felix M., *Tractatus Canonico-Moralis de Sacramentis.*—Vol. I, *De Sacramentis in genere, de Baptismo, Confirmatione et Eucharistia*, 2 ed., Taurinorum Augustae, 1928; Vol. III, *De Matrimonio*, 2 ed., Romae, 1927.

——————, *Tractatus Canonico-Moralis de Censuris iuxta Codicem Iuris Canonici*, 2 ed., Taurinorum Augustae, 1925.

Carena, Caesar, *Tractatus De Officio Sanctissimae Inquisitionis*, Bononiae, 1668.

Carriere, Joseph, *Praelectiones Theologicae,—De Matrimonio*, 2 vols., Parisiis, 1837.

Castropalao, Ferdinand de, *Opus Morale de Virtutibus et Vitiis contrariis*, 7 vols., Lugduni, 1682.

Catholic Encyclopedia, 15 vols., New York, 1907-1912.

Cerato, Prosdocimus, *Matrimonium a Codice I. C. Integre Desumptum*, 4 ed., Patavii, 1927.

——————, *Censurae Vigentes Ipso Facto a C. I. C. Excerptae*, 2 ed., Patavii, 1921.

Chelodi, Ioannes, *Ius Matrimoniale iuxta Codicem Iuris Canonici*, 3 ed., Tridenti, 1921.

——————, *Ius de Personis*, 2 ed., Tridenti, 1927.

————, *Ius Poenale et Ordo Procedendi in Iudiciis Crimi-nalibus iuxta C. I. C.*, Tridenti, 1925.

Cipollini, Albertus D., *De Censuris Latae Sententiae iuxta C. I. C.*, Taurini, 1925.

Cocchi, Guidus, *Commentarium in Codicem Iuris Canonici*, 8 vols., 2 & 3 ed., Taurinorum Augustae, 1925-1927.

Corblet, Jules, *Histoire Dogmatique, Liturgique et Archéolo-gique du Sacrament de Baptême*, 2 vols., Genève, 1881-1882.

Cornelius a Lapide, *Commentaria in Sacram Scripturam*, editio Xysto Riario Sfortiae, 10 vols., 1854-1859.

Cornely, Rudolphus, *Commentarius in S. Pauli Apostoli Epis-tolas, (Cursus Scripturae Sacrae).—II. Prior Epistola ad Corinthios*, Parisiis, 1890; III. *Epistolae ad Corinthios Altera et ad Galatas*, Parisiis, 1892.

Corradus, Pyrrhus, *Praxis Dispensationum Apostolicarum pro utroque foro*, ed. in Germania 2a., alias 5a., Coloniae Agripinae, 1697.

Covarruvias, Didacus, *Opera Omnia*, 2 vols., Antverpiae, 1638.

Cronin, Charles J., *The New Matrimonial Legislation*, 2 ed., London, 1909.

Dale, Alfred William Winterslow, *The Synod of Elvira and Christian Life in the Fourth Century*, London, 1882.

D'Annibale, Josephus Card., *Summula Theologiae Moralis*, 3 ed., 3 vols., Romae, 1892.

Dandino, Anselmus, *De Suspectis de Haeresi*, Romae, 1703.

Dargin, Edward Vincent, *Reserved Cases According to the Code of Canon Law*, Washington, 1924.

De Angelis, Philippus, *Praelectiones Juris Canonici ad Metho-dum Decretalium Gregorii IX Exactae*, 6 vols., Romae, 1880.

De Augustinis, Aemilius M., *De Re Sacramentaria Praelectiones Scholastico-Dogmatico*, 2 vols., New York, 1879.

De Becker, Iulius, *De Sponsalibus et Matrimonio Praelectiones Canonicae*, 2 ed., Lovanii, 1903.

De Coninck, Aegidius, *De Sacramentis et Censuris*, 2 ed., 2 vols., Antverpiae, 1619.

De Justis, Vincentius, *De Dispensationibus Matrimonialibus Tractatus in tres libros digestus*, Lucae, 1726.

De Lugo, Joannes, *Disputationes Scholasticae et Morales*, editio nova accurante J. B. Fournials, 8 vols., Parisiis, 1868.

Dens, P., (*Theologia Mechlinensis*), *Tractatus de Sponsalibus et Matrimonio*, Mechliniae, 1861.

Denzinger, H., - Bannwart, C., *Enchiridion Symbolorum Definitionum et Declarationum de Rebus Fidei et Morum*, 14 & 15 ed., Friburgi Brisgoviae, 1922.

De Smet, Aloysius, *De Sponsalibus et Matrimonio Tractatus Canonicus et Theologicus*, ed. 1909, Brugis, 1909. [When this edition is quoted in this study it will always bear the date of 1909].

——————, *Tractatus Theologico-Canonicus de Sponsalibus et Matrimonio*, 4 ed., Brugis, 1927.

Durandus, Gulielmus, *Speculum Iuris*, 3 vols., Venetiis, 1577.

Durandus a Sancto Porciano, *In Petri Lombardi Sententias Theologicas Commentariorum libri IV.*, Venetiis, 1586.

Durieux, P., *The Busy Pastor's Book on Matrimony*, translated by Rev. Oliver Dolphin, Faribault, 1926.

Duskie, John A., *The Canonical Status of the Orientals in the United States*, Washington, 1928.

Duysseldorpii, Franc., *Tractatus de Matrimonio non ineundo cum his qui extra Ecclesiam sunt*, Antverpiae, 1636.

Eichmann, Eduard, *Das katholische Mischehenrecht nach dem Codex Iuris Canonici*, Paderborn, 1921.

——————, *Das Strafrecht des Codex Iuris Canonici*, Paderborn, 1920.

Engelmayr, Angelus, *Series Impedimentorum Matrimonii Dirimentium iuxta principia Theologiae Moralis*, 2 ed., August. Vind. & Graecii, 1845.

Esmein, A., *Le mariage en droit canonique*, 2 vols., Paris, 1891.

Estius, Guilielmus, *In Quatuor Libros Sententiarum Commentaria*, 2 vols., Parisiis, 1696.

——————, *Absolutissima in Omnes Beati Pauli et Septem Catholicas Apostolorum Epistolas Commentaria*, 2 vols., Rothomagi, 1709.

Fanfani, Ludovicus I., *De Iure Parochorum ad Normam Codicis Iuris Canonici*, Taurini-Romae, 1924.

Farrugia, Nicolaus, *De Matrimonio et Causis Matrimonialibus Tractatus Canonico-Moralis iuxta Codicem Iuris Canonici*, Taurini-Romae, 1924.

————, *Commentarium in Censuris Latae Sententiae Codicis Iuris Canonici*, 2 ed., Melitae, 1921.

Featherston, John Joseph, *The Impediment of Disparity of Cult*, (Licentiate Dissertation, Catholic University), Washington, 1913.

Feije, (also Feye) Henricus Joannes, *Dissertatio Canonica De Matrimoniis Mixtis*, Lovanii, 1847.

————, *De Impedimentis et Dispensationibus Matrimonialibus*, 3 ed., Lovanii, 1885.

Ferraris, Lucius, *Bibliotheca canonica iuridica moralis theologica nec non ascetica polemica rubricistica historica*, 9 vols., Romae, 1889.

Ferre, Vincentius, *Tractatus de Virtutibus Theologicis et Vitiis eis Oppositis*, Romae, 1669.

Frassen, Claudius, *Scotus Academicus seu Universa Doctoris Subtilis Theologica Dogmatica*, 12 vols., Romae, 1723.

Fulton, John, *The Laws of Marriage*, London, 1883.

Funk, Francis X., *A Manual of Church History*, translated from the German by P. Perciballi; edited by W. H. Kent, 2 vols., London, 1914.

Gardiner, Samuel Rawson, *History of England from the Ascension of James I to the Outbreak of the Civil War 1603-1642*, 10 vols., London, 1884.

Gasparri, Petrus, *Tractatus Canonicus de Matrimonio*, 3 ed., 2 vols., Parisiis, 1904.

Genicot, Eduardus, - Salsmans, I., *Institutiones Theologiae Moralis*, 10 ed., 2 vols., Bruxellis, 1922.

————, *Casus Conscientiae*, 5 ed., Bruxellis, 1925.

Giovine, Petrus, *De Dispensationibus Matrimonialibus Consultationes Canonicae*, 2 vols., Neapoli, 1863.

Gobatus, Georgius, *Operum Moralium Tomi I, Pars II, hoc est Experientiarum Theologicarum de Septem Sacramentis*, Duaci, 1700.

Göpfert, Franz Adam, *Moraltheologie*, 2 ed., 3 vols., Paderborn, 1899.

Gury, Joannes Petrus, *Compendium Theologiae Moralis*, ed. in Germania 4., Ratisbonae, 1868.

Hefele, Carl Joseph von, *Conciliengeschichte*, 2 ed., 9 vols., Freiburg im Br., 1873-1890.

Heiner, Franz, *Grundriss des katholischen Eherechts*, 5 ed., Münster i. W., 1905.

Heiss, M., *De Matrimonio Tractatus Quinque*, Monachii, 1861.

Hergenröther, Joseph Card., *Handbuch der allgemeinen Kirchengeschichte*, 3 ed., 3 vols., Freiburg im Br., 1884.

Hergenröther, Philipp, *Lehrbuch des katholischen Kirchenrechts*, 2 ed., Freiburg im Br., 1905.

Hilling, Nikolaus, *Das Eherecht des Codex Juris Canonici*, Freiburg im Br., 1927.

————, *Die allgemeinen Normen des Codex Juris Canonici*, Freiburg im Br., 1926.

Hurter, H., *Theologiae Dogmaticae*, 6 ed., 3 vols., Oeniponte, 1889.

Hyland, Francis Edward, *Excommunication, Its Nature, Historical Development and Effects*, Washington, 1928.

Juenin, Gasparis, *Commentarius Historicus et Dogmaticus de Sacramentis in genere et specie*, ed. 2 Veneta post 6 Lugdunensem, Venetiis, 1740.

Kearney, Richard Joseph, *Sponsors at Baptism according to the Code of Canon Law*, Washington, 1925.

Kelly, James Patrick, *The Jurisdiction of the Simple Confessor*, Washington, 1927.

Kelly, M. V., - Geniesse, J. B., *Efficax Antidotum ad Matrimonia Mixta Praecavenda*, Romae, 1923.

Kenrick, Franciscus Patricius, *Theologia Moralis*, 2 ed., 2 vols., Mechliniae, 1864.

King, James Ignatius, *The Administration of the Sacraments to Dying Non-Catholics*, Washington, 1924.

Knecht, August, *Grundriss des Eherechts bearbeitet auf Grund des Codex Iuris Canonici*, Freiburg im Br., 1918

Konings, A., *Theologia Moralis*, 7 ed., 2 vols., Neo-Eboraci, 1889.

Konings, A., - Putzer, J., *Commentarium in Facultates Apostolicas*, 3 ed., Neo-Eboraci, 1893.

Koudelka, Charles J., *Pastors, Their Rights and Duties according to the New Code of Canon Law*, Washington, 1921.

Kubelbeck, William J., *The Sacred Penitentiaria and its Relations to the Faculties of Ordinaries and Priests*, Washington, 1918.

Labauche, L., *The Three Sacraments of Initiation*, authorized translation, New York, 1922.

Laemmer, Hugo, *Institutionen des katholischen Kirchenrechts*, 2 ed., Freiburg im Br., 1892.

Lambing, A. A., *Mixed Marriages—Their Origin and their Results*, 3 ed., Notre Dame, 1879.

Laymann, Paulus, *Theologiae Moralis in Quinque Libros Partitae*, Venetiis, 1719.

Leech, George Leo, *A Comparative Study of the Constitution "Apostolicae Sedis" and the "Codex Juris Canonici"*, Washington, 1922.

Lehmkuhl, Augustinus, *Theologia Moralis*, 3 ed., 2 vols., Friburgi Brisgoviae, 1886.

————, *Casus Conscientiae*, 2 vols., Friburgi Brisgoviae, 1902.

Leitner, Martin, *Lehrbuch des katholischen Eherechts*, 3 ed., Paderborn, 1920.

Leurenius, Petrus, *Jus Canonicum Universum*, 5 vols., Venetiis, 1729.

Lingard, John, *The History of England from the First Invasion by the Romans to the Ascension of William and Mary in 1688*, 5 ed., 10 vols., London, 1849.

Linneborn, Johannes, *Grundriss des Eherechts nach dem Codex Iuris Canonici*, 2 & 3 ed., Paderborn, 1922.

Loening, Edgar, *Das Kirchenrecht im Reich der Merowinger*, 2 vols., Strassburg, 1879.

McNicholas, John T., *The New Legislation on Engagements and Marriage,—Commentary on the Decree "Ne Temere"*, Philadelphia, 1908.

Malderus, Joannes, *De Virtutibus Theologicis*, Antverpiae, 1616.

Mansella, Ioseph, *De Impedimentis Matrimonium Dirimentibus ac de Processu Iudiciali in Causis Matrimonialibus*, Romae, 1881.

Maroto, Philippus, *Institutiones Iuris Canonici ad Normam Novi Codicis*, 3 ed., 2 vols., Romae, 1921.

Mastrius, Bartholomaeus, *Disputationes Theologicae in Quartum Librum Sententiarum*, Venetiis, 1698.

Matharan, M. M., *Casus de Matrimonio*, Parisiis, 1893.

Mazzei, Franciscus, *De Matrimonio Conscientiae vulgo nuncupato liber singularis*, (accessit de Matrimonio personarum diversae Religionis Dissertatio), Romae, 1771.

Mercerus, Guilielmus, *Commentarius in Tertiam partem S. Thomae Aquinatis a Quaest. 60*, Lovanii, 1630.

Mergentheim, Leo, *Die Quinquennalfakultäten pro Foro Externo. Ihre Enstehung und Einführung in Deutschen Bistümern*, 2 vols., Stuttgart, 1908.

Michel, Augustinus, *Theologiae Canonico-Moralis*, 3 vols., Augustae Vindel. & Dilingae, 1710.

Migne, Jacques Paul, *Theologiae Cursus Completus*, 28 vols., Parisiis, 1860.

Mirbt, Carl, *Das Mischehenrecht des Codex juris canonici und die interconfessionellen Beziehungen in Deutschland*, Tübingen, 1922.

Motry, Hubert Louis, *Diocesan Faculties according to the Code of Canon Law*, Washington, 1922.

Murphy, George Lawrence, *Delinquencies and Penalties in the Administration and Reception of the Sacraments*, Washington, 1923.

Navarrus, Martinus Azpilcueta, *Opera Omnia*, 6 vols., Venetiis, 1618.

Neuberger, Nicolas J., *Canon 6, or the Relation of the Codex Iuris Canonici to Preceding Legislation*, Washington, 1927.

Noldin, H., *Summa Theologiae Moralis*, 17 ed., 3 vols., Oeniponte, 1924.

Ojetti, Benedictus, *In Ius Antepianum et Pianum ex Decreto "Ne Temere" de Forma Celebrationis Sponsalium et Matrimonii Commentarii*, Romae, 1908.

——————, *Synopsis Rerum Moralium et Iuris Pontificii*, 3 ed., 4 vols., Romae, 1911.

O'Keeffe, Gerald Michael, *Matrimonial Dispensations, Powers of Bishops, Priests, and Confessors*, Washington, 1927.

Pappiani, Albertus, *Doctrina Christiana de Sacrosanctis Ecclesiae Sacramentis ab Heterodoxorum erroribus vindicata*, 3 vols., Florentiae, 1772.

Pastor, Ludwig Freiherr von, *Geschichte der Päpste seit dem Ausgang des Mittelalters*, (Band XII), Freiburg im Br., 1927.

Perathoner, Anton, *Das kirchliche Gesetzbuch (Codex Juris Canonici)*, 3 ed., Brixen, 1923.

Perez, Martinus, *De Sancto Matrimonii Sacramento—Opus Morale Theologicum*, Lugduni, 1646.

Perrone, Io., *De Matrimonio Christiano*, 3 vols., Leodii, 1861.

Pesch, Christianus, *Tractatus Dogmatici*, 9 vols., Friburgi Brisgoviae, 1897.

Petra, Vincentius, *Commentaria ad Constitutiones Apostolicas*, 5 vols. in 2, Venetiis, 1729.

Petrovits, Joseph J. C., *The New Church Law on Matrimony*, 2 ed., Philadelphia, 1926.

Petrus Lombardus, *Petri Lombardi Libri IV Sententiarum*, studio et cura PP. Collegii S. Bonaventurae in lucem editi, 2 ed., 2 vols., Ad Claras Aquas, 1916.

Phillips, Georgius, *Compendium Iuris Ecclesiastici*, edidit Fridericus Henr. Vering, Ratisbonae, 1875.

Pichler, Vitus, *Jus Canonicum*, 2 vols., Ravenae, 1741.

Pighi, Jo. Bapta., *De Sacramento Matrimonii*, 2 ed., Veronae, 1921.

—————, *Censurae Sententiae Latae et Irregularitates quas habet Codex Iuris Canonici*, 7 ed., Veronae, 1922.

Pignatelli, Jacobus, *Constitutiones Canonicae*, 11 vols., Coloniae Allobrogum, 1700.

Pirhing, Ernricus, *Jus Canonicum Nova Methodo Explicatum* 2 vols., Dilingae, 1678.

Pohle, Joseph, *Lehrbuch der Dogmatik*, 2 ed., 3 vols., Paderborn, 1906.

Pollock, Frederick, - Maitland, William F., *History of English Law before the Time of Edward I*, 2 ed., 2 vols., Cambridge, 1899.

Pontius, Basilius, *De Sacramento Matrimonii Tractatus cum Appendice de Matrimonio Catholici cum haeretico*, 2 ed., Bruxellis, 1627.

Porpora, Agnellus, *Theologia Moralis*, Neapoli, 1854.

Pourrat, P., *Theology of the Sacraments*, authorized translation from the third French edition, St. Louis, 1910.

Prümmer, Dominicus M., *Manuale Theologiae Moralis*, 2 & 3 ed., 3 vols., Friburgi Brisgoviae, 1923.

—————, *Manuale Iuris Canonici*, 3 ed., Friburgi Brisgoviae, 1922.

Quigley, Joseph A. M., *Condemned Societies*, Washington, 1927.

Raymundus de Pennaforte, *Summa*, Veronae, 1744.

Reiffenstuel, Anacletus, *Jus Canonicum Universum*, 4 vols., Romae, 1838.

Rossi, Joseph, *De Matrimonii Celebratione iuxta Codicem Iuris Canonici*, Romae, 1924.

Rupprecht, Theodorus M., *Notae Historicae in Universum Jus Canonicum*, Venetiis, 1764.

Sabetti, Aloysius, - Barrett, Timotheus, *Compendium Theologiae Moralis*, 29 ed., New York, 1920.

Sägmüller, J. B., *Lehrbuch des katholischen Kirchenrechts*, Freiburg im Br., 1900.

Salmanticensis Collegii, *Cursus Theologiae Moralis*, Venetiis, 1714.

Sanchez, Thomas, *De Sancto Matrimonii Sacramento Disputationum, Tomi tres*, Lugduni, 1669.

Santi, Franciscus, *Praelectiones Juris Canonici*, 5 vols. in 2, Ratisbonae, Neo-Eboraci et Cincinnatii, 1886.

Sasse, Joannes Bapt., *Institutiones Theologicae de Sacramentis Ecclesiae*, Opus posthumum cura Augustini Lehmkuhl, S. J., 2 vols., Friburgi Brisgoviae, 1898.

Scavini, Petrus, *Theologia Moralis Universa ad mentem S. Alphonsi M. de Ligorio*, 9 ed., 4 vols., Mediolani, 1869.

Scherer, Rudolf Ritter von, *Handbuch des Kirchenrechtes*, 2 vols., Graz, 1886-1898.

Schmalzgrueber, Franciscus, *Jus Ecclesiasticum Universum*, 12 vols., Romae, 1844.

Schmier, Franciscus, *Jurisprudentia Canonico-civilis, seu Jus Canonicum Universum juxta quinque libros decretalium,* 2 vols., Venetiis, 1754.

Schönsteiner, Ferdinand, *Grundriss des kirchlichen Eherechts,* Wien, 1925.

Schulte, J. Fr., *Handbuch des katholischen Eherechts nach dem gemeinen katholischen Kirchenrechte und dem österreichischen, preussischen, französischen Particularrechte, mit Rücksichtsnahme auf noch andere Civilgesetzgebungen,* Giessen, 1875.

Scotus (Joannes Duns Scotus), *Quaestiones in Quartum Librum Sententiarum,* (*Opera Omnia,* Volumen XIX), Parisiis, 1894.

Skalnik, Franc. Xav., *De Mixtis Matrimoniis,* Leutschoviae, 1835.

Smisniewicz, Leon M., *Die Lehre von den Ehehindernissen bei Petrus Lombardus und bei seinen Kommentatoren: Albert d. Gr., Thomas v. Aquin, J. Bonaventura und J. D. Scotus, den Hauptvertretern der Hochscholastik, dargestellt nach Massgabe der vierfachen Kausalität der Ehe,* Posen, 1917.

Sole, Iacobus, *De Delictis et Poenis—Praelectiones in Lib. V Codicis Iuris Canonici,* Romae, 1920.

Soto, Dominicus, *In Quartum* (quem vocant) *Sententiarum* Tomi I-II, Venetiis, 1575.

Sporer, Patritius, *Theologia Moralis Sacramentalis in IV Partes divisa,* 3 ed., Salisburgi, 1711.

Suarez, Franciscus, *Opera Omnia,* 26 vols., Parisiis, 1856-1861.

Sylvius, Franciscus, *Commentarius in Tertiam Partem S. Thomae Aquinatis et in ejusdem supplementum,* 2 ed., Duaci, 1622.

Tanquery, Ad., *Synopsis Theologiae Moralis et Pastoralis,* 9 ed., 3 vols., Romae, 1922.

——————, *Synopsis Theologiae Dogmaticae,* 18 ed., 3 vols., Romae, 1921.

Tepe, G. Bernardus, *Institutiones Theologicae,* 4 vols., Paris, 1896.

Thomas Aquinas, *Summa Theologica,* ed. 2 Romana, Romae, 1894.

——————, *In Omnes D. Pauli Apostoli Epistolas Doctissima Commentaria*, restituit F. Remigius Florentinus, Venetiis, 1562.

Tirinus, Jacobus, *Commentarius in Universam S. Scripturam*, 5 vols., Taurini, 1882-1884.

Tournely, Honoratus, *Praelectiones Theologicae de Sacramento Matrimonii*, Parisiis, 1743.

Trombellius, Joannes Chrysostomus, *Tractatus de Sacramentis —De Matrimonio*, Tomus III, Bononiae, 1783; *De Baptismo*, Tomi IV & V, Bononiae, 1772-1773.

Vacandard, E., *The Inquisition*, translated from the second edition by Bertrand L. Conway, New York, 1908.

Van Steenkiste, J. A., *S. Pauli Epistolae Breviter Explicatae*, 3 ed., 2 vols., Brugis, 1878.

Vazquez, Gabriel, *Commentariorum ac Disputationum in Tertiam Partem Sancti Thomae, Tomus III*, (Opera Omnia, Volumen VIII), Lugduni, 1631.

Vecchiotti, Septimus M., *Tractatus Canonicus de Matrimonio*, Taurini, 1868.

Vering, Friederich, H., *Lehrbuch des katholischen, orientalischen und protestantischen Kirchenrechts, mit besonderer Rücksicht auf Deutschland, Oesterreich und die Schweiz*, 3 ed., Freiburg im Br., 1893.

Vermeersch, Arthurus, *De Forma Sponsalium ac Matrimonii post Decretum "Ne Temere"*, Brugis, 1908.

——————, *De Formulis Facultatum S. C. de Propaganda Fide Commentaria*, Brugis, 1922.

——————, *Theologia Moralis*, 2 ed., 3 vols., Romae, 1927.

Vermeersch, A., - Creusen, J., *Epitome Iuris Canonici*, 2 & 3 ed., 3 vols., Mechliniae, 1924-1925.

Vlaming, Th. M., *Praelectiones Iuris Matrimonii*, 3 ed., 2 vols., Bussum in Hollandia, 1919-1921.

Wernz, Franciscus Xav., *Ius Decretalium*, 2 ed., 6 vols., Prati, 1912.

Wernz, F. X., - Vidal, Petrus, *Ius Canonicum ad Codicis Normam Exactum*, 3 vols., 1923-1927.

Westermarck, Edward, *The History of Human Marriage*, 5 ed., 3 vols., New York, 1922.

Winslow, Francis Joseph, *Vicars and Prefects Apostolic*, Washington, 1924.

Wouters, Ludovicus, *Commentarius in Decretum "Ne Temere"*, 4 ed., Amstelodami, 1912.

Woywod, Stanislaus, *A Practical Commentary on the Code of Canon Law*, 2 vols., New York, 1925.

Zhishman, Joseph, *Das Eherecht der orientalischen Kirche*, Wien, 1864.

Zitelli, Zephyrinus, *De Dispensationibus Matrimonialibus recentissimas sac. urbis congreg. resolutiones Commentarii*, Romae, 1887.

PERIODICALS

American Ecclesiastical Review, The, Philadelphia, 1889————.

Apollinaris - Commentarium Iuridico - Canonicum, Romae, 1928————.

Archiv für katholisches Kirchenrecht, Mainz, 1857————.

Homiletic and Pastoral Review, The, New York, 1900————.

Irish Ecclesiastical Record, The, Dublin, 1864————.

Jus Pontificium, Romae, 1921————.

Nouvelle Revue Théologique, Paris, 1868————.

Theologisch-praktische Quartalschrift, Linz, 1832————.

Zeitschrift für katholische Theologie, Innsbruck, 1877————.

UNIVERSITAS CATHOLICA AMERICAE

WASHINGTONII, D. C.

FACULTAS IURIS CANONICI

1928-1929

No. 51

DEUS LUX MEA

——

TITULI

QUOS

AD DOCTORATUS GRADUM

IN

IURE CANONICO

Apud Universitatem Catholicam Americae

CONSEQUENDUM

PUBLICE PROPUGNABIT

FRANCISCUS JOSEPH SCHENK

SACERDOS ARCHIDIOECESIS SANCTI PAULI

IURIS CANONICI LICENTIATUS

HORA XI, A. M. DIE II IUNII A. D. MCMXXVIII.

IUS CANONICUM

ROMAN LAW

VIDIT FACULTAS:

PHILIPPUS BERNARDINI, S. T. D., J. U. D., *Decanus.*

LUDOVICUS H. MOTRY, S. T. D., J. C. D., *a Secretis.*

VALENTINUS T. SCHAAF, O. F. M., S. T. B., J. C. D.

FRANCISCUS J. LARDONE, S. T. D., J. U. D.

VIDIT RECTOR UNIVERSITATIS:

✠ THOMAS J. SHAHAN, S. T. D., J. U. L., LL. D.

BIOGRAPHICAL NOTE

Francis J. Schenk was born April 1, 1901, at Superior, Wisconsin. After a grade school education at Gaylord, Minnesota, he was graduated successively from the high school and collegiate departments of the College of St. Thomas, St. Paul, Minnesota, where he received the degree of Bachelor of Arts. His philosophical and theological studies were made at the St. Paul Seminary, and upon their completion he received the degree of Bachelor of Sacred Theology from the Catholic University. He was ordained to the Holy Priesthood on June 13, 1926. In the fall of the same year he was sent by Archbishop Dowling to the Catholic University to pursue a graduate course of studies in Canon Law.

CATHOLIC UNIVERSITY OF AMERICA
Canon Law Studies

1. FRERIKS, REV. CELESTINE A., C. PP. S., J. C. D., Religious Congregations in Their External Relations, 121 pp., 1916.

2. GALLIHER, REV. DANIEL M., O. P., J. C. D., Canonical Elections, 117 pp., 1917.

3. BORKOWSKI, REV. AURELIUS L., O. F. M., J. C. D., De Confraternitatibus Ecclesiasticis, 136 pp., 1918.

4. CASTILLO, REV. CAYO, J. C. D., Disertacion Historico-canonico sobre la Potestad del Cabildo en Sede Vacante o Impedida del Vicario Capitular, 99 pp., 1919 (1918).

5. KUBELBECK, REV. WILLIAM J., S. T. B., J. C. D., The Sacred Penitentiaria and its Relations to Faculties of Ordinaries and Priests, 129 pp., 1918.

6. PETROVITS, REV. JOSEPH J. C., S. T. D., J. C. D., The New Church Law on Matrimony, X-461 pp., 1919.

7. HICKEY, REV. JOHN J., S. T. B., J. C. D., Irregularities and Simple Impediments in the New Code of Canon Law, 100 pp., 1920.

8. KLEKOTKA, REV. PETER J., S. T. B., J. C. D., Diocesan Consultors, 179 pp., 1920.

9. WANNENMACHER, REV. FRANCIS, J. C. D., The Evidence in Ecclesiastical Procedure Affecting the Marriage Bond, 1920. (Not Printed.)

10. GOLDEN, REV. HENRY FRANCIS, J. C. D., Parochial Benefices in the New Code, IV-119 pp., 1921. (Printed 1925.)

11. KOUDELKA, REV. CHARLES J., J. C. D., Pastors, Their Rights and Duties According to the New Code of Canon Law, 211 pp., 1921.

12. MELO, REV. ANTONIUS, O. F. M., J. C. D., De Exemptione Regularium, X-188 pp., 1921.

13. SCHAAF, REV. VALENTINE THEODORE, O. F. M., S. T. B., J. C. D., The Cloister, X-180 pp., 1921.

14. BURKE, REV. THOMAS JOSEPH, S. T. B., J. C. D., Competence in Ecclesiastical Tribunals, IV-117 pp., 1922.

15. LEECH, REV. GEORGE LEO, J. C. D., A Comparative Study of the Constitution "Apostolicae Sedis" and the "Codex Juris Canonici", 179 pp., 1922.

16. MOTRY, REV. HUBERT LOUIS, S. T. D., J. C. D., Diocesan Faculties according to the Code of Canon Law, II-167 pp., 1922.

17. MURPHY, REV. GEORGE LAWRENCE, J. C. D., Delinquencies and Penalties in the Administration and Reception of the Sacraments, IV-121 pp., 1923.

18. O'REILLY, REV. JOHN ANTHONY, S. T. B., J. C. D., Ecclesiastical Sepulture in the New Code of Canon Law, II-129 pp., 1923.

19. MICHALICKA, REV. WENCESLAS CYRILL, O. S. B., J. C. D., Judicial Procedure in Dismissal of Clerical Exempt Religious, 107 pp., 1923.

20. DARGIN, REV. EDWARD VINCENT, S. T. B., J. C. D., Reserved Cases According to the Code of Canon Law, IV-103 pp., 1924.

21. GODFREY, REV. JOHN A., S. T. B., J. C. D., The Right of Patronage According to the Code of Canon Law, 153 pp., 1924.

22. HAGEDORN, REV. FRANCIS EDWARD, J. C. D., General Legislation on Indulgences, II-154 pp., 1924.

23. KING, REV. JAMES IGNATIUS, J. C. D., The Administration of the Sacraments to Dying Non-Catholics, V-141 pp., 1924.

24. WINSLOW, REV. FRANCIS JOSEPH, A. F. M., J. C. D., Vicars and Prefects Apostolic, IV-149 pp., 1924.

25. CORREA, REV. JOSE SERVELION, S. T. L., J. C. D., La Potesdad Legislativa de la Iglesia Catolica, IV-127 pp., 1925.

26. DUGAN, REV. HENRY FRANCIS, A. M., J. C. D., The Judiciary Department of the Diocesan Curia, 87 pp., 1925.

27. KELLER, REV. CHARLES FREDERICK, S. T. B., J. C. D., Mass Stipends, 167 pp., 1925.

28. PASCHANG, REV. JOHN LINUS, J. C. D., The Sacramentals According to the Code of Canon Law, 129 pp., 1925.

29. PIONTEK, REV. CYRILLUS, O. F. M., S. T. B., J. C. D., De Indulto Exclaustrationis necnon Saecularizationis, XIII-289 pp., 1929.

30. KEARNEY, REV. RICHARD JOSEPH, S. T. B., J. C. D., Sponsors at Baptism According to the Code of Canon Law, IV-127 pp., 1925.

31. BARTLETT, REV. CHESTER JOSEPH, A. M., LL. B., J. C. D., The Tenure of Parochial Property in the United States of America, V-108 pp., 1926.

32. KILKER, REV. ADRIAN JEROME, J. C. D., Extreme Unction, V-425 pp., 1926.

33. McCORMICK, REV. ROBERT EMMET, J. C. D., Confessors of Religious, VIII-266 pp., 1926.

34. MILLER, REV. NEWTON THOMAS, J. C. D., Founded Masses According to the Code of Canon Law, VII-93 pp., 1926.

35. ROELKER, REV. EDWARD G., S. T. D., J. C. D., Principles of Privilege According to the Code of Canon Law, XI-166 pp., 1926.

36. BAKALARCZYK, REV. RICHARDUS, M. I. C., J. U. D., De Novitiatu, VIII-208 pp., 1927.

37. PIZZUTI, REV. LAWRENCE, O. F. M., J. U. L., De Parochis Religiosis, 1929.

38. BLILEY, REV. NICHOLAS MARTIN, O. S. B., J. C. D., Altars According to the Code of Canon Law, XIX-132 pp., 1927.

39. BROWN, BRENDAN FRANCIS, A. B., LL. M., J. U. D., The Canonical Juristic Personality with Special Reference to its Status in the United States of America, V-212 pp., 1927.

40. CAVANAUGH, REV. WILLIAM THOMAS, C. P., J. U. D., The Reservation of the Blessed Sacrament, VIII-101 pp., 1927.

41. DOHENY, REV. WILLIAM J., C. S. C., A. B., J. U. D., Church Property: Modes of Acquisition, X-118 pp., 1927.

42. FELDHAUS, REV. ALOYSIUS H., C. PP. S., J. C. D., Oratories, IX-141 pp., 1927.

43. KELLY, REV. JAMES PATRICK, A. B., J. C. D., The Jurisdiction of the Simple Confessor, X-208 pp., 1927.

44. NEUBERGER, REV. NICHOLAS J., J. C. D., Canon 6 or the Relation of the Codex Juris Canonici to the Preceding Legislation, V-95 pp., 1927.

45. O'KEEFFE, REV. GERALD MICHAEL, J. C. D., Matrimonial Dispensations, Powers of Bishops, Priests, and Confessors, VIII- 232 pp., 1927.

46. QUIGLEY, REV. JOSEPH A. M., A. B., J. C. D., Condemned Societies, 139 pp., 1927.

47. ZAPLOTNIK, REV. IOANNES LEO, J. C. D., De Vicariis Foraneis, X-142 pp., 1927.

48. DUSKIE, REV. JOHN ALOYSIUS, A. B., J. C. D., The Canonical Status of the Orientals in the United States, VIII-196 pp., 1928.

49. HYLAND, REV. FRANCIS EDWARD, J. C. D., Excommunication, its Nature, Historical Development and Effects, VIII-181 pp., 1928.

50. REINMANN, REV. GERALD JOSEPH, O. M. C., J. C. D., The Third Order Secular of St. Francis, 201 pp., 1928.

51. SCHENK, REV. FRANCIS J., A. B., S. T. B., J. C. L., The Matrimonial Impediments of Mixed Religion and Disparity of Cult, 1929.

52. COADY, REV. JOHN JOSEPH, A. M., S. T. D., J. U. L., The Appointment of Pastors, 1929.

53. KAY, REV. THOMAS HENRY, J. C. L., Competence in Matrimonial Procedure, 1929.

54. TURNER, REV. SIDNEY J., C. P., J. U. L., The Vow of Poverty, 1929.

55. KEARNEY, REV. RAYMOND A., A. B., S. T. D., J. C. L., The Principles of Delegation, 1929.

CPSIA information can be obtained at www.ICGtesting.com
Printed in the USA
BVOW07*0939130814

362490BV00001B/2/P